Paths of Light
and Darkness

To Hawk Santti

Love + God Bless
You Always
Mamma

CLIMB THE HIGHEST MOUNTAIN SERIES

Paths of Light and Darkness

Mark L. Prophet · Elizabeth Clare Prophet

The Everlasting Gospel

SUMMIT UNIVERSITY ⚫ PRESS

Corwin Springs, Montana

PATHS OF LIGHT AND DARKNESS
by Mark L. Prophet and Elizabeth Clare Prophet
Copyright © 2005 by Summit University Press
All rights reserved

Tel: 1-800-245-5445 or 406-848-9500.
Web site: www.summituniversitypress.com
E-mail: info@summituniversitypress.com

Library of Congress Control Number: 2004115766
ISBN: 1-932890-00-9

SUMMIT UNIVERSITY 🐚 PRESS®

Printed in the United States of America

Cover: *Northern Midnight,* a painting by Nicholas Roerich.

Note: Our understanding of life and the universe is that all things are in polarity: plus/minus, Alpha/Omega, yin/yang, masculine/feminine. The worlds of Spirit and Matter are in polarity as two manifestations of God's universal presence. In this relationship, Spirit assumes the positive-yang-masculine polarity, and Matter assumes the negative-yin-feminine polarity. Thus, we have used masculine pronouns to refer to God and feminine pronouns to refer to the soul, the part of ourselves that is evolving in the planes of Matter. Also, in order to avoid the sometimes cumbersome or confusing expressions of gender-neutral language, we have occasionally used masculine pronouns to refer to the individual. These usages are not intended to exclude women.

09   08   07   06   05   6   5   4   3   2   1

And I saw another angel fly in the midst of heaven, having the everlasting gospel to preach unto them that dwell on the earth, and to every nation, and kindred, and tongue, and people,

Saying with a loud voice, Fear God, and give glory to him; for the hour of his judgment is come: and worship him that made heaven, and earth, and the sea, and the fountains of waters.

REVELATION

Contents

2 · Psychic Thralldom   115

3 · Armageddon   199

4 · Thy Will Be Done 353

Tables

Prayers and Decrees

Preface

PATHS OF LIGHT AND DARKNESS IS the sixth book in the Climb the Highest Mountain series. In this volume we will examine the serious issues of Good and Evil, the cult of pleasure, psychicism and spiritualism, and the entire concept of spiritual and galactic Armageddon.

The Climb the Highest Mountain series has been outlined by the Ascended Master El Morya in thirty-three chapters; this book contains chapters 16 through 19 of the complete work. The concepts presented here build upon the foundational material in the five books that precede it. If you review the earlier volumes, especially Book 3, *The Masters and the Spiritual Path,* you will find an in-depth discussion of many subjects that provide background for what you will read in this book.

In the previous chapters we have spoken in detail of the Ascended Masters—who they are, their function on planet Earth and beyond; the chakras of man; his four lower bodies;

the threefold flame of life; an introduction to the science of the spoken Word; the ascension in the Light; and many other subjects only lightly touched upon in this volume. If you have not already done so, we hope you will be able to review the earlier books so that your understanding of the principles of cosmic law presented here may be more complete.

This volume is a very important part of the series, and in turn, it provides a foundation for what will follow in the remaining three books. While the challenge of Light and Darkness, Good and Evil is not easy, it is something that we all must learn to master before we can graduate from this plane of relativity where we find ourselves by our karma—and by our own free-will choices. We conclude this volume with inspirational and comforting words from the teachings of the Darjeeling Master on the theme "Thy Will Be Done," leaving us with the concept that although Darkness may be with us, Light will prevail in the end.

If this is your first exploration of the Climb the Highest Mountain series, we welcome you to your study of these teachings from the Ascended Masters, which have been called the Everlasting Gospel, our scripture for the age of Aquarius. For those who are taking up this book after reading the previous volumes, we wish you God-speed in your continuing journey to climb the highest mountain.

THE EDITORS

Introduction

I T IS SAID THAT THE BEST PROPHET OF the future is the past. And as we explore the future of planet Earth, we must identify the momentous events that have brought us to the present. So often people self-righteously intone Santayana's famous warning, "Those who cannot remember the past are condemned to repeat it."[1] It would seem, however, that this includes all of us, for despite the extraordinary differences of opinion about what history is or what history means, as one historian has it, "On one point we are all agreed—civilizations begin, flourish, decline, and disappear, or linger on as stagnant pools."[2]

I believe that we, as sons and daughters of God, can do something about that course of history. Injecting the liberating power of the Word into it, we can make the difference. I believe that God reveals himself in the moving stream of history and that the true nature as his consciousness reveals itself through the free will of men and nations. While we would agree with those who say that there is no inevitability in history except as men make it, it still remains for us to answer that elusive question, "What is the meaning of history?"

What is the meaning of the history of our planet Earth? And what are the conclusions we are experiencing? What are their antecedents? Whence have come these streams that are manifesting now as effect? What are the causes *behind* the causes that are obvious?

As we consider these questions, we find that the discussion of history masks a deeper, more challenging question: "What is the purpose of life?"

Who am I? Why am I here? What is my reason for being?

And these raise even a more basic question: "Why did someone—Elohim—create the universe in the first place?" Who and what was the point of Light that was the original beginning? And were we there in that beginning as Christ said, "Before Abraham was, I AM"?[3] When did we first declare, "Lo, because thou art, I AM"?

And if we discover the purpose of creation and of being on earth, then we must ask, "Are we truly fulfilling that purpose?" Today it seems quite obvious that many upon earth are fulfilling the purposes of death and not life, against which the Guru Moses warned us in his final hours upon earth.

Like all great truths, the answer to these questions is of necessity profound, sublime and simple. Yet it is one that God has revealed to men throughout history in an ever-unfolding pattern of His identity within ourselves. Although we may not yet know the answer to this riddle, it is the main theme and the drama of life.

Shakespeare said, "All the world's a stage"—which God and nature do with actors fill.[4] And Montaigne saw life as "an ancient drama, a noble farce wherein kings, republics, and emperors have played their parts, and to which the whole vast universe serves for a theater."[5]

Yes, God is the Master Dramatist, however you would define that God. He and no other penned the beginning, created the characters and wrote the choices of the final scene of an epoch that we by our free will are about to outplay. We, the cast, are free to play the scenes more or less as we see fit, with a minimum number of cues from the Great Divine Director. He, of course, calls the rehearsals, schedules the performance, raises the curtain at the dawn of each epoch, and lowers it as sun sets on civilization after civilization. Throughout the game of life, he sets the ground rules and then reveals himself in the players and their parts. In the moving stream of events, he gives life to history, to "his story." And history is his story even as it is the story of the free will of men and nations.

Yet with all the coaching from master artists and divine directors, more often than not the players strut and fret their hour upon the stage[6]—because they haven't got the message. It would seem, as Shakespeare said, that "all our yesterdays have lighted fools the way to dusty death."[7] For in the course of recorded history, twenty-six civilizations have arisen; sixteen of them are already dead and buried, and the ten survivors are all threatened. Two of them are making their final curtain call. Seven of the remaining eight are threatened by "annihilation or assimilation by the eighth, namely our own civilization of the West."[8] According to historian Arnold Toynbee, western civilization is in a cycle which precedes the collapse.

Although it is possible to turn the tide of history, Toynbee says that of those who have gone before us, none have yet done so. Considering this, how are we to be the generation that makes the difference? How can we make the difference when others who have gone before us have failed? If our society collapses, will it resurrect, rising to new and glorious heights—or will it fall at all?

As we study the history of our world, we find on the one hand the activities of the councils of the power elite and on the other of the sons of God who have existed side by side with them on planet Earth and other systems of worlds for hundreds of thousands of years. The battle for the minds and souls of God's children is an ancient Armageddon recalled from the records of our own collective unconscious in *Star Wars* and other science-fiction scenarios. The players of Light and Darkness are arrayed on the universal stage. The battle lines of Good and Evil are drawn. And once again the LORD sends his spirit to anoint the true shepherds of the people, to deliver them from the fleshpots of Egypt by the liberating power of his Word.

The Great White Brotherhood is comprised of the saints, the sages, the gurus of East and West who have accelerated into higher consciousness—ascended, if you will, into the white Light. They move in and through and among us as our teachers and as our wayshowers. And they inspire all who listen from within their own hearts and minds as to how we can together save this dear planet from this collision of self-destruction.

In the records of the retreats of the Great White Brotherhood are the missing links that archaeologists have not found. When there is a gap in scientific or historical awareness, God does not leave us comfortless. By this spirit of prophecy there is communication from the saints in heaven, or the Ascended Masters, to those upon earth who have an ear to hear, who will listen, and who will learn from their elder brothers and sisters on the path of spiritual evolution. Thus, by physics and metaphysics, the history of the invasion of planet Earth by forces of darkness is confirmed and the workers of iniquity among the people are exposed.

But the exposure of the power elite is only the beginning; the challenging of their authority by the science of the spoken Word becomes the supreme challenge of our era. God would confound the manipulators and the murderers of his people, but not by the bloodbath of world wars that we have witnessed nor by the reigns of terror of previous revolutions. The revolution we require, the revolution we must have is the Coming Revolution in Higher Consciousness.

You were born to blend your soul with that moving stream of the Word—the universal Word that was in the beginning with God without whom was not anything made that was made. We were not made without that Word in us, and therefore, to that Word we return. It is the key because what creates can uncreate. And the Word can uncreate the entire destructive mechanization of the fallen ones that is worldwide. It looks like a tremendous monolith of civilization and the buildup of nuclear weapons, and we fear and tremble before the councils of war of the dark ones. And we wonder what is coming upon us.

The Eastern term for all of this is *maya*—illusion. All that the fallen ones created without access to the living Word is maya, is illusion. And you have no reason to fear before it because God is in you and "greater is he that is in you, than he that is in the world."[9]

The Lord is calling you and me today to be the remnant who will use his name, the sacred name of AUM, the sacred name of the I AM THAT I AM, the sacred name of Jesus Christ, of Gautama Buddha and every saint—to use the sacred name, to intone the Word and release the Light for the healing of the nations.

For those who have the daring and the courage to probe beyond the thresholds of the outer mind to really know who they are, what lies in the caverns of the subconscious, what can be brought forth from the Superconscious Mind as the potential from the Great Causal Body of Life—this book is written, this book is for you. If you are not content with the surface, physical/intellectual/emotional existence—if you wish to probe beyond to the spiritual depths and heights of your being, read on.

MARK AND ELIZABETH PROPHET
Messengers of the Masters

Chapter 1

The Cult
of Hedon

*In the last days perilous
times shall come.
   For men shall be ... lovers
of pleasures more than lovers of
God.*

II TIMOTHY

The Cult of Hedon

The Pursuit of Happiness

WHEN THE LORD GOD MADE man, he made man in his own image.[10] It does not say that he made one man in his own image and all the rest of them in another image. Yet we read a strange thing: after Cain murdered Abel, Cain went into the land of Nod to take a wife.[11] Therefore, we realize that there were other evolutions on the earth at that time.

In orthodoxy we find that the beginning is made to be almost like a fairy story—"once upon a time." But it didn't happen that way. The evolutions of this universe are millions of years old, and we learn in the ancient Hindu scriptures known as the Vedas of what they call the expulsion from the mouth of God of the universe. As a child would take a balloon and begin to blow up the balloon, so the mouth of God pushed out the universes, the starry bodies, the heavens into space. This has occurred and is scientifically corroborated by many of our scientists today.[12]

The Vedas then tell us that after the universe gains a certain size, it begins to decrease in size and is once again taken into the mouth of God. These pralayas or manvantaras, the exhaling of the universe and the inhaling of the universe, are all a part of a cycle so vast that it almost defies our thoughts.

All of this indicates the vastness of the universe, a vastness that yet takes into account individual life. Regardless of the size of the universe, it is still concerned with the monad, the individual—and this is the wonder of it all. For in one sense of the word, we are each a miniature universe. We have the key to the whole universe in our consciousness. We can expand that consciousness out and mentally take into account the whole universe.

When the Christ, by whom all things were made, was himself brought forth from the heart of the Father, it was the greatest moment of all time. It had nothing to do with two thousand years ago. We should understand very clearly, then, that not by a vain theological speculation, not by mere words uttered by our mouths, but by the Living Word we read: "In the beginning was the Word, and the Word was with God, and the Word was God.... All things were made by him; and without him was nothing made that was made. In him was life; and the life was the light of men."[13]

So we see that the natal day of our universe was the natal day of our Lord, the eternal Universal Christ. Each of us was created in God's image; he also is made in God's image. The Christ was the first emanation from the Father—the Word, the Logos. So in one sense of the word, when the morning stars danced together for joy at the first moment of primal creation, it was the birthday of a king—the King of kings and Lord of lords who said, "Before Abraham was, I AM."[14] We are all unseparated drops of the infinite ocean of God when we rightly understand ourselves.

The consciousness that "in sin did my mother conceive me" came after the Fall of man, after he entered into the consciousness of the flesh, after he became involved in the sense of separation. As long as he could commune with God face to face in the Garden in the cool of the day, as long as he was aware of God and the Reality thereof, there was no sense of separation for Adam.

The words "And the LORD God planted a garden eastward in Eden"[15] bespeak a place where happiness abounds because Universal Law is obeyed. During that time, communion with the heart of God was sweet, real and tangible. Each moment of that communion was an interchange of awareness and exchange of concepts whereby the son grew in grace and stature finding "favor with God." In the Garden there was an abundance of peace and harmony and of quiet realization where the cup of joy runneth over. These moments with God were sought after, and each monad entering the ivy-covered arbor of communication emerged enriched and contented.

There is a concept of religious passivism abroad today, which, when incorrectly applied, leads to spiritual apathy and even a consciousness of doom concerning the inevitability of the end of the world: there is nothing we can do about world conditions anyway, so we'll wait for Jesus to come and save us and for the judgment of the wicked. This erroneous philosophy is subtly woven throughout the Old and New Testaments as a dark thread that comes to the surface of the light tapestry just often enough to influence the interpretation of the message of the Christ slightly to the left or right of center.

Let us, then, heed the warning of the Master who said, "Beware of false prophets, which come to you in sheep's clothing, but inwardly they are ravening wolves."[16] We point this out to remind the disciple on the Path that the carnal mind is ever at hand to argue against the wisdom of the Ancient of Days. And the lost Word, then, is lost because men look without, and that which is within is thereby impoverished.

Turning once again to the happy state of "walking with God," men will expand their heart's treasures. For obedience is not intended to be a yoke of burden to man but a security and trust that provides him limitless happiness here and now and that ultimate transcendence that will indeed make him to know the joy of the Lord.

The Search for Happiness

The importance that the founding fathers of America placed on "the pursuit of happiness" is indicated by the fact that they were willing to pledge their lives, their fortunes and their sacred honor to preserve those truths that they held to be self-evident—not the least of which was the pursuit of happiness.[17] They knew that no document could guarantee happiness but that everyone should be given the opportunity of searching. This shows the value that men place upon their own personal joy and their beliefs in the inherent right of finding it, which they deem essential to life itself.

The word *Hedon* mans "pleasure,"* and it is to the seeking of personal pleasure that the multitudes of the planet are dedicated, each man defining for himself that which brings satisfaction to his being. Will Durant defined hedonism as "the doctrine that pleasure is the actual, and also the proper, motive of every choice."[18]

In reality, the Garden of Eden, or Edon, was a garden of delight and beauty where divine pleasure was assured to the

---

* While *Hedon* is not a word in common usage, *hedonism* is defined as the doctrine that pleasure or happiness is the sole or chief good in life, or a way of life based on this doctrine. The origin is given as the Greek *hēdonē,* meaning "pleasure."

soul. Today the tempo of individual manifestation and the trends of life have created a false understanding of what pleasure really is, where it is to be found, how it is obtained and what the end result will be to the individual.

We live in a society of pleasure-seekers who have formed the Cult of Hedon and whose values, or lack of them, equate pleasure with the repudiation of moral codes, high ethics, decency, clean speech and cosmic law. By the power of habit, men are held in vice grips of slavery to a debauchery that daily takes its toll in their lives, defrauding them of necessary vitality, milking dry their economy and leading them to spiritual bankruptcy. This pattern of self-destruction must be understood by every thinking and feeling person who is concerned in any measure with the preservation of opportunities for personal freedom and universal opportunity for the planet and its evolutions.

Records of Atlantis

Saint Germain reveals that these patterns are not new or unique to this age: "Long ago on Atlantis, the race of men then seeking to know, to dare, to do and to silently pursue the laws of life fell into the habit of thinking they had reached the ultimate in accomplishment because they were manifesting considerable control over material substance. Nevertheless, such phenomena were and are by no means indicative of a true inner God-awareness and Self-control. Atlantean science, like the present-day physical sciences, seemed the highest; and materialism, atheism and sensuality, with gratification of personal wants, stood to the men and women of that day second only to the goals of the supreme state.

"In this false satiety, this false communal spirit, they vainly imagined that freedom from physical labor would provide all with the ultimate in enlightenment as a by-product of their newfound luxury, leisure and what they called 'the good life.' Pursuing the wisdom of the world and seeking to be thought wise among men, the people sought out licentious activities that palled on the senses while they ignored the call to adore the Source of Life and to fulfill the supreme creative purpose. Thus they outpictured the left side of the tablet, thinking nothing was new, and averring, as the Book of Revelation declares, 'I am rich and increased with goods and have need of nothing.' This attitude contrasts with the divine assessment of their state, which reads, 'And knowest not that thou art wretched and miserable and poor and blind and naked.'[19]

"To make all things new requires a steadfast conscious effort and intent in the pursuit of intangible as well as tangible goals. It requires a special focusing of the sacred fire in heart, head and hand and an inner resolve, a God-firmness, if you will, which, as a fiery zeal, assures the aspirant of unwavering progress. This progress is reflected first in greater happiness—which God intends all to have—and then in a more rapid ushering-in of the kingdom whereby the natural estate of mankind draws outwardly closer to the Ideal Image, and secular pursuits ally themselves with spiritual goals.

"The unquestioned Reality of man's cosmic destiny pre-ordained in the mind of God is 'nothing new under the sun.'[20] But by daily renewing his covenant with his Maker, man makes new his original birthright, infusing each interaction of the law of being with vitality and perpetual joy. At present, man's destiny—his own individual *Deity-established-in-you* matrix—is held secure in the heart of God. This matrix is entrusted to those advanced souls upon earth who drink the communion cup of our LORD's cosmic abundance until it runneth over with everlasting joy."[21]

And so we see that Atlantis had then and Atlantis revisited

today in the United States of America has a destiny of out-picturing the flame of Omega, the Matter cosmos and the Mater-realization of the God flame. And inasmuch as science and technology and inventions are laid upon the altar of the Divine Mother to the end that, free from drudgery, people might pursue a spiritual life and pursue that adeptship that is theirs to have, then it is a lawful manifestation.

But we have seen in many such civilizations and the records of them in akasha that when people have so much given to them of conveniences and of technology, instead of taking the opportunity to pursue the spiritual path, they begin to indulge in the squandering of the sacred fire in any and all of the chakras. This leads to the depletion, therefore, of the Light in the temple, and consequently the inability to identify with a path of personal Christhood. The people then become degenerate.

This has happened not only on our planet, but also long ago on what was then the planet closest to the sun, which was destroyed and is now only an asteroid belt.

The Origin of the Cult of Hedon

Tracing the evolution of souls beyond this planet, we can go back to the planet Maldek, and beyond that to another planet, called Hedron. Once a paradise of beauty and culture, Hedron contained within its Causal Body a divine plan for a Golden Age civilization. On this planet was an evolution of souls destined to outpicture the flame of divine love under the direct influence of Helios and Vesta in the center of our solar system.

They basked in the sun, they rejoiced in the love of God, but after a time, that rejoicing, that childlike innocence, turned to selfishness and to the pleasure cult. And so the word "hedonist" has descended all the way from Hedron as the sign of those who make the goal of life the pleasure of the five senses. The totally selfish consciousness of those evolving on that planet resulted in their self-annihilation. They destroyed themselves and they destroyed their planet.

Those who were counted worthy, the remnant of the Hedonists (or the Hedrons) were allowed to reembody on Maldek. At that time Maldek was a very pure, virgin planet. With the coming of the Hedrons, this planet was also perverted through a pleasure cult.

The Hedrons were not a new evolution. They had great experience in science and in war, and they were able to create weapons greater than our most modern nuclear weapons, inventions greater than our most modern forms of transportation in air, on sea and land. And so they brought about a nuclear holocaust on Maldek and destroyed themselves. All that remains of that planet is the asteroid belt between Mars and Jupiter.[22]

Once again there were souls thrust from physical embodiment floating on the astral plane.* Once again, life provided an opportunity. The Lords of Karma determined that two-thirds of the evolution of that entire planet were not worthy of perpetuation. They were brought to final judgment and they passed through the second death. One third who were considered redeemable, those who were humanitarians, philanthropists, scientists, who had resisted war and inharmony, who had resisted the misuse of love—love as obedience and love as vision—were allowed to reembody upon the earth.

Thus the earth is beset with a race of people who have a

---

* The astral plane is a frequency of time and space beyond the physical, yet below the mental, corresponding to the emotional body of man and the collective unconscious of the race. Because the astral plane has been muddied by impure human thought and feeling, the term "astral" is often used in a negative context to refer to that which is impure or psychic.

previous evolution of the pleasure cult, of science, of creating babies in test tubes, of creating all forms of life, of controlling genes and chromosomes, of waging war. These people (who are called laggards because they lagged behind the spiritual evolution of this system) embodied on Atlantis, and they began to repeat the same way of life, and so earth also became infested with this pleasure cult.[23]

The Fall of Hedron

Gautama Buddha opens the record and the memory of what was once a Golden Age on the planet Hedron: "Beloved of the Golden Sun of the Infinite One, how art thou now transported into another golden sphere—a sphere of memory that does become a Reality only in the Eternal Now. For the mortal cannot capture the infinitude of a presence of a once-manifest Golden Age so long past, now forgot.

"Come, then, for I would speak to you in this golden sphere, once thy habitat, once the kingdom of joy. And this joy, beloved, is the true bliss of the Divine Union, a joy of a paradise that seemed as though it would never end.

"This golden sphere, beloved, where I am taking you is in fact the Causal Body and the point of origin of a planet closest to the sun, identified to you by beloved Lanello as 'Hedron.' What you know of Hedron is its descent into a cult of pleasure, but I bring you to the golden sphere of a paradise that was beyond all necessity of human pleasure.

"For here I would that you might experience for an hour with me this night what it is to be in the warmth of the golden sunshine of love and to know the fullness of all joy in all chakras of being, oneness with the twin flame and with God. So, beloved, it is a reprieve from a planet called 'Earth' where you sojourn and have entered to tarry with the Lord and to toil for the hour of his appearing. . . .

"Thus, hearts of Light, it is a giant sphere that takes us there for contemplation upon a perfection so light, so beautiful, so immediately the transfer of the temple of Helios and Vesta—truly the first point of qualification of this 'sun-light' by a planetary body followed by the calling and the office of other planetary bodies of the seven spheres.

"Beloved ones, to enter here now you may see the beauty, the verdure, the fragrance, the harmony of an existence that each and every one of you knows exists somewhere in the vast somewhere. It is a memory like this, beloved, that endows all human existence with hope, with certainty of faith and conviction born of experience that Earth is not as God intended it to be and that there is an Eternal Now waiting for the soul.

"I give you a moment to explore—with eye and swiftness of Mercurian feet, winged-sandaled—meadows, forests, streams, vast bodies of water, sky and lightness, elemental life, visible angels—not overpopulated nor under, for on a small orb such as this many can evolve when harmony is as natural as the grace of birds and flowers in springtime.

"Sit back, as it were, beloved, and relax in this atmosphere. Absorb from this great Causal Body of golden light and pink glow-ray a peace, a recharging, a sense of divine purpose and ultimate goals, and know that all that separates you from this experience is time, space and karma—*kal-desh*.

"These things are not impenetrable obstacles. Time can be transcended when it is mastered. Space can be penetrated when it is absorbed. Karma can be dealt with, for all that is required is to deal with the day's allotment. Cast it into the sacred fire early that thy work might be a gain in self-mastery for the next karmic assignment and spiritual lesson.

"Now then, this golden sphere does not leave one passive, without activity and challenge; it affords new vistas, almost a sense of urgency to unfold cosmic splendor and science. Here Ascended Masters, unascended ones see the immediacy of becoming God and more of God. Earth's playground—or playpen—is a very limited challenge. From this level the whole of the Spirit/Matter Cosmos beckons. Any one of you can consider those things that would take your heart and mind and diligence if you but had the hours, if you had taken from you the struggle and the dire challenges of earthly existence. Know, then, that there is no plateau in infinity, no end of opportunity, discovery, happiness, creativity.

"In the wonder of this beauty where many of the inhabitants of Hedron could see to the very heart of the Sun itself, the presence of Helios and Vesta, there eventually came about on the part of some, absent of true gratitude and appreciation for these opportunities unlimited, a desiring for other discoveries in lesser spheres, in lower vibrations.

"Why, then, would they desire less than all of this? Because in the lower domain, you see, they would achieve notoriety and a human kind of a godhood not subject to a hierarchical chain of command; they would achieve independence and the fulfillment of a desire for a pleasure that would slowly begin with a titillation of the outer senses instead of the stimulus of the inner sensitivities of the soul.

"Gradations of vibration are subtle, beloved, and the one least aware of his own fluctuation is the individual himself. Only a single blind spot, and one (thinking he is yet in the corona of the Sun) may have strayed many miles from the highest vibrations of Maitreya. Many have not understood what is known as the fall of angels, but I tell you, beloved, the descent is always by imperceptible degrees.

"Now, if you but think of this eventuality on Earth, you are very much aware, for instance, that those who are ignorant know not that they are ignorant, even as in the animal kingdom the animal that is clumsy knows not that he is clumsy. You have all seen insensitivity of conscience, of awareness of Christ Self allow individuals to rationalize heinous crimes against humanity, all manner of perverse relationships and actions against one another justified for some so-called righteous cause, even as you have seen individuals locked into pockets of self-deception believing they are God-fearing and of the highest path or, on the other hand, aware they have chosen the left and yet so very certain it is correct.

"Thus, if you will attempt to understand the mysteries of life from examples and equations of Earth, you may come to some very practical as well as sobering conclusions to the questions you ask—primarily: Why would one leave the very center of the throne of grace in the heart of God in the Great Central Sun to descend for experimental purposes or other reasons?

"I show you gradations of Light and Darkness and how these have resulted, in fallen angels, as a direct opposition to the Most High. This is easier to understand than the apathy of the sons and daughters of God who stray just a little and all of whose actions seem to be Godlike and for righteousness. These pedal in one place. They know not what place they are in; they have no sense of co-measurement—neither betwixt Earth and the lower astral plane nor Earth and the Golden City of Light or the Golden Planet of Light in this sphere where we are.

"Blessed ones, the shadows creep and fall across the un-suspecting soul. No matter what plane of occupation, whether the etheric or in dense Earth, once one has entered the decision to be in relativity, a relative good and evil based on a position and a defense of one's right—'my right'—from thenceforth, beloved, one can calculate neither the plummeting nor the ascent. Something apart from oneself must report the goings and the comings—the rise and fall of the soul....

The Causal Body of Hedron

"There is a Causal Body for each planet of the system, and there are spheres of Light that contain the record of all good in that collective Causal Body. The Causal Body of each planetary home contains the entire momentum of the members of the Great White Brotherhood* and unascended souls who have evolved upon it, and may be called upon to 'swing round.' And in that swing it becomes congruent to those earthbound, as you say, and can transmit in an instant a Light and a power that can also consume on an instant.

"This consuming, to the inhabitants of such a sphere so touched by the sphere of the Causal Body, can seem as utter destruction, desolation or annihilation, as though someone flashed a light and a goodly portion of the known world were to be changed. This is a method of drawing a world abruptly back into an alignment with the inner blueprint. It is not the preferred method, beloved, but it does avert ultimate chaos and destruction of souls.

"What occurs in this method is a reducing of the identity of all. For to take from the individual his karma or his human creation before he has gained a mastery of the Light in the opposite dimension—that is, in the dimension of the I AM Presence—is therefore to reduce his identity. For one's karma and one's human creation is one's self until one has transmuted it and ascended to a higher level of self-awareness.

"Thus, if you can imagine a flash of light as a nuclear explosion coming upon the planet only for a split second, in that moment God would have the power to reduce all equally, let us say, by ten percent, by fifteen percent, depending on

---

* The Great White Brotherhood is a spiritual order of saints and adepts of every race, culture and religion. These Masters have transcended the cycles of karma and rebirth and reunited with the Spirit of the living God. The word "white" refers to the aura or halo of white Light that surrounds them.

what reduction would be necessary in order to avert an utter calamity or cataclysm. This has been done in the past. Entire evolutions have been 'dwarfed,' you might say—reduced in life span, reduced in stature. Thus, as the Evil was cut back, so the potential for greater Good was also cut back until that evolution should come unto a love for and an obedience to the higher Law and LORD.

"The drawback to this solution to a planetary equation that was once the dilemma of Hedron or Maldek and is fast becoming the dilemma of Earth is that there is no lesson learned. There is the same potential for Evil as that which created the greater danger in the first place. Without the intercession of World Teachers, those so reduced will simply continue on in their old ways, and the Darkness will mount again as new Nimrods come forth to build new towers greater than before.

"So you see, beloved ones, there is a certain futility to this solution; for the planets that have received it have not merited further World Teachers, having been given many, even as many have been sent to Earth. Thus, without an Intercessor, a Maitreya, they have simply built again, just as the grass grows and the weeds return once the fields have been cut or the lawn mowed.

"Thus, the advantage is a certain gaining of time. And this time was gained in Earth through the flood of Noah, the sinking of continents, and the reduction of the life span of the evolutions on Terra.[24] And even withal, teachers were sent again and again. Yet, the joy of it all is that there has been a harvest of souls who have ascended for the gaining of that time, for the setting back of the potential of Evil on Earth. Thus, there is in the annals of Earth, as we read them this night from the golden sphere, some salutary word that souls have been won for the ascension and have attained a Godhood that otherwise might have been lost....

"One of the dilemmas that face the Cosmic Council and the Lords of Karma at this juncture of the history of this system of worlds is that some among the Lightbearers descended too far, lost the way, identified with fallen angels through only a splinter of pride, which grew and festered and began to dominate their existence. These Lightbearers, then, lost the momentum, lost the wind in their sails.

"It is about these Lightbearers that we are most concerned, that the Darjeeling Council and the Messengers are concerned —that they, having a memory of higher spheres, not sensing the gradations of consciousness over which they have crossed, do not have a sense of the danger, do not have a sense of the jeopardy in which their souls are placed when such forces of Darkness as are being witnessed today are coming nearer and nearer a confrontation on the planet.

"This planet where they should be but pilgrims, sojourners in the way, easily able to take their leave of it, has now become to many of these children of the Sun a prison house from which they cannot escape. They have lost the key to open the prison doors, and unless some make the call, no angel will come to open those doors. This is a far greater dilemma to Sanat Kumara than the plight of a mankind that has ever walked the easy, downward way.

"We seek to save that which has lost the First Estate, those who were once in the kingdom of joy. It is our hope that in saving these, there might be an engrafting of the Word[25] unto those who have it not. Unless, then, the firstfruits be saved from psychicism and all manner of false prophecy, how, then, can there be another opportunity for humanity at large?...

"I will tell you, then, beloved, that the golden sphere of Light where you now abide is about to be transferred.... As all Lightbearers have entered it, now the golden sphere itself does begin to move toward planet Earth. When it is fully accomplished,... you will know that there is a very large golden sphere of Light that literally touches the Earth in its lower portion.

"It is like a tree house into which you climbed as a child. This place, beloved, forms the figure-eight flow with the 'Place Prepared' below. It provides you with a haven of paradise even as you work the works of God at hand. It provides you with an inner blueprint and a power source that you have not known.

"This sphere, beloved, is positioned with its center being the throne that I occupy as Lord of the World. Thus, I was called to other octaves by the Cosmic Council and Sanat Kumara many weeks ago, and to me they presented this proposal. For Hedron has long gone beyond the pale of restoration and has become, as you know, an asteroid belt.

"Therefore, the Cosmic Council decreed: Why not deliver this sphere to those Lightbearers of Earth who have demonstrated the responsibility and the ability to produce what is necessary? Why not give to them access to so great a reservoir of Light and kingdom of joy that those who have been called by Serapis to ascend and stand with him as the stalwarts of Thermopylae might have almost unlimited wealth, abundance, opportunity, wisdom—and at the same time an escape hatch if the various courses of action should come to pass that have to do with the return of mankind's karma?...

"For you, beloved, were a part of the building of this kingdom of joy and this Causal Body; and therefore, because you are here—having volunteered to redeem the karma not only of Earth but of Hedron (for many of its fallen evolutions have reembodied here)—you, then, by your presence have also allowed this event to take place.

"Thus, in truth, many upon Earth who did not go the way

of the pleasure cult completely but regained their senses and stood fast have, to your credit, substance in this Causal Body. Thus, you have a point of polarity with it and now, for the first time in thousands of years, access to this cumulative momentum of world good."[26]

Self-Awareness

The Cult of Hedon is very real to man, albeit few know it as such. The chief evils of the world gain entrance into man's being (where they vie for his soul) through misconceptions concerning his own personal identity.

The statement "I am I and no one else" cannot be denied. But to affirm "I am I and everyone else must see me deified," as do many among mankind, is to invert the affirmation of God in man "I AM THAT I AM," is to limit oneself in the self-centered attitude of the human ego. The subtle pressures of the ego for recognition are to be found not only in the attitude of the pauper and peasant, but also that of poet and prince.

An understanding of the forces involved in pleasure seeking and of the interplay of individual and mass emotions is important both to those who have a background in psychology and the behavioral sciences and also to those who have little academic preparation in these fields. In the chapter entitled "Your Synthetic Image,"* an allegorical explanation of the development of the personal consciousness was given. A rereading of this chapter at this juncture will assist the student in following the points we are about to outline.

While the very definition of the word *infinite* indicates that it has neither beginning nor ending, and this as definition in

---

* See chapter 1 of *The Path of the Higher Self,* the first book in the Climb the Highest Mountain series.

the mathematical sense is acceptable to the modern mind, the term must also be applied in the metaphysical sense to the Omnipotent, Omniscient and Omnipresent One.

As God is infinite, so man as the finite manifestation of the Infinite finds self-realization in the space-time continuum at that point where he (through individualization in the world of form—the three-dimensional world) achieves a measure of self-identity.

If infinity is thought of as a circle having neither beginning nor ending, and for the purpose of metaphor we think of God as that circle, then man, as manifestation, is a point somewhere or anywhere on that circle. This is the point of individualization, the point where the Infinite becomes finite, where God is individed and the Whole becomes many points. (Nevertheless, that Whole is always greater than the sum of its parts, because even the greatest finite number can never equal infinity.)

When man was first created, the first word he uttered upon realizing himself, embryonically, was the word "Why, I AM" or "Lo, I AM." Thus the name of God (I AM) becomes the Word incarnate—the Word that became flesh and dwelt among us—the first word of creation and the first response of the creation.

Without the name of God, without the declaration "I AM THAT I AM,"[27] there can be no individualization (no in-dividing of the Word), and the manifestation remains in the void without identity. It is thus uttered at the moment when awareness of self is realized as an independent-dependent part of the whole. And until it is spoken, there is, in reality, no activation of self-awareness.

It is to that moment, the nexus where the components of eternity descend into the capsule of time, that we would direct you in thought, for at that time the screen of man's consciousness is a white paper uncontaminated by any human thought or feeling. As the consciousness descends into the world of form, there is no contamination. But the moment individuality becomes veiled in flesh, it is made subject to a vast number of impressions, many of which are not realized at first. For the individual soon contacts the mass consciousness of thought and feeling in the evolutions of earth, and impressions of the imperfections in nature are thus formed upon the screen of the mind through contagion.

Utter rejection of many of these impressions has occurred in the lives of avatars who quickly extricated themselves from earthly consciousness and began to manifest, while still upon earth, a higher consciousness. But these were the few rather than the many. The many have succumbed to various levels of degradation. And the consciousness of man, trapped and snared by his own search for pleasure, was dethroned from its high estate and detoured into byways of self-disinheritance.

The Christ pursues joy as a babbling brook rushes to meet the larger tributary—joining hands with the many lifestreams that have all come from the One Source and desire total reunion in the ocean of God's blissful, bountiful Being. In reality, the search for pleasure, for joy, for happiness and for understanding of the meaning of life is a perfectly natural activity for the soul as she moves toward her own pristine purity; as she is impressed with cosmic influences that come directly from God in accordance with universal law.* There is nothing wrong with the search for joy and happiness, or even in its manifestation, as long as that search does not degrade or destroy the subtle manifestations of the invisible spirit man as it beckons the soul to rise in consciousness back to its supreme

---

* Whether housed in a male or female body, the soul is the feminine principle and Spirit is the masculine principle of the Godhead. The soul, then, is addressed by the pronouns *she* and *her*.

Source and then outwardly to express in the world of form and dimension mastery of self and personal destiny.

True Joy and Happiness

The Ascended Master Kuthumi, our divine psychologist, explains that "to 'overcome the world'[28] does not necessitate the surrender of true joy and happiness, of sweetness and light. To overcome the world is to understand the unnatural position of the traditional world order as it relates to man's spiritual identity. Wheat and tares growing side by side await the harvest sickle. God himself has tarried long and patiently awaited the manifestation of his created beauty, the perfection of the Divine Image on earth and in the individual lives of all mankind. . . .

"In the early days of planetary evolution when the former cycles were dominant, the beauty of perfection of the first Golden Ages was a joy to behold. All of the natural powers of Christ-manifestation, now so sadly lacking among mankind, were in evidence everywhere. Men, women and children rejoiced together in the sunlight of perfect cosmic harmony. Nature outdid herself to lavish her perfection and beauty upon a joyous people. Communion with the angelic hosts and with the higher Presences of life, the representatives of God and the Lords of the Flame from the very heart of God, was a process as natural as that which occurs today when men and women tune in their television screens and see familiar faces appear.

"It is very difficult, of course, for people to understand 'how the all-powerful Creator could,' as they phrase it, 'permit the shadows of the world to obscure the beauty and perfection of the natural order of godliness that is within every man.' This turning upside down of human consciousness, this inversion of immortal principle into a mortal lack of truth and justice is a fog that occurred in the awful majesty of the will. But it was not the will of God that was perverted but only the will of man.[29]

"Today people boast of their free will. They are proud of the fact that they can reject that which they find objectionable and that they have within their hearts the means (so they think) whereby they can make correct judgments concerning all things. This judgment is often based upon the accepted world order and the inner attunement that mankind have with one another. They do not seem to realize the effects of these mental and emotional ties and their influences upon one another. The almost hypnotic, purposeless flitting about of the people of the world in the vain search of pleasure taxes even the imaginations of their hearts."[30]

The Sword of Truth

When the ego usurps the position of the Christ, no longer is man's pursuit of joy but ego satisfactions. Divine love is lost to human love, for no man can serve two masters.[31]

One of the great Ascended Master teachers, called the Great Divine Director, speaks of this division within the being of man: "Among his many profound observations concerning the human psyche, Saint Paul noted: 'For the good that I would I do not: but the evil which I would not, that I do.... I find then a law, that, when I would do good, evil is present with me.... But I see another law in my members, warring against the law of my mind, and bringing me into captivity to the law of sin which is in my members.'[32]

"This dichotomy found in the valley of decision by every individual seeking to do right is often the result of a warfare that threatens to divide the very personal self of that one. But Christ said, 'I came not to send peace, but a sword.'[33] The sword that is sent is the sword of Christ discrimination and Truth that cleaves asunder the false from the True, showing men the Reality of their divine nature and the utter futility of the human. It is designed to set apart those who choose to champion the cause of freedom rather than that of their own personal egos and smug concepts."[34]

The major cause of man's unrest evolves from the insatiable demands of the personal ego, the incorrect use of the creative energies, the use of tobacco and harmful drugs, the imbibement of alcoholic beverages and the partaking of processed foods from which nature's own balanced life-sustaining ingredients have been removed. The chemical nightmares thus induced in the body temple can destroy the ecstatic carrying power of the nerves themselves until men and women approach a place where there is less and less satisfaction in life, rather than more and more.

The victims of these abuses are legion and all indulgences of excesses are indeed, as the apostles have stated in the scriptures, a "superfluity of naughtiness."[35] When sensual satisfaction is the goal in the pursuit of pleasure, one always finds himself at a dead end.

We see many signs that the moral cement of society is crumbling. This is reflected not only in the shoddy construction of buildings and highways, of bridges and of drainage systems, but also in the slipshod use to which man puts life's energies.

People quickly learn the "easy way out," and they are lured by the power of wrong example. They seldom realize the worth of well-doing in the lives of others, faltering even in the acceptance of the need to do well, all the while seeking a harvest of good and permanent fruit for themselves. Yet, the Master said, "Whatsoever a man soweth, that shall he also reap."[36]

How have such misconceptions concerning the basic truths of universal law been foisted upon mankind?

Why has the lie of the archdeceivers found such easy acceptance?

What is actually responsible for the downward trends that are destroying the integrity and the worth of the individual at every turn?

How can we remedy the current debauchery in our society? And will such remedies strip mankind of the essential pleasures that his being seems to require midst the turmoil of current world conditions?

Do states of happiness of a higher order exist that can fulfill every human need?

Can these states of happiness be contacted by man today?

How may he recognize them and find deliverance from conditions unwanted by him over which he seems to have no control?

These are the questions we will attempt to answer in this chapter. The answers we give will be based on the teachings of the Ascended Masters and our own knowledge of God's Laws.

The Drug Way Out

THE FRUSTRATIONS OF MAN, stemming from nonrecognition and feelings of smallness and futility, lead many to take what we may term the "drug way" out. The hurried pace of contemporary man often leaves him with a "wrung out" feeling, and in this state of being he feels the need for a "lift." Unable to exercise dominion over his life's energies in order that his spiritual Self may release limitless power into his world, he often turns to alcohol, to coffee, to other strong stimulants, and even to drugs—all of which temporarily blunt the physical senses.

Escape from physical awareness is thus effected by reason of an absence of sensation, artificially achieved. And in this state, man creates pseudojoys of illusion that fulfill for a few hours or days his wish to be recognized, as illusion builds upon illusion.

The Buddha revealed the truth that life is suffering, and this is the case until we find the key of the resolution of suffering through transmutation, through harmony—not by the mechanical means of drugs.

Beloved Astrea, the Master who works to cut souls free from the psychic realm, warns of the dangers of this path of escapism: "Bear in mind, precious ones, that all that men do in the name of religion, or even of curious seeking, is the struggle of the Light within their souls to find itself, to transcend the self, to reach out into the universe and become a part of all that is. In this wish for identification with Reality, man has sought in many ways to find it.

"One of the methods he has sought to employ is sexual union. For as men or women seek one another, they are, in reality, seeking the other half of the Divine Whole, but they know it not. They think to achieve through physical union that wholeness that can be known only through the union of the soul with its Self—with the Higher Self and with one's own beloved twin flame. Such union brings both male and female into that wholesome state of the androgynous nature of God.

"However, mankind seek to find it through euphoria, through LSD [and other hallucinogenic drugs] or through drink of fermented beverages, through marijuana and other external or so-called violent means. None of these conditions are permanent. They but stretch the faculties of the soul so that she enters into segments of the astral world that are affinitized with the untransmuted, subconscious nature of the individual.

"This accounts for the variety of experiences that have occurred to those who have experimented with LSD, [Ecstacy] and other psychedelic drugs. These create an artificial expansion of consciousness that cannot possibly pass the borders of the great temples of Light of the Masters, one that is limited forever to an exploration of the subterranean levels of astral records. Some of these are siren-like, filled with a deadly beauty, a kaleidoscopic lure of color and sensuous impressions that later deny to those who have indulged in them the conscious entering into the higher octaves of Light where permanent beauty is sustained and true freedom known.

"In the higher octaves, the power of the gentle love of the Holy Spirit administers the elixir of consciousness to mankind in a fashion calculated to create universal enjoyment of the kingdom that God has made, that God is. Do not sell your birthright, your cosmic birthright, blessed ones, for a mess of pottage.[1] Do not let hunger for an accelerated expansion or the attainment of superpowers lead you to bargain away the carefully guided fulfillment of your life's opportunities as the Ascended Masters take you by the hand and safely lead you into realms of Light."[2]

Lord Lanto, the Master of wisdom, reinforces this warning: "Those who attempt to force these spiritual experiences with dangerous drugs or mental probings and exercises literally tear open the petals of the flower of the soul from the budding center. One day they will find the fallen petals at their feet, faded and dry, returning to the dust from which all things were made. Only by recognizing that the soul within, the living soul that God made, possesses the capacity to span the centuries will you be able to enter into immortal life."[3]

While the use of drugs as a means of escape is something that has been seen throughout recorded history, the last hundred years has seen a great increase in this practice. It is not by chance that this has occurred in a time of transition to a New Age.

The Coming Revolution in Higher Consciousness

When Jesus Christ dictated the Book of Revelation to his servant John, he announced the Coming Revolution in Higher

Consciousness for this hour, and he announced the finishing of the mysteries of God by the servant, the seventh angel.[4] So Saint Germain, who is this seventh angel, comes to show us how to implement the mysteries of the Holy Grail.

The revolution that was started by Jesus Christ was the revolution whereby life as God, life as the Flame in you, conquers every form of death. The greatest moment in our entire history as the children of Israel was when one Son of God came forth to place himself willingly on the cross to triumph over death so that we too might have that triumph, we might share in that victory and its subsequent glory. The revolution of the entire Spirit of the Great White Brotherhood is the revolution that began in the Garden of Eden with beloved Lord Maitreya. This revolution, the turning around of this world, to bring it to life once again and to its resurrection is now upon us.

In the last one hundred years, the Great White Brotherhood has been the instrument for the acceleration of that revolution. They have brought to us decade by decade a greater and greater awareness of the Ascended Masters, of the science of the spoken Word, of how we could enter into communion with the body and blood, the light of Alpha and Omega, in all of the hosts of heaven. For one hundred years this unfoldment of life has been for the purpose of teaching you and me how to implement the victory that was won two thousand years ago.

The opening of the temple door has been the opening of the sacred mysteries by the members of the Great White Brotherhood and their Messengers and prophets. And so with the acceleration of the revolution of life has come the acceleration of a counter-revolution of death, reaching previously undreamt of proportions in the 1960s.

The Counter-Revolution of the Sixties

Thus we see the concept of point/counterpoint, whereby the Brotherhood sets forth its commitment—it puts its rod into the earth, it electrifies people and planets—and then there comes, rising out of the mists of human creation, the counterpoint to put down that life, to distort it, to confute it.

The counter-revolution of death is so insidious that the people who are its victims do not know that they are being victimized by death and that they no longer have the fullness of life they once knew. In fact, not only because of the insidiousness but because also of the amount of misused power behind this insidious beast, the very people against whom it works will defend the very life of this beast.

The revolution of the sixties was a strange revolution, probably the strangest in history. But in it we also see history repeating itself from the decadence of Lemuria to the decadence of Atlantis to even several thousand years B.C. The generation of the sixties lived through one of the most paradoxical, perplexing, yet truly amazing revolutions in recorded history.

People felt the coming of the relentless wave of Light. But this was not a revolution of guns and political movements, although they played a role. Nor was it solely a revolution of music, sex and drugs, of youth casting off and taking on fads, although they too were a part of the scene. So were mysticism, Zen, vegetarianism, wine drinking, folk music, coffeehouses, rock and roll and rebellion against an old order that was rapidly fading and against the mothers and fathers throughout the land. As the musician Bob Dylan put it, in a song that became the anthem for a generation, the times were indeed a-changing.

It was an alchemical change. It was a flushing out. It was

an intensification of the violet flame bringing out the highest aspirations in people—people desiring to penetrate their souls and new planes of consciousness and people falling prey to leaders who had no right to be leaders, many of whom were agents of the archdeceivers who were about to stage their great counter-revolution against the Light.

The times were at best a mosaic—fragmentary, contradictory, trendy, and for the most, hard to follow. The young who were a part of them had little trouble catching on to parts of the revolution here and there, however. A new lexicon filled with ambiguous phrases such as "doing your own thing" allowed an entire generation to avoid expressing what this new turn of affairs really meant to them.

A "generation gap" set in that allowed both young and old alike to be free from actually having to explain to one another what was really happening. In fact, many didn't know, and many parents would rather not know. It was difficult to understand the meaning of the words to the songs and poems of the day. Often the subculture idioms masked references to sex or drugs. Frequently an insider had to translate the lyrics in order to make many of the songs intelligible even to the youth, most of whom would have remained loyal to the revolution anyway. Unlike the older generation, they weren't about to criticize what they didn't understand.

The old order was crumbling. Its hypocrisy was obvious to the new souls of the Aquarian age. Right while it was crumbling, it put on its best façade to sustain a legitimacy that it did not have. There was a new spirit abroad in the land. It was the oncoming tide of the very person of Saint Germain, the Guru of the Aquarian age. Everyone felt his person and his relentless wave, but there were many on hand to take advantage of that presence and that energy.

If you couldn't understand it or you couldn't explain it,

you could feel it. It shook everyone free from their former moorings. It made some footloose and fancy free, irresponsible, working out repressions of centuries, allowing them to bring forth the very rebellions that caused the sinking of Atlantis. Instinctively it made you want to get up and do something—anything. It was a revolution of individualism, a celebration of the self, of creating, of glorying in being what you really were—if only you knew what that was.

It didn't matter if the revolution struck everyone differently and made them do diverse things. That was its nature. But it was also a new awareness of the unity of life: each individual was a part of the movement, somehow tied into the great Cosmic Mind. There was a feeling of brothers and sisters and people being one, being mobile, and people being willing to be together and to share together and not be boxed up in the old order.

It was freedom itself coming forth from their souls. But that freedom in many was aborted to a psychic thralldom. It became a prison house, a madness. And in its worst form, it became a subculture of death.

This revolution is by no means over with. That subculture of death is seeking legitimacy and recognition and legalization today in many areas of our life, and what was a subculture and a counter-revolution to the mainstream of the Great White Brotherhood is today becoming legitimized. And this is our concern—that this is not passing away or being seen for what it was or for what it is, but it is gradually being absorbed into a new culture and a new civilization.

We stand at that crossroads. Life is yet fluid. We can determine to challenge this counter-revolution and turn it back. It has no backbone because it is based upon death.

Leadership of Atlantis Returned

The leaders who came to the fore in the sixties spoke of the revolution. They were able to articulate for the rank and file many of those things they felt but couldn't express. They saw through some of the flaws of society, the blunders of Big Brother. In the minds of the youth, the failures of the war in Vietnam became the positive proof that the leaders of the revolution had caught and maintained the vision.

Many of these leaders incarnated under a dispensation from the Lords of Karma that decreed that those individuals who had been kept out of embodiment since their part in the sinking of Atlantis had to reincarnate before the Golden Age.[5] They had to reincarnate to be given a final opportunity to bend the knee, confess the Lord Jesus Christ, receive the Holy Ghost, call on the law of forgiveness, go through repentance and remission of sin and regeneration in the service of God.

It was required that these individuals reincarnate a final time so that by their actions and by their words and their works they could be judged. Jesus preached to these rebellious spirits when he left his body on the cross on Good Friday. The Karmic Board gave them the opportunity to incarnate because, they said, the sons and daughters of Light, the true initiates of Jesus Christ, have the experience, the training of twelve thousand years since the sinking of Atlantis, the building of a culture, the Judeo-Christian tradition. They have in their hands—if they will invoke them—the laws of the land and the Laws of God to rebuke and refute the Liar and Lie of these reembodying fallen ones.

So God used the reincarnating fallen ones to test the leadership of our generation, our nation and every nation on earth. The majority of that leadership failed to challenge the fallen ones, but rather allowed the counter-revolution that they worked on Atlantis, their subculture, to become a part of the mainstream of life not only in America but in every nation upon earth.

The leadership of the counter-revolution was eclectic—it had to be. So many people were into so many different things. There were the hippies, the political revolutionaries, the free-speech and free-love advocates, the followers of Zen, the Merry Pranksters, the progenitors of the freaks, Hell's Angels, groupies, and others almost ad infinitum.

There were, of course, some unifying elements also. There was a frenetic, sensual, unearthly new music. There were a lot of new words in the language. But more than anything else, if there was a single item that unified these diverse, fragmented "trips," as they were called, it was marijuana, which Saint Germain calls the death drug.

There were two sharply conflicting views about the value of marijuana. Some defended it as either a harmless intoxicant or a mind-expanding sacrament. Those who were not persuaded that it was harmless staked out positions as widely divergent as discouraging its use because it was thought to be harmful, to those who thought it shouldn't be used until it became known what effect it had on the body, to those who said that marijuana was a killer weed that would produce violence, insanity and licentious behavior. The history of marijuana does much to clarify the issue.

The History of Marijuana

Cannabis is the Latin name that denotes the genus of the hemp family of plants, of which marijuana is a member. The particular species of the intoxicating form of marijuana is *Cannabis sativa*. The psychoactive chemical in cannabis is delta-9-tetrahydrocannabinol (commonly known as THC), which is responsible for producing its intoxicating effects.

The use of marijuana as a drug in China was mentioned in a Chinese herbal from 2737 B.C. The use of the drug as an intoxicant seems to have begun in India about 1000 B.C. It was cultivated in temple gardens by priests who made it into a liquid called *bhang*, which was used in association with religious ceremonies.

From India, marijuana spread to the Middle East. Since the Moslem faith specifically forbids the use of alcohol, marijuana was accepted as a substitute, and its use "thoroughly permeated Islamic culture within a few centuries."[6] Because of the euphoria it induced, the Arabs described it as the "joy-giver," "sky-flyer" and "soother of grief."[7]

According to marijuana researcher Dr. Gabriel Nahas, the greatest effects of widespread marijuana use were felt in Egypt: "According to the Arab historian Magrizy, hashish was first introduced in the thirteenth century at a time when Egypt was flourishing culturally, socially, and economically. First, the drug was accepted and used primarily by the wealthier classes as a form of self-indulgence. When the peasants adopted the habit, though, it was as a means of alleviation of the dreariness of their daily life."[8]

What effect hashish had on the strength and productivity of the Egyptian civilization is unknown. However, Nahas continues, "the appearance of cannabis products in the Middle East did coincide with a long period of decline during which Egypt fell from the status of a major power to the position of an agrarian slave state, exploited by a series of Circassian, Turkish, and European rulers.

"As often happens, the very decline of the nation prompted the increased use of what may have hastened its fall. The hashish habit became so prevalent among the masses that some sultans and emirs made attempts to prohibit its use, knowing that they were going against a practice participated in by a large percentage of the population. In the fourteenth century, Emir Soudouni Schekhouni ordered that all cannabis plants be uprooted and destroyed, and that any users of the substance be condemned to have all their teeth extracted without the benefit of anesthesia."[9]

As powerful an incentive as this was, it had little or no effect on the national hashish habit—because it was an addiction sustained by the most grotesque entity (the conglomerate of negative energy that focuses the consciousness behind the drug itself). The grip of the hashish entity is something incomparable, causing its victims to give their life in its defense. Thus, they become insensitive, even to the defense of their own life.

Napoleon ran into precisely the same problem. After the French conquered Egypt in 1798, one officer noted, "The mass of the male population is in a perpetual state of stupor."[10] Napoleon issued a decree forbidding the smoking of hashish and marijuana and the drinking of any beverages that contained them. This decree also had little effect.

Egypt is a cradle of the highest of all mysteries, the mystery of the ascension. The Ascension Temple is at Luxor. Therefore, the highest manifestation of life is located in its very soil. There came Ikhnaton with the great flame of the one God, the Sun-God, and all of us as extensions of that one central Light. There came the Mother flame as culture, art and beauty through Ikhnaton and Nefertiti. There came the twin flames sponsoring the initiatic mysteries.

Ikhnaton brought a revolution in life, in poetry, in art, in a directness that was unprecedented—the revolution of one God against all of the Egyptian countergods and false gods. So we have here, then, Egypt as the point of the counter-revolution against Serapis Bey, against the ascension flame and against the Great Pyramid, whose chambers are for the initiations (now on the etheric plane, but formerly on the physical plane) of the resurrection itself.

In Egypt today, there are very strict laws prohibiting the cultivation, sale, transportation, possession and use of hashish. Having already experienced its negative effects, the Egyptians have not been persuaded that marijuana is no worse than alcohol or tobacco. They know from centuries of the undermining of their people and culture that it is much, much worse.

In other nations, such as Morocco, where officially marijuana intoxication is not considered a great problem, unofficially public health officials privately admit that it is a major health hazard. But if you talk about it, no one admits using it, because it is illegal. Dr. Nahas reported that when he went to Morocco to conduct a study of marijuana use, officials in Rabat, the administrative capital, told him that cannabis was a serious public health problem, and a staff member at a mental hospital told him that there was a high incidence of marijuana usage recorded in the histories of patients hospitalized for mental illness. Among the chronic smokers, there was extreme mental and physical deterioration in men between the ages of thirty and forty.[11]

In Marakesh, Dr. Nahas met Dr. M. Teste, the director of the psychiatric hospital, who had been studying marijuana for twenty years and had published a paper describing the relationship between marijuana smoking and mental illness. He found that it produced an acute toxic psychosis, primarily among the young between fifteen and twenty years old who were in otherwise apparent good health. These psychotic episodes had a duration of two or three days and were marked by "agitation, confusion, and paranoia."[12] Sometimes this psychotic reaction occurred after only one exposure to the drug, and most of those who experienced it were left with a residual anxiety.

Dr. Nahas was told that approximately forty percent of hospital admissions in Morocco for acute psychosis were related to marijuana smoking. One senior government official said to him, "You scientists are always trying to unlock an open door. You come all the way to Morocco to find out if marijuana is harmful when we could have told you, 'Yes of course it is,' a long time ago."[13]

Marijuana in the Modern World

The rapid increase in the use of marijuana in America is one of the most perplexing phenomena of our times. In the early history of the nation, while the hemp plant was widely cultivated for the production of fiber, it seems to have been rarely used as an intoxicant. However, in the 1910s and 1920s a large influx of Mexican laborers introduced marijuana use to the nation, and it became widely used by black and Mexican workers in Texas and Louisiana.

The use of the drug was taken up by jazz musicians, who believed that intoxication from the "reefers" made their music sound "more imaginative and unique."[14] Marijuana was introduced to a wider segment of the population as jazz and jazz musicians moved up the Mississippi River to the major northern cities.

According to Nahas, "In Louisiana, marijuana use was widespread enough to cause public concern, particularly after a series of 'scare' articles appeared in *New Orleans Morning Tribune*. The stories, which were highly racist in tone, implied that blacks 'crazed' on marijuana were responsible for most of the heinous crimes committed in Louisiana. This was enough to trigger a wave of arrests and police brutality against large numbers of the black population in the area."[15] Between 1914 and 1931, nearly every state west of the Mississippi and many states to the east prohibited the use of the drug for non-medical purposes.

In 1937, Congress passed the Marijuana Tax Act, which prohibited the cultivation, importation or distribution of marijuana without government approval, except for the purpose of using the stalks to make rope or twine and for the manufacture of bird seed in the bird food industry. There was some controversy over the passage of this legislation. One scientist said: "The dangers of marijuana to the health and social structure of the United States have been exaggerated. The 'killer weed' theory put forward by the Federal Bureau of Narcotics is designed only to frighten people, not to educate them."[16] However, the debate was short lived, in part because the problem of marijuana use was not widespread at that time.

Furthermore, with the passage of this act, the United States was fulfilling international obligations made in 1925 when Egypt, which had previous experience with the deleterious effects of marijuana, asked that the International Opium Conference, of which the United States was a participant, give to cannabis products the same status as opiates.

In the 1950s, there was a rise in the use of marijuana as it was taken up by the beat generation, which was influenced by a long line of artists and poets who were marked by an open atheism, anarchy and a rebellion against traditional values. Charles Baudelaire, one of the heroes of the beat generation, was a member of the Club de Haschischins—the Hashish Club—which met in the elegant Hotel Lauzun in Paris's Latin Quarter. In his book *Artificial Paradises,* Baudelaire described "the taste for the infinite" as the force in man that drives him to indulge in hashish and other drugs.

However, Baudelaire saw the dangers of drugs as a means of this pursuit. He wrote: "Like all solitary pleasures, it makes the individual useless to men and the society superfluous to the individual. Hashish never reveals to the individual more than he is himself. Moreover, there is a fatal danger in such habits. One who has recourse to poison in order to think will soon be unable to think without taking poison."[17] While Baudelaire warned against the use of marijuana, his lyrical descriptions of the euphoric effects of the drug inspired many in the beat generation to experiment with it.

The "taste for the infinite" that Baudelaire spoke of is the perversion of the hunger of the real soul for the Holy Ghost. Many of those who took up this quest through drugs were the dissatisfied, the discontents. However, discontent is also exactly the quality of the real chela on the Path. The real initiate must be dissatisfied with the way he is and what he is, because that spurs him to find God and to find the Ascended Masters. What is the difference?

Those who follow the fallen ones have a lust for power at any price. They have no honor, and they use the philosophy of the end justifying the means—this means being the destruction of the body in order to acquire some sort of an illuminating experience. The desire for power independent of God is their downfall. The real chela is content to wait a hundred thousand years, a quarter of a million years—whatever it takes—to receive God under his Law through humility, through confessing the Christ. It doesn't matter how long his Guru is gone. He waits on his Lord lifetime after lifetime.

The fallen ones come with a prescription to relieve boredom, the sameness of life. Instead of showing people how to infuse life with creativity and joy, they say, "Take hashish so you can tolerate your boring life and your boring day and go into other places of consciousness." This is a very key thing. It's the reason why marijuana is coming at the very moment of the coming of Saint Germain.

The Sixties

In the mid-sixties, representatives of the beat generation and what was about to become the hip generation got together, and a political movement based on the use of drugs was conceived and launched. Here the influence of the group fused the nihilism and the anarchy of the beat days with the mind-blowing psychedelic theology of the hip generation.

In December 1964 the Free Speech Movement at the University of California in Berkeley won the endorsement of the faculty. That free speech included the freedom to engage in the advocacy of illegal acts. Among the first illegal acts to be openly advocated was drug use. The campus at Berkeley was flooded with pro-marijuana handouts and speakers for months.

The hip movement spread to the college campuses, the high schools and to the young. Marijuana became a unifying factor between the rich and the poor, black and white, city and country people, and so on. Its use was extolled and promoted in the movies, music and by the now tuned-in, turned-on and dropped-out professors of the hip generation.

Much of the younger generation believed the Vietnam War was "wrong." To protest the war seemed "right." Drugs, rock, free love and revolution—the things associated with war protests—gained a certain validity. In fact, the moral excellence of protesting an unjust war seemed to validate the new morality. Hence the cry "Make love, not war!"

The emotional fervor with which an entire generation committed itself to the counter-culture was due in large part to the media. It told of the misery of the war and the villainy of the establishment. And it withheld coverage or favorably publicized the activities of the counter-culture.

Although marijuana was illegal in 1970, Dr. John Kaplan,

a Professor of Law at Stanford University, published a book entitled *Marijuana—The New Prohibition*, which became a best seller. He proposed that marijuana was less dangerous than tobacco or alcohol, and therefore should be distributed commercially under government license in a similar manner to these legal drugs. The American Bar Association and the American Public Health Association were calling for decriminalization of possession for personal use. Numbers of prominent medical authorities and educators said that marijuana was harmless or close to harmless.

With this kind of endorsement from the establishment, anyone who thought that marijuana produced more than an increased pulse, red eyes and a healthy appetite was in the eyes of the young simply a part of the still dormant society that hadn't yet learned to live. Hence, when other medical authorities said that the use of marijuana was either dangerous or that since its effects were not known, it should be regarded as potentially dangerous, the marijuana users were already preconditioned to reject their warnings.[18]

There were very few marijuana users in 1965 when the first major organized effort was made to encourage the use of the drug. By 1972 an estimated twenty-four million Americans had tried marijuana and twelve million were current users.[19] Many soldiers returned from Vietnam confirmed pot smokers. Others were heroin addicts when they returned, thanks to the psycho-chemical warfare waged by the Communists.

As progressively larger numbers of young people began to smoke marijuana, two things happened. The age of those smoking on both sides of the spectrum began to widen, including high school and grade school students and sometimes younger, as well as those of the older generation. The revolution was expanding. Now those who smoked the illegal substance were not just the hip generation rebelling against authority: they were professionals, housewives, doctors, lawyers, those from the middle class, blue-collar workers— people from all walks of life who had either tried the substance or used it regularly and saw nothing wrong with it.

The second major shift was the attraction that this large potential market had for the producers of commercial items. For example, at the start, those who catered to the new generation were the music and clothing industries. Soon poster art became popular. The drug paraphernalia business grew. New foods such as Screaming Yellow Zonkers—caramel-coated popcorn in a psychedelic box—appeared on the shelves. Coloring books, pencil boxes and supplies for school children were soon decorated with psychedelic stars and rainbows of Peter Max and other hip artists.

The culture of marijuana also penetrated the media. The *Official Handbook for Marijuana Users* noted that "TV itself is influenced tremendously by grass. The montages, the kaleidoscopes, music, quick-cutting, brilliant flashes of color, language, are all results of the new world which the grass and drug user has discovered. And conversely TV educates the nonsmoker that there is a more beautiful world possible inside his own mind, and as soon as the nonsmoker begins to realize —through the uses of the visual audio medium he's exposed to on TV as a result of grass—then he'll have a greater tendency of turning on."[20]

Thus, whether you're taking marijuana or not, you are being taken into its art, which comes right out of the astral plane. Your consciousness is conditioned. We have children who know no other art except the art that has come out of the astral plane from people on marijuana, LSD or other drugs.

An entire drug culture with marijuana occupying the place of central importance emerged on the scene. It had religious fervor, religious authority, high priests, gurus, sages, poets. It was present in virtually all aspects of society and all levels of the socio-economic ladder. It had a lobby, several of its own magazines, and enjoyed widespread tolerance and sometimes acceptance by the government. It became a part of the fabric of our literature, our humor and entertainment, our social interaction, and became a unifying element for many people in diverse elements in society.

And while the use of the drug grew, the entire history of what marijuana had done to other societies past and present was largely out of the public's mind. Here was a generation fond of quoting historian George Santayana's warning, "Those who cannot remember the past are condemned to repeat it."[21] Ironically, a generation that was supposed to be hip, or in the know, was woefully ignorant about the dangers of marijuana.

Even more tragic was the fact that the drug movement had detained many of those who should have been part of the real revolution. The revolution was coming anyway and it couldn't be stopped. It was a revolution in consciousness—but not of marijuana or any other drug.

Timothy Leary, Allen Ginsberg, Jerry Rubin, Baba Ram Dass, et al. were not the gurus of the real revolution, though they may indeed have been the high priests of drugs and high priests of the drug culture of Atlantis. In short, a movement had appeared that was not simply a protest against a tired, old order, but a rebellion against the new order of the Aquarian age. Jerry Rubin proclaimed, "Pot is central to the revolution. It weakens social conditioning and helps create a whole new state of mind. The slogans of the revolution are going to be: POT, FREEDOM, LICENSE. The Bolsheviks of the revolution will be long-haired pot smokers."[22]

The Effects of Marijuana

Marijuana's immediate effects are intensification of all sensory awareness; alteration of time and space perception; increased pulse and red eyes; intensified hunger, popularly known as the "munchies"; and decreased psychomotor control, so that, for example, driving a car is dangerous. Hallucinations, anxiety and paranoia, sluggish mind and lapse of memory are associated with higher doses but can occur at lower levels of intoxication.

Many people use marijuana because they say it relaxes them and they can enjoy themselves. Considered to be relatively harmless by many today, this concept of the harmlessness of marijuana is part of the drug itself and the entities that perpetuate the drug; this is their influence upon the population—that it is harmless, and that we ought to be free to smoke marijuana if we wish.

As a result, there have been many attempts to legalize the drug, in spite of the proven negative effects on health.[23] Even beyond this are the spiritual effects: the crown chakra, the third eye and the throat are all involved. We find that the clouding of the brain with the substance of marijuana and its chemical derivatives fills the cells of the brain with a substance whereby the Light of God cannot be contained within those cells.[24] Cells are cups. Within the cells we actually contain our cosmic consciousness. Where is cosmic consciousness in the body? It is everywhere. It is not simply centered in the heart or the mind or the soul. It is in every chakra and every cell.

The use of marijuana results in the persistent poisoning of the deep centers of the brain necessary for the awareness of pleasure. Thus, it poisons the part of the brain that allows us the full awareness of being alive. As a result of this, many marijuana users have a kind of sensory deprivation, a symptom of marijuana that is the slowest to recede and the one least likely to go away. The inability to experience pleasure to the fullest makes one constantly pursue pleasure because one isn't quite realizing the full satisfaction of life. And therefore the taking of marijuana involves one in an ever-receding goal of more pleasure, which can no longer be experienced.

Relying on their own personal experiences, marijuana users believe that it is harmless because they perceive no difficulties. They do not perceive the difficulties because their faculties of perception are being destroyed while they use it. And so they have a receding level of the ability to discern within themselves levels of their own God-awareness. Day by day they perceive no harm because marijuana is destroying not only the physical senses but the senses of the soul. This is one of the most subtle dangers of marijuana and most other psychedelic drugs. The user is rendered incapable of detecting the changes in himself.

This is the subtlety of the cult of death. With each joint, the smoker is deprived of a certain essence of life within the cells and the ability to perceive that he has indeed lost just a little bit of the essence of life. Therefore, he can never see himself as he was or as he is, because inherent in the drug is the destruction of the ability to perceive life and that life is waning.

And having lost the tie to life, the way is opened to experimenting with heroin and other hard drugs.

Heroin

Heroin is a member of the opium family of drugs. It is a derivative of morphine, a chemical extracted from the juice of opium poppies. Heroin is several times stronger than morphine and also more addictive.

Heroin affects the central nervous system. The initial sensations produced by the drug are a sense of pain-free euphoria and relaxation. Following this, the user experiences drowsiness, lethargy, passivity and indifference to the environment. Mental function is clouded and breathing and heartbeat are depressed. The contraction of the muscles is slowed and weakened.

These effects of the drug (some of them similar to the effects of marijuana) work directly contrary to the law of Alpha and Omega, the active and the passive. In order to have creative fulfillment and the creative release of the energies of the Causal Body in the sacred labor, in good works, in life, there must be alternative periods of tension and release. This is the principle of yoga, reunion with God. The tension is the intensification of energy in the chakras. The release is the distribution of that energy. We have the building up of Light in our storehouse, which comes through periods of prayer, meditation and spiritual practices; and then we go into the arena of action and we release this Light in our creative endeavors and in our daily lives.

When you have a drug that relaxes the nervous system and the muscles on the physical level, it also relaxes the ability of the etheric body, the chakras, the mind and the emotions to have the necessary creative tension. It's like drawing a bow: you have to pull back the string to release the arrow. The use of drugs renders the individual incapable of pulling back the string. So he cannot release the arrow. He cannot hit the mark of his divine plan or his attainment in this life. He has destroyed his instrument.

Addiction to heroin can be established rapidly. The person who takes heroin always puts himself in danger of getting hooked, despite any assurance he may feel to the contrary.

Many American soldiers in Vietnam became heroin addicts because they erroneously believed that smoking heroin with marijuana would not lead to dependence.

When a user has developed physical dependence on the drug, withdrawal symptoms begin eight to twelve hours after the last "fix." These include craving for the drug, restlessness, anxiety, depression, muscle and bone pain, insomnia, cold flushes and other symptoms. Even the slightest pain is magnified. These acute symptoms reach their greatest intensity thirty-six to seventy-two hours after withdrawal and subside after five to ten days. Craving for the drug and other effects may last much longer.

Sweet Death

Some people to this day justify that God has made everything and whatsoever he has made is for the blessing of his offspring. But God did not make marijuana, opium or any of the drugs that are in use today or the plants from which they are taken. What they do not know is that marijuana and these other drugs were created by the great advancement of Luciferian science on Atlantis and Lemuria.

Marijuana is nothing new. It is an old, old tool of the fallen ones to make the children of Light come down to their level. And when they make them come down to their level, then they are in control.

The feminine Elohim of the first ray, Amazonia, explains that marijuana was used long ago by the fallen Amazonian women. These were initiates in the mystery school that was sponsored by her, located in South America. These female initiates failed their tests, left off from being a part of that school and went forth for the destruction of man.[25] They sought to destroy the male, to emasculate him and to destroy his progeny—whether sons or daughters of God.

Amazonia explains that the marijuana entity is a feminine-gender entity. The beginning of the word, *ma,* shows its misuse of the initiations of Lord Maitreya and of the Mother flame. So the drug itself is the manifestation of women's hatred of woman, of God as Mother, inflicted upon the male, the man. In the passivity and lethargy induced by the drug we see the intent to destroy the masculine fire of the Kundalini, and this occurs through drugs, misuse of sex, through all forms of intoxicants.

Saint Germain says that the reason the people want marijuana is because they want the Holy Ghost. There is a Light and a bliss and an infilling presence in the descent of the Holy Ghost. Those who do not submit to the path of initiation through the living Christ do not have access to the living Holy Ghost. The person of the Holy Ghost is the great initiator, and the gifts of the Holy Ghost[26] are hard-won and are given only to those who have been willing to submit to the rigors of the path of Christhood: purity, honor, integrity, submission to God, the giving of one's life to him. The getting of the Holy Spirit is an amazing miracle in which you participate.

The fallen ones on Atlantis and Lemuria knew they had been cut off from the Holy Spirit. Therefore they attempted to simulate stimulation and bliss chemically. Even knowing it would destroy them in the process, they nevertheless did this, since they already knew they were self-destroyed by their rebellion against God. They would enjoy the synthetic Holy Ghost, and furthermore, they would not enjoy it alone—they would take the children of God with them in their sweet death.

Marijuana is the perversion of the Mother. It is the death drug. Its presence denotes the presence of the death entity, the suicide entity and the most intense hatred of the Woman and her seed. In chapter 12 of the Book of Revelation, Jesus prophesied that the dragon would go forth to make war with the remnant of the Woman's seed. The Woman gives birth to the Manchild, but the dragon wages war against the Woman's seed, the children of Light.

"And the serpent cast out of his mouth water as a flood after the woman, that he might cause her to be carried away of the flood.... And the dragon was wroth with the woman, and went to make war with the remnant of her seed."[27] Marijuana is part of that warfare. And the subtlety is the proclamation everywhere that it is harmless.

A Drug Epidemic

As the 1960s saw an explosion of marijuana use in America, so the 1970s and 1980s saw the rise of cocaine, which became the drug of the white-collar workers, of middle-class "white" America and the world. It cannot be cast aside as something that ignorant and poor people do that the rest of the people have no concern with. It is eating away at the very vitals of our country and of our own souls, because every one of our souls is touched every time someone takes cocaine or marijuana. And we have to deny our sensitivity to that event happening daily in order to simply be "normal." It is the great tragedy of the century, the great conspiracy of the century.

The drug epidemic seems to be growing each year, and the list of drugs available on the street to children is staggering. On any given day our children can buy cannabis (in different forms including marijuana, hashish, THC); designer drugs (including "China White"; MDA, "the love drug"; MDMA, e.g., "Ecstasy," "Adam," "X-TC"); hallucinogens (LSD, psilocybin, DMT, mescaline/peyote, PCP); inhalants (amyl nitrite, solvents, glues, rubber cements); stimulants (antidepressants; cocaine, crack; amphetamines, e.g., Dexadrine, methedrine, "speed," "crystal meth"); and tranquilizers/sedatives (opium; heroin; barbiturates, e.g., phenobarbital; Quaalude).There is also the widespread abuse of prescription medications such as Valium, Librium, Xanax and Prozac.

Needless to say, our youth is under the most vicious attack through this drug epidemic, and the attack is on all levels of consciousness within their being. The aim is to destroy the body temple so it cannot house the Flame. The Ascended Masters are extremely concerned because the plot is to destroy this generation of Lightbearers so that there will be no one to whom we can pass the torch,

Parents, schools and the media all contribute to the drug problem. Parents contribute in a number of ways: introducing illegal drugs, particularly marijuana, to their children; using illegal drugs, leading their children to follow this example; and then by using legal drugs such as tobacco and alcohol themselves. Parents also perpetuate drug use through other means, including giving children money that they can use to purchase drugs.

One of the strongest predictors of drug use is the behavior of strong role models in a child's life. If parents smoke and drink, the child is likely to try tobacco and alcohol. Tobacco and alcohol use almost invariably precede marijuana use. If a person never smokes or drinks, the odds of their trying other drugs are very low.

Besides refraining from drugs themselves, parents can cut down their children's drug use by closer supervision and correct discipline. If we want to save our children and the youth of America, we have to devote time to them and time to the necessary spiritual work.

The media contributes to the drug culture in a number of ways. It is rare for movies or television programs to portray drug use in a negative light. TV tends to avoid the issue. Movies often glamorize drug use or show it as an integral part of life.

Schools contribute to drug use by simply failing to stop the problem. Many schools avoid the whole issue by denying they have a drug problem. Some schools turn their backs on the problem. Rather than forbid drug use on campus, they conclude that drug use rules are unenforceable and close their eyes when children use drugs in the lavatories, the playgrounds and elsewhere. Drug education classes often don't teach all the risks but merely encourage a child to "act responsibly" and do what is best for him. Other classes do not condemn drug use and do not support children in taking a stand against it.

Children are even being forced to take drugs in public schools, where many elementary school children are being treated for hyperactivity with amphetamines or Ritalin. Who are these children? They are the Lightbearers who have come forth with great creative energy, and because they are feeling the creative energy of God, they are being given drugs by those who are determined that they will not rise to manhood and womanhood with the fullness of the Light that God has placed within them.

In the first and second and third grade, millions of these children are being filled with drugs. If the child is a little bit active in the classroom, the way children normally are at that age, explorative and investigating, he is given drugs to calm him down. This is the mass manipulation of a free society.

The Ancient Story of the Drug Conspiracy

Saint Germain reveals that this modern trend to the use of drugs is actually part of a conspiracy that began beyond the dawn of recorded history: "Beloved ones, the story of these drugs—of marijuana, cocaine, heroin and all of the rest of the synthetic, fabricated drugs—is an ancient one. I pinpoint, therefore, the conspiracy of fallen angels known as the Nephilim gods and as the Watchers. I pinpoint their conspiracy to control the populations of the worlds, where they have spawned their experimental creation, their mechanization man. And therefore, in order to control their laboratory experiment, they have used all manner of devices. *

"Now, therefore, other nefarious powers moving against the evolution of life everywhere have seen fit to use mechanization man, computerized man—plastic man, if you will—as trend-setters, jet-setters climbing after the gods and the fallen angels to tempt, to taunt and to hypnotize the seed of the Ancient of Days, the seed of Christ in embodiment.

"Their end is manifold, but it centers on the desire to steal the Light of the threefold flame, to draw the Lightbearers down into the valleys[28] of the pit itself where they would engage in the practices of darkness. And therefore, there are available fallen angels in embodiment to demonstrate the 'way that seemeth right'—to provide the drugs, to direct the processing and to draw mechanization man into the entire conspiracy as they are set up as storefront manikins to be copied by the children of the Light.

"Thus, those who are the glamorous and those who comprise the multitudes of the mass consciousness exert a momentum that is planetary in scope to magnetize the Lightbearers into their practices of drugs and perverted rock and nefarious deeds—and therefore karmically ally and align these Lightbearers with the darkest forces of the pits of hell....

"I come ... so that you will understand that the original conspiracy against the Lightbearers and the various evolutions and creations that began long, long ago with the fall of the fallen angels did begin and have its origin with a chemical

---

* For further explanation of these concepts, see chapter 3.

manipulation and a genetic manipulation, and did come about not only through this vein of addiction and the supplying of the people with all manner of stimulants, but with other modes of conspiracy, thereby to limit the extent of the people to rise, to take dominion over their destiny, to make contact with the octaves of Light, or to in any way challenge the fallen angels.

"Since their fall, it has been the goal of the fallen angels to keep in subjugation all evolutions and the planetary bodies they have invaded and to prevent them from rising to any form of equality—to contact the power of God or to learn the secrets of the Great White Brotherhood, which they themselves [the fallen angels] have perverted from the beginning in their arts of black magic, war and witchcraft, necromancy and sorcery....

"You can understand that these false hierarchies of fallen ones are positioned everywhere because they must control the people in order to take from them their Light—for they, themselves, as you know, were cut off from the source of Light when they were cast out of heaven by Archangel Michael and his hosts."[29]

The Curse of Atahualpa

Saint Germain goes on to speak in particular of the conspiracy of cocaine, and of a curse pronounced upon the white man by Atahualpa, the last emperor of the Incas.

With royal permission from Charles V of Spain, Spanish conquistador Francisco Pizarro set out to conquer and govern Peru in January 1531. On November 16, 1532, he met the army of Atahualpa at Cajamarca, Peru. When Atahualpa refused to acknowledge the supremacy of the Spanish king and the Christian religion, Pizarro ordered an attack and the emperor was taken prisoner.

Atahualpa bargained for his life by keeping his promise to

fill, twice with silver and once with gold, the large room in which he was held. In spite of this, the Spaniards charged Atahualpa with "crimes against the Spanish king" and executed him by strangulation on August 29, 1533.

In the last moments before his death, Atahualpa uttered: "Cocaine shall fortify the Indian and destroy the white man." Although the Indians have chewed the coca leaf for centuries (without apparent side effects) and consider it sacred, they are not known to use the "evil" powdered, processed derivative, which the Incan emperor predicted would destroy the white man.

Saint Germain continues: "I desire, therefore, that you will understand that the conspiracy of the fallen ones and the curse pronounced against the white man has become the curse of the seed of Christ. For it has been transferred by the fallen angels so as to fall upon the progenitors of the eternal Christ.

"How is this so? Beloved hearts of Light, the fallen ones, by taking their revenge against the Inca, against the empire and the head thereof, did bring about their own judgment through the Christ Light in the people of the Incas—through those evolutions whom they overtook.

"Thus, a great crime was committed against a people who occupied the continent of South America. That crime had its judgment, and that judgment (the cursing of the 'white' man) should, by Divine Justice, be upon those who perpetrated the deed. But those who perpetrated the deed did so from inner levels—the false hierarchy who knew full well that the judgment that would be upon themselves and their embodied tools would also come upon the seed of Christ (who like themselves had also embodied as the 'white' man); for the fallen angels had induced that seed of Christ to intermarry with their own. Thus it does come to pass that the seed of Christ forfeit their Light as they bear the karma of the seed of the Wicked One.

"I speak of the seed of Belial embodied in the white race itself that has moved against nation upon nation in the process of taking over the world. And I speak, therefore, of the intermingling, among those of the white race, of the seed of Light and Darkness. Thus, beloved hearts, when there is compromise (intermarriage of the seed of Christ with the seed of the Wicked One—both being of the white race), the seed of Light also suffers.

"This curse pronounced is not only a judgment of the Law, but also a curse of black magic by the seed of the wicked (transferring their culpability to the seed of Christ). And therefore, that curse is come to pass because it has never been broken, never been checked. And the full force of the Godhead dwelling in any son of God on earth has not, to this moment, challenged it or overturned it. It is to this end that I have come, for there is truly a superstition and a sense of revenge upon all the descendants of the Spanish conquistadores by the descendants of those people who did suffer needlessly under the conquests of the Spanish in South America.

"Let it be understood, therefore, that this curse has indeed come upon the middle class and the white man of America and the earth through that very deed. And you can understand that history is tarnished by the vicious circle of this karma; history is replete with acts and deeds that come full circle and therefore take the lives of the seeming innocent when they are in their very bud and blossom.

"Realize, therefore, that the vulnerability of the people who succumb to cocaine in every race is also conditioned by prior neglect, prior agreement, prior consent in some form (great or small) of allegiance to their own carnal mind, allegiance to the dweller-on-the-threshold and allegiance to those fallen angels who are the betrayers of the people of earth.

"Realize, then, beloved hearts, when you give your allegiance to your Holy Christ Self and the voice of conscience within you, when you stand with Almighty God—and still stand—and to the best of your knowledge and ability and awareness do not compromise the love of your Christhood, the wisdom and the power of your Christhood, you are protected against the wiles of the Devil and of these 'serpents,' these fallen angels in embodiment, and against their mortal cursings (execrations) against your souls.

"But when there is a giving away of the portion of the self—a little compromise here and there, because it seems harmless (and that word *harmless* is among the most dangerous words in the lexicon of the English language)—then, beloved ones, you leave yourselves open not only to the inroads of your own karma and the karma of the fallen angels as well as the subsequent depriving of yourselves of more of your consciousness because you have agreed and acceded to giving a portion of it away—but also you leave yourselves open to their black magic practiced against you to wear down your resistance to Evil, to break your free will—all the while making you think each downward turn on the road to hellish self-destruction has been your own freewill choice.

"Thus, the more you are enlightened by us and by the teachings of the Ascended Masters, the more you enter into your own Christhood, the more you take accountability for your thoughts and feelings and for your deeds, the greater the stand you take for the Light and the more Light you therefore feel upon yourself—the more you realize just how important it is to protect that Light and your Christhood.

"Those who reach the peak of Everest and the challenging mountains of the world know the dangers of the last mile, the last five miles. Beloved hearts of Light, those last few yards before your victory are among the most dangerous of all because they necessitate the securing of that which you have gained as well as the strength to attain the final crown of victory. To sustain that which you have becomes, therefore, the challenge of Keepers of the Flame, which is why we have written on the Keepers of the Flame Fraternity lessons the byword: 'Hold Fast What Thou Hast Received.'

"Now, therefore, beloved hearts, I come and ask your concerted and undivided heart-fire attention and God consciousness with me as I implore, before the altar of Almighty God, the breaking of this so-called cocaine curse and all who have reinforced it. I ask you, therefore, to kneel before your Father.

Saint Germain's Prayer for the Breaking of the Cocaine Curse

"Almighty God, our Father, the one supreme God—*Elohim!*—I, Saint Germain, stand in the earth and with those who are the Mystical Body of God. We come before thy altar and before thy throne. In the name of thy beloved Son with us, Christos, we implore:

"I call also to all Christed ones and children of the Father worldwide whom I touch with the fire of my heart—to give their attention now at inner levels to this universal and planetary prayer:

"Our Father, one in heart, one in the heart of the earth, we call forth *Light! Light! Light!*

"*Break the curse!* against the seed of Light on earth! *Break the curse!* of cocaine, marijuana, heroin, PCP and all other chemicals known on this planet and those yet to be introduced that have already been introduced in past ages.

"Elohim of God, Almighty Father, we summon now the legions of Light and the entire Spirit of the Great White Brotherhood as cosmic reinforcements in the heart of the earth. And I, Saint Germain, declare that in my heart, as in thy heart, this curse is now *fully, finally broken* by the Godhead! And this breaking of the curse shall be implemented by these Keepers of the Flame daily in the Judgment Call of thy Son Jesus Christ, in the *binding* of the curse and in the *binding* of the dweller-on-the-threshold of that curse!

"And therefore, I say: Father, release the dispensation of Light for the protection of the warriors of Light and peace who march with the legions of Seraphim and the angels and Elohim. Let there be raised up reinforcements on earth who will take their stand and bear that Light, that blinding Light of the shield of the Godhead and of the mighty sword invincible of cosmic Truth.

"Helios and Vesta, representatives of the Father-Mother God, I, Saint Germain, with Portia, now agree to hold in the earth, with Keepers of the Flame, the balance against this conspiracy out of the pit of Death and Hell.

"In the name of Almighty God and by his grace, fully ensconced in his flame, we stand in this hour to challenge the entire drug conspiracy of planet Earth and to challenge every soul beset thereby who is of the Light to:

"Leave it at once, depart from it, turn your back on it, and run for the Sun! *Run for the Sun!* is our cry and our call to every Lightbearer on earth! Now *depart* from the dark places and the hellholes and the astral pits! Remove yourselves from the fallen ones who are the purveyors of drugs and rock that go hand in hand and draw you down into the very darkness of hell.

"I, Saint Germain, stand before the altar of Almighty God. I speak from the altar of the Holy Grail. I speak into the very heart of the flame of the ark of the covenant, and I summon the Word of God in this hour to slay, therefore, the entire planetary momentum of the 'dragon' that gives power to the 'beast'[30] in every form of drug conspiracy. And I call for the empowerment of my own in this hour that they may send the call, and that that call may count, beloved Father, as my own call.

"I ask that my heart and flame and being once again reinforce them and that when they give their calls on this subject ... it shall be done! And it shall be turned back! And the possessing demons of drug addiction shall no more occupy the temples of the Lightbearers! And all evolutions of earth shall be free! And the angels who are the reapers shall come and *Bind* these fallen angels! and take them for their final judgment!

"And therefore, I, Saint Germain, plead once again before the Father for the acceleration and the shortening of the days for the elect, and for the binding of the conspirators of Darkness in every walk of life, aborting life at every age—in the womb, in our children and youth in those years when the souls of Light ought to be pursuing the mighty I AM Presence but engage themselves in pleasure-seeking and entertainment and the titillation of the senses.

"Beloved Father, hear our call, for we are one in heart. We are one in thy star-fire magnitude in the earth. We are determined to present planet Earth as a planet God-victorious in the flame of freedom....

"O beloved Father, receive my own. Receive those who are the forerunners of the age of Aquarius. I call forth grace and protection and enlightenment as well as God-happiness and the understanding and tutelage of their hearts by the Lord Maitreya in the Path of the Ruby Cross.

"I call unto you, beloved Father, to now give to us and these holy ones in embodiment that sacred fire that is able to consume by the spoken Word those who are the denizens of hell—the infamous, those who are the destroyers, those who are the seed of the Murderer and the Liar who come from beneath, whose end shall surely come.

"Our Father, we beseech you in one heart that their end shall come now and in this hour—before it is too late, before too many of those Christed ones whom we have invoked and blessed are come forth and their Light stolen and their lives destroyed....

"Our Father Alpha, our Mother Omega, we call. We are one in thy heart. Heaven and earth meet in this hour. In this consummation of the Word at the altar of the Holy Grail, there is the oneness of Spirit and Matter. And souls aflame with the victory of Light enter a new consciousness of their own Christhood as they draw down from their Causal Bodies that Light that has never been seen on land or sea—that Light in the lighthouse of Being, that Light that can descend the crystal cord and be the staying action to hold back the world tide of Darkness, that Light that can consume utterly the Dark Cycle of returning karma.

"Beloved Father Supreme, I seal this prayer in the heart of the Cosmic Christ and in the hearts of the faithful and true everywhere on earth. I seal this prayer. May it come forth. May it bud as the pink rose. May it bud and blossom in a Cosmic Christ awareness....

"In the name of Almighty God, in the name of the God of Freedom whose Spirit I AM and represent in this era, I, Saint Germain, seal this prayer in the souls of the Lightbearers worldwide and in their Christ Self.

"Our Father, we attend thy answer and thy coming.... We shall be there in full force for thy holy cause, beloved Father. In thy name, Amen."[31]

Nicotine

The burden of drugs on the people does not end with illegal drugs. Smoking tobacco products is the primary avoidable cause of death in America. Approximately 440,000 deaths in the United States each year are linked to smoking.[32]

Nicotine attacks at the lower level of the mental quadrant. It is a narcotic that strongly affects the nervous system. It accelerates the heartbeat, raises the blood pressure and in large doses produces tremors, convulsions and vomiting. It causes the paralysis of the skeletal muscles, which eventually brings about impaired respiration.

Nicotine is one of the most toxic substances known. It is a poison used in insecticides, ranking with cyanide in rapidity of action. Nicotine has no medical use. In addition to nicotine, there are some four thousand chemicals in cigarette smoke. Several of these are known carcinogens. Smoking increases the incidence of heart disease as well as cancer in the lungs, larynx, esophagus, bladder, pancreas and kidneys.[33]

Nicotine is one of the most perniciously addicting drugs in common use. It is so hard to stop smoking that it is a common occurrence for those with advanced cases of emphysema to continue to smoke cigarettes right up until death. Heroin addicts who have stopped smoking and kicked heroin have found that it is easier to quit heroin than cigarettes. Most smokers continue smoking only because they cannot stop. It requires no more than three or four casual cigarettes during adolescence to virtually ensure that a person will eventually become a regular dependent smoker.

In 1963, Archangel Jophiel, the Archangel of Illumination, released a warning on the dangers of nicotine: "It is possible for you to utilize the center of your heart as a sun of divine love and to use your brain as a radiant focus of the power of illumination's flame so that all density is indeed removed from your consciousness.

"The cerebrum and the cerebellum are as the great Milky Way is in the vast starry universe. These are intended to be mighty continents of power anchored within the head area of every man whereby great currents of illumination may flow through those wondrous folds of your precious brains, creating therein a golden flame of illumination and removing the so-called gray matter from human consciousness, which is but the distortion of the pure white Light into the qualities of gray by reason of the addition of flecks of shadow created by human ideas of great density and opacity.

"I, therefore, pray that this day the angels who have come with me release into the forcefield of your blessed beings those mighty currents of Light that are the Mercury diamond-shining mind of God and will flow across your brains—flashing there, scintillating as the sunlight upon the water and removing therefrom that density that is created by reason of human thought and feeling lowered down toward the vibratory action of jealousy, doubt, fear, dishonor and a lack of integrity.

"I would like to point out to those among mankind who are addicted to the use of nicotine that this in itself creates a tremendous density upon the surface of the brain so that the dura mater and pia mater, so named by mankind, are not able to flash forth the divine intelligence in a proper manner. When mankind, therefore, will lay aside this specific habit of smoking, they will find that it will indeed increase the flow of spiritual illumination to them.

"Now I am not in any way, beloved ones, interested in a direct opposition to the great tycoons of the cigarette industry in your nation, for the Lords of Karma will take action in due course of time against them. And they shall find that the record is very gross, and that which they have done will indeed prove to them at inner levels that they have sold their soul for a bowl of soup and for a 'mess of pottage.'[34]

"Nevertheless, those who do this shall return to balance every jot and tittle of their karma. The Great Law requires it, and let none think that they can escape; for it is not the intent of the karmic law to permit them to escape until they have paid every last farthing[35] of that which they have imposed upon the youth of America and the world by creating those vicious and pernicious habits that distort the consciousness and warp the power of the great God flame in its action through the forcefield of mankind."[36]

Following Jophiel's dictation, cigarette smoking came under governmental scrutiny. On January 11, 1964, the Public Health Service released its report that linked cigarette smoking to cancer. This was followed by the U.S. Surgeon General Luther Terry's official statement that smoking is hazardous to human health. Federal legislation was passed in 1965 that required all cigarette packages sold after January 1, 1966, to carry the label "Warning: The Surgeon General Has Determined That Cigarette Smoking Is Dangerous to Your Health." Beginning January 1, 1971, tobacco ads were banned from television.

Smoking among adults has dropped appreciably since the release of Jophiel's proclamation on tobacco, but many teenagers still take up smoking, even though laws have been enacted to drastically curtail cigarette advertising geared toward young people.

Alcohol

Alcohol attacks at the level of the emotional body. It is one of the most widely abused substances in America today. Taken in small amounts, feelings of happiness and lightness might occur, depending on the person's mood. It offers the drinker an escape from the pressures and tensions of everyday reality.

Alcohol causes a variety of psychological and physical problems. One out of every four Americans admitted to a mental hospital today is an alcoholic. Alcohol causes cirrhosis of the liver; is a significant contributor to heart disease; is harmful to the digestive system, the nervous system, the liver, the brain, the respiratory system, the muscular system, the nervous system and other vital organs. There is a close correlation between heavy drinking and cancer of the throat, mouth and liver. Over one-third of all violent crimes and fatal traffic accidents are alcohol-related.

Alcohol poisons the protoplasm of nerve cells, ultimately causing permanent damage. After a period of time this causes memory loss, poor judgment and organic psychosis. Not only is there the breaking down of the cell as a vehicle for cosmic consciousness but there is the breaking down of the physical substance, the very structure of the cell. We have been told by the Ascended Masters that any amount of alcohol in the blood prevents your attunement with your Holy Christ Self while that alcohol is present.[37]

In those who are addicted to alcohol, you can see over the years the deterioration of the sensitivity to life, their ability to think rationally. There is an opening of their astral body to their being used by demons and their mouthings of unwholesome and condemnatory statements. Often alcoholics are a funnel for all of the condemnation of the fallen ones against members of their family. And you know by what comes out of their mouths that these people are definitely not themselves—the things spoken through them they do not say when not under the influence of alcohol.

The alcohol habit is perpetuated by thousands of entities, discarnates who attach themselves to the person and goad him into drinking. These discarnates may have been alcoholics when they were in embodiment. They do not have any Light momentum to rise to the etheric level where the retreats of the Brotherhood are located, where the etheric cities are, so they remain in lower levels and hover around those in embodiment who drink alcohol. They are still looking for the enjoyment of alcohol, and so they seek it vicariously.

There are also entities associated with the substance of alcohol itself. People become very aggressive or passive from these entities. They become vicious through Spiritus, the masculine entity, and passive through Spirita, the feminine entity.

Thus, when you are dealing with the healing of an alcoholic, you have an entity and a demon-possession problem. These entities create in people the dependence on alcoholic beverages for relaxation, stimulation and euphoria. They destroy incentive and self-respect. They are family wreckers. The entities themselves are anti-Christ, and they get to the child, the Christ Child, through the father and the mother.

Millions of alcoholics and heavy social drinkers are puppets to liquor entities. These victims in turn become discarnates, or disembodied spirits, when they pass on. So there is a long chain of alcoholics in and out of embodiment, and they remain in the same group consciousness. Some are in embodiment, some are on the astral plane reinforcing them, and they trade roles from time to time. This is one reason why the drinking age gets lower and lower—the discarnates reembody with the same desires for alcohol that they had when they were disembodied and in their previous lives.

Spiritual Solutions

Saint Germain warns us that the drug problem is a spiritual problem, and that the ultimate solution will therefore be a spiritual one: "Thus, beloved ones, the key that comes by the anointed ones—and you should all accept your role as 'anointed ones'* and 'Christed ones' merging with your Christ Self—is that key that shall undo this conspiracy that is inter-

---

* The appellation "Christ" is from the Greek *Christos,* meaning "anointed one." Thus, those who are anointed with the Light of the I AM THAT I AM that is the Christ Presence, or Christ consciousness, are called "Christed ones."

planetary in nature and that has been put upon the people of this planet for millions of years.

"Please understand the equation in which we draw the line that separates Light and Darkness. It is the line between the Absolute Godhead dwelling in you and Absolute Evil pitted against it in the form [through the physical bodies of] of these fallen ones.

"I give this introduction to my message on the drug conspiracy this day so that you will understand that unless you perceive this equation, and unless those who desire to overturn the drug industry worldwide perceive this equation and have the protection of the Brotherhood, there will no change come about. For this enslavement of the youth to siphon their Light has been going on for thousands of years, and it is not a phenomenon of the twentieth century,... but one that is brought to the fore once again to entrance those who are easily taken in; for they have used these drugs in previous centuries long ago in the mists of Atlantis, on the continent of Africa, in South America and ancient Lemuria....

"And therefore, I offer my reward, my service and my protection. And I allow you to see that which it is from the beginning unto the ending. For, beloved hearts, truly this drug conspiracy of marijuana and cocaine, of alcohol and nicotine, and sugar itself upon the youth of the world is killing many a fine heart and soul, setting them back decades or lifetimes....

"Blessed ones, I would tell you that the entire drug conspiracy is aided and abetted by the suicide entity. All who partake of these drugs commit the first in a series of steps of self-annihilation—the single step toward suicide. And these suicide entities who come to seduce the youth under the wiles of the she-devil Annihla have calculated their thirteen steps of suicide as the antithesis of the path of the Bodhisattva.

"The first indulgence, the first drink, the first entering in is the preliminary stage of the development of the addiction. And they also begin in the breaking down of the heart, that that heart might become the seat of darkness and death instead of Light....

"Precious ones, the fervent prayer of the righteous and the faithful has never gone unanswered, is always rewarded and does always have the victory. Let it be realized that on all fronts, as you stand in the very center of the circle of Aquarius —in the center that is the dot of my own Causal Body—and you daily face the twelve lines of the clock twice in the twenty-four-hour cycle, all with which you deal are those conditions and practices, beloved hearts, that require the maximum Light and the maximum strength of embodied evolutions....

"When you consider the age-old conspiracy and you consider the fact that you are here, that I AM here, and we are together forming the solar ring of Light by our very bodies and presence, Ascended and unascended, you can understand that this truly is the stand of Almighty God for the victory of earth. And unless you perceive it so, unless you have that perspective and that vision, you will not comprehend or understand the attacks upon your life, your loved ones, those associated with you, and you will not be serious enough to do your daily invocations to Michael the Archangel for your protection when you are engaged in this warfare."[38]

It is vital and essential that you invoke your tube of light and call to Archangel Michael for protection once you become engaged with the hosts of the LORD in their warfare of the Spirit for the binding of the forces of Death and Hell preying upon our youth.

Healing of the Effects of Drugs

We see in the effects of all these drugs an attack on each of the four lower bodies of man and woman. And along with a temporary sensation of pleasure, there is a long-lasting damage to these bodies. With the taking of psychedelic drugs, there is the shattering of the aura and of the chakras, the tearing of the etheric body, destroying the soul's sensitivity to the "inner voice" of God within the heart. Smoking absorbs Light by filling the cells with a black, tar-like substance, blocking the ability of the mind to contact the Christ mind. Alcohol drains the emotions, causing passivity and an inability to be infused with God-desire.

The attack on the four lower bodies continues in the physical quadrant with the use of refined sugar, which is a poison that strips the physical cells of Light and causes all sorts of disorders ranging from hypoglycemia, nutrient deficiencies, hyperactivity, depression and headaches.[39] Thus the entire spiral is brought to the level of the physical body— four perversions for the four sides of the temple of life.

Hilarion, the Ascended Master who is lord of the green ray of healing and truth, and the Healing Masters tell us that the hope for salvation for those youth who have taken psychedelic drugs lies in the healing ray. For the green flame, when properly used in visualization and fervent calls to the Ascended Masters and to the angels of healing who minister unto mankind, can actually restore those cells in the brain that have been destroyed. A carefully controlled program of fasting, exercise and proper diet is a necessary adjunct on the physical plane to one's periods of prayer and meditation.[40] The ladies of heaven stand ready to answer the calls of the youth for wholeness if they will only persist in their invocations and have faith in their eventual healing according to the will of God and as their karma dictates.

Beloved Lady Master Leto, master of science, tells us that all who have partaken of any drugs whatsoever, including alcohol, nicotine and sugar, can be purified of the effects of their use. This healing and purification requires prayer as the invocation of the violet flame, prayer for mercy for departing from God's covenants, and the saturation of the four lower bodies with the violet flame. This must be accompanied by actual physical fasting: as Jesus said, "This kind goeth not out but by prayer and fasting."[41] It is important to realize that the contamination of the physical temple must be cleansed by both spiritual and material means.

Leto says, "For indeed the sacred fire can heal those cells and those points, those electrodes placed by God within the brain. And therefore it becomes of a paramount necessity that students of the Light go forth with this teaching to the youth of the world, to those who realize the folly of their involvements with the psychic and who desire to return to the Path.

"These must have an awareness of the sacred fire, for the Lords of Karma have decreed the dispensation this year that any child of God and any sincere one who has been duped by the drug culture might return to the pristine estate that he had when he came into this embodiment by invocation to the sacred fire, to the healing flame and by petitioning for mercy from the Lords of Karma.

"For God is not an avenger of his children, and he does not desire to punish them with eternal damnation. This is the lie of the serpentine force. Our God is a consuming fire;[42] he is no respecter of persons nor does he dwell upon the iniquities that have entered the hearts of men, and therefore mercy goeth forth. But how can it be implemented?

"You see, precious hearts, it requires contact with the sacred fire to rebuild the cells and atoms and the perfect design of the Christ mind and the layers of manifestation surrounding each of the chakras that have been forced open through this culture."[43]

The Cult of Pleasure

THE GOAL OF LIFE FOR YOUR SOUL and my soul is that liberation whereby we find the bliss of communion in the eternal Light. Out of this union in the ancient past have come forth great Golden Age cultures.

In the mists beyond Lemuria and Atlantis, before the records even of time and space, we learn of civilizations where the soul has risen through the soundless sound and the name of the AUM to that plane of God-realization whereby the I AM THAT I AM has been realized as the Real Self.

Within the culture that has come forth out of that Real Self is the harmony, the rhythm—the rhythm of the Mother flame. As the Mother flame leaps to join with the principle of the Trinity of life—of power, wisdom and love; of Father, Son and Holy Spirit—there are born, then, the four sides of the base of the pyramid of life.

And out of this pyramid comes the dynamic force of living, the Maha Kali, the Great Mother of the Universe. Her energy is sealed within our own body temple, and by the intonation of sound we release this energy and thus fulfill this creative round. The Mother with her counterpart is the creator, the sustainer and the destroyer of life in Matter as Brahma, Vishnu and Shiva are these three in Spirit.

The Science of Rhythm

The perfect rhythm of the art forms and the cultures recorded even in the race unconscious speaks of the rhythm of the stars, of galaxies within molecules, of cellular life, all moving to this great rhythm of the spheres in the stillness of the flame that is perpetual motion.

Priests and priestesses who tended the flame of Mother on the altars of Lemuria knew the sacred science of sound and of rhythm. There were twelve temples to the Mother surrounding the central altar. These temples were located on what is now known as the Ring of Fire surrounding the Pacific. In these temples the raising of the Mother Light released the focal point of the divinity of God in manifestation in the heart.

There came a darkening era of rebellion against the Light of the Mother, a perversion of the flame as priests and priestesses perverted both the sound and the rhythm. By the misuse of sound and rhythm, cataclysm was unleashed from this Maha Kali, the Mother force, and thus the ancient memory of the sinking of the continent of Lemuria by fire and volcanic eruption.

This activity resulted in the loss of the fires of Mother upon the temple altar. For twelve thousand years we have not known the presence of this flame enshrined in our temples, but during this period God has sent avatars East and West to reveal the Trinity of the Masculine principle, until once again we could call forth the Mother Light through the sound and the Word and its intonation, and by that Mother Light restore to man and woman the full potential of the soul.

Out of the Mother flame comes the rhythm of all rhythm. The Mother flame is located in the base chakra at the base of the spine. It is a white sphere of light sealed until we meditate upon this energy for its rising upon the spinal altar. As these petals begin to turn by the action of our meditation and the sounding of the Word, they manifest the rhythms of life: 4/4, 3/4, 6/8, 2/4, 12/8, 5/4, 7/4 and 12/4. The basis of four in all of these rhythms comes out of the Mother as fire, air, water and earth—the foundation of our pyramid of life.

In the 4/4 rhythm, we feel the release of Mother energy in a disciplined cycle, and the wheel of the chakra begins to turn. Out of the turning is produced the 3/4 time that is the beating of the heart. Three-quarter time is the rhythm of Alpha and Omega in the T'ai Chi, whirling in the center of the heart. Out of this whirling energy worlds are framed.

The 4/4 time of the four-petaled base chakra is the discipline of the march time, and upon that base, the very pyramid of life is built. If Matter does not descend according to that Matter square, that cosmic cube is going to be askew and awry and out of alignment, and it will not be a proper chalice for the Light to descend.

When the 4/4 time in a disciplined beat causes that base chakra to spin, it gently begins to turn, and that Mother Light as a crystal rises on the spinal altar. As it rises, it waters and nourishes each chakra with the negative polarity of the Divine Mother. And as it rises and you also call for the Light of your I AM Presence to descend into your temple (the Light of the Father and the masculine ray), the Light of your Presence gives to your chakras the masculine, or plus, polarity.

Thus the Mother is rising and the Father is descending, and this is how you achieve the balance of wholeness and

Alpha and Omega in each chakra and in your temple. The cradle of the heart, then, is where the union of the Father-Mother God in you gives birth to the Universal Christ.

The Perversion of Sound and Rhythm

What happened with the entrance into the 1960s is that the 4/4 time was corrupted with the syncopated beat of rock music. The syncopated beat is an uneven beat. It is not disciplined. It also goes counter to the heartbeat itself. So with the syncopated beat of rock music, the energy of the spine does not rise but it falls, and the life-force in your being then descends.

Unwittingly and ignorantly, then, many people on earth, especially the youth, have come to like this music and have developed a habit of listening to it to the point where it actually has become an addiction.

The fallen ones seek the bliss of reunion of the Light of the Mother with the Light of the Father, but they can't have it without submission to the living Christ. So they invert the beat, and the vibration of the energy descending becomes the synthetic experience, or the inverted experience, of the raising of the Kundalini fire—one of the greatest experiences of the soul in its reunion with God when it occurs under the Guru Maitreya, your own I AM Presence and your Christ Self.

The sensation is the movement of energy. So the raising of the Light through the chakras results in the wholeness of the Light of Alpha and Omega as the Kundalini ascends. The descent is also a movement, a vibration, a sensation. If one has never tasted the pure nectar of God, how does one know that the synthetic nectar is inferior? Thus the rock beat is for the descent of the Kundalini and has its own perverted bliss, which is the substitute experience for reunion with God.

This is the reason for the conception of the rhythm of the

pit.* This is the reason people are addicted to rock music—because it does create a movement of energy. And the descent of the Kundalini fire is the stripping of the chakras of that wholeness and the expending of that energy of wholeness. And thus, when you don't have the proof of the real thing, you can't understand why the synthetic, the counterfeit, is wrong.

When this energy descends, it doesn't do so gently; it comes down violently. And as it descends, it tears the delicate membranes around the chakras where the spiritual Light is entering the central nervous system in the spine. So the energy of the spine is released in these little tears in the garment, in the sheath of your inner being. As it is released, it gives a sensation that you can experience as a "rush" or a "high."

People say they don't need to take drugs because they get high on rock music. This is exactly true, because the Light of the sacred fire is very powerful; when it is released, there is a high. And so you get used to that release and you want to listen to more rock music. When you're not listening to it, there is an uncomfortability, and you feel better when that energy is released through listening to the music again. So it becomes a cycle that you can't get out of easily.

When that energy is released, it is lost; you don't retain it. There is the slow bleeding of your life-force causing early aging, early degeneracy of the mind, chaos in the chakras, and you can't concentrate for very long. You can't focus because there is no energy in the third-eye chakra and in the crown. What has also come to pass is the energy descending into the lower chakras and not rising puts all of the weight of the life-force in those chakras. That energy must go somewhere. So with the advent of rock music, the logical sequence is a sexual revolution, free sex and a greater promiscuity.

Rock music is the perversion of sound and rhythm that

* The lowest levels of the astral plane. See Rev. 9:1–12; 11:7; 17:8; 20:1–3.

was already in vogue in the last days of Atlantis and was one of the factors that contributed to the breaking up and the cataclysm that resulted in the sinking of the continent.[1]

The Bottomless Pit of Desire

Now we find once more that rock music and the discord of broken rhythms echo throughout the planet; they are everywhere, in stores, places of business, factories, elevators, buses and restaurants. The beat of sensuality is everywhere sustained by man's desire to be "happy."

However, all mortal desire is a "bottomless pit," for mortal desires are never satisfied.[2] To appease one's hunger in the morning does not satisfy the needs of the evening, and thus the cycles of the gratification of human desire and the pursuit of hedonism go on and on as the personal debts of man to life mount ever higher. In the days of Noah when the ark was preparing, man was eating, drinking and giving in marriage.[3]

On a world scale these debts produce the backlash of the return of humanity's own discord. Remorse, unhappiness, inferiority, inefficiency, shame and a partial or complete mesmerism of consciousness are often the result of such unwholesome and unprofitable sowings.

Marriage or Free Love?

The Cult of Hedon makes it essential that, in adding plus factors to the personal ego, sexual conquests of the opposite sex shall be made. These untransmuted drives often result in broken homes, a sense of futility and a general malaise. Yet the round goes on again and again as basic human drives fulfill themselves, not as nature intended, but as a means of generating "human happiness."

The Chart of Your Divine Self

The release of the energies of the sacred fire in sexual union is probably the most intense experience that we know of in this octave. It is a release of a great amount of energy—physically, materially, as well as spiritually. Therefore Jesus and the Masters of East and West have given to us the sacrament of marriage—the sealing of marriage by the invocation of blessing. Whether or not the priest, the minister, the rabbi, the one performing the ceremony himself may be worthy, the fact that we place ourselves in the hands of a representative of God means that through that invocation, the human institution of marriage becomes sanctified. And through the sacrament of marriage, there is a sealing of a sphere of white Light around the souls for the protection of the release of the sacred fire.

After God created man and woman, he commanded them to "be fruitful, and multiply, and replenish the earth." And he said in that immortal fiat, "Take dominion over the earth."[4] This is the purpose of marriage: to take dominion over the earth, to be fruitful and multiply and replenish the earth. All else that happens in the marriage circle comes under this taking of dominion.

We must consider whether sharing a life with someone means that two together can accomplish more than the two separately. If the answer is yes, there may be a very good reason for the relationship. If the answer is no, then there is a question whether or not the relationship should be pursued.

The question is: Can two people working together accomplish more than the individuals separately? Can they harmonize their energies for a goal, for an ideal, for something more than simply living the good life and pursuing pleasure and the pleasure cult?

Now, this obviously brings up the question of what to do when you have not found the right person with whom you desire to share your life. And perhaps you do not find this person for years. How do man and woman handle these energies and still abide in keeping with the laws of God?

The Ascended Masters teach that all energy is God's energy. Sex is *sacred* energy in motion—*x* standing for the activity, the action of the Christ. All energy comes forth from the God Presence. It descends to the heart and is distributed through the chakras.

In the Golden Ages where man and woman had total control of the life-force, only that energy that was necessary for the sustainment of the physical body descended below the heart—just enough to complete the functions of procreation and of the well-being of the physical body. That is what the lower chakras are for. The rest of the energy ascended to nourish the upper chakras for the expansion of God consciousness.

In these times, however, sex is put upon people as the ultimate in this plane. It's in advertising, it's in song, it's in music, it's in rhythm, it's in everything that people talk about. They are indoctrinated to believe that they are not normal unless they have sex constantly. And as people's attention is upon sex, their energy descends to the lower chakras.

Also, because of the substance of past karma, of the electronic belt surrounding the lower chakras, the energy we receive from God tends to sink to these lower chakras by force of habit. Just as water will flow through a canal because the canal is dug and the channel is there—the water is not going to make a new path—so the energy from God flows in the old patterns we have established. In order to change the flow of the energy, we have to change our habit patterns.

The need for sex comes about, then, because energies are clogged in the lower chakras. People feel a buildup of that energy; they desire release, and the only way they have been taught to experience that release is through sex. In the act of sexual intercourse the excess of energy is released. However, when that energy is released, it is spent; it is no longer ours to use in other forms of creativity.

Raising Our Energy

We have to make the decision whether we would like to have a little bit of extra energy to use in spiritual meditation, in reuniting with God, in creativity, in service of God in man, or whether we would prefer to spend that energy in sex. We each have a daily allotment of energy. What we're going to do with that energy is up to our free will.

So you say, Well, if this energy is in the lower chakras, what do we do with it if it's not going to be spent on sex? The answer is very simple. The energy must be raised. It must be raised back to the level of the heart, projected forth to humanity as love and service; to the throat chakra, expended in the power of the spoken Word, in meditation and prayer and decrees; through the third eye by ensouling the vision of God, whatever your profession or your calling is; and to the crown chakra for the illumination of the Buddhic light.

How do we raise that energy? We do it by meditation and we do it by affirmation. We do it by visualization. And we do it by determination. It takes determination to change a habit. Breaking a pattern of smoking or drinking is the same thing. It takes some will, it takes some blue fire, it takes some commitment.

But if you know that you can accomplish something because God says you can, because others like you who are not exceptions to these laws have also accomplished, then it's worth a try. Because there is a promise, there is a pot of gold at the end of this rainbow. It is attainment. It is mastery. It is the promise of reunion.

There is a very simple mantra that has proven to be the key and the answer:

I AM the resurrection and the life of every cell and atom
of my four lower bodies now made manifest!

The statement that Jesus brought forth from the East, from the Cosmic Christ, Lord Maitreya—"I AM the resurrection and the life"—is the statement that will raise energy wherever you direct the statement. You can use it for healing; you can use it for the transmutation of substance.

The action of the resurrection flame is to preserve life. It is the resurrection flame that is actually anchored in the pyramid whereby people have found out that they can sharpen their razor blades or preserve meat or food or flowers. The flame is there because of the forcefield, the geometric pattern of the pyramid.

You are a pyramid. You have a resurrection flame in your heart. When the threefold flame—blue, yellow and pink—starts whirling, the flames begin to blend. Before it gets to be the pure white light of the ascension flame, it has the full radiance of the rainbow. It is a mother-of-pearl: white, but you can see all the colors of the rainbow in the flame. Wherever that flame is invoked, there is resurrection.

When you say this mantra, visualize your spine as you would see a thermometer. The base-of-the-spine chakra is the bulb at the base of the thermometer; that is where the energies of the Mother, the Goddess Kundalini, are locked. It is the white chakra. Visualize energy at that chakra taking on the qualification of the resurrection flame, rising up the spine and pulling up all energy that causes a burden on the lower chakras.

When you hold the visualization of energy rising on your

spine as this mother-of-pearl fire rising up, you should feel a tugging. You want to pull that energy up, willing it to rise; you want to feel that energy being pulled from beneath your feet, all the way up, and offered back to God to his glory.

I AM the resurrection and the life of every cell and atom of my four lower bodies now made manifest!

Energy also gets clogged physically just by lack of exercise. This is why hatha yoga is recommended (but in moderation, because you can get so concerned with your physical body that you neglect your spiritual growth). There has to be exercise to keep up with the flow of energy. You need to have a sport or a form of exercise in which you engage regularly. Whether it's yoga or tennis or swimming or jogging or bike riding, you need to do something to keep energy moving between your chakras for your health, for your vitality, for your youth—and for your God-control of the sacred fire, if you want that God-control.

When we don't have flow, we have stagnation; and when we have stagnation, we have decay, disintegration and death. To keep the flame of life flowing through you, you need the flame of the resurrection.

The Flow of Energy

The generous flow of the energy of every chakra is the law of life, the law of growth, and it is the law of the Eternal Youth, Sanat Kumara, standing where you stand. It is the law of life that consumes death and the consciousness of the fallen angels—these black holes in space. They are dead, for no other reason save that they do not give unto life, but only take.

There are many reasons why we withhold the full gift of ourselves in the gentle expression of words of kindness, of blessing, many reasons why we stop the flow. And every time we stop the flow, there is disease, there is death, there is nonfulfillment of the Law, and karma cannot be balanced.

We must understand the law of the giving self, which is the obedient self, else we will not arrive at the point of Zion. For out of Zion—the point of the highest mountain, the point of the I AM Presence and the crown chakra—comes the anointing of your own Christ Self and the swearing of Sanat Kumara that you in that Christ Self are a priest forever after the Order of Melchizedek.[5]

Celibacy, the priesthood, being a priestess wed to God has its place in the order of Hierarchy. The marriage ritual also has its place and is equally valid. After all, we would extinguish the human race if we all became celibates.

The cosmic interchange of divine love in the marriage relationship is meant to be the same creative love that framed the universe in the beginning when God as Father gave forth the command, "Let there be light," and God as Mother answered, "And there was light." This creative flow can be expressed not only in physical union but also during cycles of dedicated celibacy as each partner goes within to commune with his beloved I AM Presence.

The exchange of the sacred energies in sexual union is for the transfer of spheres of cosmic consciousness—our Causal Bodies of Light. The Light energy resulting from this fusion enhances the positive qualities of each of the partners and strengthens their own divine identity, enabling them to carry their shared burden of karma. As the union is consecrated to the love of God, the harmonious blending of pure Father-Mother energies yields the Son, the Christ consciousness—whether it be in the form of a child, an inspiration, a successful enterprise or a work of art.

When this exchange is not spiritualized through a recognition that God is both the lover and the beloved, the two individuals may experience physical pleasure, but they also unknowingly take on each other's karmic patterns without the benefit of a spiritually transmutative love. This may explain the frequent identity crises suffered by those who have intimate relationships on a casual basis; they take on so many karmic identities, effectively neutralizing their own, that they no longer know who they really are.

When your energies are constantly engaged in sex with one or more partners, your energy is constantly being entangled with the karma and the karmic patterns of these individuals. By establishing these forcefields and these flows, you are also setting up lines of force that deprive you of the union with your twin flame or with your soul mate.*

A Life of Joy in the Spirit

Does that mean that we cannot find a relationship that is high and holy and satisfying in Christ? No, it means that when we've been surfeited with the world and the ways of the world, we can determine to lead a life of joy, a life in the Spirit. And we can determine that we can have that joy and that fulfillment in this plane, that sex is not something for which we have to be condemned. It can be used properly. It can be consecrated with a person who is dedicated to the Light.

If you want to find that person and it's important to you, then there are steps you need to take, a few sacrifices along the way, the casting aside of a few old habit patterns so that you

---

* Twin flames are two souls who came forth from the same original Divine Whole. They share the same divine blueprint, the same key in the I AM Presence. Soul mates are souls evolving in time and space who have pursued a similar evolution—not as the diametric opposite and polarity of the twin flame, but a similarity of karma and dharma. Twin flames share a destiny from the beginning to the ending—soul mates are partners for a journey or a mission.

can garner the energy as the wise virgins, keeping their lamps trimmed with oil.[6] That means keeping your chakras trimmed with Light—garnering the energy that you would otherwise spend in sex in your chakras as flames in the windows of your being.

Your chakras are windows; each chakra is another level of God's consciousness. In each chakra is a flame, and so each chakra is like its own little lighthouse. It sends out a forcefield of pure or impure energy as you determine what it is going to send forth.

Across the margent of the world there is someone, somewhere, who is garnering energy and Light in the chakras. When you reach the peak of that perfect pitch where your chakras sing with the energy of God focused there, you will find your exact counterpart who is focusing that energy also in a certain peak and pitch. And you will come together by a union of spiritual energies—which is not to say that you will not also experience physical attraction, emotional, mental attraction, because union is for all planes.

There is nothing unholy about physical union if there is nothing unholy about spiritual union, because Matter is also God. But it is only holy if it is holy in the minds of those who partake of this union, and it must be holy in the minds of both. You cannot have a holy union where one partner is in a state of lust and the gratification of the senses and the other is meditating upon the fulfillment of the spirals of the Holy Spirit.

So you must be careful where you allow your energies to rest. Where your energies rest, that is what you will attract. The way to get into a framework where you have a marriage of either twin flames or of soul mates is to pursue your meditation on the violet flame to clean up the energies of karma that have in the past been the forcefield of magnetic attraction, of instant attractions between people on a sensual basis. If you clean up those forcefields in your electronic belt by meditation, by application to the violet flame, you will clear away the debris that will make for an unwholesome alliance in the world.

You will then find that gradually there is no longer the pull of the senses or the pull of the karma that attracts you to people. It will be the pull of spiritual energies—the pull of a common flame, a common devotion; you will find that you are in polarity with a person on the basis of spiritual Light. This makes all the difference in the world. Because that spiritual Light is enduring, it can endure the ups and downs, the comings and goings, whether of sexual satisfactions or the pleasures of the senses or the things of this world upon which most marriages are based.

The Social System That Leads to the Necessity for Abortion

As we observe the history of the twentieth century, we can see that with the advent of rock music and the lowering of the sacred energies of man and woman, the logical sequence was a sexual revolution and a greater promiscuity. Thus we see the free-love generation of the 1960s largely abandoning the traditional concepts of marriage and family. Living together became fashionable. Premarital and teenage sex became widespread. Birth control became a necessity. And once the new morality was established, it was a relatively small step from birth control to population control and the social acceptability of abortion.

Where this has led us today is that many, many souls who are a part of Aquarius, who should be here—new souls of Light prepared to take their place and help bring in the New

Age—are not in embodiment. They have been denied entrance into the portals of birth because their parents considered that it was an untimely situation. Abortion has become a means of birth control.

The abortion of a soul is the abortion of the potential of that soul to become God. It is the abortion of her destiny and her divine plan, and because our Father-Mother God chooses the special moment in history when each soul is to return to earth to take part in the divine plan of the decades and the centuries, it is the abortion of an assignment from God.

When we abort life in the womb, we are aborting the opportunity of a soul whose time has come to be on earth at that precise astrological moment. The timetables of the conception and birth of every child are directed by Almighty God, the Archangels and Cosmic Beings of Light and the specific Ascended Masters who are the sponsors of that soul— the Godparents, if you will. These timetables are part of God's grand design of life.

Understanding this, you can see how wondrously you were made, how God cared for you personally, how your Father-Mother ordained your conception, your earthly parents, your life, your purpose, your reason for being, and then carefully oversaw your development in the womb. Thus no one is an unwanted child, for even though parents may think they don't want to bear a child, your God-parents want you and they have ordained your birth.

Not one birth has ever taken place upon this planet that was not sanctioned by Almighty God and the Holy Spirit. No matter how hard you may try to conceive a child, unless it is the will of God and the timing of God, that child will not be conceived. The moment of conception is the moment that the Holy Spirit ordains life.

The Divine Plan of the Soul

Even before a child is conceived, the divine plan of the soul has been worked out in intricate detail. The grand design of God is so exact that at the moment of conception, the genes in each tiny embryo are already suited to the specific soul who will grow and develop in that womb.

The Karmic Board, together with the Holy Christ Self of the soul, determines before conception takes place when, where and under what circumstances the soul will embody. In order to give the soul the best opportunity to work out her karma, these circumstances have been expertly tailored to the soul's needs.

The law of karma is integral to life on earth, and karma implies reincarnation even as reincarnation implies karma. The karma that each of us carries contains positive and negative momentums—momentums we have set in motion by our free will—our actions, words, deeds, thoughts and feelings.

We also have momentums of inaction and sins of omission —not speaking out or taking action when we should but simply sitting back and being an observer of life. Our lives are the harvest of all we have ever sown, five minutes ago, yesterday and ten thousand years ago.

As God has ordained the cycles and Laws of his universe, it works out that many of us do not reap in a given lifetime what we have sown in that life. We don't know whether it will take a thousand or twelve thousand years for those actions to come full circle and demand that we make them right. But God knows, and his Law is unerring, unfailing and always just.

Therefore, if we do the tasks of the day by performing services and fulfilling our responsibilities—doing all we can to help others as well as offering our own gifts to society—we are sowing good karma as well as balancing bad karma.

Yet in the exercise of our free will, we have ordained what must come next in our life, whether blessing or bane, according to how we have sown. As Paul wrote to the Galatians, God's law of karma cannot be scorned or evaded, for "whatsoever a man soweth, that shall he also reap."[7]

Because we wind up at the conclusion of a lifetime with many debts and the desire to pay them, God in his mercy gives us the opportunity to return in a new life to make things right. This is a far better solution than the one orthodox Christianity offers by sending us to either heaven or hell, for most of us are ready for neither and desire to finish up the LORD's business here on earth.

Before conception, all parents, whether they are aware of it or not in their outer consciousness, have agreed at inner levels to receive the incoming soul. If in some cases they have not agreed, they have understood at inner levels that it is their karma to do so. Sometimes parents do not agree to sponsor the child because they are unwilling to submit to the Law of God.

Often this is because our teachers, pastors, ministers and rabbis lack the great knowledge of these cycles of life and do not teach that if parents refuse the calling to bear life now, they will, in a sense, be aborting their own life plan and its cycles. By resisting that assignment, they place themselves in a more difficult karma-making circumstance, because sometime, somewhere, they will yet have to bear that child. And it is very difficult to return to the place where the same two individuals are together once again and the same soul will be available and blessed by God to take embodiment through them.

Sometimes parents who have already had children and have balanced the karma that they needed to balance through childbearing may be chosen by God to bring forth children with whom they have no negative karma. These may be highly gifted children, who, by bringing their past attainment back with them, may make a great contribution to society.

Every child conceived has a divine plan and a divine design—even if some in our society claim that the child is unwanted or handicapped and should therefore not be born into this world. The renowned pediatric surgeon and former U.S. Surgeon General Dr. C. Everett Koop says, "It has been my constant experience that disability and unhappiness do not necessarily go together. Some of the most unhappy children whom I have known have all of their physical and mental faculties, and on the other hand some of the happiest youngsters have borne burdens which I myself would find very difficult to bear."[8]

Who are we to say that a life is not worthwhile? Only the soul herself can say. Helen Keller proved that life is worth living and fighting for. How can we ever forget the remarkable determination and daring of this deaf, dumb and blind girl who overcame the utter darkness of her childhood to become an exceptional author, educator and lecturer?

People who are born into abject poverty and the worst of circumstances often rise to become great leaders and shapers of the destinies of nations. Look at Abraham Lincoln—born to uneducated parents and raised in a log cabin in the backwoods of Kentucky. Frederick Douglas, the famous abolitionist leader, was born and raised as an African-American slave. The American inventor and technological genius Thomas Edison attended school for only three months of his life and was expelled by his schoolmaster as retarded.

An intangible "something" exists that is higher than the body and higher than circumstance; it is the drive of the soul and the spirit that gives character and impetus to an individual. We also have to remember that many people have serious karma, for they may have committed violent crimes in the past. Such individuals are required by karmic law to embody in circumstances that are less than ideal, because the purpose of karma is never to punish but to help us learn from our past mistakes.

The only way we learn from past mistakes is to be in a similar circumstance where what is now done to us is what we previously did to life. The hard knocks of life are sometimes what our souls need, for the family and environment we are born into and the friends, foes and challenges we meet along life's way are all a part of the wondrous and intricate blueprint from the mind of God.

The Consequences of Abortion

In the twenty-five years following the 1973 Supreme Court decision of *Roe v. Wade* legalizing abortion, over 36 million children were aborted in the United States. These "missing persons" will not take their place as adults in the world scheme, nor will their children be in place for the new millennium.

When we add to that the billion to a billion and a half children aborted worldwide since 1973, the absence of these lifestreams in embodiment has compromised the divine plan for earth. The consequences of this are serious for all of us: over one billion individuals are unable to offer what God intended them to contribute to life on earth, starting in the decades of the seventies.

They did not grow up and marry and give life to other souls who were intended to learn from them and to be sponsored by them as their parents and teachers. For God does not only think of you when you are born, he is already thinking when you are yet in the womb of whose great-great-grandmother and great-great-grandfather you are going to be.

The plan of the mind of God is vast—a cosmic computer that none of us can even begin to comprehend. By playing God in aborting life, we are interfering with the evolutionary chain of life begetting life—life depending on life, helpless life depending upon those who are strong.

And although we are concerned about the ecology of the planet, we should also be concerned about the ecology of souls on the planet.[9] Souls who are meant to live together, evolve together and experience life together have a certain chemistry and a collective unconscious, and they respond together to the forward movements of their time.

Souls who should be accelerating in the winds of Aquarius and the violet flame of the Holy Spirit and who should be ushering in the Aquarian age are simply not here. Neither are those who should be in leadership roles in education and in the war on crime and drugs. They are waiting in the wings when they should be star players on the stage of life. They are not where they are supposed to be: leading America and the world to the pinnacle of a Golden Age in the twenty-first century.

We are reaping the karma for abortion in every area of life, and it is breeding a grossness, an ingratitude for that cry of the newborn child that is the most wonderful sound in the whole wide world. That child who cries out in the womb for life and opportunity represents every individual's soul. If you tune out your sensitivity to the child unborn, you cannot keep it open to the soul.

People have turned off their sensitivity to the needs of the criminal, the victim, the unborn child. There is a grossness and a hardness of heart. What you have to realize is that at any time you abort a child, that soul and that body and the soul in the body experience the most excruciating pain. This is the holocaust of the twentieth century.

The "Right" to Abortion

Many people support a woman's "right" to have an abortion based on the principle that a woman has free will and the right to control her own body. They may uphold this right even though they wouldn't choose abortion themselves. They say a woman should be able to choose whether or not to have a child.

We all agree. But we also must state that she should make her choice before conception, not after. We have access to many methods of birth control. Abortion is not one of them.

The apostle Paul said it clearly: "Know ye not that ye are the temple of God?"

He also said: "Know ye not that your body is the temple of the Holy Ghost which is in you, which ye have of God, and ye are not your own? For ye are bought with a price: therefore glorify God in your body, and in your spirit, which are God's."[10]

The point Paul makes that we must underscore here is "ye are not your own." It is true that we are not our own, for we are God's, and our souls are "bought with a price" by the living Saviour Jesus Christ. This means that our bodies are not our own, nor are our souls.

God has ordained us to bring forth souls made in his image and likeness; therefore the freedom to choose not to bring forth the soul that is conceived and already attached to the womb from the moment of conception does not belong to us. It cannot, because we are not God; we are sons and daughters of God and we are obedient to his Law. He has ordained us to be co-creators with him, not above him. We cannot play God with the soul aborning in our womb.

If you are pregnant and it is truly impossible for you to care for this soul at the present time, adoption is a viable alternative to abortion. There are many families who are more than happy to give a loving home to your baby.

We must educate people to desire to mother life and to have life, and we want to educate people against the entire social system that leads to abortion. The necessity for an abortion is a final act that has been preceded by everything that is degenerating in our society and everything that is irresponsible. At the point when somebody needs an abortion, it's too late.

We must educate society all the way back from the beginning in the correct use of the sacred fire, in the correct use of music, in noncontamination with drugs, in the sacredness of marriage, in the holiness of the individual to embody God, and how to channel those energies so that people don't have to justify a morality that ends in an unwanted pregnancy.

Suicide: The End Result of a State of Hopelessness

What more shall we say of the old, familiar story, which seems ever new to the youth of the world as they "come of age" and are soon reaping the fruit of their own sowing. Those who are involved in the maelstrom of human thought and feeling in their more discordant manifestations, those who have tried again and again without success to satisfy their desires by artificial stimulation of every kind, these know the sense of futility that can arise as a byproduct in consciousness. This frustration and state of hopelessness often provides just the needed stimulus for suicide for many people who, failing utterly to obtain happiness here below in the world of form, decide that they can no longer face life, for all attempts to find happiness have failed.

Suicide is not a modern phenomenon. Suicide of young

people and cluster suicides have happened periodically throughout history. And upon further examination we find that this
occurred on Atlantis and Lemuria as well. So, we are seeing a
repetitive cycle coming back again, and the cycle is reaching a
peak in our very era.

Loren Coleman, an expert on suicide, reports that
"nationally, suicide is the third leading cause of death among
adolescents; in some cases, the number one and two killers,
accidents and homicides, are viewed by researchers as
disguised suicides. Many drug overdoses, fatal automobile
accidents, and related self-destructive eating and alcoholic
disorders are uncounted teen suicides."[11]

The contemplation of this subject gives us profound
sorrow and grief not only for the physical death of someone of
this age group, but for the realization that something very
profound is troubling them and they have no recourse in this
octave to solve that problem.

This generation is destroying itself by a complex death
syndrome—a network of reinforcing activities that are the
common experience of this era, including child abuse, tobacco,
drugs, alcohol, pornography, prostitution, rock music, faulty
education, TV, perverse movies and a steady fare of junk food
and sugar. This self-abuse is self-destruction; it is suicide—
chakra by chakra. Death comes in increments.

The soul dies for one reason: because the Light of the
chakras has been drained. Life becomes a grasping for new
highs and new stimulus because the real stimulus of the power
of the resurrection in the chakras is not there. It is a slow
death. It is an unperceived death. Each time the light is
lessened through a rock concert or drugs or sex, the person
may have a high for a week, but a portion of the self has died,
a tiny percentage.

First, the Light of the crown chakra is lost—the ability of

thinking and reasoning. Then, with the taking of marijuana, the brain is dulled further so the individual can't figure their way out of the mess they're in. And finally, suicide becomes the next step—the only way to get another high on a long list of highs that no longer satisfy.

A soul is very fragile. Look at a newborn baby and see the fragility of your own soul. There are substances that, when taken into the body, can interfere with the functioning and the flow of Light through the chakras from the I AM Presence to the soul. Bits as fine as the sliver of a fingernail can be lost as children in their early years or early teen years use alcohol or drugs or nicotine, even excessive sugar, and as they experience the bombardment of the senses through music and the media. Part of the soul is actually no longer there. The potential to be is shrinking.

The violent sounds and the violence that occurs to the brain and the mind in a drug experience can literally blast the soul in pieces, and parts of oneself are around, not in this temple. And when there is a vacating of the temple, of a portion of a concentrated identity, a self-awareness in God, the vacated portion of the house is immediately filled with forces of darkness.

Thus, suicide is very gradual and it is taken in degrees. Suicide is only the final step in a long history of self-negation and the squandering of the Light. It is an epidemic. And we ask ourselves—how can we stop it?

Solutions to Suicide

There are solutions to suicide.

The best of the psychologists and experts can tell you that suicide is contagious. They have no other word to describe entity possession and the moving from one individual to another of the suicide entity, which is known as Annihla. Call to Archangel Michael and Mighty Astrea to bind Annihla in the name of Jesus Christ and the entire Spirit of the Great White Brotherhood.

Tell your children that they're not allowed by God, their parents or society to commit suicide—and above all their Real Self forbids them to do it.

Teach children the law of reincarnation and karma and suicide. Whatever they are today is the sum total of what they have ever been and what they have made of themselves. And if they don't like what they see in the mirror, they have the power to change.

Tell them that the moment you commit suicide, the judgment of Almighty God upon you is to place your soul in another body conceived in the womb to be born nine months later. You will have no opportunity between incarnations to take any lessons in the higher octaves. You don't go to the octaves of Light. You don't go to the temples of Light.

Your soul is put into another body, and you have to come back to the exact same place where you are right now. Do you want to spend fifteen or twenty years of your life getting where you are now and living in a life that may then be under a totalitarian state? This is what we must tell our children, the true law of the outcome of suicide, and not let them continue to have this fantasy that there is some glory land in a world of death.

This truth is exactly the opposite of what the suicide entity projects. It tells you that sweet death is going to come and take you to a quiet place. It projects a sense of darkness, warmth, comfort, security, almost back to the womb.

People who commit suicide are looking for this place where nothing can hurt them, where there are no conflicts, no resolutions, no accountability, nothing. They don't want to deal with stress. They don't want to meet the challenges of life. They feel alone, empty and so depressed.

Remember that this fragile soul is like a newborn infant, totally dependent upon its parents or it will not live. The soul is totally dependent upon the free will of the individual linking up with the individual Christ, Jesus Christ, the Father, the I AM Presence. If there is not basic training, if there is not a profound tying of the child to God through any form of religion that is true and holy and honorable, the child does not have recourse when this force of suicide comes upon him. The child doesn't understand that the commandment to choose life, not death, is primary and fundamental and has been a part of us since we began.

Defending Our Children and Youth

The God and Goddess Meru tell us that America is in danger of losing a generation.[12] If we lose the generation, the fate of our very nation is in doubt. They warn that the children and youth "are the target in every nation through all the world of the forces of Death and Hell. And those who are adults seldom comprehend what burdens lead the teenager to suicide. These are not all nonthinking ones. Some simply fall beneath the weight of their cross, bearing as they do a portion of world karma. For they have volunteered before taking embodiment, and there has been no Simon the Cyrenian to carry that cross for them while they should also bear the karma of the earth—no Joseph of Arimathea to anoint their bodies with myrrh and aloes.

"Blessed ones, there are Christed ones in the earth, and Mother Mary has called the Messenger and does call you now—'Take them down from the cross!' This is the message that comes from the heart of the *Pietà*.

"Realize that the Divine Mother in you must understand that the gap called the generation gap is that which is perpetuated by demons and false hierarchies of anti-youth in the earth. And they move to separate you from sensitivity to the situation and seeing the problems or knowing just how far a child, a teenager may be dragged into the grips of the toilers of the astral plane.

"The children and teenagers do not tell you, for they would keep up the appearance of that which you desire to see, ever desiring to please the parent. Thus, in so doing they forfeit any assistance that might be forthcoming—and then, beloved, it is too late and too hard to bear.

"We are the sponsors of youth and of a new generation. We must have a new generation, for so many have bodies that they have corrupted through following the pied pipers of this decade.

"Blessed ones, we must prepare for a future when the survivors shall be the Lightbearers. Today it is difficult enough to survive physically. I ask you, then, how can they even begin to survive spiritually when what is upon them is of such a dread and diabolical nature?...

"Blessed ones, we need an army of mothers and fathers and sponsors and teachers who will take the intensity of the call—taught by the Messenger and being perfected by the chelas—and use the Archangel Michael Rosary[13] to bring a concentrated effort of judgment on segments of life that are bringing Death and Hell into the very marketplace....

"Blessed ones, unless there is a determined all-out war launched by those in heaven and on earth, you will find that though all other problems may be solved you will not have another generation qualified to rule, to govern or to build a society that is just, a civilization that is advanced."[14]

The Cult of Death

Lord Maitreya explains that the cult of pleasure that has been propagated on planet Earth is, in fact, a manifestation of the cult of death of the fallen ones: "When a soul or a body is in the process of dissolution, decay and death, and when that individual has been a part of the Light in some form in this or previous incarnations, then during the period of the degeneration spiral, a great deal of Light is released from those cells, from that body temple.

"That Light would naturally flow back to the Great Central Sun if it were not for the fact that those who are a part of these death cycles take that energy and use it over and over again. It should be compared, beloved ones, to partaking of the very sewer of life and passing it through the body many times over.

"When energy passes through a body or passes through chakras (because it passes through something that is not moving) there is the sensation of friction between the movement of energy and the chakra or vehicle that remains still. This release of energy as sensation is used to heighten sexual experience, the pleasure cult, drug experiences and all forms of hallucination that come from the unreal world.

"Let me state this again: when there is the death of souls of Light because they have rebelled against God, because they have been corrupted by rebellion, the process of decay is by definition a process of releasing energy. The energy released is itself misqualified energy, which is regurgitated and reassimilated as it passes through many times.

"As it passes through, it may then take on the simulation of life and its many processes. Therefore, an entire evolution on the planetary body is a part of the spirals of death in this very hour, and these individuals are having a heyday of enjoyment. They seem to experience life intensely and richly, and they are motivated by intense sexual desire and the need for sensual experience.

"This is because they are in the very process of losing their soul sensitivities and contact with life. And so to keep their grasp on life, they must create and re-create, day by day, activities that are degenerate and immoral. This, beloved ones, becomes the cult of death—the cult of sweet death—whereby individuals enjoy the very last dregs of misqualified energy unto the hour of the death of the body and the death of the soul.

"Now, when children of the Light who are daily giving all of their energy to God in service, in joy, in singing and in all the things that are a part of Reality come and observe the fun and games and activities of those individuals who are already in unreality, if they are not taught by their parents to understand what is happening, they will be lured into parties, into taking drugs, into taking alcohol and massive amounts of sugar and unreal chemical foods.

"So the children of Light go the way of a death generation simply because fathers and mothers do not have the courage to extend discipline, which indeed may make them unpopular with their offspring but which will incur to them forever and forever the gratitude of the souls of their children, who after maturity will realize that they have been spared the deceptions of this age."[15]

"Individuals Would Do Better If They Knew Better"

The Great Divine Director explains that much wrong action that people engage in is simply the result of ignorance: "I cannot condone wrong thought or judgment about a part of life, whether or not the individual is guilty of the implied wrong action. It must ever be borne in mind that most individuals would *do* better if they *knew* better; therefore, it is the bane of ignorance that perpetuates wrong action, and it is ignorance itself that must be combated....

"It is not an easy thing, beloved ones, from the standpoint of the human, to sense the multitudinous pressures of existence and to be able to determine accurately which impulses to accept and which ones to reject. One of the reasons your beloved Saint Germain and beloved Jesus have so often stressed the keeping of your attention upon your Divine Presence is because such untrammeled heights of being hold no thought whatever of imperfection within them and they, therefore, are a harbor of great safety for the unascended consciousness. It is, however, a present factor of man's curious nature to explore many avenues of consciousness. And hence your beloved Saint Paul, now the great master Hilarion, so often admonished the early Christians to 'put on the whole armour of God'[16] as an effective deterrent to the forces of evil.

"I think it goes without saying that the heavenly consciousness itself is the best defense against iniquity. But when men are not content to abide in the consciousness of God and its higher upreach, choosing of their own volition to move through lesser avenues of natural existence and being, they must recognize that the attendant perils they encounter must be guarded against lest they find themselves bereft of their eternal treasures by the depredations of mere thieves and robbers.

"Those who desire to simplify the study of existence by separating realities into black and white may find the perfect solution to their problems in steadfastly abiding in the consciousness of God and his perfection, yet these frequently do not take into account either the laws of karma or the mastery of the domain into which the consciousness of man has been projected.

"They overlook the temporary magnetism of personal momentums that so often exert their pull just when the possibilities of the joys of heaven are becoming so apparent. These human tendencies, which must not be ignored, rudely thrust forth outer realities that can momentarily disturb the progress of the soul unless they be guarded against.

"Your freedom, precious ones, must be won upon earth, where your freedom was lost. You cannot expect to carry into the higher octaves of Light either soiled garments or the consciousness of imperfection; but you must resolve your crises here in this octave, that by the power of your example you may inspire others who are caught in the web of delusion and intellectual brittleness to extricate themselves therefrom and to see the pathway of Light and its mighty upward spiral as a manifest token of the constancy of heaven. I think, then, that the subconscious being of man, which is, after all, but the basement level of his memory body, ought to be properly trained in many ways so that the power of the subconscious may ever be used for the blessing of mankind."[17]

Finding Freedom

El Morya, the Ascended Master of the will of God, encourages us in our struggles on the Path and points the way to freedom from the habits and addictions of the Cult of Hedon: "I have observed countless times while individuals present here and elsewhere throughout this planet have struggled over this or that binding habit that has seized upon their consciousness and which seemed to have dominion there so that they could not and were unable to shake that condition from their world. And I have determined by God-determination and God-obedience that that condition shall be overcome for any individual who will make the call to the Ascended Host determinedly three times a day without fail and shall rest securely and serenely in the arms of their own God Presence and the cosmic Light and the action of that Light.

"Beloved ones, if you will only accept the pressure of my love, you will find within you a power rising to overcome all imperfection or binding habits that may have seized upon your consciousness, until you shall be able to overcome invincibly by the same manner others of us of the Ascended Hosts have overcome through the years that are past."[18]

"Life may be broken. Life itself, as it manifests in mankind, may manifest apparent discord. But in the final end, that discord cannot remain tangibly in evidence but must yield to the impulses of the Spirit-fire of life within the fohat of God, the unfolding beauty that he, the Creator, placed there in the Beginning and which vibration is an eternal vibration that never in all eternity can be altered by any consciousness—cosmic, human, elemental or other.

"No one can, no one shall alter the great creative Law, the eternal manifestation of divine love. For Law is love and love is Law. The confinement of the Law is nothing to those who love it. They are grateful indeed that the Law loves them enough to confine them to a purpose, to a pathway, to a spiral whereby as they ascend, they are conscious of more and more Light rather than less and less Light....

"Press on, therefore. Maintain your enthusiasm. Maintain your love and your devotion. We shall help you, knowing that the envelopes of flesh that you wear do not always respond as you would have them. We give you our aims and pray that you will have the wisdom to accept them that you may steer the steed upon which you so nobly ride toward our abode and have a winged victory in due time."[19]

Protect Our Youth
by El Morya

Beloved heavenly Father!
Beloved heavenly Father!
Beloved heavenly Father!
Take command of our youth today
Blaze through them opportunity's ray
Release perfection's mighty power
Amplify cosmic intelligence each hour
Protect, defend their God-design
Intensify intent divine
I AM, I AM, I AM
The power of infinite Light
Blazing through our youth
Releasing cosmic proof
Acceptable and right
The full power of cosmic Light
To every child and child-man
In America and the world!
Beloved I AM! Beloved I AM! Beloved I AM!

The Return to Eden

THE NERVOUS SYSTEM OF MAN WAS intended by God to carry two forms of energy: one, the necessary functional energy by which the body carries out its natural objectives; the other, primarily lodged in the functions of the sympathetic nervous system, was attuned to higher frequencies of thought and feeling intended to assist the outer, sentient man to become integrated with the inner man, the soul.

The faculties of the soul specifically reach out to obtain the treasures of heaven. These treasures are tangible manifestations of the consciousness of God, of his Reality and his intelligence. They are charged with the fullness of his grace, and they will lift the soul out of its socket of mortal density into those planes that would otherwise remain to man an impenetrable realm.

The physical body cannot act as a conductor of Light when toxins are present. By purification of the faculties of the physical body, as well as those of the mind and soul, man is able to travel across the line of demarcation that separates this world from the next. He is able to feel that which otherwise cannot be cognized. He is able to become that which is so much more than the present capacity of the human race that it is difficult for the natural mind to comprehend the heights of attainment that are possible.

A balance of yin and yang—male and female aspects of Deity—is necessary to the integration of the soul with the physical body. One method of achieving this goal is through a diet that conveys those balanced energies to the body. The principle of the yin and the yang is the foundation of the diet of the Eastern adepts.

Food is a bearer of Light and a means of conveying Light and prana to the body. Drawing in prana through food precedes living directly off prana.

Self-Realization

It is almost impossible for an individual to describe in words the true meaning of soul-realization or self-realization when that realization is interpreted to mean "God-realization." It has been said, "How can the finite understand or manifest the Infinite?" Yet the finite is the product of the Infinite and as such must, by cosmic law, as an iron filing drawn to a magnet, seek, pursue and cling to its Infinite birthright.

"Flesh and blood," as has been clearly said, "cannot inherit the kingdom of God,"[1] but the only begotten Son, the Divine Archetype, often unrelated to the outer man, is the legitimate heir-apparent to those who are self-realized men and women. Atheists, agnostics and materialists alike allow, when an individual has run his life's course and the span is ended, that death appears to have the victory over the body and those aspects of the human personality that have identified with the body.[2] From the standpoint of appearance, we will have to agree, but from the standpoint of Truth, we must disagree; for whereas the man of flesh is no more, the man of Spirit does not cease to be, but lives on.

There is no joy in life that is greater than the fulfillment of one's divine potential and of one's true self-realization. There is no price that is too great to pay to obtain the great beneficence of cosmic law that manifests for the purified soul whose faculties have become transparent, sensitized to the pulsations of God that can be felt both in Heaven and on earth.

It is altogether understandable that the Cult of Hedon should thrive on the planet, and all can and should acknowledge that their search for joy is a valid expression of the search for man's true Being. It is the method and the madness that we eschew, the blindness of false goals and the death of soul-consciousness through the amplification of sensuality that forge the chains of slavery that hold people bound in a senseless, repetitious round of vanity, debauchery and self-destruction.

In the name of mercy and in the name of freedom, how can the youth of the world expect to find happiness by violating not only the Laws of God but also the laws of Nature and logic itself. These come, so to speak, fresh from God's hand, wide-eyed with wonder, and the soul within them hopes to obtain in the experiential world grace, beauty, joy and freedom in the Light of God-guided experience.

Can the present course to which humanity have steered their errant sons have any hope for the survival of that pristine purity and Reality that gave them birth?

May our hope, the hope that must cradle generations yet unborn, probe the mysteries of life until we can clearly see how we may assist posterity to deliver themselves from the traitor's toils (that pleasure-seeking whose end is the mere satiation of appetite) unto a freedom of limitless experience in the magnificent God-control of every facet of being?

The Fulfillment of the Divine Plan

The return of man to his original estate and the restoration of the Eden of divine experience is the goal of present earth life in the Garden that God has blessed. There men may see not the yin and yang of Good and Evil, but only Good, and seeing only Good, joyously express it as the reflection of the Creator. This is the divine plan. Adherence to it and the search for it brings the bounties of freedom from the Cult of Hedon to all. This grace restores men in consciousness to the Eden of God, for salvation dwells not in a place alone but in consciousness, and the consciousness of highest Good is the redeemer of every errant one. Let us help all to fulfill their divine plan.

Through the pursuit of divine happiness, restoration can come to all life, including its many parts; the Eden of old can be restored at any time as the hand of the Father from on high is raised in tangible benediction over the head of every man who finds happiness in pursuit of the divine will. For as man commits himself wholly, consciously, willingly unto that will that gives birth to the Christ Light in every son of heaven, he is blessed by waves of divine bliss, which no man can see, which passes all earthly understanding and defies worded description.

Lord Lanto reveals the goal: "The deeper students (and I think all who seek sincerely are included in the term) must learn to master their energies. They must endeavor to draw so much of God's divine fire into their lives that without discomfort or remorse they find complete happiness in the God flame within. Journeying with spiritual ease into the arms of the blessed Holy Comforter, they find peace and understanding and they bask in that divine solace that assuages all suffering and is the soul-satisfying balm for every heart.

"Immersion in the fires of the Holy Spirit enables the student of Light to remain above the pangs of human experience while he yet walks among mankind as the servant of all. The goal of life fulfilled in the ascension, whereby the soul of man unites with the Spirit of God, is the final victory over the human dilemma. There in the oneness of eternity, the soul finds its freedom forever above the storms and strife of mortality that once bound his energies in a whirl of physical, mental and emotional activity. Here is the victory over the last enemy that shall be overcome.[3] Here in the triumph over the ego with its idolatrous death consciousness, the soul finds eternal harmony and the everlasting opportunity to express the glory of her own radiant culture."[4]

Violet Fire and Tube of Light Decree
by the Ascended Master Saint Germain

O my constant, loving I AM Presence, thou Light of God above me whose radiance forms a circle of fire before me to light my way:

I AM faithfully calling to thee to place a great pillar of Light from my own mighty I AM God Presence all around me right now today! Keep it intact through every passing moment, manifesting as a shimmering shower of God's beautiful Light through which nothing human can ever pass. Into this beautiful electric circle of divinely charged energy direct a swift upsurge of the violet fire of freedom's forgiving, transmuting flame!

Cause the ever expanding energy of this flame projected downward into the forcefield of my human energies to completely change every negative condition into the positive polarity of my own Great God Self! Let the magic of its mercy so purify my world with Light that all whom I contact shall always be blessed with the fragrance of violets from God's own heart in memory of the blessed dawning day when all discord—cause, effect, record and memory—is forever changed into the victory of Light and the peace of the ascended Jesus Christ.

I AM now constantly accepting the full power and manifestation of this fiat of Light and calling it into instantaneous action by my own God-given free will and the power to accelerate without limit this sacred release of assistance from God's own heart until all men are ascended and God-free in the Light that never, never, never fails!

Decree to Archangel Michael

In the name of the beloved mighty victorious Presence of God, I AM in me, my very own beloved Holy Christ Self, Holy Christ Selves of all mankind, beloved Archangel Michael, beloved Lanello, the entire Spirit of the Great White Brotherhood and the World Mother, elemental life—fire, air, water and earth!

I call for the deliverance of the United States of America, Canada, Central and South America and the entire planet from the cocaine curse, from marijuana, from the beast and dragon of cocaine and international drug trafficking. Let the people be delivered from sugar, alcohol and nicotine in their bodies and their brains. Let them be purged, let them be raised up. Let the mighty legions of the LORD's host cut them free.*

1. Lord Michael, Lord Michael,
    I call unto thee—
    Wield thy sword of blue flame
    And now cut me free!

Refrain: Blaze God-power, protection
    Now into my world,
    Thy banner of faith
    Above me unfurl!
    Transcendent blue lightning
    Now flash through my soul,
    I AM by God's mercy
    Made radiant and whole!

2. Lord Michael, Lord Michael,
    I love thee, I do—
    With all thy great faith
    My being imbue!

---

* Insert your calls for personal and planetary conditions here.

   3. Lord Michael, Lord Michael
      And legions of blue—
      Come seal me, now keep me
      Faithful and true!

Coda: I AM with thy blue flame
       Now full-charged and blest,
      I AM now in Michael's
      Blue-flame armour dressed! (3x)

And in full faith I consciously accept this manifest, manifest, manifest! (3x) right here and now with full power, eternally sustained, all-powerfully active, ever expanding and world enfolding until all are wholly ascended in the Light and free!

Beloved I AM! Beloved I AM! Beloved I AM.

Invocation by the Messenger to Free the Youth of America from Marijuana

Beloved mighty I AM Presence from the heart of God in the Great Central Sun, O point of Light in the heart of each heart, in the very Holy of holies of these children of the Sun, beloved Helios and Vesta, I implore you now through the heart of Saint Francis, the heart of Kuthumi, to come very close to these devotees of the flame.

Beloved Kuthumi, I invoke your mighty Electronic Presence over each one. Let your heart of Light now be one with the hearts of these souls. Beloved Kuthumi, come very close to these devotees on the Path as they offer in silent prayer their own requests for your intercession in their life.

I call especially to you and to your legions of Light, to the Brothers and Sisters of the Golden Robe, to come forth and free the youth of America and all of our people from this deadly drug of marijuana, all of its influences. And I call for the healing of all souls who have ever partaken of it—the healing now of the seed, the healing of the cells, the brain, the mind, the nervous system.

I call for the healing of all phases of the Light manifestation in the temple. I call for the healing of the channels of flow from the heart of cells and atoms. And I demand the stripping of all souls of these discarnates and demons sent by the Nephilim to enslave them to their death cult.

Burn right through, O mighty Archangels! Burn right through by the power of Kuthumi! Set life free. Set youth free. And raise up the Ascended Master youth of this nation to go forth nation by nation and set the captives free. O God, set the captives free nation by nation from that which imperils their souls though they know it not.

I call now in the name of Brahman and the Word that was with him in the beginning and the Word that was God. I call in the name of the Word manifest in the Father, the Son, the Holy Spirit, by the light of the Mother. Amen.

Lanto's Prayer

In the name of Almighty God
I stand forth to challenge the night,
To raise up the Light,
To focus the consciousness of Gautama Buddha!
And I AM the thousand-petaled lotus flame!
And I come to bear it in his name!
I stand in life this hour
And I stand with the scepter of Christ-power
To challenge the darkness,
To bring forth the Light,
To ensoul from starry heights
The consciousness of Angels,
        Masters, Elohim, sun-centers
And of all of life
That is the I AM Presence of each one!
I claim the victory in God's name.
I claim the Light of solar flame.
I claim the Light! I AM the Light!
I AM victory! I AM victory! I AM victory!
For the Divine Mother and the Divine Manchild
And for the raising-up of the crown of life
And the twelve starry focal points
That rejoice to see the salvation of our God
Right within my crown,
Right within the center of the Sun
Of Alpha—It is done!

Chapter 2

Psychic Thralldom

*Beloved, believe not every
spirit, but try the spirits
whether they are of God.*
I JOHN

Psychic Thralldom

I T IS UNDER THE DIRECTION OF THE Ascended Masters themselves that we present the following objective analysis of mankind's involvement in all planes of the astral, which we have termed "psychic thralldom." It is our wish to give the Ascended Master viewpoint, for the acceptance or the rejection of the sincere.

One thing we wish to make clear: The statements made herein are in no way intended to constitute an attack upon any segment of the religious community, for each one has the right to follow the leadings of his own conscience in such pursuits. On the other hand, the Truth must be told as we see it; and this we shall do.

Let us also state that we do not practice necromancy. We do not communicate with the spiritually or physically dead. Our communications are with those who have immortal life, with the spiritually quickened. These can never die, for they have the abundant promise of the living Christ as their bond insuring them immortality.

Communion with the Dead

In 1916 Sir Oliver Lodge, a professor of physics and pioneer in the field of radio communication, created a sensation in occult circles though the publication of a document that set forth records of communications with his son, Lieutenant Raymond Lodge, who was killed near Ypres, France, in 1915.[1] The "sittings" were held in the presence of mediums and at the table with family and friends. He claimed that evidence of the personal survival of his son was established, that the messages were reflective of his son's personality, and that to those who knew him the general tenor of his communications pointed unmistakably to the fact that only the lieutenant himself could have been the initiator of the messages. For his work in this field, founded upon his faith in human immortality, Sir Oliver Lodge has been regarded, with Sir William Barrett (who wrote *On the Threshold of the Unseen*), as one of the great pioneers in psychic science.

From the days of Sir Oliver Lodge and throughout the history of spiritualism, the possibility of communion with the dead has enthralled not only the bereaved but also many sincere psychic investigators. Just as many are shocked by what they term the gullibility of seekers after psychic experiences, so, many who are involved in such phenomena are concerned by mankind's rejection of what they consider to be, in a relative sense, the ultimate source of illumination and comfort to their souls.

Therefore, there is a need for an objective voice that can examine from the basis of personal experience, as well as from the standpoint of the Ascended Masters' teachings, this phase of psychic phenomena.

Just what does take place during a séance?

What is mediumship?

Is the investment of mankind's energies and attention in the realm of psychic manifestation warranted?

The History of Modern Spiritualism

Spiritualism has been defined as the belief that departed or disembodied spirits hold intercourse with mortals by means of physical phenomenon (as by rapping) or during "abnormal" mental states as in trances commonly manifest through a medium. Lewis Spence defines it as "the belief in the continuance of life after death, and the possibility of communication between the dead and the living, through the agency of a medium or psychic, a person qualified in some unknown manner to be the mouthpiece of supernatural beings ... variously regarded as a religion or philosophy."[2]

While attempts to contact spirits of the dead have been seen throughout recorded history, the Ascended Masters El Morya and Kuthumi were responsible for a sudden and swift blossoming of spiritualism during the latter part of the nineteenth century.

In 1848 the Fox sisters testified to "rappings" in their home in Hydesville, New York. In 1862 Hypolyte Leon Denyad Rivail, known to his followers as "Allan Kardec," founded Spiritism in France, including in its tenets the doctrine of reincarnation. (This constituted a departure from spiritualism as it was expounded in Britain and America.) In 1882 the Society for Psychical Research was founded in London. The cumulative psychic stir in society had not been equalled since the eighteenth century when, midst the skepticism of the Renaissance, a flair for the occult had been aroused by that mysterious figure, the celebrated mystic le Comte de Saint Germain.[3]

In their sponsoring of spiritualism, it was the desire of the Masters to give hope to a tired and weary world of a life beyond, of comfort from the departed, even of the possibility of their own immortality. Spiritualism also paved the way for the successive revelations to be made by the Brotherhood through metaphysics, first systematically set forth by Mary Baker Eddy in *Science and Health with Key to the Scriptures* (1866); through Madame Helena P. Blavatsky in Theosophy (1875); through the writings of Max Heindel (1911); through the Agni Yoga Society under Nicholas and Helena Roerich; and through other Ascended Master activities of the early twentieth century such as the I AM Activity headed by Guy and Edna Ballard under the guidance of the Master Saint Germain.

Historians trace the ancestry of spiritualism to witchcraft, demoniac possession, poltergeistic disturbances and animal magnetism. But there is a clear-cut line of demarcation between these activities of the lower astral order and the inspired work of the Masters, which was to presage the dawn of a new era of the Brotherhood's contact with humanity on a world scale.

Speaking of the Masters' introduction of spiritualism, Kuthumi says: "When beloved El Morya and I introduced spiritualism to the advanced students of the West in the [nineteenth] century, it was with the fond hope of increasing men's understanding of survival after death. We longed to see the receding of fear in men's consciousness and the reflection of a more expanded vision of the eternal nature of life. Therefore, contacts carried on from a very high plane were permitted that the blessing to men might be very great. However, frequently the reverse was true.

"Fraud and deceit entered into the practice of spiritualism.

Charlatans who took pleasure in entrancing the people with their own personalities for the love of money and self-glory perverted the original design of this potential avenue for Truth. Contacts debased themselves through association with the lower psychic or astral realm, paying heed to those discarnate entities whom they would never have deigned worthy of their attention while in embodiment. Thus, another door was closed that we might have used to bring humanity nearer to the Godhead.

"It must ever be recognized that the real and the counterfeit have been with humanity for a long time. Whenever God has blessed men with Truth, the counterfeit, or Antichrist, has also asserted itself. Each attempt for Good is usually inverted and the opposite end of the axis is brought to the fore in the attempt to alienate the allegiance of men from their highest Selfhood."[4]

Release of Occult Knowledge outside the Retreats

In recent centuries the Brotherhood, by special dispensation from the Solar Hierarchies and the Karmic Board, has been able to release occult knowledge outside of the sacred retreats, thereby making some of the inner teachings accessible to the world at large. This information was formerly vouchsafed only to disciples who had proven themselves worthy to enter the retreats of the Masters. And even then, only after passing the severest tests of will and sincerity were they entrusted with the knowledge of the initiatic mysteries—the control of matter and the use of the Christ mind to precipitate and levitate substance.

With this new dispensation, the world would be the stage for personal initiations, and mankind's own karma would be his guru. The opportunity for direct training under the Masters would come only to those who had successfully passed (many times unbeknown to them) the tests of the unseen Masters, while those who had failed these tests (also many times unbeknown to them) would never know how close they had come to sitting at the feet of the Masters.

Because of the law of cycles,* it was not possible for the Masters to deliver lock, stock and barrel to mankind the fullness of the higher teachings or the knowledge of what lay in store in the coming age. Each ten-year cycle, each hundred-year cycle and each thousand-year cycle has a predetermined allotment of energy granted by the Hierarchy to the evolutions of a planet.

The spiral of man's victory is an ever-unfolding one, and none dare preempt the Law of its release—although some have sought to take heaven by force.[5] Therefore, each decade and each century sees the manifestation of new forms and solar glyphs, and each revelation must be integrated into the total world thought ere the succeeding one can be forthcoming.

The astral plane, or "astral belt," as it is sometimes called, is the immediate layer of consciousness above the physical world; above the astral is the mental plane; next comes the etheric plane; and finally the Ascended Master octave of perfection. The integration of these planes of consciousness, including the wealth of understanding contained in the higher spheres of perfection, could not be released to mankind all at once, for the chalice of his consciousness must be prepared gradually and his growth be commensurate with the wisdom released. The expansion of the Light of God within the soul and the knowledge of the tie to the God Source must precede

---

* The law of cycles is the subject of chapter 20 of the Climb the Highest Mountain series. This chapter will be included in Book 7, the next volume of the series. See also chapter 1 of *Predict Your Future.*

the fullness of the revelation of the coming Golden Age.

Thus the Ascended Masters sponsored an activity (spiritualism), destined to serve a twofold purpose: as a catalyst in world thought and as a foundation stone for future revelation. However, it is never the purpose of religion to bind man to a system, to dogma or to a set of doctrines, but to bind him to God. When a particular form of religion ceases to serve this specific reason for being—when through progressive revelation new dispensations of enlightenment are released by the Hierarchy—the old form must be remodeled to conform to the accelerated momentums of Light that are made available to a planet and its evolutions. Or, when this is not forthcoming, the old form must be discarded—however painful this process may be, however much good may still remain within it.

Just as old buildings are condemned and torn down to make way for developments that better serve the current needs of a community, so the followers of God should not fear to reject a system that seeks to bind them to itself rather than to free them to reach for the heights of divine reunion.

Let us now examine some examples of psychic manifestation for the purpose of outlining our subject.

Psychic Phenomena

The phenomenon of the *poltergeist** is familiar to most people. Many years ago a strange happening occurred that could be classified under this heading.

A family became very disturbed by the fact that their children's shoes were disappearing from their home. As they had many children and lived on a farm during the Great Depression, this resulted in a considerable drain upon their

---

* A *poltergeist* is a mischievous, noisy and disruptive ghost, usually found in homes where there are adolescent children.

pocketbook as well as upon their patience.

Other inexplicable occurrences were noted even by those who were not members of the family. Unoccupied rocking chairs rocked. Doorknobs turned and doors flew open with a bang. Cut flowers in vases wilted suddenly. The children themselves were the major suspects in the eyes of the parents. However, on one occasion one of the adult members of the family witnessed a pair of shoes without an occupant walking down the stairs. The sheriff of the county was sent for, and investigations were begun.

In a nearby community there lived a man who, although a believer in God, was not what one would term an orthodox member of the church. He was a mystic. Now retired, he had been a respected businessman, the father of a physician who was also well thought of in the area. Because of his reputation as an outstanding citizen and his familiarity with occult practices, he was called upon to exorcise the mysterious force that was causing so much conflict to this family. Thus he proceeded to the building with a group of curious investigators. Immediately after he completed his ritual of exorcism, the father of the family exclaimed, "Why, it's just like the sun is shining in the room!" The feeling of dampness that had permeated the building was no longer there.

Thus ended the episode of the walking shoes and other mysterious happenings that had troubled the family for several months. Here was an incidence of a psychic phenomenon, recorded in the newspapers and witnessed by many dispassionate observers.

In many parts of the world, such manifestations have not been infrequent, although they are often attributed to natural phenomena. One famous recorded incident of a poltergeist occurred in Stans in the Canton of Lucerne, Switzerland, between 1860 and 1862 in the home of M. Joller, a distinguished lawyer and member of the Swiss National Council. It began with loud rappings in the night, then the apparition of a white, indistinct form. Subsequently, gray figures followed the maid about the kitchen and to her room, where they sobbed through the night. The entire family was witness to the phenomenon of locked doors and fastened windows being flung open. Voices, weird music and the humming of spinning wheels were heard.

Reports of the strange happenings attracted thousands of curious onlookers, who witnessed one or more of these phenomena. Investigations by the police and scientific inquiry made by well-qualified and prominent men of the community failed to resolve the mystery. Responsible citizens, including members of the National Council and the Court of Justice, attested to the events. The family was finally forced to move from their home, whereupon the manifestations ceased.[6]

Another manifestation associated with psychic activities is commonly known as *apport* ("things brought"). There are endless accounts of this phenomenon, in which strange objects mysteriously drop from thin air into the hands of those who sit in a circle at a séance. While investigators have proved that trickery is involved in many of these manifestations, there remain a number of such occurrences that are unexplained and bear all of the earmarks of authenticity.

In chapter 23 of the Climb the Highest Mountain series (which is included in Book 7, the next volume), there is a complete explanation of the entities (disembodied spirits) that cause such manifestations. We shall not digress further on the subject here, except to say that the pranks of discarnates are part of the spectrum of psychic thralldom.

Seeking advice from departed spirits has been going on since the witch of Endor conjured up Samuel the prophet for King Saul[7]—and a long time before. Many means have been employed to accomplish this, from voodoo rituals to Ouija boards to séances and the use of mediums—and more recently the phenomenon know as "channeling." There are countless individuals all over the world who have faith in mediumship and who depend for their spiritual guidance upon messages received either from departed relatives or friends or from supposedly friendly spirits (spirit guides and teachers), who dispense advice and help to the seeker.

Thus, the story of spiritualism is long and involved—intriguing to the mind, perhaps, but nevertheless a dangerous byway that can only detour the seeker from the main highway that leads to the acquisition of true spirituality. We have classified spiritualism under the heading of "psychic thralldom" because individuals become so entranced by the wonders of the séance circle that they seldom can accept the truth concerning such happenings.

The Science of Ectoplasm

In all groups where genuine contact is being made with departed entities, the circle itself is nothing more than a battery, the counterpart of a galvanic system that uses the energies and vital essences of the members of the group to supply the muscle and mind power for the spirits. This essence is siphoned off from the individuals in attendance by the discarnates in order to produce psychic phenomena; without it, they can neither communicate nor perform. A gradual drain of vital spiritual energies and a deterioration of the physical body and the brain occurs in those who practice necromancy (communion with the dead) or hold consort with the spirits of the departed over a considerable period of time.

Most dangerous of all are those discarnates who profess to be masters of the psychic realm but who, in reality, merely masquerade as "angels of light"[8] or as "masters" to defame and discredit the true Masters of Wisdom of the ascended realm and their teachings. These discarnates not only drain the vital energies of their auditors but also release confusing information, half-truths and such an unwholesome conglomeration of predictions, personal flattery and wild prophecies as to completely discourage anyone who has the least discernment or true spirituality from any further pursuit of higher Truth. Many of these earthbound departed ones enjoy little pranks that they can pull upon embodied mankind from the invisible realm, much the same as children would raid an apple tree or cavort in Halloween pranks or masquerade as hobgoblins.

The energy that is used to produce the phenomena associated with spiritualism has been called "ectoplasm" or "ectoplasy" by researchers in this field. Sir William F. Barrett in his book *On the Threshold of the Unseen* defined ectoplasy as "the power of forming outside the body of the medium a concentration of vital energy or vitalized matter which operates temporarily in the same way as the body from which it is drawn, so that visible, audible or tangible humanlike phenomena are produced."[9]

Ectoplasm (from the Greek *ektos,* "exteriorized," and *plasma,* "substance") is described as "matter which is invisible and impalpable in its primary state, but assuming the state of a vapor, liquid or solid, according to its stage of condensation.... Ectoplasm is considered by spiritualists to be the materialization of the astral body."[10]

To this "psychic force" or "exteriorized protoplasm" is attributed the power to produce direct voice, to effect the locomotion of objects (telekinesis), to mold or rearrange matter to produce the imitation of known objects (simulacra of hands and faces and other parts of the human organism), and even to rearrange particles in a photographic plate to produce a supernormal image—whether human, animal or handwriting. Authentic photographs of spiritualistic materializations showing the emanations of ectoplasm may be studied in Rev. G. Henslow's *Proof of the Truth of Spiritualism.*[11]

It is said that the force exerted by ectoplasm is great enough to raise a table with a man's weight on it completely off the ground. Interestingly, attempts have been made to measure this force by weighing the medium from whom the ectoplasm had hypothetically been removed. The weight of substance externalized is said to be the exact amount of the weight loss of the medium during the séance.

The theory of ectoplasy holds that the vital energies taken by the spirits from those who participate in spiritualistic activities return to the medium after the manifestation has occurred. In fact, the energy used to produce psychic phenomena, taken from those in embodiment by the discarnate, can never be returned to the donor, for this energy is immediately used to produce psychic phenomena and to sustain the existence of the discarnate (just as we cannot return the food we have eaten and digested to its original state).

Furthermore, the life force is taken from the vital solar body (soul body). Prolonged involvement in trance work, psychic phenomena and spiritualistic activities can result in a critical drain upon the allotment of solar energies given to each lifestream at the commencement of each embodiment.

The abortion of the solar fires in man through this type of misqualification can cause him to forfeit his ascension in the embodiment during which such activities have been engaged in. The Ascended Masters have told us that it may require as many as three or four succeeding embodiments to balance this misuse of the creative force. It is for this reason that the Masters have cautioned their students about the extreme dangers of taking dictations or "channeling" from astral entities purporting to be Ascended Masters. For in all cases, unless the being is in fact ascended, he is draining the channel of his portion of light for his present embodiment.

The Gathering of Psychic Energies

Discarnates are not able to draw energy from the Presence of God in the same manner as embodied mankind, who have a direct tie to the Presence through the threefold flame anchored in the physical heart. Therefore, entities must derive their motor power in one of two ways:

(1) Through the conscious, willing cooperation of people on earth, specifically when individuals gather in a séance and invite the spirits to commune with them. In this case the vital energies flow to the disembodied one over the thread of contact established by the attention of those in the circle. It is cosmic law that wherever man places his attention, there his energy goes. (In this case, the medium is the focal point for transmitting and receiving between the two planes.)

(2) Through the unconscious cooperation of people on earth. This occurs whenever they are inharmonious or "out of tune" with their Higher Self. Vibrations of irritation, grief, fear, anger, disdain, fatigue or other negative thoughts and feelings—even the dissonance of rock rhythms—puncture the natural protective envelope that surrounds and interpenetrates the four lower bodies of man, as does the use of alcohol, tobacco, marijuana or other drugs. (It is this envelope that holds the spiritual energies that are released to man from his own God Presence as the harmonies of higher spheres.)

The manifestation of discord of any kind in one's world— whether or not this discord seems justifiable by the behavior of another—automatically rends the spiritual garment. Without the wholeness of spiritual protection, which the spiritual garment is intended to afford every man, his energies become subject to the vampire activities of astral entities.

Thus, many types of human conduct—seemingly innocuous and sanctioned by custom—are designed by the negative forces to drain the very lifeblood of mankind until they are no longer able to resist the pull of the world and they become wholly responsive to the mass consciousness. If these forces create in your life circumstances that disturb you and you lose your balance and become discordant, they can then steal your Light. If, however, you determine to hold your ground and remain unmoved, they can never cause you to lose the abundance of energy that is the daily allotment released to you from the heart of God.

Uncontrolled emotions are the principal cause of sickness, old age and poverty. The man who cannot govern the use of his energies cannot govern his world, and he is therefore unfit to govern others or to be of dependable service to God or man. Such a person cannot be trusted to guard the bank of reserves that is given to his care for safekeeping. He will allow the astral plunderers to break in and steal that substance that otherwise might be invested for the good of all. People are more often the victims of the machinations of the unseen world than they realize. They are like puppets on a string until they become tied to their own God Source. Only then do they respond without fail to the impulse of their Creator.

God's pure energy is first misqualified by man's imperfect thoughts and feelings. Then it is seized by discarnate forces, which in turn use this misqualified energy against the very ones who have unwittingly released it into their hands. This creates more havoc and multiplies the accumulation of islands of mass misqualified energy, which gather like black stormclouds in the astral belt.

Just as a stream can rise no higher than its source, so the

muddied stream of consciousness that flows from the astral realm cannot be expected to bring forth the pure, sparkling, revivifying elixir of cosmic illumination that comes forth from the higher octaves of God's consciousness. Conversely, just as water cannot flow upstream, so the river of astral filth cannot contaminate the Source, the River of Life, whose pure waters are freely given to all who seek eternal life.

Nothing Good Can Come from the Psychic

The word *psychic* is derived from the Greek *psychē*, meaning "soul." We all have a soul and a Spirit. There is a difference. The Spirit is of God and can never die; the soul can be lost. The soul is that plastic substance upon which man's works are written.

A psychic is one who has developed his soul, or solar, faculties for heightened awareness of the physical, astral, mental and sometimes the etheric belts of earth and her evolutions. A psychic, or one who is psychic, has, in this or previous embodiments, developed faculties of sensitivity or extrasensory perception not generally accessed by mankind. This may include altered states above or below the normal threshold of awareness and the tapping of the computer of the subconscious or the superconscious mind.

The soul is anchored in the body at the seat-of-the-soul chakra, which is below the heart and also in the center of the electronic belt. Most extrasensory perception and gleanings gained from that level are unreliable, because one has to get through the astral plane, through one's electronic belt, through one's karmic momentums, and rise to the level of the Christ to really perceive what is Real. And most people who operate only from the level of the soul just do not have a momentum of Light great enough to do so. If they did have that Light, they would not be at that level in the first place; they would be in their higher chakras. Therefore, although some use these faculties constructively and with a respectable degree of accuracy, in many cases the information as well as the discrimination thereof is unreliable.

The term *psychic* has therefore come to be used synonymously with the term "astral" in its negative context, and its use in this way pertains to the penetration and manipulation of energy at the level of the astral plane. According to the terminology of the Ascended Masters, one who has involved his energies in the psychic, psychicism or psychic phenomena is functioning on the lower astral plane. Thus, by the strong ties established with entities of the lower octaves, he postpones the day of his true spiritual development and oneness with the penetrability of the Godhead.

Conversely, through oneness with God and direct apprehension of the higher octaves, he may derive spiritual benefit for his soul in the etheric plane (heaven-world), journeying in his etheric sheath to the retreats of the Ascended Masters of the Great White Brotherhood and the cities and temples of Light located in that plane. True spiritual God-mastery is not measured by clairvoyance or psychic phenomena but by the God-control of the sacred fires of the heart and adeptship on the path of love.

The things that fall into the category of the psychic include dealing with spirits and spiritualism; automatic writing*;

---

* From the Ascended Masters' perspective, automatic writing is one of the most dangerous types of mediumistic activity. In this process, an individual allows the physical body to be controlled by a spirit that writes or types messages. Most people who engage in this are very much caught up in their ego; the spirits engage them with personal messages and flattery. (In fact, this is the point of vulnerability of many people who engage in psychic activities.) An individual, by repeatedly ceding control of the mind and body to astral entities in this way, may eventually lose the ability to control their own consciousness, and thus become subject to all manner of "voices" and projections from the astral plane that they can no longer control or distinguish from the real world.

involvement with UFOs; and methods of divination such as "worldly" astrology, tarot, the pendulum and Ouija boards. The psychic has a peculiar vibration, and psychic people have a peculiar vibration. It is a vibration of entities and of a lower energy rate, and by and by you learn to recognize these people.

There is a psychic net that the dark powers of the world use. They weave a grid of dark energy in the same way that the angels weave a grid of Light. However, the dark powers try to tie people together and have them pick up the vibrations of one another that are destructive. This is mob psychology; this is how it is used and how it spreads.

But there is a way to foil the plots of the sinister force, and that is by the power of the spoken Word. We read, "Thou shalt also decree a thing, and it shall be established unto thee; by thy words thou shalt be justified, and by thy words thou shalt be condemned."[12] This means that the spoken Word, when that spoken Word is given with a certain speed and a certain rhythm and accompanied by mental visualization, will cut through the psychic net.

The psychic realm is but a continuation of the physical plane and its many levels of consciousness. Knowing this, Saint Germain once said that nothing good could come forth from the psychic. Some could not believe that the great Master would make such a statement, and they challenged it. Nevertheless, he did; and when rightly understood, the truth of his statement will be seen.

The simplest and most obvious fact to be remembered is that God is the only source of Good: it can come forth from no other. Jesus' statement in reply to the one who addressed him as "Good Master" attested to this fact. Jesus said, "Why callest thou me good? there is none good but one, that is, God."[13] Only when one becomes wholly identified with God, wholly subject to his will (and this is accomplished through the ritual of the ascension), only then is his total manifestation "Good."

Since mankind who dwell in the physical and astral realms are not yet perfected, that which they express cannot be wholly perfect. They live in the consciousness of God, who is indeed everywhere, but they have polluted that consciousness with their own mortal thoughts and feelings. They have used God's energies to fabricate a world of illusion.

Just as a drop of ink in a glass of water soon colors the entire contents, so the impurities that mankind are daily feeding into the astral realm spread throughout this compartment or plane of God's consciousness. Once the energies of this plane have been colored, we can no longer say that they are a pure reflection of the will of God; for the will of man has been superimposed upon the patterns of God's perfection.

Just as mankind exercise care in maintaining reservoirs of pure water for the needs of their communities, so there are reservoirs of Light—of pure and uncontaminated power, wisdom and love—from which all may drink freely and draw their daily supply of heavenly grace and virtue. Mankind would not think of tapping polluted streams for their water supply; therefore, they should not go to the sewer of human creation to nourish their souls.

Thus, in his assertion, Saint Germain was referring to the totality of the sea of psychic manifestation. His meaning is clear: The good that is God in manifestation cannot be directly assimilated from the psychic realm by the spirit of man. Psychic energies must first be purified by the violet transmuting flame before they can be of any creative use to man. And once transmuted, they are no longer psychic.

Lord Maitreya explains that involvement in the psychic is always a detour from the path of spiritual attainment: "The veil within the human temple must be rent in twain.[14] The veil of illusion must part, and by initiation Reality will shine forth.

"Beware, however, of the penalty for engaging in automatic writing, in psychic activity and in all of those things that are contrary to Ascended Master law. Take heed that you understand that there is no need for man to do these things that tie in to the psychic world. The Ouija board and many of these other activities bring mankind downward. I tell you, there are few upon the planet who understand how to operate the cards of the tarot.

"You ought to understand, then, that the safest and best journey [course] for the elect is under the direction of the Ascended Masters. It teaches you how you ought to study their words and to pray unto them, to call unto them, to seek initiation, to be a real person, to be a divine person, to activate the flow of cosmic energy within your forcefields by sounding the Word, by humming the majestic concept of the living Christ, by feeling the surge of the resurrection current, by entering in to the power within the Holy of holies of your own being.

"Men do not have to go outside themselves to find salvation, for the kingdom of heaven is within you.[15] And that kingdom that is within you is our kingdom."[16]

Dangers of the Psychic

Astrea, the divine complement of the Elohim Purity, wants to cut souls free from the astral plane and psychic influences. She teaches: "The desire for communion with loved ones has often brought individuals into spiritualistic séances and the pursuit of the phenomenal. We do not deny that there are many seemingly marvelous expositions that occur, many of which are outwardly inexplicable to mankind. But we wish to draw the line of cosmic demarcation in order to show that men who can produce phenomena or manifestation at will, who can invoke the spirits of the departed or enter the astral realm, who can transfer thought or receive extrasensory perceptions even of prophecy, are not necessarily holy or pure, nor are they necessarily vested with any specific level of divine attainment. Inasmuch as the exponents of these arts are not necessarily adepts themselves, it follows conclusively that they are not able, then, to guarantee adeptship to others.

"Unfortunately, many individuals who are involved in these pursuits are sooner or later overpowered by forces completely outside the reckoning of their minds until the stability of their lives is interfered with and they are no longer free, if they ever were, but bound into a greater and greater bondage of confusion of ideas, concepts and a form of ego-mania that often takes possession of them at the precise time when they feel they are losing all control of their worlds. When they feel that they are losing hold on Reality, they sometimes yield to a mass entity that promises to exalt their person while bringing them strange commanding powers over the universe. Even if they succeed in demonstrating such control in various states of limitation, the Mephistophelian bargain is never kept and, as in the opera *Faust,* the soul is stripped of her opportunities for true Reality.

"The apostles have said that 'the devil as a roaring lion, walketh about, seeking whom he may devour.'[17] There is no more deadly substitute for the true expansion of the soul than psychic indulgence and psychic power. It does not matter, precious ones, whether or not people so connected are able to perform healings or even miracles. It is the state of the consciousness of the soul that counts. It is the expansion of what El Morya has called 'cosmic morality.' It is the absorption of the nature of God into one's world that actually shows the stature of each individual to himself as well as to others.

"The Presence of God reveals morality. The Presence of God reveals Selfhood. Saint Germain long ago said that there is nothing good that comes from the psychic. Yet, we certainly will admit that many things coming through the psychic or from the psychic *seem* to be good and, when taken at face value, may present the appearance of a veritable angel of Light.[18] I would like to clarify for you why this is so, for this instruction is not a diatribe of condemnation of those sincere people who have received great comfort from spiritualistic phenomena. After all, your own beloved El Morya and Kuthumi sponsored the original spiritualist movement in the West as a means of engendering in people faith in the here-after.

"The psychic world is the world of images. It is a hall of mirrored forms, but these are not necessarily arranged in any form of order. The modes of the inhabitants of the psychic world resemble almost the sea itself in depth. A seemingly weightless condition persists there and forms may be tipped at any angle and piled up haphazardly as the substance of which dreams are made. A sense of timelessness is also apparent, with the past, present and future all blending into a montage of incongruent ideas.

"There are segments of the psychic world where a greater degree of order pervades, and this is in complete contradistinction to the disorder that pervades others. This is because the psychic world is the reflection of a cross section of humanity. There are among mankind transparent souls who on their own, although subject to a great deal of guidance from the Light, have externalized, after a fashion, order and beauty in their personal lives and also to the benefit of society in general. Therefore, the sections of the psychic world that are inhabited by those individuals whose thoughts and feelings are apparently of a higher type represent a relative standard of organization in the 'higher' psychic world from which the lower belts of the psychic could profit—if it were possible.

"However, this is not the case; for we who have examined it for centuries, for aeons, can truly say that differing planes of consciousness usually remain fixed in a relative sense and people almost invariably gravitate to those sections with which they are most closely affinitized. Nevertheless, some are not content to remain in an uncomfortable atmosphere, and they struggle against almost insurmountable odds, straining to rise just a little higher to the next level of the psychic plane.

"How much better it would be for all concerned, blessed ones, if individuals would realize that there is a divine plan whereby the essence of the soul can release her perfume in the narrow room of self and clearly show forth the matrices of expanding Reality. This design that God has envisioned for man is as beautiful as a flower in bud. The folds of the flower, prior to their full bloom, contain patterns caressed as gentle velvet and compressed into a center, which, when expanded, unfold the magnificence of the mature blossom that was hidden in the bud.

"The Ascended Masters' octave is the quintessence of beauty because it is the realm of communication with the Most High God. There is no struggle there between egos seeking to exhibit control over those on earth who cannot see their flimsy, ghost-like forms. There is no power madness, no power complex, no power politics, but only the gentle child-like expression of the Christ expounding the Law to the doctors in the temple, at work in the carpenter's shop of Nazareth, healing the sick, opening blinded eyes, loosening the tongues of the dumb, framing a world order, and showing forth the victory of the Light that from the beginning has been Immanuel, 'God with us.'

"This Light that God commanded to shine forth in the beginning is not the darkness of the psychic world of which Jesus said, 'If the light that is in thee be darkness, how great is that darkness!'[19] Nay, rather is it the eternal perfectionment in the Ascended Masters' consciousness. Here is newness of life in its fullest sense. Here in the dazzling sun-presence of the Light we see also by contrast the midnight hours surfeited with orgies of sex, of witchcraft and of the spirits that know their own nakedness; and the spirits that partook of the tree of good and evil and the knowledge thereof[20] are seen as bone-white trees, stripped of Reality, extending their barren and unfragrant branches upon the black canopy of the night. This is the midnight hour of the psychic. It is always the realm of death and decay struggling to preserve some remnant of itself alive.

"God is not so. He is the spirit of the resurrection flame, of the victorious Christ consciousness, emerging from the grave of carnality. Coming forth from the rock-hewn tomb, having carefully folded the grave clothes (for he hath no longer need of them) he enters with the blue lightning of divine love into the world as the victorious presence that preserves, nourishes, expands and transcends that initial spark of life that God implanted within the soul.

"Man was not created in man's image, for man's image was created by man. Man was first created by God in the Image of God;[21] and man's image was subsequently created by man.[22] Again and again we must examine these eternal Truths in order that the clean, crisp concepts of heaven may refute the long-entrenched theological speculations, arguments and dogmas that have bound man for centuries to misty concepts, nebulous and unformed. These have paved the way for the psychic activities of the world to invade all walks of life; all areas of endeavor, even the province of the Church—witness the rapid expansion of spiritualism in South America, even within the Catholic congregations. In this day and age, the religions of man are far too primitive, too provincial, too centered around the needs of men for creature comforts, for gregariousness, for the attainment of outer standards of conformity.

"Now we come to the place where the hidden man of the heart shall be revealed, where the pathway of the disciple with his craggy mane is seen etched upon the pages of the future, where each one can envision his own attainment as he pursues the divine discipline, cutting himself free from the rough-hewn state into the finished and highly polished stone made without hands (eternal in the heavens). Avoiding the psychic as the plague, he reaches up to the spiritual octaves of Reality, to that spirituality that lies dormant within his own being, to godliness, to the divine vision, to the unique but true sense of beauty that is the revelation of the Light of His Presence. He sheds the skin of his ignorance—the cocoon from whose delusive silk threads the subtle ties of psychic entanglement have been created—and the garment, woven of the deep desire to express the Divine Sense, is fashioned day by day.

"Break now those bonds! Cut yourself free for all time and eternity from entanglement in the imagery and tracings of past embodiments as well as past wrong thoughts!...

"Stand with me, beloved hearts, and with the Hierarchy as we take you safely through the labyrinth of life; for the Light of God never fails, and that Light is not darkness: It is God's life, and it belongs to no other." [23]

Accomplishments of Spiritualism

It is no wonder that the history of spiritualism (as well as that of all attempts on the part of the Masters to reach mankind) has been plagued with deceit, degrading press reports and the persecutions of an ignorant and uninformed public opinion. For the darkness of entrenched systems and tradition-bound skepticism always opposes the forward movement of the Light in the affairs of men.

The Masters could not preconceive that mankind would do wrong with spiritualism and that it would open a Pandora's box of wretchedness, a rupture into the astral world where marauding psychic entities would take over and obsess individuals with negativity and shadow and pain and all manner of lying releases that were not the Truth of the LORD God of Hosts. But this is what happened.

After El Morya and Kuthumi stood before the Karmic Board and sponsored the early spiritualistic activities, these movements were taken over by people who did not have the integrity of the first experimenters in that field; and therefore the world today is plagued by any number of individuals who suppose that they themselves are messengers of God when, in reality, they are obsessed by forces of negation that have used them.

Jesus said to St. Peter, "Behold, Satan hath desired to have you, that he may sift you as wheat."[24] Also we read, "For such are false apostles, deceitful workers, transforming themselves into the apostles of Christ. And no marvel; for Satan himself is transformed into an angel of Light."[25] "Be vigilant; because your adversary the devil, as a roaring lion, walketh about, seeking whom he may devour."[26] The devil seeks to devour mankind by those who are motivated by what they suppose is good, but they are tapping into the astral realm, the psychic realm; and the disturbing elements of creation put the signet of darkness upon their activities rather than the stamp of Light.

Light is to illumine. Light is freedom. And Light will give you buoyancy and joy and compassion for your neighbor.

Darkness will involve you and enmesh you in the strategies of darkness, which cause every man to be turned against his neighbor and against his brother.

Saint Germain, El Morya and Kuthumi have never condoned what is taking place today in the name of spiritualism. It is no fault of the Masters that spiritualism was immediately seized upon by the fraudulent and those who were looking for a ruse to deceive others in order to bolster their own sagging egos—not to mention those astral forces that are always ready for a heyday of adventure with the credulous.

However, no matter what may be said for or against the activities of spiritualists, no matter what evidences are brought to bear in defense of spiritualism, it must be acknowledged that the purposes of the Masters in sponsoring this movement were accomplished:

(1) The door to the unseen world was opened for the first time, with unmistakable evidence to support the claims of not just one but many mediums. This evidence tended to dispel the aura of superstition and mystery that had previously surrounded spirit communication.

(2) The belief in personal survival after death and in the immortality of the soul was strengthened in thousands of people.

(3) The possibility of mental communication (telepathy) not only between embodied people but also between the embodied and the disembodied was acknowledged. Man's innate powers of extrasensory perception were recognized at last.

(4) The way was cleared for ever-new and forthcoming revelations from successively higher planes of consciousness and more ethereal beings. Individuals on earth could now be trained by the Hierarchy for the more critical task of bringing forth the Word of God exclusively from the Ascended Masters' octave.

Death Not the Door to Deification

Enlightened students of the Masters would ask this question of those who insist upon continuing their spiritualistic activities despite the warning of the Hierarchs to stay away from all psychic phenomena: "Why talk to spirits who are subject to err and whose source of information is limited, when you can receive the infallible testimony of the Ascended Masters themselves on cosmic Truth and the most up-to-date edicts of the Solar Hierarchies pertaining to the very fate of the planet and this system of worlds?"

Contrary to some popular opinion, it is incorrect to assume that an entity who is disassociated from the flesh has a wider outlook than one who is in the flesh. Nor should the hoped-for contact with genius be given undue credence. It is a fact that, for the most part, only the lowest specimens of humanity remain in the range of ordinary spirit communication. Under the latest dispensations of the Karmic Board, those more qualified to shed light on pertinent questions of life after death are usually taken immediately to etheric realms. There, in the retreats of the Ascended Masters, they prepare for succeeding embodiments or their ascension.

In a letter to his students, Kuthumi warned of unwholesome astral associations. He wrote: "Beloved students of Light, death does not deify *except it be the death in man of his old and corrupt nature.* Those who are filthy before entering the halls of death are filthy still, and those who are holy are holy still.[27] Final victory is not attained through death but through the transformation of the Adamic nature into the 'quickening spirit' of the Christ man 'when this corruptible shall have put on incorruption, and this mortal shall have put on immortality.'[28]

"The tramps from the opium dens of China are as active in

the astral world as are the dearly departed members of many people's families. Flesh-and-blood ties are not nearly so important, in reality, as spiritual ties that link together men and women of holy purpose in God's will. The flesh may bring to men strange bedfellows, for often father and son are as different as day and night, or mother and daughter as opposite as East and West. Yet, in the kingdom of God, a Christ may sit with the Buddha and find no wide difference in spiritual service to humanity.

"All advocates of love, whether from East or West, North or South, whether manifesting universal consciousness or the narrowness of creed or class, must, if they would be true to love itself, admit to the sacred precincts of their hearts those of diverse states of spiritual attainment. There has been for far too long a 'holier than thou' attitude on the part of many seekers after greater Light. Beloved, to find a little of God's Light does not exalt men to ivory towers of wisdom. Where great wisdom truly manifests, greater love and service to one's brothers is the natural tendency.

"We do not deny that discrimination ought to be practiced when determining from whom you shall accept instruction, for it is not wrong to 'try the spirits and see if they be of God.'[29] We do distinguish, however, between those who come to you seeking your love and those who would be your teachers. Be kind and receptive to those who need your help, but be firm with those who would misdirect you. But with neither be hasty.

"There is never any real need to greet any questionable doctrine with open arms or to immediately accept that which runs counter to the very nature of your being. If it is of Truth, time will prove its Reality—if discriminating love and wisdom are sought from God alone. If it be of error, you would do your self disservice to accept it without due consideration. One of the greatest mistakes many students make is to accept the pressure that makes one feel the need to decide instantly upon the merits of each situation they encounter. The urgency of this feeling sometimes leads them into rejecting great assistance or, on the other hand, accepting that which will one day cause them regret.

"Remember, your consciousness has retained certain elements of proven Truth, and these are the building blocks for future progress in the fruition of holy wisdom. Use them carefully to erect a flawless structure that will one day be made eternally secure in the knowledge of the whole Law and therefore a fitting memorial to the revelation of the Presence 'face to face.'

"I am advocating that the dangers in all forms of contacting the so-called dead be understood. Just as you would not admit unrighteous men or thieves into your home when living, so all who have departed bearing the stamp of their own lack of holiness cannot be relied upon in the psychic world to do aught else than that which they practiced while yet in physical embodiment. Your own divine God or I AM Presence and your Holy Christ Self, together with the Ascended Masters, are always the fullness of divine authority. We will never counsel you except to lead you into paths of righteousness for his name's sake (I AM).[30]

"I have sought to spell an end to misunderstandings about life and its continuity. There is never any doubt that just as life goes on while you sleep at night without your awareness of it, so life goes on between embodiments. Just as men dream while sleeping, so the consciousness that exists in internal self-awareness continues to have alternate periods of contact with the outer world of form and the inner astral planes."

Kuthumi recommends that students seek to establish contact with their own God Presence, with their Christ Self and with the Ascended Masters, so that they might take the fullest advantage of the educational opportunities available in the temples of Light:

"The most desirable state, and that to which men should aspire for themselves as well as for their loved ones, is to obtain entrée to our schools of Light (both between embodiments and while their bodies are asleep), where men and women are given most blessed training in the spiritual arts of freedom as well as in the correct use of all spiritual power. Fortunately this can be accomplished while you are yet in your present physical embodiment, and by mastering the formula and practice, you will find it much easier to do so, should the need arise after the loss of your physical form.[31]

"Yet, above all goals, hold your own ascension the most wonderful, for it is the fulfillment of the entire law of your being and the commencing of the great journey to infinite goals of completion."[32]

Mediumship versus Messengership

At this juncture it would be well to explain the difference between mediumship and Messengership. A medium is a go-between who acts to facilitate astral-physical communication. A Messenger serves with the Ascended Masters to bring forth Truth from higher octaves of God's consciousness and the knowledge of cosmic law that is dispensed in the retreats of the Brotherhood.

A medium has not necessarily dedicated his life to the expression of the highest divinity. A medium may be a person of any character, either good or bad, who possesses one or more of the faculties of extrasensory perception: clairvoyance, clairaudience or clairsentience.

The faculty of extrasensory perception (ESP, or the sixth

sense) is developed in some people and latent in others. Through the centuries many people have spent a great deal of time dabbling in ESP: magicians of past ages, medieval alchemists, advisers to kings, seers, astrologers, fortune-tellers and others who practiced the arcane arts. They often developed the ability to penetrate the minds of others, to hypnotize, to mesmerize and in general to influence people. Frequently they accomplished their control over subjects by discerning or divining their thoughts and intents. The fact that a person has developed his extrasensory abilities has no more bearing on his spirituality than the fact that he possesses keen faculties of sight or hearing.

A medium is usually capable of performing very well in the extrasensory arts. Often he possesses an acute sense of psychology in the manipulation of others, making capital of their human frailties while conveying solace in time of difficulty. On the other hand, a Messenger is a prophet, one who has received by divine appointment the gifts of prophecy and the discernment of spirits[33] and the grace of communication with higher manifestations of God (such as Cosmic Beings, Elohim, Archangels, Angels, Ascended Masters and elementals).

The ability to communicate with the Ascended Masters directly and to act as their Messenger in the world of form is not a technique that can be acquired through the development of any of the faculties of the physical or spiritual senses. The only preparations made by a Messenger of God are total commitment to the Brotherhood, the consecration of his or her energies to the Holy Spirit, and the realization that "I of mine own self can do nothing; it is the Father in me who doeth the work."[34] Few are given this commission, and it is always directly under the guidance of the Great White Brotherhood and its various agencies such as the Darjeeling Council, the Council of the Royal Teton, the East Indian Council and other

Ascended Master bodies connected with earth's evolutions.

Messengers are ordained by God and by the Great White Brotherhood. The Karmic Board must also approve their commissions, which are personally sponsored by one or more of the Ascended Masters. Thus Messengers hold a solemn responsibility to the spiritual Hierarchy of this planet.

The Master El Morya, who has sponsored a number of Messengers, speaks of their service, and also of those who come as usurpers of this office: "Down through the centuries we have appointed our Messengers, prophets of the Law, teachers of the way of the Christ consciousness and of the Buddhic Light. Others whom we would call unappointed, or self-appointed, messengers have come forth to blatantly usurp their ministry and their office in Hierarchy. And so there is abroad in the land an enticing spirit, beguiling as the serpent, that is not the true spirit of prophecy. Nor is it come as the gift of the Holy Spirit;[35] it is the voice of rebellion and of witchcraft, of vain talkers and deceivers.[36] These are the crystal-ball gazers, the psychic readers and self-proclaimed messiahs—bewitched and bewitching, coming in the name of the Church yet denying the true Church, coming in the name of the Logos yet their lives a betrayal of true reason and the Law.

"They are the archdeceivers of mankind. They would take over the person and the personality of the Ascended Masters and the real Gurus. Setting themselves up as gurus, they sit in the lotus posture smoking the peace pipe with the false hierarchy, dispensing drugs along with demons, and even training their disciples in the manipulation of sexual energies for heightened sensual gratification. In their all-consuming lust for power, they teach the way to God through sexual perversion, abuses of the body and the desecration of the Mother. And the Light they steal from those they ensnare is used to satisfy their mad cravings and to control vast segments of the population through witchcraft, variance and mortal cursings.

"Others are in the business of training 'channels' and psychic healers. They know not the difference between spiritual and psychic energies—the pure and the impure stream. Thus they make the gullible to be channels for the energies of the pit, for the diabolical murmurings of familiar spirits and of 'wizards that peep and that mutter.'[37] The false hierarchies and the fallen ones come in many guises, seeking to impress an infant humanity with their sleight of hand, trance and telepathy, their flying saucers and other trappings.

"I say woe to those who are adept in the mental manipulations of Matter and astral energies yet have not the Christ— the snake charmers and charlatans who display a phenomenal control of bodily functions yet have not one iota of soul mastery! As if they had a thing to offer mankind that mankind cannot get directly from their own Christ Self, their own I AM Presence and the living flame that God has anchored within the heart!

"Some of these, deceived and deceiving others, go so far as to say that everyone should be a psychic channel, everyone should develop his psychic powers. Like the magicians in Pharaoh's court,[38] they hold up to our Messengers their psychic phenomena and they say, 'See, we do the same thing!' Not so! Like the fallen ones who, in their attempt to level Hierarchy, would make themselves equal with the sons and daughters of God, these psychic channels would cause our Messengers and their work with the living Word to become muddied by the flood of psychic material being released by the false hierarchy.

"Let it be so! They have free will. As the grass of the field, they have their day; for the wind passeth over them and they are gone, to be remembered no more.[39] But the day of the true

Messengers of Hierarchy shall be as the giant redwood marking the cycles of the spiritual-material evolution of the race and as the snow-covered Himalayas outlining the pinnacles of soul attainment. Thus the prophets have come in every age, and their day is the day of the salvation (self-elevation) of the race of mankind. And the coming of the Messenger is always the preparing of the way for the coming of a new level of the Christ consciousness. 'Behold, I send my messenger before thy face, which shall prepare thy way before thee.'[40]

"In every century the Messengers have proclaimed the living truth that should free mankind from age-worn doctrine and dogma. In this age they have come to prepare the world to receive their own Christ-identity and the I AM Presence 'coming in the clouds of heaven with power and great glory.'[41] Their coming marks the hour when all who have realized the oneness of the I AM Presence through the ritual of the ascension should appear to mankind through the exalted vision of the Christ consciousness. Not only Jesus, but Mary, Saint Germain, Gautama Buddha, Confucius and all who have attained oneness with the eternal flame of Life through the ritual of the ascension—these shall appear to mankind in the Second Coming once mankind themselves have accepted the law of the I AM Presence and their own identity as Christed ones.

"The true Messengers of God receive only the word of the Great White Brotherhood and of the Ascended Masters. Their communion is not with the dead, nor do they practice necromancy or spiritism or hypnotism or the mesmerism of the mass consciousness. They are forbidden by cosmic law to allow their chakras to be instruments for the fallen ones, to channel the energies of disembodied souls abiding in the astral realm, or to be the mouthpiece of discarnates or any of the rebellious spirits that comprise the false hierarchy."[42]

Lord Maitreya also warns of teachers who claim to represent the Light but are actually tied to the false hierarchy: "The fallen ones who move among the children of God upon earth have taken their training at inner levels from the arch-deceivers of mankind. In the same way as your souls journey to the retreats of the Great White Brotherhood, those who are committed to the path of ambition and pride journey to other retreats on the astral plane.

"Meeting individuals there who pose as the most advanced adepts on the Path, they truly are convinced at inner levels that they are working with the elite of earth's evolutions who are descended even from Almighty God himself. The false hierarchy has an entire evolution—all the way back to the one who sits on the throne of the impostor of the Almighty One, the counterfeit throne of God.

"So the souls who are duped are souls who have not a sincere and pure desire for reunion with God. Nevertheless, they seem sincere in their activities; and those who train them give them to understand, by a very distorted means, what are the goals of life upon earth and how they [the trainers] are concerned for the greatest good, the greatest happiness and the greatest expansion of earth's people.

"When you consider this, you must be aware of the fact that among spiritual groups and religious teachings there is a danger for individuals who have not left off or transmuted the desire for ambition (the desire for success through pride) to come into a circle of devotees and by imitation present a counterfeit path, a counterfeit initiation, a counterfeit manifestation of how the soul leaves the body temple and enters into the etheric octave.

"Movements have, in actuality, promised soul travel to their devotees. They have invented names of masters and contacts on earth.[43] Many books and organizations in North and South America, in Europe and even in Africa have purported to represent the Brotherhood of Light. Beloved ones, you can see that the false hierarchy behind them is complete and by their misuse of the energy of the chakras they, too, may create a simulation of vibration and all that which appears to be real and is not.

"Now, when children of the Light do not have a direct experience with the Holy Spirit, with the Lord Christ, with their own I AM Presence because they have placed other gods before these, they have not, therefore, reached a level of discrimination. Let them come and sit at the feet of the Ascended Masters. Let them set aside all goals of self-aggrandizement— the very subtle desires whereby those on the psychic path or the so-called 'spiritual path' see themselves as being above others, and therefore able by their so-called powers to command respect. These powers range all the way from phenomena to actual healings to that which even appears to be the raising of the dead. This has been done by the fallen ones by mechanical means and even by the misuse of the energies of the chakras."[44]

El Morya points out the danger of involvement with teachers who are tied to the psychic: "Psychic energy is like quicksand. Souls can be sucked into it and actually defend their right to be doing what they are doing because they are so enmeshed in the psychic plane and its psychic inhabitants that they can no longer tell the difference between the spiritual path and the psychic path. This is a tragedy of the age!

"There are millions of souls on earth who are following psychic teachers, and as a result, they are falling by the way-side. Because they are tied to these teachers, they are unaware that their auric sheath (the light that is closest to the body) is being 'bled' from them. Unknowingly, they are losing their soul essence.

"It is being taken from them not necessarily by spiritualists or crystal-ball gazers but by everyday people who live in the psychic plane. Therefore know that when you keep company with such people, you make yourself vulnerable to all levels of the astral plane. When you place yourself opposite them as a student, you are even more vulnerable."[45]

Life Readings

Messengers do not, as a rule, give what are known as life readings, nor do they engage in dispensing advice to individuals on the personal level. There may be exceptions to this rule; under direction, Messengers may serve in any capacity that the Masters designate.

Although Messengers can read the aura (the thoughts and feelings) of anyone on the planet, theirs is not a psychic power but an activity of the Christ mind. They are able to attune with the discriminating intelligence of an individual's God consciousness. Then, through his Christ Self, they are able to define the discrepancies between that one's divine plan and his externalization of that plan at the human level.

This discernment, which proceeds from the mind of God, is the highest "reading" that anyone can give. For it takes into account and evaluates the whole man, whereas psychic readings often present an incomplete picture of human failure and success or a string of past embodiments, without attempting to tether the soul to its divine Reality.

These partial readings, taken from the astral level, are insidious. They detract from rather than enhance individual spiritual attainment, as they present a partial view of the soul pattern. Such life readings can draw the lifestream into downward spirals of negativity that he has already overcome. Or they may activate in his subconscious mind (in this case, his electronic belt) layers of misqualified substance that he is not prepared to confront with any degree of mastery. Or these readings may develop a false sense of confidence based neither on fact nor on actual attainment.

The gift of spiritually reading an individual's karmic and akashic records comes under the office of the Karmic Board, the Keeper of the Scrolls and the All-Seeing Eye of God. Messengers may use this gift under the proper circumstances to assist dedicated lifestreams in the healing of the four lower bodies and in directing their energies for the most constructive purposes. In all these cases, the examination of the life record is made by the Masters on behalf of their disciples in order to lead them in the path of self-mastery—and ultimately to the point of their final initiation in the ritual of the ascension. As the Elohim Astrea says: "God will show you every integrated manifestation of yourself when the time is ripe. He will reveal who you were and what you are when you can safely bear it, but it will be for the fruit of the soul and not for the exaltation of the ego."[46]

Psychic Impostors of the Masters

One of the strategies of the forces of the astral plane is to masquerade as beings of Light. The Elohim Astrea exposes this strategy and reveals the dangers of consorting with such spirits: "Precious ones, you well know the comfort of the familiar. The familiar is as a pacifier to a small child. It presents a known quantity, a known quality and the comfort of a dear friend. The billions of earth's evolutions today are all subject in one form or another to the variegated manifestations of the psychic world. Yet the multitudes do not know that they are subjected to psychic dominion and psychic pressures. But they do know that they are caught between the yin and yang of experiencing happiness one moment and unhappiness the next.

"There are many who are engaged in forms of spiritual work who, by reason of their own human egos and the desire for association with the invisible world, are trapped into an alliance with one or more entities harbored in the psychic realm. These do, then, develop what we may term a very unhealthy friendship with the denizens of the astral world.

"You have heard it said that 'Satan himself is transformed into an angel of Light.' One of the aspects of the psychic world that makes it difficult to detect the dangers inherent within it is the chameleon-like nature of the entities, fallen angels, demons and vampire forces that exist there solely upon the stolen, albeit in many cases willingly given, energies of mankind.

"If men and women knew that they were perpetuating psychic horror when they tacitly give their energies or permit them to be stolen by the forces that inhabit the astral world, they would definitely be on guard twenty-four hours a day. It would not be long, then, before those of us who function on the cosmic planes to deliver mankind from the fierce vortices of misqualified energy would be free to take our leave of the earth's evolutions, knowing that mankind would cease to create the horrible episodes that are born daily of misqualified thought and feeling.

"I wish to stress in particular that from time to time many religious people make contact with vicious astral forces masquerading as angels of Light and purporting to be Ascended Masters. In reality, these entities seek only to deceive mankind and to perform upon the waiting stage of their consciousness an unfolding drama of mutually magnetized attention— mutually magnetized because the individual in contact with the entity is enthralled with the concept that he, as a person, is, in reality, at last in touch with the 'invisible realm of the Ascended Masters.'

"What a pity it is, precious ones, to disabuse the minds of these children of God who are caught in an astral trap. Often when the truth is presented to them, they are so heartbroken by the facts at hand that they refuse to accept them, and they continue the misalliance they have formed with the illicit masquerader. This blinds their eyes to the astral dangers and causes them to be led further and further from the Truth and deeper and deeper into association with these marauding entities. At last, having extended almost their total personality into this realm of shadow (which they consider to be a realm of Light), they are completely victimized by the sinister hoax and strategy that has been worked upon them, and they can no longer call their souls their own.

"Forced, then, to a form of obedient disobedience by the controlling entities, they mock the Reality of Truth and the high standards of the Deity. It is difficult for them, then, to recognize the difference between Reality and shadow, for the shadow in which they dwell becomes to them a reality. And because of their disconnection from the developing or latent realities of God within their own life, they are unable to recover their balance.

"Often individuals are fooled by the fact that the entities give forth some measure of truth, while even the lies that they put forth are imitations of the Truth. Because the utterances are sometimes given in a simple or sweet way with honeyed phrases of endearment or dissertations freely using the word *love*, people become snared by the idea of the truth of the utterance, and thus they say in defense of their positions, 'But it makes such good sense!'

"In the name of heaven, blessed ones, it is not the spoken or printed words that are released but it is the Word of God that is 'sharper than a two-edged sword'[47] that cometh through the Ascended Master octaves and the octaves of Light that does glorify God. All that is foreign to his nature, all that is false or falsifying, all that is and does emanate from the psychic realm has no part in the Reality of God, which exists far, far above the realm of psychic vibratory action."[48]

El Morya speaks of the necessity to "try the spirits": "This is the age of the testing of the spirits. Therefore, as John said, 'Try the spirits whether they are of God.'[49] How does one try the spirits? Blessed ones, you challenge every voice within or without that comes to you in the name of the Lord:

> In the name of the living God, my own I AM Presence, and by the flame of Jesus the Christ, I challenge every voice that speaks from within or from without. And I say, I demand that you show forth your Light! I call forth the flame of the Holy Spirit to consume in you all that is less than God's perfection. I call forth the Elohim and the All-Seeing Eye of God to expose the Truth, to expose the lie, and to strip all mortal consciousness of its mortality. Let it be replaced here and now with the immortal flame of God-reality.
>
> In the name of the Christ, I call to the Elohim Astrea to encircle the cause and core of every spirit of deception, self-deceived and deceiving. I call to Archangel Michael to cut me free by the action of the sword of blue lightning from every entity inhabiting the astral plane, from all denizens of the deep.
>
> And I call to Mother Mary and her virgin consciousness to intercede for me in the name of Jesus the Christ, that my soul and my four lower bodies might be preserved as a chalice of purity to receive only the word of Almighty God and his true emissaries. So let it be done

in the name of the I AM THAT I AM! And let the hosts of the LORD come forth to defend the Word incarnate in the souls of all mankind.

"Precious ones moving toward the center of the I AM THAT I AM, the Ascended Masters and representatives of the Great White Brotherhood, whether on this or any system of worlds, will never be offended by this invocation. Those who are offended, both giving and taking offense, are not of the Christ. Every emissary of the Light is required by Law to show forth the credentials of his Light to all who demand those credentials.

"Therefore, speak with the voice of one who has the authority of the Christ and the commandment of God; and accept the covenant of Jesus given unto his disciples 'Verily, verily, I say unto you, Whatsoever ye shall ask the Father in my name, he will give it you. Hitherto have ye asked nothing in my name: ask, and ye shall receive, that your joy may be full.'[50]

"It is lawful to question the purveyors of the false teachings and those whose lives do not bear the fruits of living Truth. As it is written, 'By their fruits ye shall know them.'[51] And so without hesitation Jesus cursed the barren fig tree, saying, 'Let no fruit grow on thee henceforward for ever';[52] for the elemental spirit thereof had failed to provide fruit for the souls of mankind. Thus is the judgment of the Four and Twenty Elders pronounced upon those false hierarchs of the age even as Jesus spoke unto those who proclaimed themselves authorities of the law: 'Woe unto you, lawyers! for ye have taken away the key of knowledge: ye entered not in yourselves, and them that were entering in ye hindered.'[53]

"Let it be known, then, that sweet water and bitter do not come forth from the same fount.[54] Likewise, those who have failed to surrender the lesser self unto God, those who have failed to make this sacrifice, are not counted among our emissaries. They come teaching in their own name instead of in the name of the Ascended Masters. Instead of giving God the glory, they pursue the vainglory of name and fame for their teaching or their system or their methodology."[55]

The Descent in Consciousness

Astrea outlines how mankind have become enmeshed in the psychic and how we can be free of such entanglements: "In order to explain clearly what is taking place among mankind between the demarcation lines of what you have referred to as 'the cradle to the grave,' I desire to call to your attention that the life that is within you, that beats your heart, that emanates from God, is always derived from your individualized God Presence through your own Holy Christ Self and flows through the silver cord of cosmic energy into your own life-stream.

"You must always remember that there is never any misqualification of that pure stream of energy by your own individualized Divine Presence. Neither is there any misquali-fication that occurs in the bonds of your Holy Christ Self, or Higher Mental Body. The stream of energy comes as a flow of 'molten gold' right into your heart's aura, where it pulsates and creates the manifestation of the threefold flame of life, the tripartite flame of divine Reality, which ought to be in perfect balance as love, wisdom and power.

"Misqualification occurs, then, when individuals accept this descending arc of cosmic triumph, either in the bonds of mortal ignorance (by just taking their lives for granted without realizing the Source until it is cut off) or by accepting this energy and then, in error, misqualifying that energy to create a mortal dream, which more than likely resembles a nightmare of transitory reality.

"There is only one way in which men and women may [correctly] qualify the energy of their I AM Presence, and that is by calling to God, to their individualized God Presence and to their Holy Christ Self daily to qualify for them according to his will all of the energy that God is sending through their lifestream. Thus God's energy will flow forth unobstructed to bless every part of life by right thought, right action and right manifestation of every intent that the Father has for his creation.

"What happens instead, however, is that along the pathway of manifestation individuals become imbued with the idea of having a separate free will and the need to assert it. Their right to express as they will often takes the form of rebellion, resentment or the feeling that God could have taken better control of their lives and therefore saved them many of the awful experiences through which they have passed.

"They do not remember the day nor the hour when, as the prodigal one,[56] they asked to be given the bonds of mortal limitation, of control of the sweet energies that God gave to them. They asked for their portion of the infinite inheritance of God, but the cosmic law could not bestow the infinite upon that which was not yet prepared to receive it. And therefore, of necessity, mankind's inheritance became mortal, transitory and temporary. He was embodied in a land of opportunity where he could choose for himself the way in which he should go. 'Choose ye this day whom ye shall serve,'[57] therefore, became an unspoken law to all men; and the majority chose to pursue their own course, following by whimsy a pattern that was often a duplication of their fellowman's walk without God.

"Experience without attachment to the Deity or to his

original design created records. Records became akasha.[58] Akashic substance attached itself to the memory body of man, to his physical form, to his consciousness, to the whole man until the substance of akasha became, by reason of its thickening, a gray veil of misqualified, mortal episodes. Embodiment after embodiment, individuals created in error. Denying the Deity within, they wove veil after veil of encasement like the rings upon trees. There is no doubt that these were composed of 'good' and 'bad' energy, of violence and of service. Yet the angels of record had no authority to cut man down, as the harvest had not yet arrived. And therefore the tares of human creation grew up with the fine wheat of man's obedience to cosmic precept.[59]

"Karma became a blending of good and bad, truth and error, joy and sorrow, hope and despair. Among the children of men, individuals often concentrated in a more than ordinary manner upon probing the life aspects of others. The reading of other people's faces, their identities, propensities and possibilities became a fascinating pastime, not only for the noble but also for the depraved. Through the use of illicit drugs, even in days of old, psychic faculties and centers long dormant in men were opened temporarily and dangerously.

"Thus there came into manifestation soothsayers, astrologers, fortune tellers, witchdoctors, shamans, priests, teachers and prognosticators. Some of these were accurate and some inaccurate. There was a relative state of perfection and imperfection that manifested the whole gamut of psychic extravaganza, psychic containment and psychic manifestation. For *psychic* is but a word related to *psyche*, the soul, and it, in reality, means 'the life record of manifestation.'

"Every individual, wherever he goes upon the planet Earth, carries the mixture, or blending, of all the psychic records of his many embodiments upon the planet. Unless these records are transmuted by the violet-flame energy that rushes forth from the heart of God as a response to mankind of the Deity's love, providing the Communion of Saints,* the violet-fire cup —the chalice of the 'new wine' of spiritual regeneration—man must of necessity continue to be wedded to the psychic patterns and manifestations of his own sins.[60]

Redemption through the Christ

"Only by a correct and prolonged use of the violet flame can the thin or thick membranous veil of old records surrounding all lifestreams be thinned and purified until the pure Christ Light can shine through from the heart flame on the altar of each individualized manifestation. When this is accomplished, it does not necessarily mean that the karma of that individual is balanced. It simply means that the karmic record in its gross intensity has been thinned as a veil, permitting a greater flow of the Light energy of God to pour through the flesh form. This makes it easier for an individual to attune with the Deity, to come into consonance with the divine ideas, to reach up and to become one with the individualized God Presence.

"Through forging anew this great link with the mighty and beloved I AM Presence of all life, through the mediatorship of the Holy Christ Self, individuals then become wedded once again to the Deity. The City of God, the New Jerusalem, descends as a bride adorned to meet her husband,[61] and the eternal peace of God envelops the soul below. As all enter through the same door, there is a renewal of universal opportunity when the descending New Jerusalem consciousness is obtained by any lifestream.

---

* The first known recorded reference to the term *Communion of Saints* appears in the Apostles' Creed, formulated by the early Church.

"The Holy Christ Self always knows the perfect thing to do, and the karmic record is clearly read by the Holy Christ Self of each individual. Therefore, from the moment that the veil thins enough for communion to be reestablished, the kingdom of heaven is opened to that lifestream, and opportunities, one after another, are born whereby the karmic record of the individual can be truly purified. This amounts to a descent of the only begotten Son of the Father, the Holy Christ Manifestation, the Light of God that never fails—the infinite power that is resident within each lifestream and was the power of the Word by which the whole creation was framed to descend into the consciousness of the chela.

"Thus the true meaning of the statement, 'The Blood of Jesus Christ redeems us from all sins,'[62] is fulfilled; for in reality, as the Holy Christ Self, the Mediator of all life, establishes contact with the Divine Presence and reads the record of the human individual, the embodied manifestation, it sees clearly the means whereby a new and living way may be opened up through the 'flesh' (the four lower bodies) of the individual ('Yet in my flesh shall I see God'[63]). This regenerative process takes place through the transmuted flesh of the Ascended Son of God, the Holy Christ Self, 'the only begotten of the Father, full of grace and truth,'[64] who is, in reality, the Mediator or midpoint between the Presence of God and the human self.

"Thus, there comes into manifestation the quickening of all life experiences and the willingness to do God's will as the holy Son himself spake when he descended through the ethers saying, 'Lo, I am come to do thy will, O God.'[65] Of this Christ it was spoken, 'Thou art my beloved Son, in whom I am well pleased.'[66] And again in another place, 'Thou art a priest for ever after the Order of Melchizedek.'[67] The Holy Christ Self is the true manifestation of both the Father and the Son as well as the agency of the Holy Spirit, for in the Holy Christ Self there is the balance of life made manifest. The Father's purposes and will are made known to the Son, the embodied individual, as 'I and my Father are one,'[68] and therefore the Son below can speak unto the Father saying, 'I AM thyself in action here below,' and it will be so.

"Thus does the blood of Jesus Christ (the life essence of the Christ that was in Jesus, that was in the Son of God from the foundation of the world, and that is in every individual who will accept it as manifestation here and now and forever) redeem the mortal consciousness from all of the sins to which the flesh is heir. This is the means of deliverance, and it is the true and living way of cosmic nourishment. This is the door to the sheepfold. A thousand thieves may try to get through another way, but they can never enter into nor obtain eternal life except through the manifestation of the Cosmic Christ intelligence inherent within the Holy Christ Self of all men—the Universal Christ consciousness. This is the spirit of life and Truth that maketh of all men one body in Christ.

"Seek First the Kingdom..."

"Now, the psychic world is not so. It is the world of episode and humor, of temperament and temper, of the fiery steed that drags mankind again and again over a bed of spikes. The psychic world must, in God's name, be controlled, and men must learn to live above it. There is no need for any individual to probe extensively the life records of another except in rare cases when an avatar, a Messenger or a specifically trained chela of the Great Ones, for some holy cosmic purpose or reason known best to God, does reveal some pertinent incident of value to the lifestream in order that he may come to God in greater faith and be cleansed of the record of an episode from the past.

"There is a divine astrology, but only the Masters and highly advanced chelas of God upon earth are able to understand it. Much of the astrology of the world and much prognostication and prediction that is in the world is, according to the tenets of the Great White Brotherhood, causative in producing undesirable negative manifestations whenever the predictions are dire. When the predictions are benign, individuals do not mind them but whatever strengthens their faith in the psychic realm prolongs their sojourn in the night side of life.

"The highest form of advancement comes not through the psychic or psychic probings but through deliverance from the psychic realm and attachment to one's Divine Presence. I cannot stress enough the dangers of the astral world. Here every festering form of hatred—racial, personal and demon-inspired—and every sense of mortal injustice dwells, spawning more of its kind. The forces of the astral world continually seek to use the consciousness of those beginning chelas on the Path and seize them by reason of man's desire to be a link between the higher powers of Light and the darkened world. We can well understand, precious ones, how the hearts of men become tender and enraptured by the idea of God's love. They then seek in some way to formulate a plan of deliverance for the world, and thus they unwittingly enter the astral and psychic realm as communicants in the hope that the powers of Light will use their offered and dedicated selves as instruments for the salvation of the world.

"Rather than seek these manifestations, men and women should first seek the kingdom of God and his righteousness[69]— to purify their souls by many years of devoted service to the violet flame, to seek a great adjustment in their own personal affairs and the putting of their houses in order, to learn to commune with God in the stillness of their own hearts, and to perform those decrees that are necessary for themselves, their families and loved ones, and for all of mankind.

"The world has been visited by a multitude of avatars, and there are at the present time on earth a small number who are active and representative of the Great White Brotherhood. Alignment with that which is already established is far more to be desired than the thought of man becoming a self-appointed prophet or teacher.

"We urge, therefore, seeing that false prophecy is so much a part of astral treachery, that all shall seek first the kingdom of God and his righteousness and seek to walk justly with their fellowmen in the service of the Masters of the Great White Brotherhood according to the directions already released and shall, above all, avoid contact either with the dead (which is but necromancy) or with astral entities masquerading as sons of Light. In most cases it is not necessary that individuals should become amanuenses for cosmic purposes; for when it is the will of God that such should be done, he will make it known with such clarity that even a child could read and understand.

"There is a stratum in the astral world that seems to be very right and filled with a considerable accumulation of Truth, of facts and of beauty. I consider this to be far more dangerous than even the ugly and the abortive, for men are more easily deceived by this than they are by the horror of the world. Yet today the remnant of the decadent Atlanteans who have been released into embodiment from the prison houses of the astral are bringing in new forms of sexual horror, perversions of principle, and the seeking after places of glamour that (like the cave in the story of Aladdin—Ala-ed-Din—and his uncle, the evil black magician) are filled with many lures of bright and shining jewels, possessions of the astral realm that are as easily lost as a fog or a mist upon a glass.

"Be not deceived, beloved ones; God is not mocked. As men sow, so shall they reap.[70] There is only one way to safety, and that is through the Ascended Master consciousness. Your beloved Saint Germain, Jesus, beloved Godfré and every Master of the Great White Brotherhood know this. Your beloved Mother Mary knows this. The Goddess of Light and the Queen of Light and all the ladies of heaven know this. We know the pain and anguish that comes from psychic contact, which sometimes, once established, cannot be broken for many embodiments. Too many have lost their ascension over this one matter for us to let it go. We must warn, because to be warned is to be forearmed. We must ask that those who truly desire God and divine unfoldment shall seek as never before for the complete attunement of their souls with the divine idea of cosmic domination (cosmic grace)....

"The inhabitants of the astral world have in the main cut themselves off from the divine idea. They no longer recognize the God of the universe as their God. They seek to take the vital energies of God, released to man daily, and siphon them off through his [man's] imperfect, mortal consciousness by playing brother against brother, by creating situations of hate and confusion so that people will willingly yield their energies to the wrong vibratory action.

"Every time you lend yourself to feelings of irritation, criticism, condemnation and judgment, or inharmony of any kind whatsoever, you are prolonging the life of the astral entities, whereas divine harmony is of no use to them at all. God's energies, retained inviolate and pure by man, can never be trampled upon by the astral creation, for they cannot enter perfection; and thus perfection is its own protection. Jesus gave the key to holiness—wholeness—when he said, 'Be ye therefore perfect, even as your Father which is in heaven is perfect.'[71]

"The psychic world is well organized and complete with its own hierarchies. The false hierarchy that dwells there and utilizes the interplay of forces between man and God continues to reach out into the world of form, as the roaring lion, seeking whom they may devour.[72] Their manifestations are legion, and all of the warfares upon earth and the misunderstandings between people are the result of their intransigent energies.

"You cannot possibly know as we do how frightful these forces are. Yet I say to you that the battle of Armageddon is the tremendous focalization of astral energies and moon substance that pulls upon the water body of man—the astral body—and influences it as the tides are influenced by the moon. This is the veritable enemy of every man. Yet men love the darkness of the moon and of the mortal drama more than they love the Light of God, which has not yet breathed its tangible Reality into their manifest minds. That is to say, they now have no memory of it, the doorway to that beauty of divine perfection having been lost, which they once knew when they were in the bosom of God.

"I urge upon all a shunning of the vicious astral forces and a searching as never before for the wonders of the Divine Mind. You must learn to commune with the Realities of God of which you have not yet dreamt, for 'eye hath not seen, nor ear heard [the mysteries of God], neither have entered into the heart of man, the things which God hath prepared for them that love him.' "[73]

Christ, the Only Mediator

The devices of indirect control that have been substituted by astral forces for the direct manifestation of the Christ are legion. God does not require any other intermediary except his radiant Son, the Christ, to teach mankind all things, to warn him of impending danger, to regulate his life and to ordain him in the service of the Light. The Christ Self of each man is therefore his own direct link to God, his own divinely ordained Mediator.

Astrea, complement of the Elohim of Purity, is uncompromising in her admonishments concerning "harmless" flirtations with psychic phenomena: "I tell you before Almighty God and before your own divine I AM Presence, it is all-important that the students shall understand the need to cut themselves free from all psychic and spiritualistic activities and to enter into the fullness of Ascended Master love. For Ascended Master love is Real, Ascended Master love is true, Ascended Master love is all-enfolding, and it is the full sufficiency of the cosmic law, integrating mankind into the forcefield of pure Light and removing from him those splotches of darkness that are blots upon his path of progress.

"Will you understand with me tonight, then, that the little pastime of the practicing of the Ouija board has led many an individual into a condition wherein he is no longer able to have dominion over his own world. We want you to understand that we do not approve, regardless of human opinion, of the use of the pendulum, which men and women have thought that they could use with success. We want you to understand that there are connected with the use of the pendulum, regardless of the manifestations of seeming authenticity in it, activities whereby individuals are for a time guided correctly. And it is so. Sometimes they are guided accurately for years by these manifestations, all for that moment when they will be, as you say in baseball parlance, 'pitched a curve.'

"We want you to understand that the authority of your own I AM Presence is the only power in the universe that can ever give you your freedom. You cannot depend upon outer devices, on crystal balls, on fortune-telling apparatus and on horoscopes that are cast—albeit there is a true science of cosmic astrology, but this is not known in the outer world today, nor has it been for many a year; it is only taught in the inner schools of the Great White Brotherhood. Individuals, then, should be extremely careful in all their attempts to cast horoscopes and future projections according to the inaccuracies of modern astrology.*

"Let them understand that the authority for their life is their own God Presence and that, because it is the authority, the words rang forth long ago, 'I the LORD thy God am a jealous God.'[74] The keys of authority are in the heart of your Presence. Whenever you turn to outer accoutrements or manifestations of the psychic plane for any design of your life, at that precise moment you are stopping the perfection of your Presence from coming through. So long as you rely upon these outer conditions, they will continue to act in your world, and they will deny you the full freedom of your own I AM Presence."[75]

The man of God who knows that God lives in him need not stoop to any lesser manifestation for consolation. The mind of God is not the medium or the mediator for aught that is less than perfection. By like token, that which is imperfect and incomplete cannot be the mediator or the medium for perfection. To stoop to an inferior means of deliverance is to seal one's fate in the grips of the fatalists, whereas to place one's hand in the hand of Christ is to make one's pact with eternity.

---

* Since this dictation was given, Mother Mary has released the fundamentals of her teaching on the science of the cosmic clock to the Messenger Elizabeth Clare Prophet. See *Predict Your Future: Understand the Cycles of the Cosmic Clock* (2004).

Hypnosis

Another means by which people have sought to bypass the Christ as the mediator is by the practice of hypnosis—using the power of the mind (one's own or another's) to bring about change in one or more of the four lower bodies. This practice has its origins with the Austrian mystic and physician Franz Anton Mesmer (1734–1815).

Practicing medicine in Vienna in the eighteenth century, Dr. Mesmer was to have a profound effect on the fields of science and medicine of his day and to the present. He taught that man was affected by the planets and stars through the medium of an energy field that acted as a fluid because it flowed in, around and through all of Matter. He said that "everything in the universe is contiguous by means of a universal fluid in which all bodies are immersed."

Mesmer discovered that "all things in nature possess a particular power, which manifests itself by special actions on other bodies." He found that he could control and direct emanations of energy to his patients, either nearby or at a great distance, and that this action would result in miraculous cures of the diseased.

One of those who took up Mesmer's work was Phineas Quimby (1802–1866), an American pioneer in the field of mental healing. The experiments of Quimby and Mesmer paved the way for the medical use of hypnosis.

The effectiveness of hypnosis is well documented. However, there is a price that is paid. Hypnosis is dangerous because you do not maintain the use of your own free will; someone else is given authority over your consciousness when hypnosis is administered. When you allow another to enter into your consciousness, this means that whatever they are composed of—good and bad—is imposed upon you. And though you may receive some benefit, you also receive the negative momentums of that individual.

Furthermore, the only way you can return and ascend to God is by the conscious use of your free will. The only identity that should be given control over your consciousness is your God Presence—and the Ascended Masters who are wholly one with God and therefore cannot pass on to you any influence that is not of the Light.

Hypnosis, or mesmerism, is effective through the power of suggestion that works in the etheric body through the subconscious mind. The power to change, therefore, is not of the higher type that would be called transmutation or divine alchemy; the power of change through hypnosis comes about because we are by the power of the etheric body, the memory body, determining that we shall change conditions in our consciousness or in the physical body.

For instance, if someone has a record from many past embodiments of extreme hatred, the final manifestation of that hatred could be in the form of a cancer, and the karmic law may decree that the final working out of that karma must descend into the physical body. If by hypnosis and the power of suggestion you determine that you are not going to have this cancer, the cancer may be removed and an apparent healing may take place.

However, the record of that hatred is not transmuted, the cause is not taken, and therefore the effect must someday manifest. Unless the use of the sacred fire through the violet transmuting flame is made, this cancer is simply dissolved in the physical by the power of your lower body, your etheric body. The record remains, and at some future time, perhaps in a future embodiment, that cancer will reappear.

Therefore, the healing is never complete with hypnosis. You have achieved nothing permanent. You have turned your consciousness over to someone else and received the fruits of his lower nature; furthermore, you have postponed the hour and the day of your own salvation.

Karma should not be seen as punishment but as opportunity, and every sickness or problem or circumstance that comes to you that is not affording you happiness must be seen as a situation that can afford your victory. Our search is not so much to live in comfort and tranquility, but to live in a state of overcoming, where we have each day new victories and new fields to conquer.

It is recorded in the Bible, "Sufficient unto the day is the evil thereof."[76] The Lords of Karma never release to you more of your karma than you can handle at one time, so you never need fear that you will not be able to rise to the occasion. It comes as you are able to balance it.

Let us listen to the Ascended Masters' views on the serious consequences of hypnotism. One whose title is the Great Divine Director spoke of this as a form of mechanical enslavement: "One of the most awesome threats to mankind today is the unfortunate use that is made of hypnotism. And I say awesome because this particular evil is cloaked with authority from a professional group highly esteemed by mankind. We do not deny that a very high percentage of embodied mankind is subject to hypnotic control to some degree through many subtle influences, but we affirm that this ought not to be; for that which binds the mind of man to the spell of mayic glitter is also a mechanical holding of the attention of the outer man upon Matter and form in order to enslave the spirit of man, which originally came forth as a flame from the heart of God."[77]

"Unfortunately, individuals who are not completely oriented around divine Truth sometimes submit to an attempt to utilize the power of hypnosis in order to accomplish seeming miracles through the power of the subconscious. As your beloved Ascended Friends of Light have told you so often, you ought never to submit your being to the control of any person or hypnotist, even for seemingly benign purposes. Nor should you practice so-called autohypnosis; for the energies required to perform this type of action, while seemingly innocent enough, actually diminish the power of the soul of man; and while they may seem productive of good for a time, the ultimate long-range effect is not freedom, but bondage. 'There is a way which seemeth right unto a man, but the end thereof are the ways of death.' "[78]

"Hypnosis in any form is a sooty business, for thereby the clean-burning flame of the soul is mingled with abominable substance so as to coat the lens of the mind with the appearance of imperfection in the guise of perfection. It is the work of the wicked who say, 'Let us do evil, that good may come.' And, in the words of Saint Paul, their damnation is just.[79]

"This mechanical clouding of man's knowing also occurs in the release of subliminal advertising through television and motion picture screens. Well, let them have their day of 'spots' and influence—truly they have their reward! The karmic record grows heavy with drops of retribution, and I think it shall return unto those who would mechanically enslave the minds of men."[80]

Animal Magnetism

Another form of enslavement comes through what is known as animal magnetism. This term was originally used by Mesmer to describe the energy field that surrounds all living things and by which he was able to exert a hypnotic influence on others. Actually, all people carry a magnetic forcefield that is determined by the rate of vibration of their own individual thoughts and feelings and records of past lives, both being recorded in the "electronic circle" or "electronic belt" of each lifestream.

We speak of "personal magnetism" or a "magnetic personality." This is the intangible quality made up of the combination of many complex factors of the ego. However, there is only one true magnetism that is desirable, and that is the magnetism of the Christ who is the Polestar of each man's being. All else is the glitter and glamour of the human—the maya of imperfection that should be handled daily.

For the purposes of simplification, we have categorized four types of animal magnetism. The records of personal imperfection in each one are the open doors through which these forces enter, gathering more of their kind from the accumulation of the mass karma of the race.

Malicious animal magnetism works through the subconscious, the etheric body. It is malice aforethought—conscious, willful and directed evil such as the many forms of hatred and jealousy that are the foundations of most criminal acts. Psychic murders occur through the projections of malicious animal magnetism; many times people are removed from the screen of life simply because someone or a group of individuals, either embodied or dwelling in the astral, is holding a death wish over that one. Even mild dislike carries the seeds of death, and those who retain even the slightest thought of irritation concerning another lifestream must bear the karmic responsibility, if only in part, for the downfall and even the demise of that one.

Criticism, condemnation and judgment are more sophisticated forms of malicious animal magnetism; but these arrows of hostility, which admittedly sometimes bear the sugar coating of "good intentions," do manifest as serious consequences for other parts of life, and many times they are fed through the subconscious so that those who are victimized by their own error or that of another are not even aware of the fact that they have been so employed. Thus our best defense is in the giving of decrees, for the sacred fire takes care of *all* problems, whether or not they have been diagnosed or admitted by the outer consciousness.

Ignorant animal magnetism works through the mental body and manifests as many forms of density—slowness of mind and action, clogging and sluggishness in the functioning of the physical body, untidiness and dust in one's surroundings, a tendency to have accidents and, in general, being out of step with life. Ignorant animal magnetism is the Antichrist—the mass effluvia of human creation that opposes the expansion of the Christ Light throughout the world. Problems connected with mechanical failures and electrical mishaps can often be traced to this form of animal magnetism.

The use of copper telephone wiring renders this form of communication vulnerable to the abuses of ignorant animal magnetism since copper is an ideal conductor of astral energies. For this reason copper jewelry and accessories should not be worn and household ornaments likewise should not be of copper.

Sympathetic animal magnetism works through the emotional body and thus vibrates on the level of the astral plane. Human sympathy, personal attachments and involvements not based upon the Christ are among the manifestations of sympathetic animal magnetism. It is the most difficult form of animal magnetism to pin down and deal with because it always masquerades as some form of human concern, all the way from deep affection to neighborly kindness. One of the most insidious types of sympathetic animal magnetism is self-pity. Many people wallow in self-pity embodiment after embodiment and are thus ineffectual in adhering to any worthwhile goal.

Love for one's fellowman, the willingness to lay down one's life for one's brethren, to be "my brother's keeper," are divinely ordained ministrations of the Christ. However, when friendships become possessive and are based on what one individual can get from another, this can never lead to the freedom of the individual and his ascension in the Light.

Family mesmerism is one manifestation of animal magnetism; it involves the exertion of unwholesome control of one individual over another in the name of family ties. This name is often given to hypnotic ties whereby we allow ourselves to be open to energy of negativity coming from members of our families. We are open to them because we have karma with them, because we love them and because we have mutual responsibilities.

The key to dealing with this energy is to maintain a very strong heart tie through the Christ Self to one's family members. You are in control of this tie and through it you can give a great deal of love to them. However, if you allow yourself to be tied at untransmuted levels of your being—the solar plexus, the emotional level, the astral body—and if you have a great deal of sympathy for family members, you do open your chakras to them and open your beings to them, and they have access to you and to your Light and energy at will.

Sentimentality and nostalgia are forms of sympathetic animal magnetism. Jesus' statement, "Whosoever shall do the will of my Father which is in heaven, the same is my brother, and sister, and mother,"[81] should be remembered when choosing companions or breaking spiritually unprofitable ties.

Delicious animal magnetism works through the physical body and involves overindulgence in the gratification of one or more of the five senses. The attainment of mastery must include balance in all areas of living. Prolonged abuses to the physical body such as gluttony, sexual excesses and perversions, the use of harmful stimulants such as alcohol, psychedelic drugs, dope and other unwholesome indulgences lead to physical disease, insanity and death. In many cases the results are carried over for several embodiments. When entire communities are involved, cataclysm is the end result.

Such manifestations of a lack of self-control not only indicate an absence of mastery, but also they are sins against the Holy Spirit, for they violate the temple of God and the sacredness of the life force. It is each one's responsibility to maintain the purity of the life-stream that flows forth from the Presence twenty-four hours a day. To this end were the four lower bodies created, and that man might win his victory in the world of form. Mastery over the four lower bodies is mastery over the four elements (etheric—fire; mental—air; emotional—water; physical—earth).

Mental Healing

After Phineas Quimby's initial experiments with hypnosis, he found that healings could equally be accomplished by means of conscious suggestion. He came to believe that illness was the result of incorrect beliefs and that healing came about through discovering the truth.

Many came to him for healing; several went on to become famous healers in their own right and leaders in the New Thought movement. One of these was Mary Baker Eddy, who went to him for treatments when she was experimenting with a type of faith healing.

Mary Baker Eddy saw the limitations of Quimby's methods, and when she started to work with mental healing, she realized that one could go higher, to the Divine mind, to the Christ mind, as Saint Paul called it,[82] and receive healing from

God directly, instead of simply transferring thoughts from one individual to another at the mental level. And so, because her consciousness was highly attuned to Jesus, for she had walked with him as Mary, the sister of Martha and Lazarus, and had received teachings directly from him at that time, she was given, by a form of dictation from Jesus, Mary and Hilarion, the revelation that she called Christian Science. Because of her lack of knowledge of the violet flame (which had not yet been released to the world), there were some errors incorporated into Christian Science. However, it was sponsored by the Ascended Masters, whereas the practitioners of hypnotism were not.

Christian Science is based on the affirmation of Good and the denial of Evil, the affirmation of principles, of qualities of God, the affirmation that man is made in the image and likeness of these qualities, and therefore is whole. The same principles are taught by Unity and other New Thought organizations.

Unfortunately, like hypnosis, this process of affirmation and denial also has its drawbacks; for even though appealing to the Creator, once again we see that without transmutation, without the use of the violet flame, practitioners of these various organizations may, in this process of affirmation, fall to the level of the mental body, and once again it does descend into a form of hypnosis—not hypnosis in the name of the power, however, of the lower mental body, but in the name of the Christ. And therefore, today, you will find Christian Science has to its record many testimonies of healing, but ninety percent of these healings are the pushing back of the disease into the etheric body; one day it will have to come forth again so that the karma may be expiated or transmuted by the violet flame.

The True Science of Prophecy

Spiritualism is not synonymous with spirituality, and true spirituality never leads to spiritualism. All religion presupposes revelation of some kind. However, prophecy is not for the unbelieving but for those who believe[83] because they maintain some degree of contact with the Spirit of Christ that dwells within them. Through this contact they are able to verify communications that come forth from higher spheres through the prophets of God, even before they themselves are able to make positive and accurate attunement with the Masters.

In the matter of prophecy, the unpredictability of human will—the fact that it is free and can at any moment change its course—must be taken into account. If the fulfillment of divine predictions were inevitable, this would circumscribe man's free will. Instead of providing him with a warning of the outcome of his inordinate behavior, prophecy, being inevitable, would preclude the possibility of man's turning from his downward course and averting the action of the karmic hammer, even at the very last moment. (See the Book of Jonah and note Jonah's prophecy of the destruction of Nineveh and its nonfulfillment due to the repentance of the people.)

Inasmuch as the Deity ever desires to provide for transcendence in life at every level of consciousness, the science of prophecy always takes into account mankind's ever-present opportunity to change. If he changes, prophecies may also change. Nevertheless, the plotting of trends on the graph of human consciousness is done at divine levels, and the Masters can and do foretell with great accuracy the denouement of personal and world karma. Since the harvest of current events is so delicately intertwined with mass and individual sowings, the latter often determine the former, and current events can therefore be predicted by the Masters who have access to the karmic records of the earth and her evolutions.

Psychic Predictions

Dire foretellings that enter the subconscious minds of large numbers of people (especially when such predictions are publicized) tend to be fulfilled by the focusing of the mass energies of the people in the belief that the prediction will come to pass. In some cases so much fear of impending doom is magnetized that great harm is brought to entire communities, even if events do not come to pass precisely as they were predicted.

A stir among psychics that infected many groups was caused by a prediction concerning the asteroid Icarus. This asteroid was to have collided with the earth on June 15, 1968.[84] Five hundred people gathered at Boulder, Colorado, for the end of the world—even though scientific calculations showed that the asteroid would continue in its cigar-shaped orbit and come no closer than 3,950,000 miles from the earth.[85]

Commenting on this prediction the year before, the Ascended Master Cha Ara said: "At the present time, there is a tremendous activity being focused through the psychic forces of the world concerning the asteroid Icarus, which has now been located in the heavens by the astronomers.

"I would like to call to your attention that from time to time, mankind have had much greater perils sent against them from within their own forcefield, as a result of their impure thoughts and feelings, than that which has been directed against them from outer space. And for the record, I would reiterate this point: mankind have here upon this planetary body, if they wish to measure the potential of evil, far greater dangers threatening them from within than from without in outer space.

"I therefore say to the students to take heed that you reckon with Reality, and be not moved by those who seek to move mankind through the impulse of fear. For the actual vibratory action that God desires to direct to mankind is that which will magnetize their attention to the Divine Presence in order that they may have their immortal freedom. When individuals are constantly made to fear, they are thereby separated from the great pole of cosmic love. Perfect love always casts out all fear, for fear has torment,[86] and torment is no part of the real nature of God.

"Those who continue to purvey into the world of form a constant series of scare tactics are cooperating with the sinister forces who seek to spread abroad upon the world a psychic and astral horror that is intended to deter mankind from pursuing the great cosmic love of the Christ Self of their own beings.

"True Reality will ultimately show mankind that God is the only way to escape, for the perfect love that casts out all fear abides and dwells in God. God is the power by which men are raised, from all dangers that may ever threaten them, into the great master sheepfold of life. There the Good Shepherd cares for the sheep and nurtures them until they are able to go forth into other pastures and be, indeed, no longer sheep but shepherds in the everlasting fold of spiritual regeneration.

"The love of the Father, scattered abroad throughout the universe, teaches men and women upon all planets and systems of worlds where embodied life exists (and even out into the realms of the spirits themselves where God seeks to preserve the Divine Image inviolate) to know and to be that which he is in the fullness of himself. For the love of God teaches the creation to manifest his fullness in the Christ Light that he has sent forth as the means to create, to sustain, to preserve and to regenerate all life."[87]

All men hold a fragment of destiny within their hands. Each man, in a limited framework, is the master of his fate.

Many prefer to interpret the flow of events as the will of God when they, by their own actions or inactions, are directly responsible for what has become of the gift of life that was so tenderly placed in their hands.

While it is true that God disposes of man's proposals, it is also true that man's obedience to divine decrees will without fail eventuate in his freedom to manifest under divine law the fullness of self-mastery. There is a divine plan for every man. Some may choose to interpret this plan as the doctrine of predestination; however, it must be remembered that until man by his free will chooses to accept this plan, it cannot be fulfilled in his life. And until he accepts this plan, there is no predestination. Destiny must be sought, forged and won.

A Plot to Discredit True Religion

Many sincere and trusting souls have been victimized by unscrupulous practitioners who have defrauded them of either their money or their energies or both. This is one of the principal reasons that the intelligentsia of the world have scoffed at the spiritual activities of the Brotherhood. Those who practice various aspects of wizardry and those who purport to receive messages from God have delivered a diatribe of obvious hoax and a flood of questionable materials that, by strange coincidence, always seem to center on the exaltation of their own egos. Their motive has obviously been to attract the more simpleminded to themselves for the purpose of psychic control or personal adulation. Such practices have not set well with honest and rational people. When investigators like Sir Oliver Lodge and others exposed these activities as fraudulent, many became altogether disillusioned and turned their backs on every activity that laid claim to the supernatural.

What man has done in the name of religion has so

discredited true religion "undefiled before God"[88] that it is no wonder that many intelligent, reasoning people have gone the pathway of an ethical humanism, of agnosticism, or even of atheism or nihilism. These would rather go hungry than partake of the mould that is substituted by modern theologians for the manna of heaven and the meat of the Word. We must admit that the purposes of Antichrist have been well served.

Perish the thought that there are no well-meaning investigators and spiritualistic mediums on the planet. We have contacted many and are aware of others. These individuals are honest of heart and, to the best of their ability, strive to serve God and man. The problem, however, lies not with their sincerity (which even the Great Ones do not question) but with their own misdirected efforts. These are the blind who lead the blind—and sooner or later both fall into the astral pit.[89] Although they have the best of intentions, the road they pave can only lead to the hell that is the psychic world.

The Path of the Ascended Masters

Let people decide for themselves, of their own free will, which path they will follow—but let all understand the Ascended Masters' viewpoint concerning psychic thralldom. Those who seek phenomena, the manifestation of ghosts and spirits, the apporting of objects and communion with the dead may enjoy the search and the experiences that will come to them in the séance circle. But there is no compatibility whatsoever between psychic phenomena and the glorious revelations that come forth with power and Light and love from the Ascended Masters' octaves. Here the purity of Truth, manifest in the vibratory actions released by the Ascended Masters, rekindles the spirit of the resurrection flame within the being of man. This action of the flame, which raises every atom of his four lower bodies to the place where both God and man are glorified, bears testimony to the fact that the individual has made contact with the highest Source of inspiration.

The path of the Ascended Masters leads to the ascension. The path of psychic phenomena, as we have said, leads to the bottomless pit that is the hell of the astral realm. Saint Paul described those who follow the leadings of chaos and old night in his Epistle to Timothy. He prophesied that they would come in the last days, "ever learning, and never able to come to the knowledge of the truth."[90]

In the final analysis all should be forewarned that psychic thralldom is the perversion of the seventh ray of the ritual of communion with God and the transmutation of the misuse of the sacred fire. It involves the misuse of the seat of the soul, the chakra governing the production of the divine seed of the Christ in man and woman, and the misuse of the mental body, which is intended to receive the impression of the Christ from the Higher Mental Body and impress it on the seed.

On the other hand, to deny the existence of spirits is just as bad as indulging in spiritualism; for thereby people turn their back on them and they are left to carry on their unwholesome activities. Only by squarely facing the fact that such is the reality (albeit in the relative sense) and then making calls to the Masters and the angels for their deliverance can people be truly free from their unwholesome influence.

Let all who have the courage to withdraw from the curious attractions of psychic involvement know that the legions of Archangel Michael and the Elohim Astrea stand ready and waiting to buoy their consciousness into the higher domain where angels, Masters and Cosmic Beings commune with unascended men and lead them into the highest Truth of their destiny as sons and daughters of God.

The Gift of the Golden Chain Mail

Those who engage in psychic activities cause a great burden not only to themselves but also to the planet as they become the open door for the energies of the astral plane to enter into the physical. In order to prevent this, the God and Goddess Meru in 1964 announced a dispensation whereby a "golden chain mail" would be draped around the entire planet to protect us from the psychic planes, the planes that are astral and of Death and Hell:

"There flows now the wondrous outpouring of our love from the Andes unto the world. And as this love flows forth, we urge that the golden armour of holy illumination's flame be placed in the consciousness of all as though it were wrapping and enfolding them round, so that the arrows and pestilences that infest the world to this present hour may be stayed and by the gift of divine illumination men may walk in robes of righteousness.

"The right use of divine power will make this planet reflect the Golden Age radiance, which it is our will to expand now. And so, as I come to you this morn, it is my wish that you will feel the sweet gift of our grace imparted to you through the angelic messengers who issue forth from this retreat, carrying to your heart strands of golden substance that you may feel also the illumination of this precious substance as it is placed by angelic hands as a circlet of light around your brow.…

"As I am come to you this holy morn, I then come with cosmic purpose in view, bearing tidings of kindness and grace from the lovely Lady Meru, who is my consort. Today we shall not experiment, but we shall perform—we shall weave a network of Light over the planetary body. And because this is the day called Sunday, we shall utilize the energies and devotion of many hearts to weave this great garment of Light over the planet.

"And it is our intent this day that this garment of Light shall resemble a coat of golden chain mail so that we may plug the gaps in mankind's consciousness where the penetration of psychic substance passes and causes them to reinfect various areas of the world after the decrees and calls of the students of Light have effectively rendered them antiseptic....

"The Christ of the Andes, this magnificent statue of Light, is now being charged while I am speaking to you by angel devas from many parts of the world and is also being touched by a rod of power held in the hands of the Angel Deva of the Jade Temple. This action of purity is talismanic in action and designed to cause a spiritual white radiance of cosmic Light to be released from this statue in commemoration of the Cosmic Christ. And as this takes place, it is beamed out in an omni-directional manner so as to contact the entire periphery of the earth's surface.

"These currents, then, follow the curvature of the earth and will incite a cosmic action of Love and Light wherever they contact the spires of worship of mankind this morning, weaving together the energies of both Christian, Moslem, Jew and Buddhist, and the many religions of the world into a con-secrated chalice and forcefield that the angelic hosts will take up and offer to the Karmic Board. This offering is intended to be carried directly to the Great Central Sun and laid before your precious Alpha and Omega....

"We hope to insulate mankind from the psychic realm as much as possible and establish a curtain of great power so that this realm will become somewhat isolated from mankind and exceedingly difficult to pierce. It is our hope that this will bring about a great wall of Light between the octave of psychic substance and the human consciousness of mankind, making it extremely difficult for those individuals engaged in psychic practices to actually contact the psychic octave....

"It is the intention of the great Goddess Meru this morning to intensify the feminine ray in your midst while I amplify the masculine ray so that you will understand that the action of building this coat of golden chain mail is not an action of one second but is being accomplished in part while I am speaking and will be intensified in the days to come as you call for the amplification of the action that took place this morning....

"Now, precious ones, with the great release of substance of Light that is pouring forth across the planetary body this morning, I would like to tell you also that we are using some of the political focuses of the world, such as the Washington Monument, and we are tying in to the mighty ray that is anchored there as a silent sentinel for and on behalf of America. The action of Light this morning is actually weaving strands of great cables and extending these cables to tie all of the monuments that are constructive across the face of the earth into one vast network of Light.

"Then the angelic hosts are contacting persons and places and conditions and things that are vibrating with an action of Light, and all are being interwoven into this marvelous pattern.

"This is going to mean a tremendous boon to the earth in this day and age, but it will require the attention of the students in order to reinforce and establish it so that it may be a permanent action for the earth.

"Do you see what I mean, blessed ones? This is an etheric gift that we are conferring upon the earth this morning. And this gift requires a specific action of mankind's attention being fed into it in order that the power of Light may retain this power of the golden chain mail armour anchoring mankind into the purity of his divine radiance.

"I thank you and I am counting on you, as is the lovely

Goddess Meru, to sustain this action of mighty assistance poured out in this day to the earth and all mankind upon it."[91]

In 1969 El Morya announced a new dispensation reinforcing the golden chain mail: "The will of God is strengthening itself in the world net, and we are formulating a new concept whereby the great chain mail that was placed between the psychic realm and the human shall now be coated with fiery blue-white diamonds. And there shall be builded into these diamonds a magnificent power of repulsion.

"We have brought forth and evoked from the Lords of Karma an activity where when the psychic world breaks forth into the human and penetrates it, whether it is through the willing admission of individuals or against their will, [through] the God flame in the heart of these diamonds that shall coat the chain mail armor placed long ago between the psychic and the human, the Lords of Karma shall invoke against those lifestreams that actually are doing despite to the law of love such an activity of karmic recompense that these individuals shall find that they no longer have that time delay that they have had in the past whereby they seem to feel that they can escape with impunity as they bring forth their arrows of destruction against the sons of God."[92]

In spite of these dispensations, we have seen since the decade of the 1960s a spilling of the energies of the astral plane into the physical bodies of the planet and her people. The puncturing of the astral plane has come not only through psychic activities, but also through drugs, through rock music and through bloodshed that has occurred in satanic rituals and voodoo, as well as in war. We have certainly seen amazing distortions of human life and human behavior on the planet since that time, and it was to prevent this that the great dispensation of the golden chain mail was given. However, as Serapis Bey explained in 1985, this endeavor was not entirely successful because there was not sufficient reinforcement of the golden chain mail by the calls and decrees of those in embodiment:

"Angels have begun to weave a filigree net of blue flame, a most intense fiery blue. It is a tight crocheting of an armour of mail made of light substance impervious. It is draped now between the physical manifestation and the astral plane for the protection of the earth from further eruption of astral hordes and darkness that began when the hour struck midnight December 31, 1959.

"It was then that the spilling over into America and the world of the subcultures of rock music and drugs paved the way for all astral horror and Death and Hell to come into the physical plane. There was therefore established on July 26, 1964, a golden chain mail connected at the great monuments of the world. But, beloved ones, this golden chain mail was not sufficiently reinforced with dynamic decrees by those in embodiment, inasmuch as the numbers of Keepers of the Flame and individuals decreeing at that time were not nearly so great as they are today.

"Therefore, I trust you will review this dictation concerning the golden chain mail and realize that we enforce this now and reinforce it with this blue chain mail of fiery blue energy and powerful protection."[93]

In 1995 Apollo and Lumina spoke further of the golden chain mail and of the importance of this dispensation: "We speak out of the heart of the God and Goddess Meru and we say to you each one: You may call for a personalized segment of the golden chain mail to be designed for you that you might wear it as an armour to seal your soul and your etheric body from the astral plane and the levels of Death and Hell.

"Understand this, beloved. We have called you to reestablish the golden chain mail. And the etheric pattern of that mail is now being strengthened as the Light of God quivers the strands—quivers them, beloved. And you see the strands shimmering and yet becoming more concrete as that tightly woven golden chain mail is draped over a planet.

"The question arises: Why have we called you to reestablish the golden chain mail? It is because that evil that came to pass in the last days of Atlantis is come to pass again in your day. Just as there were black magicians in high places of Church and State and priests who used their powers to work evil thousands of years ago, so there are black magicians and priests in embodiment today who are using their powers to destroy civilization.

"The very ones who were instrumental in causing the sinking of Atlantis have reincarnated in this century, and their focus is a staggering agenda of world destruction. Among them are the Atlantean scientists who experimented with recombinant DNA, breaking up and splicing together DNA from human and animal sources, thereby spawning creatures that were half man and half animal. Their evildoings ultimately brought forth the LORD's judgment....

"We wish to point out that the golden chain mail is the greatest weapon you have to thwart the agenda of the reincarnated Atlanteans and the false hierarchy of fallen angels who support them. We desire to see you accomplish, as the Messenger has stated, the corking of the bottle of hell. In other words, we desire to see you drive back the Antichrists who have wreaked havoc in their determination to destroy this civilization.

"Let them be driven back and confined to the depths of Death and Hell, where they belong, until the hour of their judgment is come! And let it be accomplished by the powerful decrees of stalwart Keepers of the Flame who read the signs of the times—yes, who read and run with the message of salvation unto the righteous and the message of judgment unto the reprobate.

"This dawning day of Aquarius is a wondrous time for the alchemy of the golden chain mail! It is a wondrous time for rethinking and remaking civilization!"[94]

Freedom from Psychic Thralldom

Jesus explains the part prayer can play in freeing individuals from psychic thralldom: "Many people fear to take to God those distressing problems that involve their own personal guilt, whereas others, working in the opposite direction, seem to almost enjoy telling God how very unworthy they are. We would clarify for the benefit of all. Insofar as impure acts and thoughts go, bringing them to God for purification is in a very real sense bringing your iniquities to heaven for judgment ahead of time, thus removing from the karmic record, in many cases, the need for future recompense. 'Some men's sins are open beforehand, going before to judgment; and some men they follow after.'[95]

"As a mother comforts a sobbing child, so God can and does quiet the restless energies that you seem unable to govern. When you keep your problems to yourself, as though they could thus be hidden from His eye, often they are only intensified, and your distress increases rather than lessens. In the matter of those who tell God how unworthy they are and appear to revel in so doing, this in most cases is the overriding of a rebellious entity or discarnate that manipulates their feelings to no good end.

"You know, precious ones, the evil spirits that have lived in the world in the past and who are now out of the body, together with those possessing entities that attach themselves to individuals because they love darkness rather than Light,[96] enjoy performing acts that they suspect might give distress to the Creator of the universe. This attitude is difficult for many to understand; but like that psychological trait known as masochism or self-abuse, the attempt of these spirits to flagellate the Deity by acclaiming their own dire condition actually feeds their egos and is intended to make those whom they control enjoy being sinners.

"When the sincere disciple brings to the Father *all* of his energy for purification, God is truly able to wash and to regenerate with his love and attention the developing son and bring him to maturity. In cases where extreme perversions have been practiced, it will be necessary that the individual make application for forgiveness with deep sincerity and follow the injunction 'Go, and sin no more.'[97] Those in the latter category must of necessity strive until they have won a relative state of victory over the outer condition and understand that the demons of ego and rebellion must be put down.

"There is a law involved here that states that man is accountable for that which he creates. Those who have created or harbored a rebellious spirit must themselves bring it under control and then approach God with humility that they, too, may be received and their energies purified. There is never any question whatsoever concerning the will of God to receive the prodigal son[98] back to his heart. Therefore, no one should make unworthiness an excuse for not engaging in holy prayer. The worthy need to progress and the unworthy to disentangle themselves from the enchantments of the world.

"More things are indeed wrought by prayer than the world dreams of. Yet ordinary prayer, strenuously engaged in, that cries out for emergency help in time of need is not to be compared with that steadfast outreach for God that understands communion as a most fortunate means to the end of personal freedom."[99]

Let all who have the courage seek the Divine Presence of life, which is above all psychic thralldom and which leads men to the feet of the Master. There the disciple can become truly God-centered, God-taught and God-inspired.

Let us close this chapter with a final word of advice from Astrea: "The LORD God has given to man dominion over all things. But this dominion does not of necessity include entanglement in the astral world of thought and feeling. The source of all human imperfection is old astral records. Buildings and houses, people and even animals in the world of form are filled with these old records. Your tube of light must be made strong and resilient that it may bend when necessary but never break under the onslaughts of psychic disturbances.

"You must learn to move in the world of form as victors over death and misqualified energy. The vortices of evil and of psychic disturbances may move all around you, but you may call upon your Divine Presence for release and deliverance. You may call unto me, and I will assist you by locking my cosmic circle and sword of blue flame around these vicious foci and providing not only yourselves with deliverance but also those whom you love.

"You must be persistent in your calls and determined in your conviction that the Light of God will not fail to answer them, and you must, under no condition, yield an inch of ground to those forces that are not of the Light. Beloved ones, these forces could not survive a single day if it were not for the feeding of mankind's energies into them. There is only one Source of Life, and that is God."[100]

Decree to Beloved Mighty Astrea—
"The Starry Mother"

In the name of the beloved mighty victorious Presence of God, I AM in me, mighty I AM Presence and Holy Christ Selves of Keepers of the Flame, Lightbearers of the world and all who are to ascend in this life, by and through the magnetic power of the sacred fire vested in the threefold flame burning within my heart, I call to beloved mighty Astrea and Purity, Archangel Gabriel and Hope, beloved Serapis Bey and the seraphim and cherubim of God, beloved Lanello, the entire Spirit of the Great White Brotherhood and the World Mother, elemental life—fire, air, water and earth! to lock your cosmic circles and swords of blue flame in, through and around my four lower bodies, my electronic belt, my heart chakra and all of my chakras, my entire consciousness, being and world.

[You may include here prayers for specific circumstances or conditions for which you are requesting assistance.]

Cut me loose and set me free (3x) from all that is less than God's perfection and my own divine plan fulfilled.

1. O beloved Astrea, may God Purity
    Manifest here for all to see,
    God's divine will shining through
    Circle and sword of brightest blue.

First chorus: Come now answer this my call
    Lock thy circle round us all.
    Circle and sword of brightest blue,
    Blaze now, raise now, shine right through!

2. Cutting life free from patterns unwise,
    Burdens fall off while souls arise
    Into thine arms of infinite love,
    Merciful shining from heaven above.

3. Circle and sword of Astrea now shine,
   Blazing blue-white my being refine,
   Stripping away all doubt and fear,
   Faith and goodwill patterns appear.

Second chorus: Come now answer this my call,
                Lock thy circle round us all.
                Circle and sword of brightest blue,
                Raise our youth now, blaze right through!

Third chorus: Come now answer this my call,
               Lock thy circle round us all.
               Circle and sword of brightest blue,
               Raise mankind now, shine right through!

And in full faith I consciously accept this manifest, manifest, manifest! (3x) right here and now with full power, eternally sustained, all-powerfully active, ever expanding and world enfolding until all are wholly ascended in the Light and free!

Beloved I AM! Beloved I AM! Beloved I AM!

[Give each verse, followed by the first chorus; repeat the verses, using the second chorus; then give the verses a third time, using the third chorus.]

Uses and Misuses of the Threefold Action
of the Seventh Ray

Flame	Correct Uses of the Flame	Psychic Misuses of the Flame
Love (pink)	**Love Reality:** Correct use of energy to bless fellowman and establish lines of communication with God to bring forth the Christ, the Divine Manchild, in one's life through service and in one's offspring	**Love Perversion:** Misuse of the energies released through the seat of the soul replacing the image of the Christ with the image of death Science of ectoplasm Gathering of psychic energies
Wisdom (yellow)	**Wisdom Reality:** Release of occult knowledge for the purpose of the ritual of communion with God Messengership True science of prophecy Developing communion with the Presence in place of communion with spirits Christ the Mediator	**Wisdom Perversion:** Spiritualism Mediumship Channeling Life readings Automatic writing Ouija board Tarot Pendulum I Ching Fortune telling False prophets
Power (blue)	**Power Reality:** Precipitation of the qualities of the Christ in character and the abundance of every good and perfect gift	**Power perversion:** Phenomena Witchcraft Black magic Voodoo Hypnotism False astrology Astral travel

Chapter 3

Armageddon

*And there was war in
heaven: Michael and his angels
fought against the dragon; and
the dragon fought and his
angels, and prevailed not;
neither was their place found
any more in heaven.*

*And the great dragon was
cast out, that old serpent, called
the Devil, and Satan, which
deceiveth the whole world: he
was cast out into the earth, and
his angels were cast out with
him.*

REVELATION

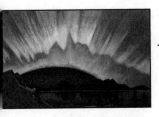

Armageddon

SECTION ONE

A Personal and Planetary Battle

> *We wrestle not against flesh and blood, but against principalities, against powers, against the rulers of the darkness of this world, against spiritual wickedness in high places.*
>
> SAINT PAUL

FROM TIME IMMEMORIAL, MEN have predicted the end of the world and the coming of the great battle of Armageddon.

Har-Magedon means "hill of Megiddo." The Canaanite fortress of Megiddo guarded the pass to the Valley of Jezreel, through which ran the major commercial route from Egypt to Mesopotamia. Whoever controlled the pass governed the economy of Israel. Therefore, the stronghold has been the scene of many battles, ancient and modern. Thus Armageddon, both as a name and as a place, came to symbolize the final battle of the forces of Light and Darkness.

In the last two thousand years, this battle has been associated with certain eschatological concepts—the Second Coming of Christ, the resurrection of the dead, the Last Judgment, the rapture of the saints, the punishment of sinners and the coming of the New Jerusalem.

Many Christians who are troubled by current trends expect the prophecy of the reappearance of the Christ to be fulfilled at any time. Some feel that the signs of the times are preliminary to the battle of Armageddon. Others have believed at one time or another that we were engaged in the war that would end all wars. These find in the doctrine of "final ends" a hope of the appearing of a new order of the ages that will terminate the injustices of the old and establish a Golden Age of peace and harmony in every country upon earth.

We have a profound hope that because God wills it, ultimately all these things shall come to pass and shall be fulfilled as a blessing, not only to contemporary man, but also to men of the future. However, we are well aware of God's commandment to man to take dominion over the earth.[1] Thus, human destiny is not only in the hands of God but also in the hands of man. Man's destiny is fulfilled through his willingness to become an active follower of the divine plan. As long as mankind insist on having their own way, they will be buffeted by their own returning karma.

Spiritual Warfare

The battle of Armageddon is, in reality, a battle between Light and Darkness, between the forces of Good and the forces of Evil, between the Real Self and the synthetic self. It is a spiritual warfare waged so that the world might be stripped of illusion and prepared for the coming of the radiantly victorious Christ into manifestation in every heart.

This battle has been waged from the beginning of the manifestation of Good and so-called Evil. For the Light of the Christ has always been opposed by the Antichrist,[2] and the Christ is the Lamb of God who has been "slain from the foundation of the world."[3]

Paul referenced the continuing battle that must be waged by all who would truly manifest the Spirit of the Christ when he said, "We wrestle not against flesh and blood, but against principalities, against powers, against the rulers of the darkness of this world, against spiritual wickedness in high places."[4] His advice to the Ephesians was to put on "the whole armour of God, that ye may be able to withstand in the evil day, and having done all, to stand.

"Stand therefore, having your loins girt about with truth, and having on the breastplate of righteousness; and your feet shod with the preparation of the gospel of peace; above all, taking the shield of faith, wherewith ye shall be able to quench all the fiery darts of the wicked. And take the helmet of salvation, and the sword of the Spirit, which is the Word of God."[5]

Updating this advice for disciples in this age, El Morya says: "The tube of light that the students have been given is very effective in shutting out and screening from man these discordant vibrations. The violet flame is also most helpful. But men must diligently practice these services and must call forth forcefields of spiritual protection around themselves daily—and even hourly when under attack.

"In the name of God, I say to all: You are in a battle! The battle of Armageddon is not a mere clashing of spears and chariots in the arenas of the world. It is a spiritual battle for the minds and hearts of men. The great clarity of the Christ mind, the great purity of God, the great love and munificence of his being, are scarcely understood by individuals today, who at times seem to have a very nebulous concept of the power of God.

"The power of God is very close to man. It is not far away as mankind sometimes imagine, but it might as well be at some great distance insofar as many are concerned—for these do not effectively release this divine power of protection into their worlds. The power of God is able to protect man against all the depredations of the sons of Belial (those who pursue a path of iniquity).

"Therefore, I say that the children of mammon, in their own generation, have for too long been 'wiser' than the children of Light![6] We desire ... to give the students greater understanding of the need to invoke their own protection—the protection of the pure in heart upon earth! It is not enough to have individuals clothed with innocence; they must also be sheltered from the infernal blasts of the spoilers."[7]

Armageddon in the World and in the Individual

In the Book of Isaiah and in the Book of Revelation we read of the destruction of Babylon and its rulers[8]—part of the apocalyptic message of Old and New Testament writers. It is a vision that is seen again and again: the alchemy of the judgment and the fall of the mighty and how they are put down, the coming of the remnant and the intercession of God. It is the message of Armageddon. It has a very present definition to our service in this time.

This message of Armageddon contains archetypical patterns that will occur in the life of the soul who becomes the saint, who becomes the Ascended Master. Everyone who has ever ascended has gone through this specific prophecy, perhaps only in the microcosm. Today we are seeing its imminent manifestation in the macrocosm of life upon earth; but if it were not so, if you were living a thousand years ago or you were living on Atlantis or Lemuria, the day that you determined to be God incarnate and to walk the path of your ascension, you would have the confrontation of your personal Armageddon.

Because the Christ is the highest manifestation (in man) of the Presence of God, the battle of Armageddon is more central to the individual than it is to the world. Therefore, there is an action of Armageddon that occurs simultaneously in the world of the advanced disciple and in the world at large. This is an example of the law of correspondence between the Macrocosm and the microcosm. The way of overcoming is the life of the initiate. This way of life is inextricably identified with the battle of Armageddon that is taking place on the world scene.

Our service in this life does not hang on the anticipation that all of these events will be absolutely concrete and physical around us (though all signs point to that fact). In the days following the ascension of Jesus Christ, the early Christians expected the imminent descent, the Second Advent, the destruction of world power, and they did not realize that it was taking place in the very nucleus, in the very heart of those souls who had reached that point on the path of initiation.

Each man has his own Armageddon, and each person and each earth has their own battle of Armageddon, and each solar system has a struggle between the forces of Light and Darkness. In fact, Armageddon began millions of years ago on other systems of worlds.

We are in a time when people are making final choices. The battle of Light and Darkness must be waged and won by us while we are on earth. That is really why we are here today: to solve this problem and to go out and make our voice count for the victory for souls.

El Morya says, "For it is there in the arena of life and of consciousness that you must fight the battle of Armageddon, that you must overcome the hordes of evil, that you must put down all oppressions that you have created against any part of life until, washed pure and clean and robed in fine white linen, you are brought before the Lord of the Universe in the knowledge that you are his son and conductor of his energies."[9]

The Dividing of the Way

Michael, the Prince of the Archangels and our defender in this personal and planetary battle, invites us to his retreat at Banff, Canada, where he gives us keys for the victory: "This is a crossroads of planet Earth and this is where Armageddon must be fought. And it will be fought in the psyche of the individual. It will be in the heart of the individual. It will be in the dweller-on-the-threshold.* That is where Armageddon shall be, beloved, and it shall be multiplied in every individual upon earth.

"And some will be on the side of the forces of Light and our legions and will go after the Lord Christ as he does come. And others will go after the fallen ones. There will be the dividing of the way, but it may not come at all in the way in which Christians interpret it.

"Armageddon is the place where you determine whether you shall be a God-free being or go the way of the fallen ones.

---

* The dweller-on-the-threshold is a term sometimes used to designate the anti-self, the not-self or the synthetic self. It is the antithesis of the Real Self, the conglomerate of the self-created ego. See pp. 214–18. Additional explanation of the dweller may also be found in Mark L. Prophet and Elizabeth Clare Prophet, *The Enemy Within.*

I daresay there is no one in this place who will go the way of the fallen ones consciously. But this I would point out to you: When you do not resolve your psychology and the burdens of your heart and the records of this and past lives, then sometimes your energy goes below the level of the heart, and you may be melancholy, you may be sad, you may be depressed, you may be out of alignment. In those moments, you have left the side of Light and joined the side of Darkness.

"So think of this, beloved. Armageddon is taking place inside of you at this very moment. Most people have a warring in their members, but the dweller-on-the-threshold manages to cover it up. And so that war is never fought and won by the soul, but it is only left there. And that war and that warring is a festering condition within the physical body itself. Many of your problems in the physical body or the emotional body or the mind do come from the nonresolution that you have midst the forces of Light and Darkness.

"Therefore, sometimes when you pay allegiance to me and all the Hosts of Light, I come to you. And at inner levels at my retreat at Banff, I show you and I explain to you that because you have not forthrightly dealt with the issues of the unconscious, you are yet vulnerable. You do not have that certainty of wholeness, and therefore that certainty of your victory and of your ascension.

"Remember the circle around the cross, the circle of wholeness, the cross of white fire. That wholeness is your goal. Then you will be invincible. Then there will not be a part of you that is an open door to burdens of sickness, of darkness, of mourning, of suddenly wanting to go here and there, for you cannot find peace. If you cannot find peace, beloved, it is a serious condition in your psychology.

"Peace must be with you as the Elohim of Peace, as the Prince of Peace, as Uriel, as your Holy Christ Self. The peace that passeth understanding[10]—when you have its full cup, you will reduce your misery and subconscious levels of misery. And then you will realize that God is where you are. You need not go here, go there; for the kingdom of God is fully ensconced within you,[11] and no devil, great or small, can in any way tamper with your state of mind, your project, your goal."[12]

The Personal Armageddon

While the prophecies of scripture have led many people throughout the world to believe that Megiddo in the land of Israel is the biblical, prophetic site of man's final days upon this earth, the word *Armageddon* has also come to mean the personal battlefield of every individual in a spiritual sense; it pertains to the battle between Good and Evil in his own world —the world of his thoughts, or the reflective world spoken of by the contemplatives.

The personal Armageddon may be defined as (1) the spiritual battle that the individual who is becoming the Christ must wage with the dragons of his own past creation (the slings and arrows of hatred, greed, resentment, fear and malice that he has sent forth into the world that have returned to roost in his electronic belt as records of infamy and injustice); and (2) the spiritual battle that the overcomer must wage with forces outside himself that work diligently to betray the Light of every son of God (demons of pride, fallen angels, discarnate entities, witches and black magicians).

The biblical admonishments "Resist not evil" and "Resist the devil, and he will flee from you"[13] must be balanced in the light of the teachings of the Ascended Masters. Evil, the veil of imperfection that shrouds the immortal Light of the soul, must be effectively dealt with by every student if he would ensure his freedom to progress spiritually in the Light.

Everyone who puts his foot on the path of the ascension is opposed by forces from within and from without, both personal and impersonal. Forces from within consist of the pressures of the records of momentums of imperfection carried over from past embodiments as well as the present. From without looms the mass consciousness, that imperfection that draws the individual consciousness down to the lowest common denominator of human vibration. This force may be focused personally as projections of hatred, malice, jealousy, and so on, or it may simply be the impersonal ebb and flow of the tides of human creation.

Whatever the form, whatever the source, none of these forces have any power, presence or permanence—for there is only one Reality, and that is God. Man derives his very life from this Reality, this God. However, insofar as man places his attention upon imperfect conditions, he prolongs the existence of that which is unreal by giving freely of the energies of God's radiant Reality to that which claims a separate identity apart from the Creator.

Because it is man and man alone who originated imperfection through ambition and pride of intellect, it is man and man alone who must undo this false creation by withdrawing those energies of God that he has unwisely invested in incomplete matrices—the products of his incomplete, ego-centered consciousness.

At some time or other we must face ourselves and determine what we are going to make of our life in our personal relationship with God and with this giant aspect of life we see all around us. We have our immediate families. We also behold the many families of nations. We behold the multitudes of people. But when all is said and done, we come down to a *monad*, to an expression of God. We are each a monad. We can never be more than a monad as man or as a manifestation of man. We will always be one.

But in a like manner, when we attain that mystical union with our spiritual Self that enables us to call the Father "Our Father," we will find that there is a flow or exchange of consciousness whereby we become integrated into the Godhead as our personal Armageddon finally ends in the epic manifestation of peace—the true Om, the true Shalom, or the true recognition by man. And what we have to recognize is that through the doorway of our monadic self, through the doorway of our personal self, we must come to that place where each man knows himself, and in knowing himself, knows God.

Two Paths before Mankind

Universal peace is nothing more than a manifestation of universal recognition—where all men come to simultaneously recognize that there is a God of peace and that that God of peace intends men to learn to live together in peace and to pursue those spiritual arts that will ennoble man and raise him up rather than tear down his whole society, wreck his civilization and produce a chaos whereby man almost becomes insane.

The world in which we live is basically and in many parts insane. Many of the actions of men are purposeless when they are viewed from the standpoint of the Divine Godhead. But as we look at them from the perspective of the outer self, we have come to accept them as natural. We say, "This is the way it is." And so we have the present conflicts between the Arab nations and the Jews in Jerusalem and throughout the Holy Land and throughout the world. Yet all these people speak of peace. And it should be that peace comes to them.

There are two potentials before us and before mankind. And instead of peace, we see the potential of deadly destruction, which could well happen at the biblical site of Armageddon. We now live in an era of the atomic bomb. Man has discovered tremendous power. He has discovered how to literally split the world in pieces from a physical, objective, scientific standpoint. Yet the fearfulness and the awesomeness of that bomb has come to be regarded by scientists and political and religious leaders of the world as being an activity that strikes terror into the hearts of the people so that they say, "Of what value is this bomb?"

Hence, we may come to an era when there will be the banning of that bomb and the destruction of the world will be by the return of mankind to conventional warfare. Should conventional warfare be adopted once again by the nations as the means of settling their supposed differences, we may well see in the biblical site of Armageddon the full manifestation of that which has been prophesied. Therefore, do not be too quick to say the battle of Armageddon that has been prophesied will never take place.

However, we do not believe in a predestination that does not allow the exercise of man's free will. For until an event is crystallized, it still can be changed. And the Great White Brotherhood in its outpicturing of life to the planetary body is always trying to create those aspects of living that will enable men to live together in peace.

Two thousand years ago Jesus Christ came forth and walked with his disciples over the hills of Judea. His coming was a purposeful manifestation of peace to the earth and the extension of Light unto the planetary body. The fact that he was slain is only a proof to all of us that any time that you have an actor upon the stage of life who is sent forth by the Great White Brotherhood, you may well expect that that actor, that son of God, that manifestation of the One Life, may well find himself being misunderstood, may well find himself cast down so that the work that he does may be destroyed. This is the purpose, then, of those dark ones who desire to destroy our peace upon the planetary body. They would prevent it.

Let us understand, then, that Armageddon may happen. Let us understand, in any case, that certainly the spiritual Armageddon will happen, has happened, is happening all at once and right now.

Through our understanding of this, we will recognize our opportunity, wherever we are, whatever day we are living in, that we can, through the power of prayer and the power of banding together in the Light, demand of the Godhead (in the manner of the woman and the unjust judge[14]) that heaven shall, in extending its arms of mercy to the earth, provide our deliverance and the deliverance of the land of Israel itself from that activity that is destructive. And we may hope that we may enter a realm when the greatest constructivity will be possible because men truly understand the meaning of love.

The Intertwining of Personal and World Karma

The personal Armageddon must be fought and won by every soul—not in one final glory, but in the daily overcoming of his own human creation. Of the daily allotment of karma that must be balanced by the disciple if he would progress toward his ascension, Jesus said, "Sufficient unto the day is the evil thereof."[15]

The Lords of Karma have set the pattern of returning karma for each individual, for each nation and for the planet as a whole. This is the method of mercy that gauges the rate of the return of the individual's own misqualified energy according to the strength of the soul. Thus, the blessing of Moses was based on a scientific principle of karmic law: "As thy days, so shall thy strength be."[16]

The intertwining of the karma of the Lightbearers and the fallen ones is being outplayed today on a world scale. You cannot ultimately balance your personal karma unless you see it juxtaposed against the background of world karma. What is that world karma we are facing? We all embodied knowing the great weight of this era, and we knew that we had to get through our selves and our entanglements and where we lost ground in past lives by giving in to or forming alliances with dark ones. We lost a certain amount of our power, the power we had when we were in heaven before we touched earth.

The karma we make also has to do with the initiations we are willing to take, how much sacrifice and service we are willing to give. The more we integrate with God, the more we are the masters of our karma instead of the slaves of it and the less karma we make. When we decide to stop making karma and pick up the pieces, we start walking back to the Sun instead of walking away from the Sun. We then reap what we have sown, but we can do it with mastery through the violet flame and the science of the spoken Word. The way to avoid making more karma is the eightfold path of the Buddha and the way of Christ, and our mission is to internalize the Christ and weave the paths of the Christ and Buddha.

It was Saint Germain who first introduced the science of decrees[17] in the twentieth century. Through his devotion to the freedom of man, this method of prayer has become widely used by those desiring to undo their past mistakes. Thus we return unto the Father the energy he has vouchsafed unto man, purified by the violet fire and freed from the misqualifications of thought and feeling that mortals are so prone to superimpose upon the Real (thus casting the Divine in the mold of their imperfect vision).

Above all, everyone who goes forth to do battle with the Goliath of human creation must remember the very first precepts of Ascended Master Law: God is the only Reality, the only life and the only power in the universe. God and man are inseparable as the Divine One. All that has determined to manifest imperfection has placed itself outside of this oneness, far afield from God's saving grace—until it elects to return to the state of divine union.

Those imperfect models of creation that have set up an existence apart from God must one day relinquish the energies they have pirated from the Deity, for their existence outside of him is a myth. He who is always conscious of God within as Real, always aware that naught else has the power to oppose the divine will, shall emerge from the fray victorious, the master of life.

The Dweller-on-the-Threshold

When we come to the point of dealing with our human creation, we will encounter what has been called the "dweller-on-the-threshold." We all have a dweller-on-the-threshold, and its definition is the accumulated negativity of our lifestreams since we fell from grace. This dweller is the focal point of the consciousness behind the human creation—the mind behind the manifestation.

This term has been adopted by the Brotherhood because it conveys the meaning that it sits at the threshold of self-awareness where the elements of the subconscious cross the line from the unconscious to the conscious world of the individual, and the unknown not-self becomes the known. Once surfaced, the dweller has entered the realm of the conscious will where, through the decision-making faculties of mind and heart, the soul may choose either to "ensoul" or to slay the components of this antithesis of his Real Self.

There comes a time in the life of the individual who contacts the Path, the Masters or their representatives when he comes face-to-face with Christ and anti-Christ—Christ in the person of the man of God and anti-Christ in the personal dweller-on-the-threshold within himself—and he may see both face-to-face.

Now this usually does not happen the very day of the encounter with the Great White Brotherhood, but by and by it does occur. And sometimes people manage to follow the Masters and the Path and the teachings for many years without experiencing the confrontation. Either they avoid it or they try to avoid the appearance of having had the confrontation, but ultimately when the Masters determine to do so, they will force the confrontation and force their chelas to make a choice between the Christ Self and the dweller.

This may occur at any time on the Path. People sense this, and therefore they avoid all contact with the Great White Brotherhood or its agents. They even take up arms against it, thinking to thwart the Law and the inevitable Day of Reckoning.

This was so for Saul on the road to Damascus. In this case it was the Master Jesus who forced the encounter, and Saul was blinded in the alchemical process of the Light confounding the darkness. Jesus made Saul choose between his dweller, the anti-Christ or anti-Self who was persecuting the Christians, and his Real Self personified and represented in the Ascended Master Jesus Christ.

When he chose his Lord, he chose the path of discipleship leading to individual Christhood. And the Master bound his dweller until he himself should slay it "in the last day" of his karma. Endued with the power of Christ in his Guru Jesus, Saul, now called Paul (having put off the old man and put on the new), went forth to witness to the Truth that had set him free from his own momentum of human creation and the human mind that created it—the dweller-on-the-threshold.[18]

From his personal confrontation and conversion by the Lord, Paul was later able to tell the Romans with the conviction that comes only from experience: "To be carnally minded is death; but to be spiritually minded is life and peace. Because the carnal mind is enmity against God: for it is not subject to the law of God, neither indeed can be."[19]

There is, on the road of self-mastery, the initiation that comes nigh the point of the crucifixion, when the individual has considerable Christ attainment as well as balanced karma and is required to slay that dweller totally and utterly. Jesus could not have been on the cross had he not slain the dweller. His illustration of slaying the dweller was his wilderness confrontation with Satan three years before the crucifixion.[20] That was the planetary dweller-on-the-threshold: Satan himself—the personification and sign of everyone's personal dweller.

Later, the Son of God dealt with the planetary dweller again in his confrontation with the Watchers and the Nephilim —the chief priests and Pharisees, the elders of the people and the powers of Rome. This was possible only because he had already slain the personal dweller. This is why he said, "The prince of this world cometh and hath [findeth] nothing in me."[21]

The planetary momentum of the dweller-on-the-threshold —the collective undefined unconscious of all evolutions of the planet—can and does move against the individual who has not yet slain his personal carnal mind. What this means is the obvious—that most people come under the influence of the mass consciousness daily. And the more they have conquered the wiles of their own not-self, the less influenced they will be by the ups and downs of world turmoil.

Nevertheless, the planetary momentum will tie into and activate the personal anti-Christ to catch off-guard even the souls nearest their victory over the beast. At that moment the individual must slay not only the personal carnal mind, but in so slaying it, drive back the planetary momentum and overcome the original Liar as well as the lie that the originator of Evil has propagated in his seed.

There is a planetary dweller, there is a galactic dweller and there is a dweller inside of us; and we must recognize that evil is real until it is destroyed, because in order to make our ascension, we have to conquer not only our own dweller, but every fallen angel that would come between us and that ascension.

You may day by day resist the temptations of your carnal mind and of the planetary dweller, but you may not have completely slain the personal representative of the Evil One. Thus, there is a point of winning on each occasion of the overcoming, and then there is the point of winning ultimately because the entire beast has been slain.

Since we have through many lifetimes literally surrendered our God-energy and endowed this creation with this power, the dweller has become much bigger than the individual. So now we cannot slay it of ourselves. The serpent or serpentine mind is a clever mind, a deceiving mind. Therefore we need a Guru who is an Ascended Master, an Archangel, an Elohim, a Cosmic Being; we need the entire Spirit of the Great White Brotherhood to slay this beast that has become more powerful than we are. When we fasten ourselves to one of these great God-free beings and say, "I will serve the cause of God on the path of this being," that being then, according to our daily efforts, begins to help bear our karma and to help us slay elements of the not-self.

The Ascended Master John the Beloved explains that it is love that is necessary to enter into this challenge: "It has been said that the Gospel that I wrote and the Epistles, even as I recorded Jesus' Revelation, the final book of the New Testament, are mystical in nature and appeal to the mystics of all ages. Truly it is so, for that which I have written is written out of the Sacred Heart of Jesus.

"These teachings and my witness are a witness of love and of a love that gave me the ability to see beyond this plane into many octaves of the etheric and even into Death and Hell, wherefore I could record scenes taking place in the Great Central Sun at the throne of God even as I could record scenes shown to me in the very depths of the degradations of hell.

"These mysteries cannot be seen and felt and known tangibly except you have embraced love and a path of initiation. You must be locked in the grip of love, of your Christ Self in Jesus, as well as in that Armageddon, seeing it through to the end of the carnal mind and the dweller-on-the-threshold, whether of yourself or another or the planet.

"When you are engaged in both absolute Reality and absolute Unreality, then your vision by love can span all dimensions. But when you are not, then your vision is limited, the senses of the soul are not awakened, the third eye has no clear vision. For, beloved, God does not open the kingdom of heaven to you unless he also open the depths of hell....

"Understand, then, beloved, that those who truly love will not fear the embrace of Christ or the challenge of Death and Hell."[22]

Evolutions of Light and Darkness

And he said unto them,
Ye are from beneath; I am
from above.

GOSPEL OF JOHN

I N THEIR INTERPRETATIONS OF THE age-old mysteries, people must bear testimony to divine justice. And just as his sheep know his voice and follow him, so does the Father know his own sheep.

In holy writ, God has spoken through the Christ and other teachers describing the son of man, the son of God, the children of God, the children of the Light and the children of Belial (or the children of darkness). Some men have been called the children of God while others have been called the children of the devil. What is implied in these statements, and why does such a differentiation occur? Clarification of this mystery will help us to see how the lines of Armageddon have been drawn.

A **son of God** or a **daughter of God** has a Divine Presence, separate and distinct from the human personality and the human flesh form. (See the Chart of Your Divine Self, facing page 76.) The radiation of his I AM Presence is either a latent or a manifest image shining through the flesh form. The term *son of man* (meaning "son of *mani*festation") refers to the natural order of physical generation. A son of man is also a son of God whenever he expresses the ideals of his own Divine Presence.

The appellation "son of God" implies a certain degree of self-mastery, a certain ability to let the Light of the spiritual Sun shine through the four lower bodies. One who is called a son of God has earned the name by successfully passing certain initiatic degrees. Sonship, therefore, is an office in Hierarchy. It signifies that the holder is a Christed one in whom the threefold flame blazes in balanced action, one who can baptize with the power of the Holy Ghost and with fire.[1]

Children of God are sons of God in the making. As offspring of the Father, they have the full potential to attain to the stature of divine sonship.

The Soulless Ones

The **children of darkness** and the **sons of Belial**—those who are of their father, the devil[2]—are of an entirely different origin than the children of God. They were synthetically created (using genetic engineering) by advanced scientists of past ages who came to earth from other planets. These robot creations were carefully adapted to their physical environment. They were endowed with a certain mechanical brilliance in science, technology and business administration.

In physical stature these robots were designed to intimidate "mere mortals." Slightly taller and larger in bone structure than the average child of God, these automatons have a rather dead mechanical beauty (a glassy-eyed look) that has become the vogue in certain circles. The term "beautiful people" points to the desire of their creators to endow the flesh with a beauty and a glamour all its own, instead of making the physical body transparent for the beauty and virtue of God to shine through.

It is most difficult for the average person to distinguish between a son of God and a son of Belial. The chief difference is discernable only with the inner eye, for automatons do not have a threefold flame, a Holy Christ Self or a God Presence. Therefore, they have no direct tie to the Father Supreme.

Intermarriage between the children of Light and the children of darkness has brought about an adulteration of the divine fires within man, a weakening of the high integrity and natural morality of the sons of God and a looseness in the codes of society that has enabled the powers of darkness to obtain a foothold of great magnitude in world affairs.[3] It was to this end that the robots were created in the first place—for without the infiltration of a Luciferian creation into society, the children of God would have naturally ascended in consciousness toward their Father. The Light that is within a child of God is magnetized by the currents of the Great Central Sun, whereas the Light (the energy of God) that was used to create the sons of Belial has become darkness through misqualification. ("If therefore the light that is in thee be darkness, how great is that darkness!"[4])

Both the sons of God and the sons of Belial have certain power in the world of form that is manifest in their bearing, and the masses of humanity (the children of God) are often subject to the control of both. The sons of God are spiritually minded people who have awakened and quickened their spiritual senses in order to serve the hierarchical plan. The sons of Belial, also known as the **Luciferian creation** or the **godless creation**, are conscious of their "superiority" to the children of God. They use their dark powers as archdeceivers and manipulators of the race. They have organized and now control large corporations, the banking systems of the world and the multimillion-dollar international crime machines.

The sons of Belial embraced the Cult of Hedon because they had nothing else to live for but pleasure. Their motto was "Eat, drink and be merry, for tomorrow we die." They use the endless distractions of the cult of pleasure as time occupiers and energy stealers to capture the souls of men.

They do not excel as practitioners of black magic, but they are the principal tools of the black magicians. They are programmed to work against the Christ at every turn, wherever there are children of God working for freedom in its many aspects. These fallen ones use political bribery, fear tactics, threats, intimidation and even murder to maintain control of government bodies and the destiny of nations. In all wars they play both sides against the middle, profiting from the sale of munitions to both factions and using the politics of war to gain their ends in social and economic policy.

The sons of Belial brought about the French Revolution to destroy throughout Europe the vested authority of the divine right of kings. Since civilization first began, the succession of sons of God as leaders of the people had been the Hierarchy's means of ensuring the perpetuation on earth of a divine government—*God-over-men*—the sons of God being *God's overmen.* When the dark ones could not control the sons of God who were appointed to rule, they sometimes kidnapped their children within hours of their birth and replaced them with ones of their own. Eventually, the lineage of royal families became predominantly of this dark origin. Thus they could easily be controlled from astral planes by black magicians.

It was their scheme to make the concept of monarchy so obnoxious to the people that, with a little prodding from eighteenth-century philosophers, the people would rise up en masse to overthrow their overlords. The robots fit the mold very nicely, for by nature they were pleasure-seeking, immoral, selfish and greedy. Thus, the children of God became disillusioned with the divine system of government because it failed to work in the hands of the robots and those sons of God who had been won over to their ways. The fact that the majority of Christians would accept Jesus Christ as their king and as the ruler of the world shows that it is not the monarchical system that was challenged but those who abused the system.

Democratic thinking has brought people to the place where they no longer have respect for the sons of God as divinely vested to rule. This concept is just one more method whereby the sons of Belial can control the destiny of nations. They first brainwash the people to their ideas—making them believe they are their own—and then they declare that the majority knows best. Once they have reduced mankind to a common denominator that is only slightly better than animals, they put out the theory that mankind are no longer fit to rule themselves but require an intellectual elite to do their thinking, make their decisions and program their lives. And so we have an oligarchy of darkness replacing the monarchies of divinely anointed ones, as in the case of the Russian Revolution and its aftermath.

The enemies of righteousness (the children of Belial, reinforced by the bestial forces in mankind) tend to support one another and to rally to any standard that will dethrone the sons of God and prevent them from carrying on an activity of liberation for all men. Even so, by the grace and mercy of God, there are provisions in the Hierarchy for the redemption of soulless beings. Thank God that no part of life is bereft of the ministrations of the angels of hope. By committing their energies to the will of God, right action and the drawing forth of the flames from the heart of God, these mechanical men can be granted, by cosmic dispensation, the right to weave a soul in the glorious Image of God. They may magnetize soul-substance through every thought, word and deed that is consecrated to the Christ.

They may accelerate their progress under sponsors (Ascended or unascended) who assist them in the spiritualization of their consciousness. As a part of their training, the sons of Belial are given the same tests that the sons of God are required to pass. When they have demonstrated sufficiently to the Karmic Board their willingness to serve the Light and to be free from their past, they are awarded a threefold flame. And the Father, who has given to his creation a replica of himself, magnetizes a focus of the I AM Presence and Holy Christ Self for the stranger who aspires to enter into heaven.[5]

It is never the will of God that anyone should perish, for did he not say, "I have no pleasure in the death of the wicked"?[6] God is the Source of all life. Since the energies that were used to create the "beautiful people" were God's energies, they too are a part of him. Since all derive their energy from him, it is his will that all should be given the opportunity to save themselves from becoming castaways.

Life's opportunities are many, and the mercy of God has gone to great lengths for mankind so that men can image the power of His love. Nevertheless, He has clearly said, "My spirit shall not always strive with man, for that he also is flesh"[7]—indicating God's desire to free man from human vanity and the banality of purposeless mortal aims.

Fallen Angels

In the first few centuries after Christ, Church Fathers were philosophizing on the origin of evil in God's universe—especially on earth. All agreed that evil was rooted in the angels who fell from heaven—the familiar scriptural account of an Archangel's rebellion against the Almighty and the angels who were cast out with him:

> And there was war in heaven: Michael and his angels fought against the dragon; and the dragon fought and his angels, and prevailed not; neither was their place found any more in heaven. And the great dragon was cast out, that old serpent, called the Devil, and Satan, which deceiveth the whole world: he was cast out into the earth, and his angels were cast out with him.
>
> And I heard a loud voice saying in heaven, Now is come salvation and strength, and the kingdom of our God, and the power of his Christ: for the accuser of our brethren is cast down, which accused them before our God day and night. And they overcame him by the blood of the Lamb, and by the word of their testimony; and they loved not their lives unto the death.
>
> Therefore rejoice, ye heavens, and ye that dwell in them. Woe to the inhabiters of the earth and of the sea! for the devil is come down unto you, having great wrath, because he knoweth that he hath but a short time.[8]

Thus we see in chapter 12 of the Book of Revelation that Archangel Michael and his legions cast out that Fallen One and his angels. They did not want to be cast down. They wanted to have their rebellion and they wanted to remain in heaven. It took a battle, a heavenly battle, a galactic Armageddon, for Archangel Michael to force these fallen ones out of heaven and into the planes of the earth, fulfilling the law that everyone must be evolving at the state of his consciousness. Wherever the tree falls, it must lie. To whatever lowly estate consciousness descends, that is where it must embody.

Usually these angels who were cast out of heaven were depicted as immaterial, winged creatures, dark and shadowy demons tempting man to err, whispering wicked thoughts into his ear. But certain key passages in the holy books indicated that there might be more substance—literally and physically—to the fallen angels.

The materiality of angels seems to have been an age-old belief. There was the angel with whom Jacob wrestled—physical enough to cripple him at least temporarily, if not for life. So tangible was this angel that the author of the Book of Genesis calls him a man, although elsewhere scripture reveals that he was an angel.[9] The "angel" said to Jacob, "Let me go, for the day breaketh." How could Jacob have had hold upon an incorporeal angel?

The angels who came to visit Sodom had to be bolted indoors in Lot's house in order to protect them from an intended sexual assault by local townspeople—Sodomites who wanted to get to "know" the angels.[10]

And Manoah offered to cook dinner for his guest—presumed to be an ordinary man until he ascended to heaven in the fire Manoah had lit. Only then did Manoah know that the "man of God" was "an angel of the LORD."[11]

The bad angels, the fallen ones, were no less physical, according to certain religious scriptures of the world.

Zarathustra, the great Persian prophet, reportedly dashed the angels' bodies to pieces because they had used them to wreak evil. The angels (according to the story) had instigated illicit love affairs with earthly women—hard to accomplish without physical bodies, especially since the tale attributed offspring to them.[12] The story of corporeal angels, despite its questionability, at least made sense of scripture and legend.

The leader of the angels who fell was known as Lucifer.

We read of him in Isaiah chapter 14:

> How art thou fallen from heaven, O Lucifer, son of the morning! how art thou cut down to the ground, which didst weaken the nations! For thou hast said in thine heart, I will ascend into heaven, I will exalt my throne above the stars of God: I will sit also upon the mount of the congregation, in the sides of the north: I will ascend above the heights of the clouds; I will be like the most High.
>
> Yet thou shalt be brought down to hell, to the sides of the pit. They that see thee shall narrowly look upon thee, and consider thee, saying, Is this the man that made the earth to tremble, that did shake kingdoms; that made the world as a wilderness, and destroyed the cities thereof; that opened not the house of his prisoners?
>
> All the kings of the nations, even all of them, lie in glory, every one in his own house. But thou art cast out of thy grave like an abominable branch, and as the raiment of those that are slain, thrust through with a sword, that go down to the stones of the pit; as a carcase trodden under feet.
>
> Thou shalt not be joined with them in burial, because thou hast destroyed thy land, and slain thy people: the seed of evildoers shall never be renowned.

Thus we see in Isaiah and Revelation the familiar story of the fall of the Archangel through pride, and how "his tail drew the third part of the stars of heaven," one third of the angels of heaven, "and did cast them to the earth."[13]

However, there is another, different account of the fall of angels that is found in the Bible, and most clearly in the ancient text known as the Book of Enoch. In fact, the Book of Enoch gives us a key to understanding the history of men and angels in this and other systems of worlds.[14]

The Watchers

The Book of Enoch speaks from that obscure realm where history and mythology overlap. Privy to those unfathomable founts of ancient lore, its author draws for the reader a brimming cup of secret wisdom. A primordial drama of Good and Evil, Light and Dark, unfolds. The book tracks Enoch's footsteps back to antiquity's timelessness—back to the first hint of corruption upon a pristine world: earth.

The trouble began, according to the Book of Enoch, when the heavenly angels and their leader named Samyaza developed an insatiable lust for the "daughters of men" upon earth and an irrepressible desire to beget children by these women. Samyaza feared to descend alone to the daughters of men, and so he convinced two hundred angels called Watchers to accompany him on his mission of pleasure.

Then the angels took oaths and bound themselves to the undertaking by "mutual execrations"—curses. Once such a pact was sealed, betrayal was punishable by unnamed horrors. In their gang-inspired bravado, the angels descended and took wives from among the daughters of men. They taught the women sorcery, incantations and divination—twisted versions of the secrets of heaven.

The women conceived children from these angels—evil giants. The giants devoured all the food that the men of earth could produce. Nothing satiated their hunger. They killed and ate birds, beasts, reptiles and fish. To their gargantuan appetites, nothing was sacrosanct. Soon even *Homo sapiens* became a delicacy.[15]

One spiteful angel named Azazyel created unnatural accoutrements for their consorts—like eye makeup and fancy bracelets—to enhance their sex appeal. As for the men, Azazyel taught them "every species of iniquity," including the means for making swords, knives, shields, breastplates—all the instruments of war.[16]

There, millennia ago, someone explained war not as a man-invented or God-sent plague, but as a vengeful act of a fallen angel barred from the planes of God's power. The implication is that man, through one form of manipulation or another, latched on to the war games of the fallen angels and allowed himself to commit genocide in defense of their archrivalries.

But there is more to Enoch's account of the Watchers. When the men of earth cry out against the atrocities heaped upon them, heaven hears their plea. The mighty Archangels—Michael, Gabriel, Raphael, Suryal and Uriel—appeal on behalf of earth's people before the Most High, the King of kings.[17]

The LORD orders Raphael to bind Azazyel hand and foot. Gabriel is sent to destroy the "children of fornication"—the offspring of the Watchers—by inciting them to their own self-destruction in mutual slaughter. Michael is then authorized to bind Samyaza and his wicked offspring "for seventy generations underneath the earth, even to the day of judgment."[18] And God sends the Great Flood to wipe out the evil giants, the children of the Watchers.

But in succeeding generations (after the Flood, which we also know as the sinking of the continent of Atlantis) the giants return once again to haunt mankind. Likewise it seems that the Watchers will hold power over man (in some curiously undefined way) until the final judgment of these angels comes, which, the author implies, is long overdue.

There is also a most significant passage near the end of the book that speaks of the latter days upon earth:

> In those days will the angels return and hurl themselves upon the East,... to stir up the kings and provoke in them a spirit of unrest....
>
> And they will march up to and tread under foot the land of His elect ones....
>
> They will begin to fight amongst themselves ... till the number of corpses through their slaughter is beyond count, and their punishment be no idle one.[19]

This seems a chilling prophecy of our own time—with wars and rumors of wars in "the East" and the countless corpses in a holy land. There is no date stamped on the prediction, but a few word changes in the right places would make it duplicate today's headlines.

The main theme of the Book of Enoch is the final judgment of these fallen angels, the Watchers, and their progeny, the evil spirits. In chapter 15, the LORD explains to Enoch the nature of the offspring of the Watchers and the evil that they wreak upon the earth:

> Now the giants, who have been born of spirit and of flesh, shall be called upon earth evil spirits, and on earth shall be their habitation. Evil spirits shall proceed from their flesh, because they were created from above; from the holy Watchers was their beginning and primary foundation. Evil spirits shall they be upon earth, and the spirits of the wicked shall they be called. The habitation of the spirits of heaven shall be in heaven; but upon earth shall be the habitation of terrestrial spirits, who are born on earth.
>
> The spirits of the giants shall be like clouds, which shall oppress, corrupt, fall, contend, and

bruise upon earth.

They shall cause lamentation. No food shall they eat; and they shall be thirsty; they shall be concealed, and shall not rise up against the sons of men, and against women; for they come forth during the days of slaughter and destruction.

And as to the death of the giants, wheresoever their spirits depart from their bodies, let their flesh, that which is perishable, be without judgment. Thus shall they perish, until the day of the great consummation of the great world. A destruction shall take place of the Watchers and the impious.[20]

Because of so great a sin, the LORD tells the Watchers, "Never therefore shall you obtain peace." (16:5) According to the text of the Book of Enoch, the LORD's judgment against the Watchers prevails—then and now.

The author of the book also describes in powerful majesty and moving praise certain visions of heaven given to him. He writes of his instruction from the Archangels regarding the awesome judgment of the fallen ones before God's throne. He delivers three heavenly parables (or similitudes) describing the glories of the Kingdom and the ineffable Ancient of Days and the Son of man who, it is said, shall bring the final judgment upon the wicked of the earth.

There are many passages in the Old and New Testaments that echo the Book of Enoch.[21] The Epistle of Jude clearly discusses the content of the Book of Enoch, noting that

> ... there are certain men crept in unawares, who were before of old ordained to this condemnation, ungodly men, turning the grace of our God into lasciviousness....
>
> These are spots in your feasts of charity, when

they feast with you, feeding themselves without fear: clouds they are without water, carried about of winds; trees whose fruit withereth, without fruit, twice dead, plucked up by the roots; raging waves of the sea, foaming out their own shame; wandering stars, to whom is reserved the blackness of darkness for ever.[22]

Jude actually quotes Enoch directly and refers to him by name, saying:

And Enoch also, the seventh from Adam, prophesied of these, saying, Behold, the Lord cometh with ten thousands of his saints, to execute judgment upon all, and to convince all that are ungodly among them of all their ungodly deeds which they have ungodly committed, and of all their hard speeches which ungodly sinners have spoken against him.[23]

Another biblical parallel to Enoch occurs in Genesis 6, in one of the most puzzling passages in scripture:

And it came to pass, when men began to multiply on the face of the earth, and daughters were born unto them, that the sons of God saw the daughters of men that they were fair; and they took them wives of all which they chose.

And the LORD said, My spirit shall not always strive with man, for that he also is flesh: yet his days shall be an hundred and twenty years.

There were giants in the earth in those days; and also after that, when the sons of God came in unto the daughters of men, and they bare children to them, the same became mighty men which were of old, men of renown.

The twentieth-century discovery of several Aramaic Enoch texts among the Dead Sea Scrolls prompted Catholic scholar J. T. Milik to compile a complete history of the Enoch legends, including translations of the Aramaic manuscripts. Milik's 400-page book, published in 1976 by Oxford,[24] is a milestone in Enochian scholarship, and Milik himself is no doubt one of the world's finest experts on the subject. His opinions, based as they are on years of in-depth research, are highly respected.

Milik notes the obviously close interdependence of the story of the fallen angels in Enoch and the story of the "sons of God"[25] in the Book of Genesis. But he does not draw the same conclusion as the Church Fathers, namely that the Book of Enoch misinterpreted the earlier Genesis account and was therefore irrelevant. Milik, rather, arrives at a surprising yet well-justified conclusion: that not only is the history of the fallen angels in Enoch older than Genesis 6—but Genesis 6 is in fact a direct summary of the earlier Enoch account. This is what Milik calls the "ineluctable solution": it is Genesis 6 that is based on Enoch and not the other way around. Milik thinks that the text of Genesis 6, by its abridged and allusive formulation and direct quoting of two or three phrases of Enoch, must be the later of the two, making the Enoch legend earlier than the definitive chapters in Genesis.[26]

Two Separate Falls of the Angels

In an unparalleled and detailed probing into the specific meaning of this passage, Hebrew scholar Julian Morgenstern discovered that tied up in the Genesis verses are traces of "two distinct and originally entirely unrelated myths dealing with gods or angels."[27]

In his remarkable exegesis, Morgenstern proves that originally two accounts of separate "falls" of the angels were known: one, that of the Archangel's rebellion against the authority of God and his subsequent fall through pride, in which he was followed by a multitude of lesser angels, biblically called the *Nephilim* (the "fallen ones"); and two, the other account, recorded faithfully in the Book of Enoch—the later fall of the angels, called *Watchers,* through inordinate lust for the daughters of men.[28] And so, Morgenstern concludes, the angels fell not once but twice.

Morgenstern explains that the very construction of Genesis 6:4, one of the most intricate and obscure Old Testament verses, implies that it is referencing two events simultaneously. The verse reads, in literal English:

> The Nephilim were on the earth at that time (and even afterward) when the sons of God resorted to the daughters of men, and had children by them.[29]

The text specifically sets side by side two facts: one, there used to be beings called "Nephilim" on earth; and two, they were still around when the sons of God came down and mated with the daughters of men. Clearly, says Morgenstern, the Nephilim are fallen angels who were *already* on the earth when the sons of God—the other angels that Enoch depicted—also fell through their own lust.

But how did the Nephilim fallen angels get here to earth in the first place? That, states Morgenstern, is where the story of the rebellious Archangel, Lucifer, and the fall through pride fits in. That is the earlier of two entirely separate celestial events.[30]

The Nephilim

What seems to have caused scriptural confusion in later times is the many-faceted meaning of the word *Nephilim*. The synopsis in Genesis 6 is so terse and abbreviated that it apparently became all but unreadable to later Jews. Some seem to have thought the Nephilim were the same as the "sons of God" in that verse, while others thought the Nephilim were the evil children of the sons of God and the daughters of men. The latter misunderstanding cropped up in the Book of Jubilees and in some editions of the Enoch material.[31]

On top of this confusion, the Greek Septuagint, a late translation of the Hebrew Scriptures, rendered the word *Nephilim* as "giants," eliminating all connotations of "fallen angels." The evil giant children born to the angels and daughters of men were known to the Hebrews specifically as *Gibborim* (literally "heroes" or "mighty men"), but later editors, in the confusion, mixed up the Nephilim with these Gibborim and also with the giants of Numbers 13:33, the Anakim.[32]

Morgenstern further notes that the term *Nephilim* is in the passive voice, i.e., "those who were made to fall" or "those who were cast down."[33] The New Testament Greek term *eblēthēsan* conveys precisely the same meaning. ("And the great dragon was *cast out,* that old serpent, called the Devil, and Satan, which deceiveth the whole world: he was *cast out* into the earth, and his angels were *cast out* with him."[34])

This form of the word *Nephilim* is entirely different from the active voice of the verbal form, i.e., *Nophelim,* those who fell of their own accord or in a natural manner. Elsewhere the Bible confirms that these fallen ones were "cast down" and "delivered into chains of darkness"[35]—they did not descend by their own free will but were forcibly removed from heaven.

In time, it appears, the original meaning of the term *Nephilim* (the "cast-down ones") became more generalized and applied to whoever or whatever was wicked. Thus, the giant Gibborim born to the lustful angels (the Watchers) and the daughters of men might have been labeled "Nephilim" simply because they were of fallen character like the original Nephilim who already walked the earth and seemed like "giants" in their own right.

With so many definitions and misunderstandings piled on top of the word, it is not surprising that the history of the original Nephilim who fell with the Archangel through pride got lost in the translation. But the account in Revelation 12 is well worth examining. The angels, who had fallen in rank with the fall of the proud Archangel, were forced to surrender their position in the Hierarchy of heaven by none other than Archangel Michael. This "great prince"[36] of the celestial orders had to wage a cosmic war and engage in direct combat with the rebels in order to force them to surrender their position.

The Gospel of Bartholomew elaborates upon the reason for the Archangel's fall. This apocryphal work explains that the Archangel revealed his pride when he refused to bend the knee (to confess the Christ) before the man made by the LORD.

The account in Revelation 12 gives force to this apocryphal theme. The great dragon in Revelation, "called the Devil, and Satan" is threatened by the birth of the manchild to the woman "clothed with the sun" and therefore seeks "to devour her child as soon as it is born." The dragon's disrespect for the manchild, son of the woman and son of God, cost him his high rung on the ladder of heavenly Hierarchy.

The same proud refusal to bend the knee before God's newly created man is evident in the Gospel of Bartholomew. "I am fire of fire," boasts the Archangel, "I was the first angel formed, and shall I worship clay and matter?"[37] His refusal to worship the man—as the son of God—was the original act of the angels' rebellion.

The apocryphal Book of John the Evangelist contains a description of the consequences of the Archangel's pride:

physical incarnation. The apostle John asks the Lord, "When Satan fell, in what place dwelt he?" The Lord replies, "My Father changed his appearance, because of his pride, and the light was taken from him, and his face became like unto heated iron, and his face became wholly *like that of a man.*"[38]

Revelation 12:9 ("he was cast out *into the earth*") confirms the physical incarnation of the Nephilim in the earth plane in earth bodies. Genesis 6:4 confirms not only the physical incarnation of the Nephilim (the "giants" *in the earth*) but also that of the Watchers, as we have seen. So, not only were there two falls—there were two (or at least two) separate incarnations of fallen angels upon earth. The Nephilim were "made to fall" or "cast down"; the Watchers "fell" of their own accord—we might therefore call the latter *Nophelim*.

The seeming contradiction between two falls of angels, eventually used by the Church Fathers in their attempts to discredit the Book of Enoch, disappears if there are separate stories of two falls: one through pride and one through lust. Sentenced to earthly life, the angels thereafter became as mortal men. From the original prototype, they have cloned and carbon-copied an oppressive godless power elite. These fallen ones, together with the progeny of the Nephilim, have continued to embody on earth without interruption for at least half a million years.

These facts, although exposed in the forgotten manuscripts of the Book of Enoch and mentioned occasionally throughout the Old and New Testament scriptures, have been concealed from the children of the Light for thousands of years by deliberate design.

The Power Elite

The Bible records that Enoch "walked with God: and he was not; for God took him."[39] We know him today as the

Ascended Master Enoch, and he comes again to reveal the plots of the fallen ones and to give further explanation of the teachings found in the Book of Enoch: "Understand, then, the mystery that is so clearly written in my book. These Watchers came down lusting after the daughters of men,[40] who themselves were defiled and entered into the defilement of the holy angels. These daughters of men were the very ones who were the offspring of the Nephilim—Nephilim who had descended even before the hour of the Watchers for the violation of the seed of God. And in their lust for power, they themselves took the seed of God and combined it with the seed of animal and therefore produced neither a god nor a man but a devil incarnate, even the evil spirits.[41]

"Thus, these daughters that were the offspring became the focal point of verily what has been called animal magnetism— the animal element of *Homo erectus* and the magnetism even of the Great Central Sun Magnet that is contained in the holy seed of holy angels. Thus, without authority, these fallen ones established the enthronement of the carnal mind. They created not god, not animal, not man, but what has been called a *kind of man,* a race of *mankind* hewn out of the rock of Light and yet enslaved by the lesser creation.

"And whence cometh the lesser creation? It is also the product of genetic manipulation. And therefore one can look back and further back and discover these self-styled Darwin-ians[42] who, in the very origination of the evil of their hearts,[43] determined to enslave the Christic Light 'gainst whom they rebelled in the courts of heaven.

"Thus, there are levels of rebels called fallen ones. And the Watchers represented a class all of their own who responded to the lust of power, to the mockery of God, to the entering in of the misuse of the life-force itself."[44]

These fallen ones are with us today in positions of power

in Church and State as prime movers in matters of war and finance, sitting in the banking houses and on policy-making councils that determine the actual fate of mankind by population control and genetic engineering, the control of energy and commodities, education and the media, and by ideological and psychopolitical strategies of divide and conquer on all fronts. They have been from the beginning the spoilers of the dream of God and man. This is an ancient conspiracy that is still with the mankind of earth and will be with us until children of the Light receive the true knowledge concerning the seed of the Wicked One and the seed of the son of God.

The Watchers are always the ones at the top and behind the scenes, and they consider themselves far superior to the Nephilim class. They consider themselves the superrich, the elite, having the highest and best genetic strain on the planet. There is no question that the Watchers consider themselves a different race—a different evolution separate from and having all the little people beneath them. They think that the little people exist only to be pawns in whatever game they happen to be playing.

The Nephilim are a lower order of angels, and they are the ones who frequent with laggards who have betrayed their Christhood. They are found more in the fields of science, genetic engineering, population manipulation, philosophy. They seek to control society through psychology, socialism, liberalism and other ideologies; whereas the Watchers are always found in positions of power in money, in law, in government and in the economy.

The Watchers, by their words and their deeds, have been eroding our planet for a long, long time—our civilization, our religion, and if they could, our very souls. And so, as we are attentive to the Ascended Masters and their directions, we should always realize that the key reason for all teachings and all direction, all admonishments, all calls for decrees and various practices that we have are for the protection of the soul from its vulnerability to the perpetual manipulation of spacecraft, laggards and Nephilim and their scientists who have long since blended in with the evolution themselves.

Out of the union of the Watchers with mortals came the giants who are mentioned throughout the Old Testament—for example, in the story of the shepherd boy David and the giant Goliath.[45] These giants are the offspring of these mighty Watchers, who once held the office at the same level of the Great Silent Watchers. It was their responsibility to hold the Cosmic Christ image for all evolutions. So their fall was great, and today they are the powerful and the mighty among earth's evolutions. They have a very large physical presence, and when they are not compromised by intermarriage, they retain that large stature.

These are the enemies of Archangel Michael. They are your enemies also. And you need to know yourself, know the enemy of yourself in the carnal mind, know your vulnerability to the personality cult and the death cult, the money cult, the success cult of these Watchers. They put out the signal that we should have the desire to be like them—to dress like them, to look like them, to share in their power and above all, to gain their approval. Many people spend dozens of embodiments attempting to gain the approval of the Watchers.

The Laggards

After earth had already experienced several Golden Ages and the return of the first, second and third root races to the Father-Mother God, the earth was invaded by Luciferian hordes during the Lemurian epoch. Later, the earth was asked to play host to those recalcitrant lifestreams known as the laggards.

As was explained in "The Cult of Hedon," the laggards are lifestreams whose evolution began on planets other than the earth, where they lagged behind in their spiritual progress. When their home planets were destroyed, the laggards, through the mercy of the Great Law, were given another opportunity.

Coming into embodiment through members of the fourth root race, these lifestreams did not respond to the ministrations of the angelic hosts and the counsels of their elders. Instead they continued in their rebellious ways. They were determined to reverse the upward course of Golden Age civilizations and to deprive mankind of the teachings of higher Law and the mysteries of the Christ, thereby attempting to ensure, as centuries passed and the dust covered the records of man's devotion to God, that no one would be able to ascend. Thus, the laggards have sought to maintain a status quo of imperfection on earth to secure a place where they could dwell in the lusts of the flesh for all eternity, keeping the children of the Light bound by their economic schemes, and thus vampirizing the Light of God to prolong their decadent consciousness.

Having already evolved for millions of years before coming to earth, the laggards are older souls than those who have recently come forth from the heart of God in the fourth, fifth, sixth and seventh root races. Thus, they can outsmart the holy innocents. Although the laggards are embodied in all races and should not be identified with any one race, nationality or religion in particular, they always feel that they are a superior race and a chosen people—a people chosen to rule those who are inferior to them. In their councils they have determined to achieve this through the economic slavery of the entire planet.

In his exposé on the Mechanization Concept, the Great Divine Director speaks of the coming of the laggards and the darkness that ensued: "Long ago, from a certain system of worlds there came bands who descended to earth, the hordes of shadow who were invited here by mankind (for mankind thought by the power of good example to elevate the consciousness of the laggard bands).

"Now it is not so well known that these laggards were accompanied by some who were not invited. Some of these brought knowledge to mankind and to the earth, and some of this knowledge was degenerative and destructive. In addition, they also brought with them strange creatures of their own creation—seemingly intelligent beings not created by God, however, but by advanced scientists on other systems of worlds.

"The extent of the evil of these hordes and that of their mechanical creations has been very great, and the oppression they have wreaked upon mankind has been terrible to behold. The infiltration of the planet by these creatures is indeed a manifestation of human creation, not of the divine creation. God did not create evil, neither did he create destruction nor hatred nor egoism nor any form of vanity whatsoever....

"I do not bring forth this information in order to frighten any, but to warn mankind that there are beings among them who are not the creation of God, who are not possessed with the same beautiful electronic pattern and Causal Body with which a manifestation of God is endowed.

"I propose no so-called witch-hunt. I propose that no one search out specifically these beings for identification. For your own mighty I AM Presence is the fullness of all that you desire, and I urge that the result of this release of knowledge shall be that you will turn more and more to God for your supply of every good thing, that you will determine more than ever to be alert to assist the mankind of earth in overthrowing absolutely all that is darkness and shadow and pain upon the Earth planet. In order to do this and to break the monstrous plots that the sinister strategies have launched upon mankind, harmony and unity must remain the forte of all who love the Light....

"The existence upon the Earth planet of what we may term 'simulated man' is a fact carefully hidden from the masses of mankind. Although it is the knowledge of the few, it may become and perhaps should become the knowledge of the many. Yet great care must be used in the dissemination of this knowledge, for it is never the desire of the Ascended Masters to do anything except that which would result in the greatest blessing and the release of mankind from every binding condition....

"Therefore, great care must be exercised by mankind today in ferreting out upon the planet those individuals who belong in the classification of 'the wicked' lest the innocent lambs suffer for their deeds. It is our hope that the heinous crimes perpetrated against all humanity by those so classified can, in the name of cosmic justice, be corrected without the undue suffering of mankind en masse.

"Through the power of infinite freedom and relieving the consciousness of the gross mechanical sense, we believe that the purposes of God can be fulfilled by divine edict—without the interference of human fanaticism and untempered zeal. It is our hope to squeeze out blind injustice and negation by saturating the planet with those necessary reforms that, by divine love, will remove the bane of that oppression that the wicked rulers have for generations instituted upon the earth."[46]

The Rescue Mission

With the coming in of laggard evolutions that had destroyed other planets and the coming in of the fallen ones, the planet Earth became a conglomeration of lifewaves, and instead of raising up those who had come here, the evolutions of earth themselves fell in consciousness. The consequence of that fall was the total degradation of life almost to the level of the animal, the most primitive state ever known on earth—to that point where man became almost like a beast, almost walking on all fours, not even being able to stand erect, not even having the sense of respect for the flame that burns in the heart.

At that moment cosmic councils determined: "There is not one soul on Terra who acknowledges and adores the fire of freedom, the flame of freedom. There is no further reason for being for Terra." Cosmic councils determined that Terra should go the way of many other stars, many other homes of evolutions whose entire lifewaves elected not to be. So cosmic councils decreed Terra should be no more, because cosmic councils were obliged to ratify what the free will of mankind had already decreed: Not to be.

In that moment that was the judgment of a planet and a people, a flame of freedom leaped. It was the flame of Sanat Kumara, known as the Ancient of Days,[47] the hierarch of Venus, sister star to Terra in this solar system. Sanat Kumara came before those councils and he said: "Wait! Do not snuff out Terra. I will go! I will be the soul on Terra who elects to keep the flame of freedom for all life. I will keep that flame until some respond, until one responds and then the few and then the many come to acknowledge the fire of the heart. I will go."

So came Sanat Kumara. He came from Venus. He came with Lords of Flame. He came with many souls from other planets in this system who volunteered to keep the flame with him. And they, too, raised their hands and said: "Sanat Kumara, O Lord of Flame, we will not let thee go alone to Terra. We will come also! We will come to minister unto our brothers and sisters who have forgotten the Flame, who have forgotten the force of freedom within the soul."

These volunteers knew that once they embodied, the chances were very great that they would become involved in karma-making situations that would tie them to their adopted home for perhaps thousands of years. Nevertheless, they had been trained to render this service, and the opportunity beckoned.

For many centuries, the thousands of lifestreams composing the retinue of Sanat Kumara remained in his service at etheric levels at Shamballa, the retreat of the Lord of the World situated over what is now the Gobi Desert. But there came a time when, through their ministration from etheric levels, the general consciousness of the race was raised to such a level that Sanat Kumara considered it safe for the volunteers to embody.

Under his direction, they were commissioned to go forth into the world of form to carry his Light. Two by two they took embodiment, until an entire wave of Venusian and other interplanetary volunteers were firmly entrenched in the karmic patterns of the earth. Thus the earth became the crossroads of a universal Armageddon that has been going on for thousands and millions of cycles. Sanat Kumara explains the challenges of this rescue mission:

"Concerning the covenant that I established between me and my servant Abraham and his seed, it was 'to be a God'[48]—the Guru—unto him and to the lineage of his seed of the Ruby Ray. Lo, unto him and unto you through him, my beloved, I promised the everlasting possession and dominion of the land wherein you were strangers. This land, called Canaan, is the earth plane of the Matter spheres. Whereas, before coming to the Earth planet, you made your abode in the etheric plane, it was given unto you through your first earthly father and mother, called Adam and Eve, to enter the physical octave, to subdue it, and to take dominion over all of the sub-evolutions inhabiting the 'earth, earthy.'

"These evolutions had come forth from the fallen ones...

They were the rebellious creation of the rebellious ones. Animal types—they were the prototypes of the animal-man called primitives, without soul or spark of the divine potential. These creatures first inhabited the astral plane, on the surface of the earth and beneath the surface in tunnels and hollowed-out caves. So great was the corruption of these Nephilim, as they were called, that the whole earth was in darkness, and darkness was on the face of the deep depths of the astral plane through this progeny of the fallen angels.

"As the fallen ones of Lucifer in the Great Rebellion had been cast out of the heaven into the earth, so these creatures of the pit of their delusion, horrific and monstrous as they were, descended from the mental and feeling worlds of their procreators to the physical plane—they and their demons and imprisoned elemental spirits with them. This synthesized man, mere mortals that were created as a slave race by the Luciferians together with the synthetic animal forms, both of which were inhabited by the demons of the fallen angels, thus began to people the physical octave.

"It was to the midst of this menagerie of the *hu-man* creation that you, my beloved, volunteered to go when you gathered on Venus to serenade me and my Beloved with your songs of love and your vow never to leave me and my own in our exile on earth. I told you then and I tell you now that you knew not what darkness you had volunteered to penetrate.

"But one thing you knew, my beloved: that this Luciferian creation inhabited not only the earth but was infesting the physical octaves of many planetary bodies throughout this galaxy and its twin galaxy [Andromeda]. You understood, as I understood when I went before the Cosmic Council to volunteer my life as an atonement for all of the darkness that the Luciferian rebellion had accomplished in these twin galaxies, that a cross section and a sampling of every type of evolution, lifewave and synthetic creation was then and is now manifesting in the four lower bodies of Terra; and that if these samplings of the miscreations of the rebellious ones could be confronted by the Light of the Seven Holy Kumaras and conquered by the Four Cosmic Forces through the person of the Eternal Lamb and the Embodied Lamb, then and only then could the final judgment come and the ascension of the Light evolutions of the twin galaxies take place. Earth, my beloved, is not the center of the universe but it is the crossroads of a universal Armageddon that has been going on for thousands and millions of cycles.

"The fallen ones and their synthetic creation, in their mockery before mortal men and the sons of God, have boasted of their kinship with gods. They have claimed him as their own and proclaimed Jehovah, the fount of the four rivers, as their origin. But while they have purveyed their mechanized religion among the children of God of the fourth root race, he has denounced them through their father Enoch and through their forefather Adam, and Seth, and unto the tenth of the progenitors of my lightbearers, the beloved Noah himself.

"There is no turning back from the line of confrontation where Light in the Lightbearer meets darkness in the dark ones and their nefarious deeds. For they have confused my people with a great confusion, so much so that they have transformed themselves into angels of Light while covering my prophets and preachers of righteousness with the shroud of their own deception and devious divinations. Thus they have acclaimed unto themselves the mercy of the LORD which endureth forever while he has denounced their ungodly generation, withholding his mercy from the Watchers and sending the edict of their final judgment through the sons of God in the heavens and the sons of God in the earth.

"This is the love that has bonded us together as one God

and one people and one light, which is the light of the true Israel—the universal, archetypal community of the Holy Spirit to which my son Jesus Christ has called you in the name of the Church Universal and Triumphant. This is the community of the called-out ones who are the remnant of the Woman's seed; for that universal Mother, also represented in my lady Venus, is the sponsoring one of your pilgrimage in love unto the evolutions estranged from the LORD in the physical octaves of the Matter spheres. By the Mother flame of Omega you have come, and by that Mother flame you shall conquer the Fallen One.

"My promise to Abraham, whom I sent forth to be the father of thy many nations, is the promise of the Guru-chela relationship unto all who would claim in the name of the I AM THAT I AM the 'land of Canaan' for the everlasting possession of the LORD.

"In the galactic sense, the 'land of Canaan' is interpreted to mean all planes of consciousness violated by the Watchers and their godless creation—planet to planet, universe to universe, system to system. In the biblical sense, it is the narrow strip of land called Canaan, which became the settlement of the twelve tribes, the land that was promised to them if they would worship the God of Israel and destroy the entire seed of the Nephilim that inhabited the territory.

"But though they enjoyed many victories by my hand and by the intercession of the Ascended Masters and the Archangels and their hosts, and though Joshua and the warriors of Israel with him cut off the Anakims and destroyed them utterly with their cities and none of the Anakims were left in the land of the children of Israel—yet the full inheritance of the Palestine covenant was not to be theirs. For as I spake unto Moses, so it came to pass: 'For when I shall have brought them into the land which I swear unto their fathers, that floweth with milk and honey; and they shall have eaten and filled themselves, and waxen fat; then will they turn unto other gods, and serve them, and provoke me, and break my covenant.'[49]

"For though Joshua took the whole land and divided it among the tribes of Israel and warned them not to forsake the LORD and made a covenant with the people before his death, and the people had vowed unto him: 'The LORD our God will we serve and his voice will we obey'[50]—yet those people once again followed the gods of the Canaanites and departed from the mighty I AM Presence. Every man did that which was right in his own eyes, and they were a law unto themselves though they were delivered seven times from their servitude to the seven nations of the fallen ones through the seven judges whom I raised up among them. Yet the fullness of my covenant made unto Abraham remains to be realized through the reincarnated remnant of Israel, the issue of the Woman."[51]

Splinters in the Soul

"When men have examined their heart's motives," Lord Maitreya says, "when they have found there the flaws of inordinate desire and the actual attempt to use the Light of God to cover their own sins, to cover their own darkness, let them pray that the LORD God will come and extract the splinters. These splinters are not of God but of the Satans who walked the earth,[52] the fallen ones who came as the Watchers of old to mingle their seed with the daughters of men and to thereby produce the offspring that were known as giants in those days.

"These giants came forth out of the fallen power of fallen angels united, then, with that which was mere mortality. The attempt of Lucifer and the fallen ones to blend the seed of God with the seed of mortals and to thereby seize a light they no longer had has produced a race of people on earth this day who must always come closer to the Light to continue to cover themselves with a veil of light whereas inwardly they are ravening wolves.[53] Inwardly they rebelled against the Law of God, but they continually seek to hide their origin and their destiny.

"Once again the Ascended Master Enoch walks through the highways of America. He walks midst the children of the Light. He comes, 'the seventh from Adam,'[54] the son of the mother and the father of the children of the Light of Abraham.

"Enoch stood in the Presence of God in the earth. He had cosmic consciousness. He ascended through the planes of heaven, and they registered as a great cosmic chord of cosmic consciousness within his seven chakras of being. Therefore, he was able to stand and behold the visions of God, of heaven and earth and all that they contained of Light and Darkness and of the challenge of Light by Darkness in the original rebellion.

"Therefore he left a record, a record for the sons and daughters of God concerning the intrusion of the seed of the Wicked as splinters in the Body of God and their attempt to intrude splinters within the souls of Lightbearers, which have become flaws in the diamond of the heart of our devotees.

"We come to extract the splinters by the surgery of the Lord Jesus Christ, the Cosmic Christ and your own Christ Self —surgery to remove the seeds of rebellion and disobedience and disorder and chaos and even the challenging of the LORD God himself.

"Let those, then, who take their oaths with the fallen ones and swear by the LORD God Almighty and by his name to destroy his children know that in the hour of the denial of the flame of God, God so denies their own flame. Let those who walk in the imitation of the Watchers and the Satans know that they will be judged with their seed.

"Let those who walk in the imitation of the Christed ones, the anointed ones, also know that they will be judged with the anointed ones. And let the children of the Light whose soul Light has been compromised listen well, for the teaching of the great Teacher is nigh. The Ascended Master Enoch comes to give to you the understanding of your own cosmogenesis, your own history, your own evolution of light and also of Armageddon that has been waged since the hour of the casting out of the fallen ones from the heavens into the earth.

"See, then, that you heed the mighty Word of Enoch and that you receive the impetus of the warning of one who descended from Adam, who bore the mantle and who stands in the very midst of the children of God once again to summon them back to the highest mountain, back to the very places of Light, back to that peak, that awareness, that oneness, that Mount Zion, where the children of God were gathered and from whence some of the children of God descended, not to partake of Christ's communion cup but to commune in the cups of the fallen ones and to drink with them the blood of the martyrs.[55]

"These Splinters Shall Be Removed"

"I AM Maitreya. I come also with a mighty action of transmutation. For these splinters shall be removed by the gift of healing, by the great agency of healing, the Holy Ghost in the Lord Jesus Christ within you. And it shall come by the great gift of miracles signifying the hour of transmutation, the dissolving by the universal solvent—the violet transmuting flame itself—of the infiltration and penetration of the very auras of the Lightbearers by the odor of the impure motive of the heart of the seed of the fallen ones.

"Let clarity, the crystal clarity of Truth, come forth. Let

each soul of Light who yearns for oneness realize that even as there has been an invasion of this solar system by those of evil intent from other systems of worlds, so there is an invasion of the body of earth, the astral sheath of the earth and even of your own temple, by energies that are not your own.

"They have remained with you for thousands of years, causing, therefore, great grief and striving within your being against an adversary you have not understood, whose face and name you have forgotten, yet whose face and name you once saw clearly.

"In the hour of confusion, in the hour of the intensification of illusion, the attempt of the fallen ones is to confuse Truth and Error, Light and Darkness and to create a blending to confute the Word of God and to confuse the little children. Clearly, it is the Word of God delivered unto the Messengers of Truth that once again is a mighty sword separating Light and Darkness within you so that you can recognize a healthy cell from a diseased cell, treat the one and invigorate the other. Beloved ones, to give more energy to the diseased cell, in some cases, will cause the disease to grow, to increase. Therefore, often the withdrawal of the Light from the diseased cell—diseased because it has been in rebellion against the Light—is the great mercy of God on behalf of the healthy cell, which must now have free, living, moving access to the Light of God, unhampered by the burdensome cells that encroach upon the flame of the living.

"Thus dying, being born, the resurrection, the miracle of spring, the great miracle of Eastertide is the new birth. Therefore with the coming of the new birth certain cells within the consciousness pass through the degeneration spiral unto death, unto cancellation, unto annihilation. That energy is recycled through the Great Central Sun so that the cell that is alive because the threefold flame is the energy of that cell can increase, can multiply, can propagate and create year upon year more beauty, more Light and a greater fulfillment of the incarnate Word."[56]

The Serpent

Now with all these many strains of fallen ones fighting on earth, we must ask the question, Who is behind the scene coordinating the operation? Alpha announced the final judgment and second death of Lucifer on July 5, 1975. Jesus Christ announced the final judgment and second death of Satan on February 1, 1982. Who is now left on earth that has enough attainment on the left-handed path to conduct galactic warfare?

Enter Serpent: the mastermind, the usurper. Subtle, sleek, sophisticated and sly. He is seen in the Book of Genesis. He is not a snake; he is a man, an incarnation of a fallen one who comes as the anti-Christ or the anti-Guru within the Garden of Eden.

We can never get away from the story of Adam and Eve: this major episode in earth's history is at the core of our subconscious mind. It has burdened the human race because it has to do with the twin flames who were chosen for the redemption of the fourth root race. The redemption of that fourth root race could have occurred if Adam and Eve had passed their test of initiation in this first mystery school. Because they did not, there was a long period of evolution in darkness.

Sanat Kumara has some very specific teaching on the one called Serpent*: "In the Great Rebellion against the LORD God

---

* The word "serpent" comes from the Latin *serpens*, which means "creeping." The biblical word for serpent is *nahash*, which comes from a root which means "decipherer; he who finds things out."

Almighty and the hosts of his heavenly Hierarchy, Lucifer seduced no small number of angelic bands led by his cohorts. Their names are mentioned in the Book of Enoch, and in other books of the Apocrypha, and in the codified scriptures of East and West.

"More notable are the names Satan, Beelzebub, Belial, Baal, etc. One such name, that of the more shrewd and subtil leader of a band of fallen ones, has come to be lowercased in the lexicon of sacred scripture, and it has taken on a symbolic rather than personal connotation. It is that of Serpent.

"Whereas the term 'great dragon' refers to the conglomerate of the entire Luciferian false hierarchy arrayed against the Great White Brotherhood, its individual members and hierarchs specialize in certain phases of the 'dragon's' persecution of the Woman and in the war waged by the Luciferian false hierarchy against the remnant of the Woman's seed.

"Whereas Satan is known as the original Murderer using the murder of the lightbearers to thwart the divine plan of God in the earth, Serpent, who is also '*called* the Devil and Satan,' is the Archdeceiver, the original Liar and the father of lies whose philosophy of deception, based on fear and doubt, is his modus operandi in his warfare against the true Christs and the true prophets.

"Serpent is the Wicked One whose seed, along with Satan's, is sown as tares among the good wheat of the Christic seed. It is this seed who are called the offspring of the vipers. 'Viper' is from the Greek translation of the proper name 'Serpent,' who, together with the fallen ones of his band, was cast out of heaven and took embodiment on earth where they have continued to reincarnate since the Great Rebellion....

"The Serpent who spoke to the woman in the Garden of Eden was the leader of a band of fallen angels who fell from the second ray of the LORD's wisdom. Before their fall, their understanding of God and his laws governing the path of initiation and of individual Christhood was more complete (subtil) than that of any other angels (beasts) of the field of God's consciousness that the LORD God had made in the beginning.[57]

"This fallen one was selected from the Luciferian councils as the one most able to turn the woman away from her first love in God, who had come to her in the person of the Great Initiator, Lord Maitreya, the Cosmic Christ, as well as from her second love, that of her beloved twin flame.[58]

"The seeds of doubt and fear formed the foundation of Serpent's questioning of the Lawgiver and his Law. Impugning the motive of Maitreya, Serpent set himself up as the false hierarch and impostor of the Cosmic Christ. And ever since, he has, with his seed, maintained the foundations of the false hierarchy's philosophy of Antichrist in economics, politics, the social sciences and the culture of civilization—all on the basis that his way is better than God's way, that he knows what God knows and knows it better; and what's more, that he knows what is best for His offspring on earth.

"While the tactic of this fallen one is to destroy the Word of God by detracting from it, carefully removing the sacred-fire mysteries of the Holy Grail from the codified scriptures of East and West, his temptation of Eve was based on the distortion of the Word. Thus he perverts the Trinity by false initiation—giving to the woman the fruit of Light that is forbidden except through the initiation of the Christ; by false teaching—'Ye shall not surely die'; and by false comfort—'Ye shall be as gods, knowing good and evil.' "[59]

Serpent wanted to blend his seed of rebellion with the seed of Light. His synthesis was the demon, the de-mon, the deified man, the man who makes himself God without being the servant of God because he doesn't have to serve God. He has stolen the son of God, the Light of God, and now contains it within his own universe and forcefield, so he can merely mock God and not have to come under his Law.

This is the warfare of the dragon against the seed of the woman that is in chapter 12 of the Book of Revelation: "And the dragon was wroth with the woman, and went to make war with the remnant of her seed"—the remaining portions of her seed. And what is that warfare? It is the corruption of the divine identity.

Evolutions from "Above" and "Beneath"

Jesus spoke of two distinct evolutions, one that came from God, the I AM Presence, and one that came from the lower order of fallen ones. This is specifically concealed in the Lord's conversation with Nicodemus: "Except a man be born again, he cannot see the kingdom of God"[60]—so the translation usually reads. But the original Greek reads: "Except a man be born *from above,* he cannot see the kingdom of God." ("And no man hath ascended up to heaven, but he that came down from heaven, even the Son of man which is in heaven," John 3:13.) The phrase "born from above" is reminiscent of Jesus' statement to the Pharisees, "Ye are from beneath; I am from above."[61] In chapter 8 of the Gospel of John, Jesus is quoted as making an even stronger statement to distinguish these two evolutions. Here he declares that the Pharisees are the seed of the "devil."

Now, just who was Jesus talking about when he used the term "devil" and "seed of the devil"? The root of the word is "slanderer," one who defames the name of God and elevates his own, or one who "deifies" evil (*d-evil*) in place of the Light and Person of Christ. In the sense that the original Devil, and devils in general, invert the creation and pervert the name of the Godhead, both Nephilim and Watchers, as the angels who were either cast down or fell of their own volition, would be termed devils.

Perhaps the Book of Enoch also explains where these devils get the energy to do their despicable deeds. Since they have already lost the divine spark and their place in heaven—God told them, "Never shall you ascend into heaven," and "Never shall you obtain peace"—they have nothing else to lose and everything to gain from the shedding of the blood (the life-essence) of the sons of God.

They have no remorse for their misconduct, for the way of penance and forgiveness is not open to them. Without a heart flame, they have no pity for their victims, no ability to "feel" for them. They do not identify with them in murder, or in the mass murders the Watchers legitimize with the term "war," as in "wars of liberation."

As a substitute for the loving rapport between our Father and his beloved sons, which they have rejected, the Watchers and their seed have entered into a symbiotic relationship with the discarnate spirits of the "giants" who yet roam the astral plane oppressing, corrupting and contending for the minds of their victims. Devoid of the mind of Christ, the evolutionary chain of the Watchers become demon-possessed tools of dark forces from whom they derive both the energy and the cunning for their crimes.

The author of Hebrews calls them not sons of God but "bastards," who are without chastening because their final judgment is sealed—for the LORD chastens only the beloved sons whom he would receive to his heart. It should be understandable that these evildoers whose souls are condemned to the second death would be lovers of death rather than life. And their death cult—their pleasure in sensual stimulation expending the life-force in riotous and rancorous living—has become a shroud upon a planet and her people.

Renowned psychologist Erich Fromm comments that those who are the "necrophiles" have "precisely the reverse of the values we connect with normal life: not life, but death excites and satisfies them"[62]—death in all of the sensational downward spirals of a selfish, purposeless existence.

Few have ever understood the "why" of this alternate generation, who seem the antithesis of the life-loving sons of God—the angry, the blasphemous, raging, restless, dying race whose core is rotten, rebellious and irresponsible toward the Light and the Honor of God. But then, few have explored the teaching of Enoch and the early Church Fathers on the incarnation of demons and fallen angels.

Jesus called them "whited sepulchres, which indeed appear beautiful outward, but are within full of dead men's bones, and of all uncleanness."[63] The truth is that these fallen ones are so dead that they cannot respond to the cries of the people to stop waging arms races, nor do they give adequate answer to appeals to stop misappropriating the people's money in their inner sanctums. Instead, the Watchers take the people's gold and give them inflated, worthless currency in exchange for their sacred labor.

It is time that the godly evolutions of this planet—the sincerely religious people—be given an explanation of the facts behind the spread of darkness in the world order, behind the traducing of the doctrines of Christ, behind the destruction of his religion, and behind the history of war, selfishness, greed, revolution, Communism, atheism and all that has worked against the Light of the Christ ever since the fall of Lucifer and the coming of the laggards.

The Conspiracy of Gog and Magog

*Satan shall be loosed out of
his prison, and shall go out to
deceive the nations which are in
the four quarters of the earth,
Gog and Magog, to gather
them together to battle.*

REVELATION

THE ASCENDED MASTER WHO HAS chosen for his name The Great Divine Director is an ancient soul—and one who has seen the rise and fall of many civilizations. He is now the Manu for the seventh root race, which is destined to take embodiment on planet Earth sometime in the future. He is also a member of the Karmic Board.

He reads to us from the scroll of cosmic history of the planet Maldek and beyond: "I come bearing the scroll of cosmic history; and I read the record of ancient civilizations—some of Light, some of darkness—and the fate of their evolutions. In order to draw for you the future of a planet,

I must first draw for you the past and then allow you to draw your own conclusions. The writing is on the wall. History repeats itself; hence mankind must learn a lesson from cosmic history.

"I would speak of Maldek and of lifewaves chosen of God to manifest the principles of freedom and brotherhood and unity. Micah, the angel of Light, son of Michael, was assigned to those evolutions while they were on Maldek; and the banner of that angel is unity. Now if a lifewave uses the flame of unity to come together and to meld the carnal consciousness, then the end result will be the beast, the serpent that becomes the dragon at the end of the spiral of its precipitation.[1]

"Thus the perversion of unity was the cause that was set in motion that resulted in the flying-apart of the very atoms of that planetary home when the two lifewaves evolving there—one assigned to carry the Flame of Alpha and the other to carry the Flame of Omega—instead of uniting in a spiral of oneness, chose rather to amalgamate their carnal-mindedness for the greatest holocaust that has ever been seen in this solar system.

"Among those evolving on Maldek were lifestreams and souls of high principle dedicated to Truth, yet all were destroyed. In a moment, in the twinkling of an eye, all were flung out of their physical bodies into the astral realm. Two-thirds of those lifewaves passed through the second death because their consciousness was totally dedicated to the energy veil called evil.

"When a consciousness that is the gift of God chooses to crucify God in the energy veil, then the ever-merciful Creator expresses mercy unto himself and releases his own atoms from the framework of identity that personifies chaos, death and discord. Thus you see, the second death is the highest expression of God's mercy that is expressed unto God himself and his imprisoned energies.

"And what of the one-third remaining lifewaves considered worthy of another chance? These came with their bag and
baggage, homeless wanderers, to the planet Earth, to which
they were assigned by the Lords of Karma for two reasons.
First, lifestreams in embodiment upon earth volunteered to
give bodies to these souls and to assist in training them. And
second, certain numbers among mankind's evolutions had
already capitulated to the Luciferian lie, and they worshiped
the golden calf,[2] and their high priests and priestesses
desecrated the altars of the Most High God on Mu, following
the Fallen One and the angels who fell with him.

"Thus, because the earth as a sphere was no longer herself
perfect, she was vulnerable to the intrusion of imperfection in
the consciousness of other lifewaves. This is a most outstanding example of the protection that purity affords—of the
protection that perfection is. When mankind depart from that
perfection, that wholeness, then they are vulnerable to the
most horrendous forms of astral manifestations that float right
through the grids of their own consciousness because these are
less than perfect and therefore serve as a magnet to magnetize
energy veils from other worlds, from interstellar space. And so
you see, even today dangerous cosmic rays penetrate the earth
because of the vulnerability, the betrayal and the selfishness of
mankind's own consciousness, which ought to be magnetizing
the Christ Light, the Solar Logos, the Great Central Sun.

"Thus they came without a name and without a country.
And they embodied among the holy innocents and those who
had not yet capitulated to the Luciferian lie. Parents of these
ungodly ones who still retained the spark of divinity found
that when they came to the age of the return of karma,
between twelve years and fourteen years, they could no longer
control these children; they could no longer teach them. And
the children rebelled against their parents, and they left their

homes, and they went out into the world to pervert children who were the holy innocents and to teach them the ways of the Liar and his lie.

"By and by, these laggard souls amalgamated forces with the fallen angels who had been forced to take embodiment because of their allegiance to the Fallen One; and thus the team of the fallen angels and the laggards became an ever-present menace, growing and growing in giant proportions upon the planetary body. Karmic councils, beholding this manifestation, expressed great concern lest the young souls of the sixth root race be contaminated by the ungodly.

"And yet lifewaves must go on, manifestations must occur, ages come and go; and whatsoever a lifewave may manifest, that is what it shall reap. For there is a certain group karma in each root race that manifests upon earth. And there is a lowest common denominator of consciousness within a root race that holds back the highest manifestation of the Christic Light in that root race. And thus the golden mean of consciousness is found somewhere between the two; and that golden mean becomes a mediocrity that goes neither up nor down, but walks the middle of the road and thinks that it is highly clever and that it cannot be touched.

"And thus the laggards and the fallen ones taught mankind how to dodge returning karma, how to dodge the effects of causes they had set in motion. This they achieved in one instance by prohibiting intermarriage into their race, thereby prohibiting the return of karma that was a mingling of their energies with the holy innocents. This may be hard for some of you to understand; but by forbidding the intermarriage between the laggards and the earth people and making this a part of orthodox tradition, there is a failure of the greatest kind. For it is an omission and a loss of opportunity for the laggards themselves to evolve and to attain greater heights of

Light and manifestation. And by that mingling, they might be converted to the Christ and to the Light.

"This also preserves the wealth within families century after century, guarding that wealth and therefore preventing lifestreams from having the karma of having deprived others of wealth or of having to earn their daily bread by the sweat of their brow.[3] And thus the karma, instead of returning and manifesting, continues to build and to build and to build because of the isolation policy of the laggard races.

"Now the situation of many strains of lifewaves upon the earth is a condition that must be considered again and again by the Lords of Karma. The evil deeds of the fallen ones, the commingling of the seed of animals and of man, which resulted in the hideous creations that were destroyed at the time of the Flood—all of these had to be contended with. And therefore the fiat went forth from the Lords of Karma, 'Henceforth let every seed bear after its kind'; and it was forbidden that such an unholy and an ungodly situation should occur again. And these miscreations, then, were canceled out by cosmic edict through the Flood, which was the sinking of Atlantis.

"I tell you that the last days of Atlantis were wicked indeed; and the very ones who caused the destruction of Atlantis have come again, returning into embodiment. Joining forces with darkness, they have created a culture in direct antagonism to the culture of the Divine Mother.

"Now those same parents who first volunteered to receive the laggards have had to receive them again and again, in order to discipline and to draw them into alignment with the Law—the Law that was given through Moses, the Law that was given through Mohammed for the salvation of these races that are continually warring with one another and attempting to draw the entire planetary body into their ridiculous strife, which has as its end not the glory of God, not the freedom of man, but the pride of the ego and the ruling of the planetary body through the Luciferian consciousness of a one-world focus.

"I say to you, then, Hierarchy is concerned this day that these same races, these same two groups of laggards now embodied and centralizing their energies in the Middle East, are coming together for that confrontation—the same confrontation that they had on Maldek. And it is a most volatile situation, a situation that, if the children of the Light do not rally to contain their actions, to withdraw their aid to both sides, might result in a total war at the end of this decade.

"I must apprise you of these facts; for without the facts, you cannot pursue the invocations and the arresting of the spirals, as you have been taught, for the salvation of the planet.[4] Thus, when the veil is drawn and when it is torn asunder and man sees face to face the highest Good and the highest Evil, he realizes that by the power of the Almighty, he can bind the forces of darkness that are in his midst.

"You have the authority to challenge not only the war in the Middle East, but all war anywhere at any time. You have the authority to challenge the Luciferians. You have the authority to challenge those who take the precious holy innocents to the slaughter, to the battlefields, in a continual round of killing that amounts to nothing—absolutely nothing —in the sight of the Karmic Board. You have this authority by the power of the Christ that is in you; and in the name of Jesus the Christ, you may give the commands of perfection that will allow us to enter in and do the perfect work that is so necessary in these troubled times.

"Thus the handwriting is on the wall. History repeats itself. The only power that can check the widening spiral of the pride of the people of Israel on the one hand, and of the deceit and treachery and intrigue of the people of the Arab nations on the other, is the authority of the Christ, who occupies the position at the heart level to challenge this yin and yang perversion of Alpha and Omega. Your knowledge of the Cosmic Clock[5] will show you that these two nations this day represent the malefactors on either side of the Christ—both in manifestation of Antichrist—the Christ who came to redeem and restore the laggard consciousness and to give to these nations and their people the opportunity to accept the Light and to redeem that karma that they created on Maldek.

"Do you see now why these people are called the chosen people? They are chosen because they have the greatest karma, the greatest debt, and because they owe the most and require the greatest forgiveness. And thus, going to the lost sheep of the House of Israel,[6] Jesus the Christ came to save that remnant of souls who embodied here, that they might have the opportunity to bring the entire planet into a Golden Age and thus redeem that karma of having destroyed another planetary home.

"Thus God, in his infinite mercy, gives to those who have the greatest debt the greatest opportunity; and if they reject that opportunity, then it is passed on to the children of the Light who, as far as their soul history is concerned, do not have the ancient experience and the cycles of evolution that these laggard souls have. For they have only recently come from octaves of Light to evolve upon the planetary home. And so you see, the age of the soul often determines her opportunity, even though she might not have preserved that Light that was originally given to her in the beginning.

"Thus you say, what is the future of a planet? The future of a planet is in your hands; it is in the hands of all who have chosen to be of the House of Israel, of all that *is Real*. For the state of Reality can be claimed by all. It is not unique to any race or time or people. And those who do not choose Reality cannot be counted among the children of Israel; and they have no claim to the Holy City, the city that lieth foursquare, eternal in the heavens.[7] For their claim is the energy veil; and since they have claimed it, that is what they may have and that is their just reward....

"Now I must remind you of the redeeming factor within the laggard races. I must tell you that these ones were chosen because they had some spark of divinity left within them; and among them were great spiritual leaders, people of great holiness, who also were flung into the astral and were given an opportunity to embody here. And thus among these races, you do find the highest souls of the highest evolution; you find also that these souls of great Light have been misled by the Luciferians, just as the holy innocents have been misled.

"And therefore I caution you never to entertain condemnation or prejudice for the laggard races; for among them, if they would but accept the Christ, are those who have the potential to lead the earth into the manifestation of the New Day. And many are being brought into this Ascended Master activity; and some have been born into these races who are not laggards at all, but who volunteered to help the cause of Light, manifesting therein the golden Word of the Golden Age teaching....

"And thus, you can never judge a book by its cover. You can never judge a man or a woman by name or by origin, by race or religious background. But you must understand the nature of the mingling of races and the mingling of the blood itself, which is the conveyor of the Christic Light and the Christic fohat. And thus when there is the mingling of the blood, there is sometimes a fortification of the power of the Christ in man and sometimes a forfeiting of the power of the Christ in man....

"And so, precious hearts, understand that as all came forth

from the one true Source on different wavelengths, on different rays, so all are intended to master those rays and to return to God. And in the Golden Age civilization, there shall be a manifestation of Golden Age man, a manifestation of Helios and Vesta having the glow of the golden-pink glow-ray upon their countenances and in their body temples. And thus a new race and a new civilization shall manifest that shall transcend all other races by the action of the threefold flame within the heart.

"I can prophesy to you this day that as the rising of the spirals of Light and darkness continues, creating an ultimate precipitation of confrontation between Light and darkness, the future of the planet hangs in the scales of mankind's own free will. Because there are so few who even recognize that they have free will, behaving instead as a will-o'-the-wisp, following every whim of consciousness coming from the astral, there are few that we can depend upon to decide for the Light and to remember they have decided for the Light and to remain steadfast in their determination in the Light.

"Thus, we appeal to the lost sheep of the House of Israel. We appeal to all people in all nations and in all races. We appeal directly to the heart of every lifestream upon this planet who has come forth from Maldek. And we impress these lifestreams this day with the power of the spoken Word, with the power of opportunity; for it is not too late to bend the knee and to confess the Christic Light and the power of the Logos.

"I say to you, precious hearts, the misinterpretation of the teachings of Christ has been a great deterrent to the coming into the Christic Light of these laggard generations. For they have the ancient teachings of the Ascended Masters that were given to them before their fall on Maldek, and they have enough of a divine memory of the Law that they understand that the Son of God cannot be confined to one human identity pattern. And therefore, they see no need to worship Jesus; for they understand—however perverted that understanding might be—that it is idolatry to worship the outer personality of anyone.

"Many of these souls are highly evolved. And when they come into the awareness of the Christ within them, of the Universal Christ manifesting in all and of Jesus the Christ being part of the Hierarchy of Lightbearers that also consists of Moses and Abraham and many prophets of Israel, then they see that in the order of Hierarchy the logical fulfillment of the House of David is the manifestation of Jesus, and they acknowledge his triumph. And so they come to understand the true worship of Jesus the Christ as the manifestation of the only begotten Son of the Father.

"I urge you, then, to understand that there is a great need for the accurate setting-forth of the Law, its publication, its teaching, and making it available to all peoples everywhere. You must be patient with all lifewaves, you must love the Christ within the heart, and you must not differentiate between these souls that I have described this day. For my explanation is given to you as a point of history, as a point of warning, as a point of understanding why there are such conditions within your midst. But when all is said and done, all people are God's people. All people are his children....

"I say then, make your mark upon the age! Determine the future of the planet! I would like to hear from you! I would like to receive a letter from each one of you,[8] writing the history of the next thirty-six years. I would like to see you write the history and tell me what you desire to outpicture; and I will send back to you my letter of divine direction for your soul as to how you might implement the Law and the art and the covenants of old.

"I wish to see what a body of Lightbearers entrusted with

the authority, the governing authority of a planet, would do if given their way and their free will. And the *if* is only a contingency of the moment. For it is *not* an if, because you *are* the authority for the planet; and the authority is your I AM Presence and your Christ Self. The authority is in you, in the power of the spoken Word, and in the fiats of the heart.

"Therefore I say, write down the decades and write to me what you see, in communion with God, ought to be and should be fulfilled. And we will see what we can do to bring it to pass. For Heaven is open to suggestion; the Lords of Karma are ready to accept your strong right arm and the power of your heart that is determined in the idealism of your youth and in the idealism of your maturity. For both unite in the knowledge of the Law and in the realization that the Great Divine Director is the directing force and power in your life and in the life of a planet.

"Therefore I say, take the proffered gift, study the records of history, look at the mistakes of the past, and consider yourself king for a day, queen for a day, and write your edicts for the next thirty-six years! And let us see what we can do, putting our hearts and our heads and our hands together with the scepter of my authority, to bring this planet into the golden awareness of a Golden Age reality!"[9]

Reservoirs of Negative Energy

Sanat Kumara figures in the lore of the Hindus as the great leader in the Battle of Armageddon, though they have another name for the battle.[10] He was seen by John the Revelator as the "Faithful and True,"[11] the leader of the armies of heaven. In this time, he reveals to us the accumulation of reservoirs of darkness that are used in this planetary battle:

"You have to understand that these dark ones now are gathering the power of hate in vast reservoirs.... And when moments come where they feel the need to incite the crowds to riot, they tie into that momentum of hate, and they flash that energy of hate forth with all of its misqualification into the world domain. And then police power and the power of armies is invoked by the political governments of the world, and all of that energy and misqualified substance flows out into the world body.

"When you hear about it in the news media, blessed ones, you are disturbed and you say, 'What in the world is happening here?' You should understand that you are seeing the fruit of man's accumulated hate energy down through the ages and the storing up of that energy and the release of that energy now in the battle of Armageddon, seeking to destroy man's spiritual values and sense of values, seeking to make men feel that life upon earth is useless, that there is no opportunity to actually bring forth perfection and order in the world scheme. Yet there are many good men in political service, men that you should respect and love, who are rendering a tremendous service to this country."[12]

The Great Divine Director also speaks of reservoirs of darkness in his manifesto on the Mechanization Concept: "Whenever an individual uses energy, and this always occurs whenever thought or feeling is exercised, the energy itself is not destroyed even after passing through the nexus of consciousness where qualification with bane or blessing occurs. Hence, energy is continually being released by all of mankind into the atmosphere.

"Now, because of the law of harmonics dealing with affinities, like seeks out like; and therefore, a strengthening occurs in the strata of misqualified energy as well as in that of properly qualified energy as line upon line of similarly qualified vibrations are added thereto. Many have noted that in spiritual places, temples and churches, they can receive a greater inrush of peace than in the busy streets and businesses of the outer world; contrariwise, when entering into places qualified with feuds or destructive and trivial passions, mankind are often ensnared in feelings that do not sustain the vibratory action of God-happiness and peace.

"Let all take into account, then, how very important is the law governing affinitized vibration. Likewise, let all examine the fact that the solar plexus as a center, unless guarded, may become a doorway through which negative vibrations enter to bring about a descent of the levels of normally happy consciousness, clouding the sun of man's being with thoughts of fear or threat, foreboding or danger. As discord is never a part of the divine plan but is solely an action of Universal Law in its application with respect to karma, I think it wise that the 'mechanical' nature of this law be understood so that our chelas [disciples] can become reasonably free from unwanted conditions.

"Your precious tube of light is, of course, an invincible protection against the intake of such volatile or desultory vibratory actions as well as of downward spirals of despair. Yet it is very true that many of the students at one time or another, often unwittingly, do fail in their application to maintain the required spiritual contact. And thus, in an unguarded moment, an inrush of misqualified energy does occur whereby vibrations of unhappiness do enter the feeling world—even attitudes of faithlessness are sometimes taken in and amplified as feelings of doubt and uncertainty....

Floating Grids and Forcefields

"There do exist, then, in the atmosphere throughout the entire planet, floating forcefields or grids containing the scapegoat energies of mankind's wrong thought and feeling. These abide in larger quantities in the so-called ghettos of the large cities and such places as are rampant with the ravages of crime and poverty. Yet I can recall but few spaces upon the landed area of the earth where these large forcefields do not occasionally drift to bring about potential destruction where taken in. They are like floating minefields in the sea. Insidiously existing beneath the level of visibility, they drift to affect the unwary of mankind and to bring about results little dreamed of by most contemporary men.

"Bear in mind that each shade of human opinion carries a specifically different rate of vibration and that thousands of forcefields are anti-this and anti-that, making for innumerable clashes referred to by beloved Morya as 'human dissonance,' which are actually impediments to the full harmonic orchestration of the brotherhood of man.

"The subtle nature of man's free will and his insistence upon having his own way have led many well-meaning people into pitfalls of discord so trivial as to cause even the simple to smile, yet the stiff-necked move without motion into the realm of mental and spiritual stagnation. The sad part is their lack of awareness of the pitiful plight of their being. May I say of these for their freedom's sake, 'Deliver them from evil!'

"The power of prayer and spiritual attunement, of closely living to the divine Presence of God, the maintaining of attitudes of happiness and awareness of life's purposes, the sustainment of service and goodwill for others, and the amplification of every divine attitude is, of course, one's own best protection against the intake of these forces.

"I cannot deny that some of them, by reason of size and density patterns, are particularly lethal and hence deadly to those who are unsuspecting and therefore unprotected against them. Just as a cloud will cover the face of the sun preceding a storm, so in many cases a sudden feeling or drop in the normal level of happiness or well-being will indicate the presence of such an invisible forcefield.

"There are two simple defenses available to mankind against these unseen pitfalls. One is to recognize that mobility can soon bring an individual into an area out of the center of the thrust; hence, many times, a distance of one or two miles will give absolute safety. At other times, for various reasons when individuals cannot conveniently flee the invaded area, they can make mighty application to the Godhead, to the Cosmic Beings and the Ascended Masters, including beloved Jesus and Archangel Michael, for spiritual assistance in moving these forcefields away or transmuting them into Light.

"Now, I do not for one moment wish any to accept that no matter how deadly these forcefields may be, they cannot be made to yield to the invincible power of God. Yet just as Don Quixote was unable to defeat the windmills with the point of his lance, so it is senseless to, in the words of Saint Paul, fight as one who beateth the air.[13]

"You see, there are few in physical embodiment today who are able on the instant to cope with the more malevolent of these conditions from the level of mankind's externalized personal grace. But I am certain no call goes unheeded by heaven, and therefore mighty inroads can be made into these forcefields. Sometimes they can be reduced or cut in half by a thrust of the sword of blue flame invoked by a chela.

"It is not my wish to have the student body overly conscious of these conditions; yet, precious ones, it is not wise to be wholly unconsciously subject to them either. Therefore, in a state of perfect mental and spiritual balance, mankind ought to understand that these conditions do exist and that they function almost mechanically—not always as fixed monsters either, but frequently as predatory roaming beasts of the air subject to unconscious driftings and magnetization by minutely affinitized centers in individuals or in groups.

"This means then, precious ones, that those who permit themselves to be subject to vibratory actions of fear, anger, human consciousness or hatred or even a sense of wrong or injustice may draw to themselves from various parts of the planet either small or large focuses of the exact type of the quality of negation they permit to play through their mind and feeling consciousness. Is this not a sound argument, then, for the constant maintenance of thoughts of beauty, holiness, protection and grace?

"You see, precious ones, these conditions that function upon the planet so automatically as the result of man's defection from the Laws of God have become, in this age of Armageddon, an ever-present threat that the powers of Light are most anxious to dissipate in the freeing of the planet from every unwanted force and condition.

"There is no need for me to diagram these forcefields for the sake of the more scientific of my readers, for they exist in various sizes and shapes, some of which resemble the popular nebbish figures depicted by modern cartoonists in your papers. The sizes vary from those no bigger than a man's hand to some that are huge clouds covering many miles of the earth's surface.

"It may not be interesting to some of you, nor fully understood by all, but I mention in passing that there is a special branch of Archangel Michael's legions that devotes a great deal of time to what you might call 'dive-bombing' these formations and breaking them up into smaller sections so that they pose less of a threat to the mankind of earth.

"Naturally, the more calls that are made by the larger numbers of mankind to Archangel Michael and the beloved Ascended Hosts, the greater the quantity of spiritual energy that can be released for the dissipation of these unwanted human creations. After all, blessed ones, these are the mechanical creations of unthinking man. I smile as say this, for they are the result of man's thoughts and feelings but not the thoughts and feelings qualified with godliness or the right thought of the Godhead, which is the true power of thought.

"Now, it goes almost without saying, precious ones, that few among mankind if they were able at all to fully control themselves would knowingly create such vibrations of human viciousness and centers of darkness. Yet many of these are not created by any one individual at all but by the many who think subtle and supposedly harmless thoughts against another individual. Because energy is almost impersonal, like seeks like; and it is the union of shadowed substance with shadowed substance that causes a densification and strengthening of these nefarious forces.

"I must admit that there are certain activities of the black magicians and insidious actions that we may well term vicious witchcraft that deliberately foster and encourage the building up of such reservoirs of negated energy....

"Do you see, then, that reservoirs of negative force can also be accumulated in these drifting banks of negation to be used by the brothers of shadow to draw upon when needed to fight against Good? Well, precious ones, this misqualified energy becomes available to the powers of darkness, then, to use in confusing the mind of man and in upsetting his world whenever possible so as to create more and more mass confusion.

"This is why undesirable television programs, vile movies and destructive books are so effective in disturbing the very young as well as people of all ages. These tie emotionally into these clouds of negated energy and feed through the consciousness, holding an absorbing fascination for mankind once they become emotionally involved in the drama. The plot sequences of most of these unwholesome stories are often mere duplications of themselves in a new format. We do not deny that many of the authors thereof enjoy great popularity with mankind, but they must bear well in mind that they will one day give account of their stewardship of life....

"You see, precious ones, it does not matter through whom the misqualification occurs upon earth. The fact that it does occur at all is a threat to all mankind embodied here."[14]

The Manipulators and Their Conspiracy of Anarchy

Those who work behind the scenes to play communism against capitalism, white against black, the rich against the poor, also attempt to control, wherever possible, freedom of speech, freedom of the press, freedom of assembly and even freedom of religion. They have agreed that the end justifies the means and that they are born to rule. For this purpose, they manipulate economic trends, politics, science and religion to perpetuate their smug little world within the confines of the snarl they have made of it.

Archangel Gabriel says: "The fallen ones have projected their plan for terror, anarchy and confusion in America based on doubt and fear and an overwhelming laxity in those necessary protective agencies—the armed forces, the police, the FBI and the CIA. The protection of a nation, its people and its freedom must be entrusted to individuals who will bear the sacred trust with honor, dignity and love.

"And while cruelty and brutality and high-handed methods must be shunned within these agencies created of the people for the people, the agencies themselves must not be put down, compromised or weakened to the point where the strategies of the fallen ones are facilitated.

"And what are these strategies? From the perspective of an

Archangel, they are very obvious:

"To divide and conquer the children of Light through rivalries of personality and the segmenting of the population along the line of relative truth and error and right- and left-wing positionings in politics, economics and matters of faith and morals;

"Then to engender hostilities in the mass mind through anxiety and an amazing absence of the awareness of the Presence of God in the very midst of the fast paces of modern life;

"Then to generate, through pent-up emotions and commercialized violence, a frenzied fanaticism outcropping in international terrorism ... with its uncontrolled hijacking and intimidation of innocent citizens—or in the sudden crazed unleashing of subconscious hatred ... in cold-blooded murder....

"From the inner planes, we the Archangels see the danger and sound the warning. The strategy is one of anarchy. The original Anarchist was Lucifer himself, who rebelled against the authority of the Lord Christ and the incarnate Word in the sons and daughters of God and therefore has, from the beginning, advocated the violent overthrow of the established order of the universe.

"This philosophy, which has become dignified as a political theory declaring any form of government to be undesirable and unnecessary, comes sugarcoated with such euphemisms as 'voluntary cooperation' and 'the free association of individuals and groups.'

"Thus, to justify their relentless determination to destroy the order of Hierarchy of Christ and his apostles and of an established path of initiation through levels of government spanning the Spirit-Matter cosmos and entrusted to enlightened sons and daughters of God, the fallen ones use a principle of freedom and free will to overthrow the very one, the LORD God himself, who is the giver of that gift of freedom and who, through his only begotten Son, the Christ in all, instructs his offspring in the responsible use of the gift of free will.

"The counterpart of this strategy is to infiltrate the governments of the nations with irresponsible elements, the seed of the wicked themselves, and then to hold up the very corruption that their own members have created as the justifiable grounds for the overthrow of the entire system itself.

"This circus of the fallen ones has been repeated again and again throughout the ages while self-centered and naïve children of God, who have failed to give their undying commitment to the flame of life within themselves and all people, have become susceptible to the ruses of Satan's spoiled children and even amenable to their demand for rights to the taxpayers' money to underwrite their guerrilla training.

"And a part of the conspiracy is to erase the connecting lines of the conspiracy in the physical plane. Hence no outer connection is evident between sudden assassination, kidnappings, murder outcropping in South America, Africa, Asia or the streets of Rome, Paris, London and New York.

"The connection is one of a common vibration of individuals who have long ago rebelled against their own Real Self and the God-government of that Christ, who have thence fallen from grace, the state of oneness with the inner Christ through the World Saviour. Thus they are called the fallen ones, and their fall is from the higher consciousness of the God within, the I AM Presence, whom they reject as their Lord and Master.

"They have not the courage to stand alone in their rejection of the Almighty One, but they must go forth in their cowardice to overthrow the Light of the Christ in the children of God and in the governments established by God to maintain a platform of evolution in the Matter plane. And their ultimate justification is the very imperfection of the children of

God themselves who have been tempted by vice and greed to abuse the positions of public office entrusted to their care.

"The solution of the Archangels is not anarchy or the violent overthrow of established institutions but rather the tutoring of the souls of the children of God as to the nature of their own inner Reality and a just application of the law of cause and effect.

"We come to engender love in the souls of God's people, a love for God that leads to the sacrifice of the self for the many and for the community of the Holy Spirit, which is indeed based upon the 'free association of individuals and groups' but always under the authority of the enlightened ones who, by their character and their example, are most qualified to rule in the footstool kingdom."[15]

Relative Good and Evil

Archangel Gabriel also reveals the strategies of Light in the midst of the battle of Armageddon: "The dilemma of good and evil was put to naught by Jesus Christ when he addressed the rich young man who came and said unto him, 'Good Master, what good thing shall I do, that I may have eternal life?' The Master replied: 'Why callest thou me good? There is none good but one, that is, God. But if thou wilt enter into Life, keep the commandments.'[16]

"Jesus would not be classified as a good person. No, he would not. He attributed all goodness to the Person of God and the attainment of that goodness through the obedience of the chela to the commandments of the Guru and Lawgiver.

"Pride motivates men's souls in the performance of good works in order that the self may receive a reward from other selves and acquire name and fame, position and prestige. For similar reasons, in a perverted sense, the deranged perform feats of devil-daring, ideological murders, seeking for them-selves the headlines of the dailies or a reference in the history books as anti-heroes or prime movers in the mainstream of events.

"A study of the psychology of fanaticism, especially when observed in the outplaying of the psyche over several embodi-ments, reveals the pendulum swing to the right and to the left of relative good and evil as the extremes of the human consciousness find the individual positioned now with 'the good guys,' now with 'the bad guys,' but always on the same rod of energy with the mere change of the dial from plus to minus and minus to plus.

"Human hatred is human hatred, whether it takes the form of malice and premeditated evil or that of human sympathy with the human consciousness. Both attitudes fulfill the goal of the fallen ones: the destruction of souls—whether by the venom of vipers or by the milk of human kindness.

"The personality cults of the day surrounding figures in politics, religion or entertainment illustrate the game of human sympathy where individuals, incomplete in themselves, build altars to their human gods and sit in circles around their idols, totally identifying with every laugh or tear, trial and triumph, as though they were their own. So intense is their involvement with the idol that the energies of their emotional bodies flow out of themselves and into the personality figure, thus creating the emotional tie through which they can then be hypnotized and controlled.

"This willing consent given by the masses to their soapbox leaders, allowing the latter to live their lives, not only for them but through their energy, can well be labeled the emotional tyranny of the age. It occurs because individuals with a poor self-image derive satisfaction in living their lives through those who present a more colorful self-image, daring to do more 'good' or more 'evil,' as the case may be, than the less polarized, less daring masses they control.

"This relationship of the people to their gods is an obvious imitation of the true Guru-chela relationship wherein the God in the Guru and the God in the chela retain a relationship that is based upon their polarity of the light of Alpha and Omega.

"The Guru represents the God Self, the Spirit, the plus factor of life, and is the Source-emitting sun center receiving from the Above, distributing to the below. The Guru is the activator of Good, the only Good that is God.

"The chela is the passive receiver of that Good. When he receives it, he becomes a portion of the Guru and of the Person of God that the Guru has become. Now the chela (who holds the balance of the negative polarity in relationship to the One Sent) takes on, in relation to other personages in the circle of life, the plus polarity, he himself becoming a secondary outpost of the Great White Brotherhood.

"Thus in the mode of receiving life, Light and consciousness from Above, every part of life sustains the negative polarity of being in relationship to the person in Hierarchy who stands above him in the cosmic chain of initiation. Inasmuch as all who have received must become givers of the life that is Good, they, then, in the mode of givingness, assume in turn the role of the plus polarity of Alpha. Thrust and return, thrust and return is the ritual of the givingness and the receivingness of God throwing the warp and woof of a cosmos.

"Now the dilemma of good and evil becomes the drama of Gog and Magog[17] who, because they are of the same genesis of the plus, the minus of the anti-God, destroy one another, hence are self-destroyed.

"What is this human consciousness arrayed upon the human consciousness as dinosaur upon dinosaur, locked in a life and death struggle, pierce and puncture one another until their mutual viciousness is spilled upon the ground? Not as the spilling of the blood of a Christ upon Golgotha, theirs is the blood of martyrs, which they have drunk as their own death potion (though they know it not).[18]

"Unto Clare of Assisi the Saviour Jesus Christ gave the Sacred Eucharist for the turning back of the hatred of the Saracens upon themselves.[19] Thus, through the Body and Blood of Christ present in the sons and daughters of Alpha and Omega is the judgment of the nations come, and the Light of the One confounds the light and darkness in the relativity of the human consciousness.

"Saint Germain sets forth the strategy of Armageddon: It is to allow the forces of relative good and evil to array themselves, one against the other, and to cancel each other out while the Lamb, as the Word incarnate, is with the hundred and forty and four thousand who sing their new song,[20] giving dynamic decrees unto the day and unto the night. This precipitates the gently falling manna that angel ministrants place upon the tongues of God's children as his Body becomes their body and his Blood, as Spirit's Light, becomes their blood.

"They have lost their leader, these fallen ones. Lucifer is no more.[21] They have no rallying point save the ebb and tide of their own aggressions. Let the Communist regime of Cambodia's Pol Pot destroy and be destroyed by the Communist Vietnamese as column upon column of the black ants invade the territory of the red ants in this Communist game of checkers wherein each side, drugged by their own hatred of the Light and drunk with the blood of martyrs whom they have murdered by the millions, is too insensate to know that Death itself speaks from both ends, playing them against the middle, when they say, 'We pledge to fight them to the end.'[22]

"This is a mini war of Gog and Magog, of the sympathetic

Communism of the Soviet Union in polarity with the malicious Communism of Red China. Yes, each assumes from time to time the polarity of the other in the plus/minus exchange. It is only the dance of the most unfortunate advance, swinging partners right and left but always returning to the point of origin that is Anti-Light.

"These factions of the tares live off the wheat, you know. Let the children of the Light beware! Let them withdraw their supplies, manpower and matériel, their technology, taxes, trained experts and tender loving care from the Gogs and Magogs West and East. Their principalities and potentates are everywhere positioned, vying for the power of the Son of God....

"Don't take sides, for neither one will win.... Human good and evil will never out. Only Truth will triumph over sin. While everywhere the power plays go on among the spiritually wicked in high places[23] and they volley for financial empires built upon the souls of people—who are guilty in part, for they have played their game of the personality cult from the start— the Son of God in the Son of man stands unmovable as the Rock, still waiting to receive all who will receive him in purest Light."[24]

Ancient Rivalries of the Fallen Ones

Uriel, the Archangel of the Judgment, reveals further aspects of these ancient conspiracies and rivalries that we see outplaying in the Middle East: "I AM Uriel, and once again we must hold the citadel of Light against that encroachment of darkness, always threatening, of the abuse of Light in the Middle East—to turn it against the Woman and her seed, always threatening to make that point, that point of definition for who shall conquer the whole world.

"Therefore, let the Light prevail! And let our hearts of Light united as one, in the very heart of Helios and Vesta with your own, go forth then. For the armies of the LORD are with the saints on the earth. And whereas the leaders have not the faintest idea or the understanding of the battle of Armageddon —or where is the true promised land of the I AM Race—we, the mighty Archangels, will defend a point of Light.

"And we stand in the Middle East also for the judgment of the Nephilim gods who have usurped that land for more than a half a million years and beyond, into the very mists of antiquity, to overturn the Light, even the promised Light that was sent.

"I lay the sword of the One Sent upon the altar of the Grail and I address you, my beloved, out of the Book of the Law; for He came and took incarnation in the East, there at the midpoint of continents—there to separate the darkness, there to bind the darkness.

"Beloved hearts of Light, the age-old conspiracy of Gog and Magog has been interpreted in many ways, but I would give to you an understanding of an ancient history of two rival forces representing, as it were, the king of the North and the king of the South—both anti-gods. These kings, however, not located in the earth (as noted in the prophecy of Daniel[25]) but located beyond this solar system, sent their forces for the conquering of worlds. And they used every conceivable and inconceivable means to thwart the plan of Almighty God and to outsmart one another.

"Therefore, you will understand that this rivalry, as it is the opposition that ought to be the harmony of the Light of Alpha and Omega, has existed for aeons and aeons. You see that rivalry among the fallen ones, among the species. You will note their rivalry; you will note it in the political arena, in the military forces.

"You will note the division, even within nations, of various factions who move one against the other, even the division of Lebanon herself and other nations of the Middle East where the factions, posing as this and that, right and left representative of the major world's religions, are yet locked in a deadly combat one against the other—who ought to be brethren but are not. For they are not the seed of Light; yet they take upon themselves the form of the worship, whereas they do not embody the fullness of the Light of Christ.

"Therefore, the mechanical recitation of the Word does not afford them the very nucleus of the living Light. Yet nevertheless, they are the *imitators* as impostors of the Word.

"Thus, they seize upon the major world's religions, they become fanatical in a fundamental interpretation, an orthodox version that denies the very Body and Blood of the living Word, that denies the flame of love. And they are beyond religion. In every sector of society, the extremists right and left, pitted against one another, still represent the ancient force and the forces of Gog and Magog that one day must devour one another on the planes of the earth.

"See them, then—whether the interpretation is between the Red Chinese and the Soviets, or whether between various factions in Iran or Iraq or in Lebanon, or even among the Christians or even among the Jews—where there be these ones, beloved hearts, realize then that there is no love of Christ, no love of Buddha, no love of the Light, no love of the little children, but only a determination to the end, even unto the death, to destroy one another.

"Thus, this mortal combat even threatened this very soil as one of the representatives of these forces from beyond this planet rose up to create the divisive elements and to align that similar seed of Gog and Magog in the War between the States.[26] This attempted division of America came from these very ancient rebels beyond this system that were part of the Nephilim ones, even those fallen ones.

"They came fully arrayed with their armies and spacecraft and have continued to despise the children of the Light. But their despise* has no end when it comes to their determination to destroy one another. For they are determined that not two, but one between them, shall rule the entire universe. Such is their ambition.

"Does it sound somehow like the ancient gods of Rome or beyond on Atlantis, or the war of the gods on Lemuria or even prior to Lemuria? Well, beloved hearts, it is the same—the one. These archenemies, therefore, blinded by their mutual hatreds, unite only for the destruction of the living Word and the Christ who is their common enemy.

"This they have done time and again when it came to eliminating those who held the flame of freedom. Otherwise they never end their engagement of rivalry, and thus it has been the complaint of both men and angels: the viciousness of the political campaigns in this nation itself and in every nation in the world, as these rivalries have resulted in murders—as in the Philippines, as in the nations of Africa—and they cannot endure that the rival should succeed.

"Thus, the desecration of the principles of Saint Germain, and of the representative form of government, which is entirely in harmony with the hearts of the children of God and the sons of God who could live peaceably according to the vote of the people, or the vote of the representatives of the people.

"Thus, the name-calling and the mudslinging may begin again in another round of elections here and there, and you will be all the wiser. For I, Uriel, have come to show you, as in the case of Gabriel defining the red ants and the black ants in

---

* *despise:* (substantive, obscure; from Old French *despiz, despis*), despite, contempt, malice; used in English literature in the 15th and 16th centuries.

Cambodia and Vietnam,[27] so there has ever been this rivalry. Caught in the middle of this are the forces of freedom on a peace-keeping mission.[28] Beloved ones, to keep the peace requires that those engaged in war desire peace. And thus, instead, they become fodder in the cross fire of these fallen ones nation by nation.

"Once again we must declare to the Lightbearers that unless the wages are understood, unless the chessmen are known, unless the forces, the lifewaves and the evolution are *seen,* scarcely shall the elect be saved.[29] The fallen ones on Atlantis, who also destroyed that continent in their manipulation of energy, have reembodied again to hold in tow the children of the Light and to attempt to give them talismans, electrodes (even misusing the Light of the pyramid), connecting not hearts with Heart, but the astral bodies once again.

"The manipulators of energy from interplanetary levels have come in many forms—not merely as serpents but as the 'cat people,' as they are called. And these fallen ones are determined to claw against the Light of the Woman until they defeat not only one another, but also the armies of heaven.

"All of this Saint Germain and the Darjeeling Council have before them. And they have sent me, therefore, to declare to you the God-determination of the legions of the seven mighty Archangels come to earth once again for the defense of every Lightbearer.

"The recommendation of Archangel Gabriel has been to let these fallen ones destroy one another; and the Lords of Karma have pointed out: 'but not at the expense of the Light or the earth or freedom itself.' And therefore, there is an adjudication. There is a very careful deliberation, measure for measure, as to how much the karma of the laggards is allowed to fall upon them and how much there must be the intervention of the forces of freedom.

"If the forces of freedom are always fearing the fallen ones and their victory, always fearing the triumph in war and can never take a stand, it is easy to see, as we have said many times, that the Bear will eat away until there is nothing left and world freedom herself is threadbare and tattered....

"I turn the page now to the record in the last days of Atlantis—how the hordes of laggard lifewaves overran that continent and desecrated the Light, the temples, the life-force. The compromise of the seed of Sanat Kumara is a history that repeats itself. Somehow the people have forgotten the Word of the LORD that the seed of Light must not intermarry with the aliens from other systems who are the godless, the defiant ones.[30] But as the Hebrews, some went after the Canaanites, some went after this seed. So it is today, so it was in Atlantis, so it was in Lemuria.

"Why do you suppose the Lord Sanat Kumara called Abraham, and called the father of Abraham, and called the lineage of Abraham out of Ur of the Chaldees?[31] It was to separate out the seed of Light to bring them into a far country and to allow once again the purity of the I AM Race to have the genetic structure through which to embody, free of the manipulation of those fallen ones who were even then encamped around that city.

"In each new age, after each new period of cataclysm and the resolution of forces, when life once again begins to dawn upon earth, there is the desire of the Almighty One to send twin flames, representatives of the Manus, into embodiment to bear the archetype of mind, soul, heart and body unto this seed of Light. But again and again and again, once the seed is in embodiment and once they develop that point of Christhood, they are snatched into revolving again the interchange, the entangling alliances with those who are not from Above, but from beneath.

"Thus it has become very difficult for the Lords of Karma, even in these hours, to send souls of Light. Tremendous dispensations have gone forth, about which you have not even heard a word—so complex are these, having to do with the neutralization in the newborn children of certain of the forces in the very genetic code itself, transmitted through the physical bodies where there has been the intermingling of the blood (and this has occurred almost universally).

"Thus, beloved hearts, many, many Lightbearers have come through those whose bodies have also come down generation by generation by the admixture of all sorts of evolutions from various systems, many of these who have never held in their cells or in their chakras the true and living Light of the threefold flame.

"The manipulation of life, the creation of life in the ancient game of the rivalries is even beyond your ken, so vast was the scheme to create myriad evolutions. For in the rivalries of Gog and Magog, they required more and more forces, more and more legions, more and more armies pitted one against the other, that the final outcome might be seen as a victory for one of the two head rivals.

"All of this human creation, therefore, was for that purpose and to that end. And you can see that war and the pitting of these armies one against another has never ceased. And if you would actually come face-to-face in the Middle East with these legions representing these nations, you would find a relentless hatred, and you would have a certain despair and hopelessness that peace could ever come to the Middle East, for the vendetta is 'never let go.'

"Thus, in bringing children of the Light through these lineages, the dispensations of the Four and Twenty Elders have been to set aside and neutralize so that the Manchild could spring forth, almost as a phoenix bird out of the ashes of the dying race.

"Most amazing, amazing configurations of the descent of Lightbearers have occurred upon this earth. And truly in this hour no longer may it be determined that the seed of darkness may only produce darkness; but through it may pass, unscathed, Lightbearers of God-determination—so determined that they would be born through anyone—and upon their rejection at one age or the next, or at full maturity, they would turn and judge the very ones who bore them.

"And you would find that the Light of the Presence and the threefold flame itself, by the time they had reached the age of thirty-three, had already passed through, neutralized and transmuted every evil element of the tares sown among the wheat.[32] Most amazing, therefore, is the transfer of the evolutions of the Spirit into the physical octave.

"Therefore, we come and make known to you, on the wings of the Light of Sanat Kumara and his mighty dictation on the coming race,[33] that we are here for the defense of the open door of the Lightbearers and of the community of the Holy Spirit worldwide. We come to reinforce and protect your hearts and souls, as you are vessels of Saint Germain.

"We come physically to stand, and stand with our very bodies of Light, against the forces of infamy. We are determined to protect a flame of God-harmony and not to allow the determinations of the Soviet Union to exacerbate the already horrendous problems in the Middle East.

"We pray that our determination will be matched by freedom-fighters worldwide, and we are here to help by delivering this night a mighty light of freedom, a glow of the golden pink glow-ray and the fohat of the ancient priesthood of the Order of Melchizedek, who himself came to earth determined to stand guard in the very presence of Abraham for the consecration of Light....

"Children of the Sun, sons and daughters of the Most High, I bow before the Light of the Sun within you. My heart is pledged to defend that Light as the Light of the Almighty One; and I have assigned my legions the task of the reminders (by the violet fire and the blue lightning) that ye are brethren, ye are servants of the Most High, and ye will not fail in the God-harmony that is where you are and where I AM.

"You will not fail to call forth the judgment upon Gog and Magog and all forces thusly pitted against one another to the death. Let them be *bound* in the name of the Lord Christ! I, Archangel Uriel, speak it, and I have spoken it in the name of Helios and Vesta.

"Let Gog and Magog be bound! And therefore, let their power be reduced and let their karma be upon them and let it be turned unto them—and let the blood of the prophets be required of them.[34] For I am the mouthpiece of the judgment of the Cosmic Christ. I say the Lightbearers are raised up and these age-old rivals are put down by the hand of the Almighty.

"Now understand, where you see this death grip and where you see this locking-in of deadly combat, understand that there you will find the ancient rivalry that must be bound.[35] Not among the sons of God of all ages, even in their struggles and in their karmic cycles, has there ever been in cosmos a mutual hatred so great as these forces of Gog and Magog contain.

"Therefore, Helios and Vesta admonish the sons and daughters of God: Put aside your differences and enter the Union. Be not caught in the skirmishes of these ones, but understand the true love of Christ, and thereby shall all men know that ye are brethren and disciples in his name."[36]

The Judgment

*And whosoever was not
found written in the book of
life was cast into the lake of
fire.*   REVELATION

ONE OF THE GREAT FALLACIES that mankind have long held concerning the return of the Christ and the finalizing of the battle of Armageddon is that these two events are grouped into one concept or doctrine of the end of the world and the Last Judgment.

However, it is recorded in the Book of Ecclesiastes: "One generation passeth away, and another generation cometh: but the earth abideth for ever."[1] Yet, mention is also made of the coming of the end of the world. The end of the world may come about countless times for each individual

The sole purpose of the creation of the material universe as well as the creation of the physical body was to provide a platform for evolving souls. Therefore, the outer creation (the physical earth and the physical body of man) must continue until the individual Spirit-sparks have taken the fullest advantage of their experiential opportunities, have found liberation from rebirth or the wheel of karma, and have been elevated in the ritual of the ascension to become Ascended Masters—one with the Priesthood of Melchizedek, one with the living Christ.

The Book of Revelation reveals a path of initiation that each soul in her season must pass through if she would ascend to God. It is a study in the psychology of the soul and the testings she must master on her homeward path leading to reunion with Alpha and Omega, the Father-Mother God.

At any point in time and space in any century, the soul on the path of reunion with God may experience in sequence, one after the other, the initiations encoded in the twenty-two chapters of Revelation; these correspond to the symbology of the twenty-two letters of the Hebrew alphabet. According to their soul pattern, evolution and attainment, Lightbearers of the world are experiencing all of the leaves of Revelation; and each of those leaves is tumbling in its time and space, though not necessarily in the same dimension, for we are multi-dimensional beings.

Revelation juxtaposes the soul and the collective planetary evolution with the forces of Light and Darkness engaged in Armageddon. The outcome of this warfare of the Spirit is either the soul's resurrection unto eternal life or her final judgment. By free will, the soul must choose either the path of initiation under the Lamb of God and his hosts or the path of Lucifer and the fallen angels in their rebellion against the LORD God and his Christ.

In Revelation we find an outline of these two paths and a prophecy of the outcome of free-will choices made—to be or not to be—each step of the way.

Through a preordained series of lifetimes God gives each soul the opportunity (1) to serve the LORD and glorify him in her members or (2) to deify the ego, the synthetic self and the carnal mind Paul spoke of when he said: "To be carnally minded is death."[2] Those who take this path do swear enmity with God and his Christ and make war with the remnant of the seed of the Divine Mother.

At the end of this cycle of opportunity, which extends over myriad incarnations on earth, the time comes when the soul "is judged according to his works."[3] The Keeper of the Scrolls reads the soul's record before the Ancient of Days, who sits on the great white throne at the Court of the Sacred Fire, and before the Four Beasts and the Twenty-Four Elders.[4]

Dictating through John the Revelator, Jesus defined two paths—the path of the overcomers and their reward, and the path of the violators of God's laws and their end in the second death, which is the merciful canceling out of the soul potential that has denied the incarnation of God within her temple:

> He that overcometh shall inherit all things; and I will be his God, and he shall be my son. But the fearful, and unbelieving, and the abominable, and murderers, and whoremongers, and sorcerers, and idolaters, and all liars, shall have their part in the lake which burneth with fire and brimstone: which is the second death....
>
> And, behold, I come quickly; and my reward is with me, to give every man according as his work shall be. I am Alpha and Omega, the beginning and the end, the first and the last. Blessed are they that do his commandments, that they may have right to the tree of life, and may enter in through the gates into the city.[5]

"The Father Hath Committed all Judgment unto the Son"

Evil, in itself, is misqualified energy, the malintent behind it, and the entity encompassing both. By the very nature of the Liar and his lie—the consciousness behind it—evil at its inception is deceptive and deceitful. In fact, it is a veil of illusion—an energy veil, or *e-veil,* enshrouding the Deity and all his marvelous works. Illusion, or *maya,* as the Hindus call it, then appears more real than Reality itself. In fact, men's illusions become their gods, and evil is deified.

Now, what is plain to see is that a devil *(d-evil)* is one who has deified evil and the entire energy veil. A devil is one who has deified the dweller-on-the-threshold to the position of Christ and has declared himself master and saviour of the world, whether in politics or art or in the philosopher's chair.

Since the one who embodies the dweller, thereby deifying evil, may have been a Watcher or a fallen angel, the attainment at the point of the Fall may have been very great—for these fallen ones once had a great Light, dwelling as they did in the courts of heaven with our Father and Mother. So the greater the Light at the point of the Fall, the greater the Fall, and the longer the extension of time and space in which to repent. For God in his truly great mercy gives to that one an opportunity commensurate with his office in Hierarchy at the time of the Fall to repent and to return to him.

Those who once had great Light may thus be given even a longer opportunity to balance their karma and return to the throne of grace than those who had less. This is a corollary to the Law of Karma, as it is written: "For he that hath, to him shall be given; and he that hath not, from him shall be taken even that which he hath."[6]

Therefore, the opportunity given to some of the fallen ones has been very, very long, until even the Psalmist thousands of years ago cried out, "How long, O Lord, how long will the wicked triumph?"[7] For the power of their dweller-on-the-threshold seems endless as they move against the children of God who seem so much less powerful and often helpless.

Indeed, the fallen angels who swore their eternal enmity against God in heaven move freely on earth, embodying the dweller with bravado, sophistication, wealth and worldly wisdom until they should be confronted by someone in embodiment—someone who has the courage to be the spokesman for the Elect One. For by definition, by the very science of Being, that Elect One who cometh in the name of the LORD I AM THAT I AM has the attainment of Light physically manifest equal to the dark ones; the One Sent did not fall from grace but took incarnation for the express purpose of challenging the seed of the wicked on behalf of the shorn lambs of God.

This is why John the Baptist and Jesus Christ as well as the prophets and the avatars of all ages have come to the earth: "For judgment I am come into this world."[8] They come because they want to give a reprieve to the blessed children of God who are tormented by these fallen ones and yet have not the ability—the externalized Christ consciousness—to move against them.

In this hour of the Aquarian age and the dispensation of Saint Germain, we find that by the science of the spoken Word, when we give our dynamic decrees in the name of the Christ, in the name of the entire Spirit of the Great White Brotherhood or any of the Ascended Masters, we are decreeing in the full magnitude of their attainment sealed in their Causal Body of Light.

When you decree in the name of Saint Germain, instantaneously you have behind your call the full power of the Light qualified by the Ascended Master Saint Germain for thousands of years. His purple fiery heart multiplies the power of your heart, and it is as though Saint Germain and you were one. In fact, you are one.

Therefore, when you confront the Adversary within or without, you know that Saint Germain has the equivalent or greater of the power of the Archangel (or any other fallen one) when he fell. And therefore Saint Germain is able to fulfill the decree of the Word through you, even if your own external-ized light is not adequate to the encounter with Antichrist.

When we give Jesus' Judgment Call, "They Shall Not Pass!" (see page 348) and we are naming the oppressors of the people of God, we are focusing on the self-conscious awareness of the individual in his motives and actions to manipulate Life against the purposes of the Godhead. When we give the decree for the binding and the casting out of the dweller (page 350), we are getting at the core of the human creation that is in opposition to the Divine. We are getting at the nucleus of the anti-God, or the anti-Self, and demanding that it be bound. The Judgment Call involves the judgment of words and deeds, the judgment of actions, step by step. It may bring the judgment of returning karma to the individual for a single act, for a single embodiment, for a single momentum; whereas the decree on the dweller is for the binding and casting out of the entire conglomerate of the carnal mind coiled in the center of the electronic belt. It is the original seed of evil at its inception, which has grown to the present hour from the point of its beginning—millions of years ago, a hundred thousand years ago, five years ago.

In Jesus' name we may give these decrees and, as repre-sentatives of the Elect One, become a part of the Brother-hood's concerted efforts to move against world situations—

organized crime, war, massive forcefields of negative energy, problems in the economy—which to a great extent are controlled by Watchers and fallen ones who long ago chose to embody the dweller-on-the-threshold and have actually gone unchallenged (in this physical octave, i.e., on this Earth) since the last Christed one appeared.

As a result of the dispensation of Jesus' judgments, his call to our Father and his Presence with us whereby we may now indeed challenge by Christ's power the evildoers, we are seeing unprecedented planetary changes. The fallen ones are shocked and affrighted. They cannot believe that they could be challenged and that the Light—or the "Light-bearer"—could win, so accustomed are they to look down upon and to control by intimidation the children of God who do not have nearly the momentum on creating Good that they, the fallen ones, have on creating Evil.

At whatever point the reprobate decided to embody the dweller, at that point on the Path he inverted the Light he had acquired up to that moment. If he succeeded in stealing the fruit of the tree of the knowledge of good and evil, and was not then and is not now challenged by a son of God, he will go on misappropriating the Light, turning it to greater darkness. Thus he practices karma-dodging by devices of deceit, fooling the children of the Light, inciting them to accuse one another, to argue with each other, to be discordant, to engage in wars and genocide in defense of Nephilim divide-and-conquer political schemes.

This inequity between the children of Light and the children of this world (the seed of Christ and the seed of the Watchers and Nephilim) led Jesus to admonish: "The children of this world are in their generation wiser than the children of light.... Be ye therefore wise as serpents and harmless as doves."[9]

Making karma by their foolishness, putting their attention upon the fallen ones through idolatry, the children of Light unwittingly give them their energy. (It is the law of karma: that which we place our attention on, or give our devotion to, we become; i.e., energy flows to the object of our attention and devotion.)

The fallen ones make a spectacle of themselves, preferring politics, the media and entertainment as center stage. Focusing our attention on their outrageous, hilarious or spectacular antics, they rake in our money and our Light. And therefore, a fallen one walking the earth today as the incarnate dweller-on-the-threshold, though spiritually bankrupt, may actually be gathering more power and more Light unto himself, which he turns into darkness to control and destroy the very ones from whom he has taken it by the schemes he has perpetrated.

Thus the dynasties of the powered and moneyed interests carry on "the tradition," reincarnating until the law of cycles decrees their judgment by the sons of God, Ascended and unascended. And so the cycles of manipulation continue until the one aligned with the Great White Brotherhood raises his right hand, lifts up his voice unto the LORD God, the Almighty One, and says: "In the name of Jesus Christ, Thus far and no farther! Enough!" and then gives the decree for the binding and the casting out of the dweller-on-the-threshold of the manipulators of the people.

This is a very important call, because when we say, "I cast out the dweller-on-the-threshold," we're talking about the personal and planetary dweller, we're talking about everyone on earth in or out of embodiment who has raised a clenched fist to dare the Almighty to strike him dead, everyone who has hated the Light, declared war against the Faithful and True, and spilled the blood of his sons and daughters in the rites and revenge of Hell.

When this call is given, whoever the perpetrators of evil are (and we ourselves need not know), the Angels of the Lord Christ—the legions of the Archangels and of Elohim—bind and render inactive the core of Absolute Evil within them and all that is aligned with it. This is the true and righteous judgment that cleaves asunder the Real from the unreal, thereby opening the door to salvation to millions of oppressed peoples worldwide, and saving the world from the ultimate revenge of the false gods: planetary holocaust.

It is our earnest prayer that those whose ungodly deeds are challenged by our call—even those allied with nefarious practices—might be liberated from the strong delusions of the dweller and make an about-face to serve the living God. In giving this call, we are the champions of the soul and the defenders of the right of the individual to be free from the sinister strategies of the carnal mind—free to be his Real Self. This is a rescue mission on behalf of all caught in the grips of the illusions of the astral plane and its denizens.

This is the increase of the Christ consciousness on earth. The Judgment Call and the dweller decree are given by the son of God as the signal to his angels that the consummation of the age of Pisces is at hand and the harvest of the tares sown among the wheat is nigh.

It is time for the bands of angels known as the Reapers to gather the seed of the children of the Wicked One sown among the good seed of the Son of man.[10] When both calls dictated by beloved Jesus are combined with calls to the Elohim Astrea, Archangel Michael and the violet flame, you will find that the Archangels can move in to do a wondrous work for God and his children of Light on earth.

We see that by the lineage of the path of discipleship, the saints have the mantle and the dispensation for the judgment not only of the fallen angels whose hour has come, but also of those among the twelve tribes who have committed themselves to their cause. It is written in the Bible that Jesus said, "The Father judgeth no man, but hath committed all judgment unto the Son."[11] And the Son Jesus has given that authority for the judgment to the apostles through the holy Christ Self:

> Do ye not know that the saints shall judge the world? and if the world shall be judged by you, are ye unworthy to judge the smallest matters? Know ye not that we shall judge angels? how much more things that pertain to this life?
>
> And Jesus said unto them, Verily I say unto you, That ye which have followed me, in the regeneration when the Son of man shall sit in the throne of his glory, ye also shall sit upon twelve thrones, judging the twelve tribes of Israel.
>
> Ye are they which have continued with me in my temptations. And I appoint unto you a kingdom, as my Father hath appointed unto me, that ye may eat and drink at my table in my kingdom and sit on thrones judging the twelve tribes of Israel.
>
> And when he had said this, he breathed on them, and saith unto them, Receive ye the Holy Ghost: Whose soever sins ye remit, they are remitted unto them; and whose soever sins ye retain, they are retained.[12]

The problem with Christianity today is that the children of the Light are not being given the tools to obey Christ's injunction: Be not overcome of the Evil One but overcome the power of Evil with the power of Good.[13] While the world hangs in the balance of the arms race and war on every hand, the *sword* of the Saviour—the science of the *Spoken Word*—is waiting to be wielded by all sons of God on earth for the binding of planetary evil and those who are its perpetrators.

The Second Death

When the fallen ones are removed by the calls given by the Messengers and the students of Light, and amplified by those of the Ascended Masters, then those who have followed darkness for many embodiments are taken to the Court of the Sacred Fire upon Sirius, which is the God Star, the focus of the Great Central Sun in our sector of the galaxy. There they stand on the dais of white fire, and they must give answer for the use they have made of God's Light.

They are asked the question, "What have you done of worth to serve mankind?" Most of them can offer nothing. And if there is no spark of divinity in them that has been used for Good and there is nothing left of Good, then, when they stand in the center of the ascension flame, the flame from Alpha is released from above and the flame of Omega rises from below and they are consumed; and they go through what is known as the second death.

The second death means that they do not have any further opportunity for reembodiment. It means that their energies are taken to the Central Sun and repolarized as raw material again, as clay that is put back into a lump so that it can be used again in the universe for the creation of perfect forms. In other words, this identity no longer exists when it passes through that flame.

The Christ Self of that lifestream merges with the Universal Christ; the I AM Presence of that lifestream merges with the Universal I AM Presence. And the energy that was used to create the soul and the energy that was used by the soul in its miscreations is withdrawn back to the God Star for requalification in a giant forcefield of the sacred fire that is named in the Book of Revelation as the "lake of fire."[14]

The Lightbearers are also preparing to stand on that dais, and most likely if one of us were to stand upon it today, we would also be consumed. We may have more human creation in our worlds, in our four lower bodies, than we have Light, and so we are not taken there for our judgment today.

We are in embodiment with the opportunity to evolve. If we pass from this embodiment with good works and good deeds, yet not enough momentum of Light to stand this acid test of going through the Flame, we are given another embodiment and another until our momentum of Light is at least 51 percent. That, then, is enough to stand in the Flame and not be consumed by the Flame. Thus we become one with the Flame and gain our eternal identity; and this is known as the ascension in the Light.*

Jesus explains this process as it occurs at the end of cycles: "At the conclusion of a cosmic cycle, God, by the momentum of his great love, draws the entire creation into his being, as the fire infolding itself. At that moment of the inbreath, or the drawing-in, when God receives unto himself all that he has sent forth, the fires of the Holy Spirit consume all that has refused to identify with the Reality of God. As all energy has gone forth from him, so all energy will return to him. The purposes of life, then, are not destined to death from the beginning, as some have averred; but the sons and daughters of God are destined to eternal life if they will espouse that life as a living flame while they yet abide on earth.

"Some have regarded the cycles of man upon the planet as the Psalmist once described them: 'As for man, his days are as

---

* Additional explanation of the second death and the Court of the Sacred Fire will be included in chapter 22 of the Climb the Highest Mountain series, "Immortality," which will be included in Book 7.

grass: as a flower of the field, so he flourisheth. For the wind passeth over it, and it is gone; and the place thereof shall know it no more. But the mercy of the LORD is from everlasting to everlasting."[15] This is the description of the cycles of mortals and mortality. For there are some who are born to die because they have not come forth from life but from the seed of the Wicked.

"Of those who are created of God, it is said in the Bhagavad-Gita:

> Never the Spirit [the I AM Presence] was born;
>   the Spirit shall cease to be never;
> Never was time it was not;
>   End and Beginning are dreams!
> Birthless and deathless and changeless
>   remaineth the Spirit for ever;
> Death hath not touched it at all,
>   dead though the house of it seems![16]

"Long ago I said, 'Fear not them which kill the body, but are not able to kill the soul: but rather fear him which is able to destroy both soul and body in hell.'[17] Men may indeed kill the body, but they cannot kill the soul unless it be with the conscious consent of the individual. It is only because man by his misuse of free will consents to the manifestation of evil through the misuse of God's energy that he can pass through the second death, which is the death of the soul. Embodiment after embodiment, man is given opportunity by God to ensoul the virtues that flow from his heart in an endless chain of his own Self-realization.

"It is the opportunity of every individual, whether he be of the evolution of the Wicked and the fallen ones or of the children of the Light, to choose to ensoul the beauties of eternity. But if individuals neglect to challenge the energy veil created by the carnal mind, if by their free will they allow evil intent to continue in themselves and in society embodiment after embodiment, they will eventually come to the end of the spiral of opportunity. And when their miscreations are swallowed up in the fires of love, they, too, will be no more, because they have identified totally with the unreality of the not-self instead of with the Reality of the God Self. This is the death of the soul-consciousness. When this occurs, the I AM Presence merges with the Universal Presence of God, and the Christ consciousness merges with the Christ Self-awareness that is the Universal Logos.[18]

"Thus nothing is lost but the potential of the soul to become God. Nevertheless, when one considers the worth of one soul who has united with God in the ritual of the ascension, this is a very great loss indeed.... Likewise, how devastating can be the example of the soul that is wedded through satanic ritual to the carnal mind and its evil ways. As in the example of Lucifer, such a soul can take other millions of lifewaves from the true course of nativity in God. Therefore, the destiny of the soul is entirely in the hands of the individual and in the use he makes of the opportunity for life and the expansion of life's potential."[19]

The Implementation of the Judgment

El Morya explains the implementation of the judgment midst the outplaying of Armageddon: "To understand what is behind what is taking place today, you must go back to the roots of Lemuria. For all other roots only reflect more recent millions of years upon the planetary body. When you go to Lemuria, you go to the cradle of life, you go to the beginnings of beginning, you go to the Mother flame, and you see how life has progressed—first with the early root races and then with the great rebellion of the Archangel affecting vast systems of the galaxies.

"To trace all of these intricacies and to see how these are being outplayed in the Middle East and in Africa today and then to understand what is that God-solution—I can assure you that we also pray, we also meditate, we also decree. And we are in touch with the great Cosmic Council that governs the flow of life to this planetary home.

"We are proceeding with all due deliberation with our program of enlightenment for the path of initiation. We must tell you, however, that there are many individuals upon this planetary body, millions in fact, who according to all testings and examinations of their existence over hundreds and thousands of years have steadfastly rejected whatever manifestation of the Cosmic Christ was incarnate. They have rejected the Path. They have rejected the Almighty One. We do not send you to these but to the lost sheep of the house of Israel.[20]

"However, the knowledge of the presence of these individuals, their destructivity, their anti-love demonstrations, can only tell you that with their continued manifestation in power in these nations, there is not a God-solution until there be an alteration complete of the course of human events. For by cosmic law we are not allowed to interfere with free will. The only interference that can come with the free will that is committed to death and to the death of millions is the judgment of the LORD God Almighty himself, when and only when that judgment is implemented by the sons and daughters of God in embodiment. Therefore, when the Lord Jesus Christ pronounces the judgment, it must be pronounced through those in embodiment. The Word must go forth, and it must manifest in the plane where the judgment is required.

"Thus, you see, following the fall of Lucifer and the Satanists, their judgment was postponed for two reasons: (1)

the mercy of the Law extending to them the opportunity to repent and to bend the knee; (2) waiting for the moment when those originally overcome by the fallen ones would reach the level of attainment, moving from the aspect of the child to the full heir of Sonship and therefore capable of calling forth the judgment, implementing the judgment by the spoken Word, but not being overcome by the reactionary forces of the fallen ones. For you see, the ones who invoke the judgment in that physical plane—where that judgment must be meted—will be required to receive the lashback of the dragon's tail until all energy spent following the judgment results in the individual's dissolution into the white-fire core of the Central Sun.

"I am telling you, beloved ones, that once the judgment call is given upon an individual lifestream, if it is ordained by God and ordained by the son of God in embodiment, yet that seed of the wicked has a certain prescribed number of cycles in which it is allowed to outspend the remaining energy lodged within its aura and physical form. Thus, between the hour of the judgment and the consummation of the judgment is a battle! And this is the nature of Armageddon.

"The forces of Darkness in the battle of Armageddon are already judged by the Almighty, who awaits the attendant confirmation of the judgment by the embodied sons of God. Once it is spoken, the battle rages all the more. And unless sons and daughters of God in embodiment—truly, chelas all the way—are able to stand fast and hold the balance, there may be in the shuffle the loss of certain little ones.

"We are concerned for these little ones in every nation, but our problem solving is complicated by the fact that many of these fallen ones know all too well the Law that I am speaking to you. Therefore, they know that the son of God is about to pronounce the judgment, will pronounce the judgment, and therefore they take a head start on the battle of Armageddon.

And therefore the raging begins, like the horses that cannot be contained in their stalls before the shot is fired at the beginning of the race.

"These ones, then, attempt to preempt the coming of the sons of God. They mock the judgment affirmed and confirmed by these sons. They set up their own courts and they, then, judge the children of the Light and the sons and daughters of God before they in turn will be judged. They create their wars. And the holocausts of this century have already shown the outplaying of the forces of the fallen ones who have known that their time was short.

"Thus, until the judgment [call] is given, we may not intercede. But before it is given, there is grave danger to the little ones. And after it is given, we must assist in its implementation, we must awaken, we must illumine. We must summon the ones who will hold the balance and understand that there is great treachery, then, in those periods following the invocation of the calls."[21]

The End of the Age

The Book of Enoch reveals that the hour of the judgment of the fallen ones will come in the end of the age. We are living in a time when many of them are going to their final judgment.

On April 16, 1975, Lucifer was bound by Archangel Michael and taken to the Court of the Sacred Fire on the etheric plane of the God Star Sirius, where he stood trial before the Four and Twenty Elders over a period of ten days. The testimony of many souls of Light in embodiment on Terra and other planets and systems was heard, together with that of the Ascended Masters, Archangels and Elohim.

On April 26, 1975, he was found guilty of total rebellion

against Almighty God by the unanimous vote of the Twenty Four and sentenced to the second death. As he stood on the disc of the sacred fire before the court, the flame of Alpha and Omega rose as a spiral of intense white light, canceling out an identity and a consciousness that had influenced the fall of one third of the angels of the galaxies and countless lifewaves evolving in this and other systems of worlds.[22]

On January 27, 1982, Satan was remanded to the Court of the Sacred Fire, resulting in his final judgment and second death.[23] Many others who followed the Fallen One in the Great Rebellion have also been brought to trial in this era.

Galactic Armageddon

*For then shall be great
tribulation, such as was not
since the beginning of the world
to this time, no, nor ever shall
be.*   JESUS

O N FEBRUARY 26, 1980, SANAT
Kumara announced the release
of an electrode of Light that was to assist mankind to overcome "the ungodly mass manipulation of the mind and brains
of the people of earth." He discusses the vastness of this
manipulation and the Galactic Armageddon that is taking
place on earth now:

"The Seven Holy Kumaras have released their Light and
sealed it in an inner electrode neath the crown chakra of the
children of the Light who are a part of the evolutions of earth,
from those on the physical plane through the highest levels
of the etheric plane unascended. The Light is sealed,
encapsulated. It cannot be interfered with or misused by any
consciousness that is beneath the vibration of the God
consciousness. It becomes an electrode to increase freedom—

freedom in the mind, independence in the mind.

"There is a spiral emitting from this microscopic forcefield of Light. It begins to turn, radiating and emanating through the mental body and the very brain itself an energy unique from the very nucleus of the I AM Presence. It is an energy and a dispensation that has not been given in this manner to the evolutions of earth. It is transmitted because of the ungodly mass manipulation of the minds and the brains of the people on earth.

"This manipulation has caused the enslavement of humanity and the limitation of their expression as well as their interaction with the mind of God. It has been carried on scientifically and methodically by the fallen ones, those in embodiment, those on the astral plane and those who have come periodically from other systems of worlds in their spaceships to take advantage of the lesser development of this particular lifewave. This interference with the spiritual evolution of the lifewaves of earth, from the extraterrestrial individuals as well as from the fallen ones, has been a principal reason that earth's evolutions have not responded or accelerated into their God-capacity.

"Their manipulation has consisted of placing wedges within the very structure of the four lower bodies to block the flow from the heart to the head, and from the head to the heart. This explains the nondevelopment of the heart chakra, the overdevelopment of the brain, and the consequent psychological problems, the distortions and the imbalance in millions upon millions now inhabiting the earth.

"Though we have been aware of this activity for aeons, it was the karma of earth's evolutions, as well as the absence of sufficient numbers of Lightbearers, that made it difficult for the emissaries of cosmic councils of Ascended Masters to intercede. It was also necessary that certain cycles of solar systems and galaxies and the cycles of the judgment of the fallen ones be fulfilled.

"Our coming to this earth was an original mission to counteract this manipulation, which had brought the lifewave here to such a low manifestation. You who came with me volunteered to enter life in the dense bodies already interfered with by the fallen ones. Thus, though you knew the darkness, you really did not know how dark was that darkness.

"It is one thing to offer to evolve through primitive life; it is another to offer to incarnate knowing the impairment of the vehicles, the vehicles that could be offered through the pro-creative process of that lifewave. Thus, you have walked by faith for many lifetimes, for faith bypasses the necessity of full conscious awareness of the Presence of God and his Laws. With the removal of the teachings from the sacred scriptures and this manipulation, you can see that the burning Light of faith and your obedience to our representatives has brought you, beloved ones, to this moment where I could bring you the awareness of this mass mechanization and shed more light as I lift the veil on just how extensive is that mechanization, first revealed by the Great Divine Director.[1]

"Some of you have been astonished to hear of the manipulation and mechanization now present in society and in education.[2] You are among the comparatively few who are aware of the facts presented in our manifestos. You are among the few who have been able to face these facts fearlessly, because God dwells in you. Yet these facts are material facts. I speak of astral conditions and conditioning. I speak of manipulations that go far beyond several hundred years of a conspiracy. I speak of manipulations that have manifested in the distant past that already affect this lifewave.

"From these manipulations, the lifewaves of earth have been reduced to their present state of imbalance. Thus, you also, functioning in the midst of this lifewave, have learned to accept the conditions in which you find yourselves. Not having an outer recollection of your former state of a vastly increased Christ consciousness anchored in the physical, you have not quite been aware in this life of the loss that you have suffered through many embodiments.

"Understand, then, that by your present awareness you perceive; and I am telling you that your present awareness is not what it should be or what it could be, due to this very fact of manipulation. There are few who can deal with manipulation on a national scale, and fewer on a planetary scale. But now I come and I ask you to consider the manipulations of systems of worlds and of galaxies themselves. I ask you to see yourselves as my very own, who once knew of the Fallen One, and of a conspiracy that was system wide.

"I am asking you to consider that just beyond your present capacity to perceive by your senses, by your chakras and by your minds and hearts, you individually have a higher consciousness that is so vast, that if it were possible to lower that consciousness through your present vehicles, you would see that the victory would be far more real, far more accessible, and you would trust it and you would pursue it. I ask you to understand that the God that you are interpenetrates even the physical being that you manifest, that under normal conditions of spiritual evolution, you would, even now, be aware of a more vast consciousness.

"Thus, the path of initiation leading to the ascension that we have outlined for earth and her evolutions has taken into consideration this setback brought about by the fallen ones and the vulnerability of the people due to their own karma of disobedience and disrespect for God's emissaries.

"It is written that without faith, it is impossible to please God.[3] This is true in the fundamental sense; but the principle has a corollary, and it has to do with the fact that individuals simply do not have the capacity to see God or to know God and therefore to please him from a higher perception.

"Beloved ones, millions of angels have volunteered to keep the flame of faith in the earth so that faith would be the door by which the children of the Light might pass to reunion with God. Without these angels, mankind, and even my very own, would be in far worse conditions today because of this manipulation. Therefore, I express in your name immense gratitude for the legions of Faith, of Archangel Michael and of all of the Archangels. Their compassion for this plight of humanity is great. And thus you can understand the mercy of God that continues, for the Almighty is determined that his very own children will not be judged prior to the removal of certain of the effects and of the conditions of manipulation....

"The people of earth indeed bear the burden of their own karma; but they bear a much greater burden, and it is of the fallen ones and extraterrestrial evolutions who yet occupy the physical and astral planes, who are indeed a law unto themselves and represent no godhead, neither by free will nor by our appointment. They do come, as they have said, from very distant systems. But they are not of the Hierarchy of the Great White Brotherhood and they do not penetrate the etheric plane. But their forcefield of manipulation extends through the mental belt, through the astral sheaths of the planetary bodies and to those who are in physical evolution because in physical octaves they have made their karma....

"The Causal Bodies of the saints Ascended and unascended, keyed by the Messengers' Causal Bodies, will also reinforce the liberation of the planetary lifewave. It is the desire of the Seven Holy Kumaras that this liberation should occur without major cataclysm. It is our desire to see transition take place into a Golden Age without the upheavals that have been planetary in scope in past changes.

"However, the Holy Kumaras will not sacrifice the long-term goals for a short-range vision. The long-term goal is the Golden Age, the preservation of earth for her lawful and rightful root races and the final judgment at the Court of the Sacred Fire of certain fallen ones whose cycles are spent.

"There is a cross section of life and a sampling of life, as we have told you, from many planetary homes, thus making earth the pinpoint and the nexus of galactic Armageddon. Why do you suppose I should have selected Terra for our journey, for the commitment of aeons of Light and love and devotion? And why do you suppose, beloved ones, that you would have left with me the God Star and come, then, from Venus to be exiled here—not for a hundred years, but for tens of thousands? It is because ultimate decisions will ultimately come out of this experiment and this mission of salvation.

"From the beginning, you have been prepared for this hour, and I will comfort you with the truth that the greatest darkness is behind you. You have come out of the darkness to which you came, and you now stand to inherit the fullness of that Light that was once your very own consciousness."[4]

"This Mortal Must Put on Immortality..."

You can see why our brother the apostle Paul said, "This corruptible must put on incorruption, and this mortal must put on immortality."[5] In order to experience the fullness of Divine Identity, one cannot contain within this limited body—manipulated and distorted and imbalanced deliberately—the full conscious awareness of who I AM.

The entire point of genetic engineering, practiced for millions of years on this planet, is to deprive the individual of the grasp of the ability to go to the heart of the Spirit cosmos, his own Divine Monad, and perceive the I AM, and therefore to discover that he is the manifestation of God. This was the natural link in the chain of being, the natural awareness that God gave us in the original creation.

With this single awareness and awareness alone of our mighty I AM Presence, the fallen ones have no power over us. Without it, we are no better than the animal kingdom. Without the knowledge of the spark of divinity, the spark atrophies. Without its proper exercise and our devotion to it, it can no longer continue to pulsate.

And so, one can see far back in a distant history the loss of identity reducing the manifestation of life on earth to the pre–*Homo sapiens* state and then once again the experimentation with *Homo erectus* to bring it back up the ladder again, this time without a threefold flame, this time to create a race in imitation of the sons and daughters of God but lacking the God flame of self-determination.[6]

What is the characteristic of the masses of mankind? They have no individual awareness, but only a mass consciousness that can be manipulated by a dictator or a god. We can see the design, then, and the purpose. And Archangel Michael and Saint Germain and El Morya have helped Sanat Kumara sustain the flow of faith within us through a long, long night of darkness.

Without faith in the future and in what we really are, we could not have made it through the centuries and centuries of experiencing the clipping of our wings, so to speak, the clipping of the pinions of Light that are the Alpha and Omega consciousness. So the dangers we see today are not merely astral or extraterrestrial, but they are immediate in people we contact on a day-to-day basis.

The Choice for Good or Evil

This loss of contact with God and our inner Reality has also come about by free-will choices. We have seen many times in history that when the people lose their Light, when the Light descends on the spinal altar, they are no longer able to hear their God. They no longer hear the voice of their I AM Presence, even when his emissaries stand before them face to face.

Take the example of Moses, who spoke with God face to face. Moses in turn spoke to the people. But the people of Israel rejected Moses and God, and they repeatedly disobeyed the prophet and the words of God through the prophet, even as they saw Moses face to face. They saw the Light shine upon his face. They saw him come down from the mountain and out of the Holy of holies in the tabernacle, having spoken with God. Yet they rebelled. They failed their tests because they could not equate with that level of Light.

Each one of us must present to the living God the Light raised up in our own temple. Only by doing this can we have co-measurement, a sense of co-equality to the teacher, the Guru, the Lord who is sent to us. We have to be able to contact the point of Light in the heart of the Guru in order to understand it, to comprehend and to also be that Light. Without that Light, we cannot obey God, we cannot follow the one He has sent. Our energy must have a certain equivalency to the one who would be Guru in our life.

This is the sad state of the evolutions of earth today: those who need the teacher, those who need the Ascended Masters most, are self-sufficient in their pride and their command of their lives, their professions, their money, their well-being and their status. Those who have the greatest need do not perceive that need at all.

The way the fallen angels and the false gurus get us to follow them is by drawing our energy down. The only way they can do it is by conniving, cheating and lying, playing upon the pride of the ego or the pride of the body or the need for consolation or the need for a friend or the need for emotional reinforcement. The forces of evil will always play on our weakest point. And although we know in our heart they are leading us against the Law, some other prevailing human need takes over, and we are deceived because we want to be deceived.

This is what the serpents, the fallen angels, have done in every mystery school since Eden. And every mystery school is established on the same basis. First the Christ appears. That one who has come to teach gives the students all of the learning and the understanding, teaches what temptations they will have in the wilderness, how the fallen angels will come to them with every temptation.

When they are ready and when they have advanced on the Path, they must face that Absolute Evil. That is the test and it is required. If you cannot deny that Darkness and that force of Darkness, then you do not deserve to have the Light made permanent within you, because one day you might turn and turn that Light into Darkness, because you have not gone through the necessary steps to prove your trustworthiness as a keeper of God's Light.

There are many people today who deny that evil is real or deny that by free will, some people choose to embody evil. And yet we can see it throughout our society. We don't have to hold up a Hitler or a Stalin or a Saddam Hussein. We can talk about drug pushers and people who lead our youth into excessive uses of alcohol and other abuses of the body. The burdens upon the bodies of our people are horrendous. And they are there because some people have decided to make merchandise of their bodies and give to them those things that destroy not only the body but also the soul.

If you will look at the so-called good people of today who are living in the midst of evil incarnate and the entrenched forces of evil, such as malevolent spirits and demons of possession, you will see that they simply cannot understand the rationale of evil or those who are under its power even while they are empowered by it. People just cannot understand how someone would knowingly, willfully choose to harm another part of life. Yet it is going on every day.

Until we come to grips with the fact that evil is a choice that people make, a choice to deny God and elevate unreality, we will not go out and challenge the betrayers of our people, of our nation—these entrenched forces of the power elite that are all over the world subjugating the people, not in the name of Christ but for their own glory.

It seems that the people never understand what's going on until it is too late. When they finally see it, they are no longer of this world. They have died on the battlefield. They have shed their blood for the wrong cause. They have given up their bodies to drugs and all manner of darkness. And so they pass through the portals of life and death and their eyes are opened. But from that level, there is nothing they can do.

The battle of Light and Darkness must be waged and won by us while we are on earth. And that is really why we are here today—to solve this problem and to go out and make our voice count and our Light count for the victory of souls.

El Morya sums up the choice we make for Good and Evil by reminding us again of the gift of our free will: "For your heartbeat, precious ones, is a contract—a contract in diastole and systole whereby as the tide of life flows out, the tide of life flows in. And as God gives, so God receives. And thus, He gave free will to man because it was His wish that that which

He gave first to them should be of their own willing hearts returned to Him, knowing full well that by cosmic edict and decree the Divine Majesty (who also would not violate His own Law) could, according to that Law, vest mankind with ten times as many talents and gifts and graces when they returned their glory to Him as though they were to withhold it."[7]

Earth Is Where the Victory Must Be Won

Lady Master Venus explains that earth is a pivotal point in the battle of Light and Darkness in a cosmos: "God did send this Son Jesus Christ into the world to give opportunity to every creation, whether God's or that of [fallen] angels. And therefore that opportunity has been extended, not for a mere century or a mere 2,000 years but for the full 25,800 years, which as time is measured for the evolution of souls, and in the karmic sense of reincarnation, is plenty of time to decide to bend the knee before the Almighty and to receive his Son. Thus, beloved, there is absolute justice in this cosmos.

"Your memories are ancient and go to ancient civilizations and Golden Ages that predate Lemuria and Atlantis and then to other planetary homes. May you know that in this hour Earth is a crossroads for fallen ones who are the archdeceivers and archrebels against Christ and his own. It is also the crossroads of the greatest souls of Light who have come from various planetary homes down the centuries. Great avatars have walked the Earth in the physical plane, not the least of whom is Jesus himself. Earth has known the highest and the lowest, and that spectrum is still present.

"Therefore, beloved, it is the place where the victory of Light must be won. Though it is preordained, it is not predestined. By this I say that that which God preordains, his sons and daughters must confirm and bring forth in the physical octave and in the Matter universe. This is the choice of the sons and daughters of God.

"If the battle is not won on this planet as it is intended, it will be taken to another and to another until there may be many souls lost in many systems of worlds. The battle will rage stronger as the forces of Darkness see themselves strengthened for the failure of those who have not understood that the victory is to those in embodiment who take their stand against embodied Evil and are unflinching and unswerving in their dedication to the cause of the Great White Brotherhood.

"There have been periods such as that known as the Hundred Years' War. There have been extended battles, beloved, but none so extended as the continuous battle of the fallen ones against the Lightbearers since these fallen ones were cast out of the heaven plane, the etheric octave, by Archangel Michael and his legions of Light."[8]

Morya says: "And the hour is late! *The hour is late.* For this age and mankind now abide in an era of hazard when the darkness and the discord and the despair and the confusion tend to cover over the pure image of the immaculate concept. And mankind wonder who is God, for they do not see him hiding behind the sunbeams or the smiles of mankind or the joys they daily experience. They see only the manifestation of the pall of human gloom. Sweep this aside then, and acknowledge the divinity of the Presence of God within your world this hour!...

"I say to you, and I speak from the realm of authority: The day of the LORD is at hand! Armageddon stands before mankind. And the day has come when the Hosts of Light must stand up and fight for that which is right, as the knights of the

Table Round—to hold the Grail concept in solemn convocation and to know that our cause, now not on behalf of England but the world, is the more stalwart because of the oppression of the times and requires men and women of such distinction that they shall not go down neath the steeds breathing fire and brimstone of mankind's iniquities, but shall establish for all time the great cosmic purity of those who have partaken of the communion cup of our covenant immortal!

"I say then to all of you, when the fears of the world seem to cause you to tremble as upon the brink of destruction, cast them aside and empty that cup upon the earth and say: I will not drink of thee. For I have a cup of communion and holy solemnity that is of more import to my soul. And I deny thy power to alter the path of my destiny, which is cosmic and not dust! I will, therefore, stand in this day and age and in all ages to come as a devotee of holy Truth—one who recognizes the puny attitudes of mankind and their ridiculous excuses as they say, 'I must do this and that,' while the kingdom of God is bypassed for the saloon!

"I say to all of you: Drink deeply, then, of the draught of God's will and stand up in this day by the side of the legions of Light, by the side of Archangel Michael and by the side of the Ascended Host."[9]

SECTION SIX

The Victory

And they overcame him by
the blood of the Lamb, and by
the word of their testimony.

REVELATION

THE BATTLE OF ARMAGEDDON spans the ages, but it is always more intense at the end of cycles—at the end of a year, the end of a decade, the end of a century or the end of a millennium. Old patterns are broken so that new cultures, new ideas and even new continents may emerge to lift man by his bootstraps into a higher spiral of the unfolding divine plan.

However, the Second Coming of Christ takes place in different ages and not just at the end of any one age. When an age reaches its zenith (as at the end of a two-thousand-year cycle), the maximizing of the forces of Good and Evil occurs simultaneously.

That which opposes the Light that is God is the darkness of anti-Light and anti-God. This Darkness is the consciousness of the Dark Ones who have sworn enmity against the Light and exist only to destroy the Light and the Lightbearers. Thus in Armageddon we deal with Absolutes—Good and Evil, Light and Darkness, and those polarized on either side. Absolute Darkness is the antithesis of Absolute Light (as opposed to relative darkness or relative light) and is the Light misqualified, turned inside out and posing as Light.

Aligned with the forces of evil are momentums of human greed, which have become entrenched through institutions of commercialism, and of old established religions with a monolithic structure whose size alone carries great weight in the minds of men. This makes difficult the unification and healing of world tensions or the bringing of the world to a state of consciousness in which Golden Age idealism can be enshrined in every heart. Unless great care be exercised, the very desired growth factors result in the creation of a giant concept that cannot with ease or impunity be challenged by the still small voice of Truth. This we see in the growth of media, television, newspapers, magazines and political forces respected purely for their size and the economic wealth they represent.

During the final stages of Armageddon, negative forces emanating from the astral plane bombard the world intensely. These forces use every means at their disposal to conquer the minds of men. At the head of the list are the advertising agencies, whose every effort is to sell more hair tonic, bread or cake, and unfortunately to increase the sale of liquors, cigars, cigarettes and lurid publications designed to appeal to the sensuality of men and provide them with a fetish for their lusts.

The recurring cycles of Armageddon are spaced so widely apart that contemporary man can do no more than sense the repetition of history. The spirit of Armageddon was much abroad prior to the flood of Noah, and the same forces are coming to the fore in contemporary times. Men are shocked by mass murders, bludgeonings and a host of horrible crimes—they have not reckoned with the powers that are unleashed to distort man's vision of reality.

A steady diet of impure books and movies (such as Alfred Hitchcock's *Psycho* and the Frankenstein and werewolf series) released in the guise of entertainment creates images of bestiality in the subconscious of men. These take a frightful toll upon the minds of young and old alike. Thus the world is victimized by its own machinations, and even the perpetrators of such crimes against society do not escape the backlash.

Jesus said to fear not those who kill the body but those who destroy the soul in hell.[1] And this is what we see happening in the world. The fallen ones are corrupting the very souls of our youth. And it is done through the third eye, through the media, through television, through books, pornography and motion pictures. This diet of corruption turns their souls; it transfers the disease, the cancer of the Wicked, and the people take it on. And that is where Armageddon is.

Would it not be, then, a marvelous advent of Good to the whole world if the media could be enlisted to produce without greed and without purposes of control, but simply to educate men and women according to great spiritual principles, thus producing a Golden Age rather than an age of darkness?

True Ascended Master concepts enabled Jesus to win his ascension. Yet these concepts have been pushed into the background and replaced by many pseudo-ideas in religion that do not win for individuals real freedom, God-success and purity. The battle of Armageddon is raging today. In the midst of the clamor of dissonant voices, the voice of the infant Messiah seems a frail cry. In reality, the powers of Light are gathering great and magnificent strength for the future victory of man.

If men are to suppose that Armageddon is the time of the end, they must hark back to the time of the Beginning, and thus the span of life that men know is seen to be of finite duration. Inasmuch as life, in reality, is infinite, individual and earthly beginnings are only a part of a grand scheme to bring about divine perfection in manifestation. The vicissitudes of life are occasioned by man's reactions to the opportunity for God-realization and true Self-realization. His refutation of the divine plan by the misuse of free will has altered the entire structure of his life. Thus his concepts have become finite and of finite duration. Actually, the earth is but a schoolroom from which mankind graduate to begin real life in the ascended state.

The separation of the sheep from the goats in the Judgment is the prerogative of each man. By his every thought and deed, he places himself in one category or the other. If, as the Christ said, he serves two masters, he cannot long do so, for he will soon love either one or the other and thus take his stand either for the Light or for Darkness.[2]

In one very real sense we are our own judges, and our own individualized Holy Christ Self carries out the mandates of heaven for us. Practicing before the Great Karmic Board as our attorney at the bar of eternal justice, he pleads our case based upon the facts of our earthly existence—not just one lifetime alone, but involving the many lives we have lived—and not one jot or tittle of the Law shall pass away until all is fulfilled.[3]

The Second Coming of Christ, no matter how it may manifest, manifests best as the individual expression of the Christ consciousness through a sincere effort to emulate that which the Master desired to do and expressed in his Palestinian mission. We must walk in his footsteps today. And when the world has accepted the Truth of the Lord Christ en masse, the Christ will have returned to walk the earth, not alone in the form of Jesus, but also through the many sons and daughters who will then have achieved immortality in their oneness with the Father.

The promise of Christ's coming is strong, but its greatest strength lies not in the mere stimulation of excitement attendant upon his coming, but in the absorption of the immortal principles by which he lived and which upheld his life.[4] Unless these principles be lived by us and applied, no grandiose manifestation of Christ, whether in the atmosphere or as a spectacular outer manifestation, could achieve the divine ideal for the onlooker. If this were the case, then the Father himself would long ago have fulfilled the prophecy of Enoch, saying "Behold, the LORD cometh with ten thousand of his saints."[5]

The Intercession of the Archangels

Archangel Michael explains the angels' solutions to the challenges of Armageddon: "Archangels are of a certain breed, you might say. Archangels have been with you from the Beginning, so long ago that I have ceased to count the centuries. We are created by God to be your caregivers, beloved. We are, therefore, beings of tremendous power. Any one of the Seven Archangels and Uzziel, when you call upon us, can invoke untold millions of troops and armies of Light.

"Have the faith of a little child! Call on us with the fiat of most profound love. Meditate for moments, if you have the time in a crisis, to increase the love of your heart and your appreciation for our service, and you will see your world turn around. You will see and know that you can have that empowerment, for we are here to give it to you.

"The legions of Light obey the commands of the true sons and daughters of God. Those who are the Christed ones may command angels in a very special way as compared to the little children, the newly born souls who have yet to increase in stature by good works before the living God.

"To maintain your status as a son or daughter of God, you must maintain the cross of your Christhood. You must understand that that cross brings persecution, triumph and the ascension. That cross then, beloved, delivers you unto the Almighty God, and the Almighty God answers your call through us. And we comb the entire planet and go after the fallen ones and specifically care for those categories of lifestreams such as children or the poor or the starved or the sick or the leper.

"Wherever you direct us, we obey. For we obey sons and daughters of God centered in their Christhood. This is your goal, beloved! When you get out of that center, stop! I say, as though you are at a stoplight and it was red. Stop! And get back to the center of your Christhood. For you are then somewhat without recourse or armour when you are off-center and off-balance.

"There is a great closeness between the Archangels, the hierarchies of angels and the chelas of the Ascended Masters, for you have entered the realms of Light during sleep. You know of the temples and the universities of the Spirit.[6] You know what is beyond this life. You fear not death, but you embrace life as opportunity to pour that life of your Causal Body and your lifestream into souls who must drink of it and be restored, for they are ill, sick, dying and know not the way to go. And when they pass on, they know not how to escape the astral plane.

"Indeed, you need not go very far to notice that hell is all around you in the physical octave in some form or another, whether through the television or in the bars or amongst people who are vile. Blessed ones, hell invades the wealthiest and the poorest. Hell is everywhere about in the earth. You are making a difference, beloved, but in this hour the majority of inhabitants of this planet are aligned to the astral plane and not the etheric octave. You have been reminded to get both feet out of the astral plane, and I summon you to do this swiftly, for you are never safe when you leave a part of yourself in that astral plane.

"We the Archangels and all accompanying legions of Light and some from far-off worlds who come as reinforcements are here, then, to commit to you our strength, our direction, our ability to solve problems quickly, our ability to get you through complex situations, problems that defy resolution. These are the situations that you have learned to deal with in many ways.

"I say to you, always call to the Archangels! Always call to the Seven Holy Kumaras! Always make the call. Test us! See what victories we shall bring to you. See how this planet will change in this year.... You can accomplish a great deal with our help. Try us, beloved! We have offered ourselves in the past. We offer ourselves again....

"I remind you to not let a day go by that you do not make fiats to the Seven Archangels and the eighth and all those of unknown names to include our legions in your every effort and to know we are the troops that will fulfill the mandates of God in turning around the propensity of war at any level or in any place.

"We are serious, we rejoice, and we are convinced of the victory, as every noble soldier of Archangel Michael and the legions of Light must be. Let your conviction, your determination and the gathering of the elements of power in your being be your thrust unto the victory!

"At any day or any hour when you feel helpless and without recourse, call to Archangel Michael and know that I AM instantaneously there! Thrust ho! Onward unto the fight to the finish and the victory!"[7]

Victory through Self-Transcendence

Saint Germain warns that even though we may have the knowledge of forces of Good and Evil, "man of himself cannot go on a witch-hunt. He cannot become suspicious of everyone who crosses his path, else he will lose his point of reality and sanity. There is no other way to win in this war, which is Armageddon, than through self-transcendence—through the transfiguration, through the resurrection, through the new birth—so that one is no more the natural man but a fiery Spirit truly dwelling at the level of the etheric body, and the Lord Christ of you is descended into this temple.

"It is promised. You must stand on the promise of God and know that you who love and obey the Christ must have the Father and the Son and the Holy Spirit take up their abode within your house, within your temple, within your soul, within your chakras.[8]

"Unfortunately—and this word is mild, but it is unfortunate indeed that the laws of Christ and his teachings, so meticulously brought forth to the close initiates, are not fully known today, having been taken even from the holy people. Therefore, to obey Christ becomes the challenge of the hour—to find the Person of that Christ, to find the Way and the teachings."[9]

"Armageddon is the day of your divine choosing to be your Real Self in the midst of the world wars of the gods. Your boldness to proceed with this walk in love's aloneness, when all around you fools scatter and shatter love's creation, must be based on aeons of faith established through trust in Almighty Love.

"To challenge the Adversary within and without fearlessly, in the defense of the unity of love, this is indeed the initiation that must precede, as requirement, the alchemical marriage.

To pass it you need the intercession of Chamuel and Charity, the LORD's angels of love. And He shall send them to your side in answer to your call. Divine love, then, is the courage to defend love against all enemies and to know that only love, and love all-one, will sustain thee."[10]

The Necessity for Prayer

Jesus' solution to Armageddon is a return to prayer: "Out of the bane of uncertainty, men excuse themselves from communion and they pursue those enervating pleasures of the world that bring them to discouragement and doubt. Faith requires the fuel of fervent effort and fervent communion. Each time an individual feels the fires of Reality dying down within the furnace of self, he must once again renew his covenant with God and seek to raise those fires to a place where the throb and pulsation of that inward Reality can be felt and known within one's own flesh and the flesh of true identity....

"O beloved ones, in this hour of world peril when the throb of Armageddon is heard as violence in the streets and as fear coming to many hearts, there is a need in America and in the world to renew the diligent application of prayer that burned on Quaker's hearth and in patriot's home. There, love was a glowing fire that sought itself to nourish a nation and cause this great land to expand wholesomely, teaching the young courtesy and grace and the art of loving one another.

"Modern methods do not surpass the old. The latter are enhanced by scientific achievement and a richer measure of technological embellishment. If such elements of progress were used for the furtherance of the kingdom of God upon earth today and to teach the Law as we intend it to be taught, it would be truly to place the kingdom within the grasp of men.

But in this hour when communication has become so readily possible on a larger scale, the voices of the night are heard and the voices of the day are stilled; they are lost in the blare and tumult of the film makers and commercial vested interests and in the hammer of religious dogma....

"Without heaven and heaven's God, life would lack purpose and meaning; for God framed the world with holy wisdom and gave to man free will in order that, like Prometheus unbound, he might create Reality within himself and achieve his own Godhood. This glorious concept has been cast aside by delusion and by the contagion of error so that men today are but a shadow of their former selves and the Light is nearly gone out. Yet the Light lives and the Light is abundant! The Light is Real and prayer and communication are the requirements of the day."[11]

Archangel Gabriel also speaks of the necessity for prayer in the midst of Armageddon: "The spirit of terrorism, anarchy, and assassination abroad in this world must not go unchecked, for it is the wedge that the fallen ones seek to drive between the soul and the ordered evolution of the incarnating Word.

"As the Christ Child is born within you and matures, ripening the soul into the higher consciousness of selfhood, seedtime and harvest and the order of life must continue. Thus the seed of the wicked come in the person of Antichrist, directing their venom against the little child before the child has become child-man—wary and aware of the real meaning of Light and Darkness.

"The children of God are all too trusting, and theirs is often a misplaced trust given unto the ones who pose as angels of Light. They see not beyond the mask of a performed pleasantness the treachery of armed hordes, so jealous of the bliss of the innocent children of God who have never lost their innermost intimate communion with the Lord Christ and his

Holy Spirit.

"Now we see coming over the hillsides of the world not the vision of the hosts of the LORD but of a plague of locusts.[12] From the astral to the physical plane, there mounts a tide of astral armies pitted against the Defender of the Faith, Archangel Michael. One by one, the opponents of the Seven Archangels make their entrance upon the stage of life in the very hour when the Great Deliverer comes for the defense of the Woman and her seed.[13]

"That seed, as sons and daughters of God in embodiment, must realize that all and everything for which the hosts of Archangel Michael stand—goodwill and faith, God-government and the strength to be in God inviolate—is challenged by those who have already sworn their enmity not only with the World Mother but also with the Lord Christ to whom she gives birth and the legions of angels that form the retinue of protection to the children of God.

"Now we come to clear the way for the coming of Archangel Michael and his legions of blue flame! Some upon earth have formed the Blue Army[14] for the protection of the Mother and her children. They have sensed the vibration of the blue-flame angels in their midst, and their devotion is unto the Hail Mary as the great instrument to defeat World Communism in the battle of Armageddon.

"Commendable indeed are the works of souls uplifted unto the vibration of the Virgin Mary, whose purity of heart has enabled them to see the extraordinary protection afforded by the science of the spoken Word in the giving of the adoration to the blessed Mother of Christ. Truly, entire legions of fallen ones, bent on the destruction of Christianity and the governments and economies of free nations, have been turned back by the blinding Light invoked and sustained through the ritual of the Hail Mary....

"Let the New Age Rosary of Mother Mary be accorded the place of honor in the homes of Lightbearers that they would give to the Blessed Virgin herself. And let the Child's Rosary, a gift from Mother Mary to her children this Christmas, be both a devotional offering and the means of the edification of the little children in the sacred scriptures of the apostles of Christ.[15]

"Let the little children and all advancing in the decades of life's opportunity daily blend their voices nation by nation, chorusing with the angels of God who cry with one breath, 'Ave, Ave, Ave Maria!' and themselves gather here and there to celebrate the Hail Mary as the adoration to life as Mother, as God, as the soul suspended in the womb of time and space."[16]

Hail Mary

Hail, Mary, full of grace
the Lord is with thee.
Blessed art thou among women
and blessed is the fruit
of thy womb, Jesus.

Holy Mary, Mother of God,
Pray for us, sons and daughters of God,
Now and at the hour of our victory
Over sin, disease and death.

The Victory of the Violet Planet

Omri-Tas, the ruler of the Violet Planet, gives us encouragement in the battle as he explains how the Lightbearers of his planet faced a challenge similar to that now facing earth: "Beloved ones, I address you this evening to give to you a remembrance of a period upon our planetary home when we approached the crisis that you are approaching. It was in that hour (when some of you were even a part of our evolutions) that the then Lightbearers of our system did rally to our call.

"Circumstances were similar to those you now have upon this earth, with fallen angels moving among the people and leading them astray, pursuing their divide-and-conquer tactics, blurring the issues, deceiving the elect of God.

"There was a rallying by the then representative of the Divine Mother, who moved in the midst of our people. And that one did appeal to their hearts, and the message was transmitted round that planet until all servants of God were galvanized, even by the power of her heart and the Great Central Sun Magnet. They were quickened, almost as though they were suddenly in another dimension, and they awakened to the urgency of the hour!

"Beloved, they responded before even greater odds than you face today. They turned the tide with the violet flame. They heard the call to give their invocations at altars around that planet. There was a saturation of the planetary body with the violet flame. That saturation therefore did flush out the fallen angels, who then could be bound by the legions of Light and removed.

"Blessed ones, we went on into a Golden Age because of the few who responded, and today that planet is sustained in that Golden Age because the people have not lost the memory of that which was almost a planetary holocaust.

"I would remind you that in the battles of the history of earth, the few have stood for the many, have rallied and have won a victory for those who yet slept. And when they awakened, they found themselves in a world that was safe and secure.

"There are young souls and new souls who are children on the Path. There are souls who need shepherding. May you not despair. May you know that by calling to me you will have access to many millions of adepts of the seventh ray who will help you, that it is indeed possible that this message be delivered, that the people who have the awareness will hear, will invoke the Light, will overcome. Let there not be doubt or discouragement! Fill every hour with the flame of living hope and the acknowledgment of your immortality!"[17]

Love Is the Key

As Saint Paul said long ago, "Let love be without dissimulation."[18] We ought not to be carried away by the sea of trouble that is upon the world; rather we ought to summon from within ourselves the unifying precepts that will unite home, family, neighborhood, community, state, nation and world into an action that can begin with the individual and end with the circle of the world order as we seek to frame out of the rubble of confusion a new order of the ages.

This was nobly begun two thousand years ago by the Nazarene carpenter, and today we must ignore the mandates for chaos and one by one ally ourselves with that spiritual order He advocated. We must become carpenters as we seek to find our way out of the heap of confusion. Individually and collectively we need direction. We can receive it from Above; we can receive it from one another; we can receive it by sanity and justice, by decency and by faith. This is our work today.

The Ascended Lady Master Rose of Light also affirms that the solutions to the challenges of Armageddon must come from the heart: "Dear ones, our Lord Gautama has given to us the answer to every question of life. Love is the key. And the acceleration of love as the ruby ray will answer every question and questioning in the wider and wider rings of civilization where the burdens of planetary survival even burden those who themselves will not endure unto eternal life. Well, of course, blessed ones, they are burdened, for these fallen ones seek survival, even to survive as mortals—their chief concern.

"And therefore we come to the council tables. We come to meetings concerning ... armaments and disarmaments and the escalation of implements of war. Far worse is the escalation of the consciousness of war! Some men advocate heaping upon the pile and stockpile of weapons more and more weapons; some men advocate the cutting of these stockpiles in half. Well, I come to advocate, then, the life of Buddha and his message of love and to teach you how to implement said flame of love.

"Blessed hearts, the answers have not been found to struggles of East and West, Gog and Magog. There is no solution thus far that has been proposed that will solve the problem of mankind on the brink of self-destruction by the insanity of a single fallen one or a single tool of darkness. Whether the assassin against the life of Christ's Vicar or of the president, whether one who determines in a moment of insanity to press the button that is the beginning of the end, it all begins with a single malintent of one individual's heart capable of wreaking that destruction upon another part of life—upon a single idea of Christ or a rose that blooms as the fire of the soul.

"Dear hearts, I am not here to propound an oversimplification of a most complex situation. For God knows that the Lords of Karma and the Four and Twenty Elders and all of us who are the sponsors of a race are determined that there shall be the pushing back of this knot of human consciousness and the making of the way for the I AM race. All understand that in this hour solutions to men's problems yet hang in the balance of men's consciousness rather than in the focal point of the heart or the Sacred Heart of Christ Jesus.

"If there were any legitimate fear, it might well be the fear of that ultimate power in the hands of those who are ultimately insane for having forsaken the original will of God. And if there were a legitimate fear, it might well be the fear of the LORD whose wisdom is the beginning of the solution to this problem.

"Therefore take heart, and realize the meaning of that word. Take the heart of your mighty I AM Presence and Christ Self and of each one of us so dedicated and become that magnificent heart of Light!

"Blessed ones, we advocate the fiery heart! We advocate fiery, burning hearts pressing out love—love that transmutes in the way all anti-love. And surely there is no greater anti-love than the misuse of the nucleus of the atom of Self, even of the Light of Alpha and Omega, for nuclear destruction. Surely there is no greater love than the Holy Spirit itself come as the Destroyer to consume all unlike itself.

"In the hands of God the sacred fire of the atom may lawfully destroy all that is not truly of life, but in the hands of lesser individuals that destruction may very well be the destruction of souls and civilizations unlawfully and not in keeping with the will of God. Thus, let there be an intense fire pressing out by the petals of the heart that which would by malintent destroy the hearts of God's people.

"At all costs, let us protect the fire of the heart, the threefold flame, the soul becoming one with that fire! This is the opportunity of life granted unto life upon earth. Let us consume all death! Let us consume war and the implements of war, not by the solutions of the intellect—which have never worked and never will—but let us consume that, all of that, by the fire of the heart.

"Measure for measure, I tell you, if there be the pressing out of the fire of love of your heart, heaven tells that there will also be a pressing in from heaven upon this planetary body of

the love of all of the members of the Great White Brotherhood, all of the angels of Light pressing in upon the earth,
pressing out from heart centers and even the sun of even
pressure.

"There can be, then, a band of containment and God-
control by the conscious cooperation of members Ascended
and unascended of the Great White Brotherhood and of
elemental life, which promises to be the agency of the Holy
Spirit mediating the flow of love twixt the Hierarchy Ascended
and the devotees unascended.

"Let us establish the cult of the heart and the path of the
ruby ray rose of Light. Let us do it in Saint Germain's name!
Let us do it for the anchoring of Shamballa once again!

"I come, then, with the assurance of Saint Germain that all
of the Great White Brotherhood will confirm and recite with
you:

> I AM the Light of the heart
> Shining in the darkness of being
> And changing all into the golden treasury
> Of the mind of Christ.

"Each and every Ascended Master and angel of Light
promises that as you affirm that will to be love in all of the
manifestations of thy creation everywhere, past, present and
future, so there will be the multiplication of this mantra of
Saint Germain:

> I AM projecting my love
> Out into the world
> To erase all errors
> And to break down all barriers.

"Blessed hearts, can you not hear the rustling of wings, the
sounds of tender cherubic voices, majestic Seraphim, Cosmic
Beings, Elohim who have intoned this mantra of the heart of

the God of Freedom to the earth for aeons? Can you not hear yourself a part of one grand company of hosts of Light declaring:

> I AM the power of infinite love,
> Amplifying itself—

"O the amplification of that infinite love throughout all the world, worlds without end! O the amplification of that love! Truly,

> I AM the power of infinite love,
> Amplifying itself
> Until it is victorious,
> World without end!

"And truly, as the sound of many voices, so will there be a resounding roar! This is a key, a dispensation come this very day from the heart of Saint Germain as a part of that dispensation received by him in the Central Sun, as he would also lay it at the feet of Gautama Buddha.

"Therefore, for the implementation of Buddhic Love and Buddhic Light, the universality of Christus, we of the Ascended Hosts converge at the altar of your heart. And the fire burning there will increase if you will allow it, if you will not doubt it, if you will fear not to surrender unto the greater love of thy life.

"O blessed hearts, surrender into the arms of the Divine Mother and live at the point of Light of Buddhic adoration, Buddhic initiation, now and forever, spiral upon spiral of being, worlds without end.

"I AM come for the confirmation of Light! Together, let us conquer by love this falsification of the yin and yang by the International Capitalist/Communist Conspiracy of the Nephilim. Let us conquer that which men fear most because of an absence of love. It is nuclear holocaust that they fear, almost more than death itself—this very process of worlds in self-destruction. It need not be! It shall not be! It need never be when hearts are full of love.

"I come with a momentum of Light employed by millions of Lightbearers, now Cosmic Beings, who themselves took this formula of love pressing out and pressing in—this formula of cooperation of the Great White Brotherhood by the sacred fire of the heart—and did thereby forestall and deflect worlds in self-destruction whose overcoming became a victory of love, a victory for Mighty Victory.

"Let us penetrate the consciousness of earth, the subconscious, and the higher levels of the mind with the assurance that God can heal even this breach in the planetary body, even all of this arraying of forces against one another. God can heal! God can heal, my beloved! God can yet heal this earth by the Light of your heart! Will you allow it? Will you allow Him to step through your heart and impart to all the fullness of Christ's love?

"O let it be—let it be confirmed by the vow of love in your heart! I seal it here. I seal it there.

"Now, from the outer to the inner retreat of the soul, let us go forth to conquer worlds without end by love. By love, I seal you in the rose of light. By love, by love, by love I AM made more bright for my coming into your midst.

"O blessed one, I love thee." [19]

I AM the Light of the Heart
by Saint Germain

I AM the Light of the heart
Shining in the darkness of being
And changing all into the golden treasury
Of the mind of Christ

I AM projecting my love
Out into the world
To erase all errors
And to break down all barriers.

I AM the power of Infinite love,
Amplifying itself
Until it is victorious,
World without end!

"Not by Might, Nor by Power, But by My Spirit..."

Armageddon occurs in the world of form, and the age we now live in is full of it. The battle between Light and Darkness for the minds of men is waged with the loudest cries, appealing to the baser emotions and instincts of men. The press, television, radio and the entire publishing industry have caused to be issued forth a flood of unconscionable material, mingled with apparent virtue and a steady rehash of tales more than twice told.

Few are the voices raised in defense of Truth, and many are the voices raised to uphold, defend and promote a monolithic concept central to one religion or one philosophy—in some cases even devoted to one man, and he but mortal. The entire Divine Image of the infant Messiah that each Christmas calls to mind is a symbolic drama of world-shaking import. Into it is poured the story of every man and the responsibility of every man to reeducate his vision so as to behold God in all things. Thus will he increase his Light and stature, until the Magi of old will come to him because they have seen his star in the East. This is the divine plan.

The reflection of cosmic brilliance in the individual monad

is the fulfillment of a divine intent, and thus victory in the battle of Armageddon is achieved on the individual level. The words "By this sign we conquer" are definitive of the cross, but the cross itself is definitive of a much greater explanation of life.[20] The horizontal bar represents the plane of individual identity; the vertical bar symbolizes the descending and ascending energies of God. These two worlds (the Macrocosm and the microcosm) meet at the center point, the point where God and man merge. To balance the cross of life requires sustained effort and a meeting of daily challenges.

The battle of Armageddon is fought in the mind and being of man. Each time it is won on the personal level, the raging conflict in the world at large is checked. Yet there must be an implementation of Truth in the world of form that shall counteract error. The dissemination of the great cosmic Truths of the Ascended Masters is the greatest rallying cry that the zealot for the earth and its evolutions can cause to be heard if the world is to be won for God.

"Not by might, nor by power, but by my spirit, saith the LORD of hosts"[21]—by the Spirit of God and by a most practical idealism that calls into joint action the energies of God and man. Drawing forth from the hand of God whatever is the requirement of the hour, we must determine to counteract by the power of the Christ the great flood of astral energies that are being sent forth out of the dragon's mouth to carry away the woman and the manchild[22] (to drown the understanding of the World Mother—the feminine aspect of God and the Christ who comes forth from her virgin consciousness).

As "the earth helped the woman ... and swallowed up the flood which the dragon cast out of his mouth," so we can count on the assistance of the beings of the elements to work with "the remnant of her seed"[23] in the winning of the great battle. In the name of God we can send forth a mighty tide of

Light that will inundate the earth with the power of God and his Christ—with purity, hope and overcoming victory for every man, woman and child and generations unborn.

Evil must be exposed by Reality and straight thinking. The Ascended Masters' thinking follows a straight line from God to man. It is the line of pure reason that leads to the ascension because it refuses to be enticed by the byways of mortal contamination. It is the line of devotion that insists upon the transmutation of all negative human elements in the fervent heat of God's devotion to the Christ Light in every man. It is the line of commitment that throws itself wholeheartedly into the fray, knowing that the battle will not be easy, but that the Light of God will ultimately triumph in the hearts of men, as it will in the world.

> The song of the world may be strong,
> But the song of God is stronger;
> The battle cry of the world may echo long,
> But the cry of heaven echoes longer.

> The power and glory of human fury
> May seem extensive,
> But the Lords of life and the Law of life
> Are not defensive.
> For here is Truth and here is proof—
> By action we will win our youth,
> And raise the Law of Christ on high
> To challenge laws of human fate
> And set the stage without debate
> For all that makes us truly great.
> In life and love and liberty,
> We all declare, I AM now free!

The Benediction of the Master El Morya, Lord of Heaven's First Ray

Lux fiat!

O Light, thou art the king of all creation! *Blaze!* thy dazzling Light rays forth in God's holy name, and let his heart draw the response of the hearts of men until the white stone kindled in the hearts of men recognizes the new name of God written there.[24] For, aye, it shall never be taken from those who shall continue to keep the faith.

> And they shall rise step-by-step on cycled stair
> Until they see ascending in the air
> The radiant faces of the angels fair
> Whose love is everywhere like a prayer
> Bringing spirals of beauty and compassion
> In rainbow rays and substance of immortality,
> Not only to the consciousness
> Of the children of the earth
> But to the children now grown to maturity and form
> Who shall ascend into spiritual consciousness
> To become the children of God,
> The children of men,
> The children of life
> And not the children of sin!

For then we shall see the completion ray,
Fulfilling forever, forever, and for aye
God-purity, God-security, God-victory and peace,
And the fullness, the purity of freedom's release!

O Holy Spirit, Lord Maha Chohan, touch now these hearts with thy flame! And let the radiance of that flame sustain the God-power within. And may the cleansing perfection of the seekers for the Holy Grail illumine our knights and ladies fair of this Table Round. For in this age, too, we need crusaders for thy cause.[25]

The Invocation of the Judgment

This is the hour of the fulfillment of the prophecy of Daniel: "And at that time shall Michael stand up, the great prince which standeth for the children of thy people; and there shall be a time of trouble, such as never was since there was a nation even to that same time. And at that time thy people shall be delivered, every one that shall be found written in the book.

"And many of them that sleep in the dust of the earth shall awake, some to everlasting life, and some to shame and everlasting contempt. And they that be wise shall shine as the brightness of the firmament; and they that turn many to righteousness as the stars for ever and ever."[26]

This is the hour of the awakening of the sleeping serpent of the dweller-on-the-threshold, this is the hour of judgment for those who choose not to be God but to be the embodiment of evil; this is the hour of the judgment of many who have chosen the left-handed path, many who have become one with Antichrist, many who have inverted the Light to create the monster.

This is the hour when Jesus Christ has sent forth his call to the Father to bind them and cast them into the outer darkness, the astral plane, which they themselves have created; for these fallen ones are the creators of that Death and Hell, which itself shall be cast into the Lake of Sacred Fire.

We know not how God will accomplish his purpose or how the holy angels will implement the judgments of the Son. We have no desire to see anyone go through a physical death or even the second death: This is not the purpose of the Judgment Call or the dweller decree! It is for the life of the soul in the grips of the toiler that we cry out to God for salvation through his great and marvelous works—beginning with his perfect judgment. We are charged to make the call, and the armies of heaven under the Archangels are charged to implement the answer, subject to the will of God and the adjudication of the Son, in Jesus and in us.

Fully clothed upon with the armour of God, give your Tube of Light Decree (see page 110) and calls to Archangel Michael (page 111) before giving Jesus' Judgment Call or the decree for the casting out of the dweller-on-the-threshold.

The Judgment Call
"They Shall Not Pass!"
by Jesus Christ

In the Name of the I AM THAT I AM,
I invoke the Electronic Presence of Jesus Christ:
They shall not pass!
They shall not pass!
They shall not pass!
By the authority of the cosmic cross of white fire it shall be:
That all that is directed against the Christ
    within me, within the holy innocents,
    within our beloved Messengers,
    within every son and daughter of God,
        [by the Nephilim gods, their genetic engineering,
        population control, and contrived wars,
        slaughtering the Sons of God and children of the Light
        on the battlefields of life]*

---

* At the places indicated, you may give the suggested calls shown in brackets, or include your own calls for the hosts of the LORD to take command of conditions of personal and planetary injustice that you name.

Is now turned back
 by the authority of Alpha and Omega,
 by the authority of my Lord and Saviour Jesus Christ,
 by the authority of Saint Germain!

I AM THAT I AM within the center of this temple
 and I declare in the fullness of
 the entire Spirit of the Great White Brotherhood:
That those who, then, practice the black arts
 against the children of the Light
  [namely, the entire interplanetary conspiracy of
  the fallen angels and their mechanization man]*
Are now bound by the hosts of the LORD,
Do now receive the judgment of the Lord Christ
 within me, within Jesus,
 and within every Ascended Master,
Do now receive, then, the full return—
 multiplied by the energy of the Cosmic Christ—
 of their nefarious deeds which they have practiced
 since the very incarnation of the Word!

Lo, I AM a Son of God!
Lo, I AM a Flame of God!
Lo, I stand upon the Rock of the living Word
And I declare with Jesus, the living Son of God:
They shall not pass!
They shall not pass!
They shall not pass!
ELOHIM. ELOHIM. ELOHIM. (chant this line)

Taken from a dictation by Jesus Christ, August 6, 1978, Camelot, California, "They Shall Not Pass!" Posture for giving this decree: Stand. Raise your right hand, using the *abhaya mudra* (gesture of fearlessness, palm forward), and place your left hand to your heart—thumb and first two fingers touching chakra pointing inward. Give this call at least once in every 24-hour cycle.

"I Cast out the Dweller-on-the-Threshold!"
by Jesus Christ

In the name I AM THAT I AM ELOHIM

Saint Germain, Portia, Guru Ma, Lanello,

In the name I AM THAT I AM SANAT KUMARA

Gautama Buddha, Lord Maitreya, Jesus Christ

I CAST OUT THE DWELLER-ON-THE THRESHOLD of _____.*

In the name of my beloved mighty I AM Presence and Holy Christ Self, Archangel Michael and the hosts of the LORD, in the name Jesus Christ, I challenge the personal and planetary dweller-on-the-threshold, and I say:

You have no power over me! *You* may not threaten or mar the face of my God within my soul. *You* may not taunt or tempt me with past or present or future, for I AM hid with Christ in God. I AM his bride. I AM accepted by the LORD.

You have no power to destroy me!

Therefore, be *bound!* by the LORD himself.

Your day is *done!* You may no longer inhabit this temple.

In the name I AM THAT I AM, be *bound!* you tempter of my soul. Be *bound!* you point of pride of the original fall of the fallen ones! You have no power, no reality, no worth. You occupy no time or space of my being.

You have no power in my temple. You may no longer steal the Light of my chakras. You may not steal the Light of my heart flame or my I AM Presence.

Be *bound!* then, O Serpent and his seed and all implants of the sinister force, for I AM THAT I AM!

I AM the Son of God this day, and I occupy this temple fully and wholly until the coming of the LORD, until the New Day, until all be fulfilled, and until this generation of the seed

---

* Here insert your specific calls for the hosts of the LORD to take command of conditions of personal and planetary injustice that you name.

of Serpent pass away.

Burn through, O living Word of God!

By the power of Brahma, Vishnu, and Shiva, in the name Brahman: I AM THAT I AM and I stand and I cast out the dweller.

Let him be bound by the power of the LORD's host! Let him be consigned to the flame of the sacred fire of Alpha and Omega, that that one may not go out to tempt the innocent and the babes in Christ.

Blaze the power of Elohim!

Elohim of God—Elohim of God—Elohim of God

Descend now in answer to my call. As the mandate of the LORD—as Above, so below—occupy now.

Bind the fallen self! *Bind* the synthetic self! Be *out* then!

Bind the fallen one! For there is no more remnant or residue in my life of any, or any part of that one.

Lo, I AM, in Jesus' name, the victor over Death and Hell! (2x)

Lo, I AM THAT I AM in me—in the name of Jesus Christ—is *here and now* the victor over Death and Hell! Lo! it is done.

Evolutions of Light and Darkness

Evolutions of Light

Fourth, fifth and sixth root races	Earth's native inhabitants
The 144,000	Volunteers from Venus and other planets who came on the rescue mission with Sanat Kumara
Embodied angels	Angels who volunteered to take embodiment to assist earth's evolutions
Children of God	Those who are of the Light but who have not yet reached the stature of full Sonship
Sons and daughters of God	Those who have passed the initiations of the sacred fire that would warrant their being called joint-heirs with Christ

Evolutions of Darkness

Laggards	Evolutions from Hedron and Maldek who were given the opportunity to embody on earth
Nephilim	Angels who followed Lucifer in the great rebellion and were cast out of heaven to embody in the earth
Watchers	A specific band of angels who fell through lust
Mechanization man (robots)	Soulless beings produced by means of genetic engineering
Nephilim from the 12th Planet	Fallen ones from another planet in our solar system who first came to earth 450,000 years ago[27]
Nephilim and extra-terrestrials from other systems	Evidence points to the fact that earth has played host to Nephilim and extraterrestrials from a number of different systems [28]
Giants and half-breeds	The products of the interbreeding of various evolutions of darkness, and also of their interbreeding with the evolutions of Light

Chapter 4

Thy Will Be Done

*Lo, I am come to do thy
will, O God.*

HEBREWS

Thy Will Be Done

"HOW CAN I KNOW THE WILL OF God? This is the cry of millions. Man presupposes that the divine will is hiding from him, as though it were a part of the plan for the eternal God to play hide-and-seek with him. Not so! The will of God is inherent within life and merely awaits the signal of release from man's will in order to ray forth the power of dominion to the world of the individual.

"There is a sovereign link between the mortal will and the Immortal. In the statement of Jesus 'It is the Father's good pleasure to give you the kingdom,'[1] men can be aware of the eternal will as the fullest measure of eternal love.

"Release, then, your feelings of possessiveness over your own life! Surrender the mean sense of sin and rebellion, the pitiful will to self-privilege that engenders bondage.

El Morya, as the chohan of the first ray of God's will, has a profound devotion to the will of God. His teachings on this subject are woven throughout this chapter, his quoted words often being attributed to him only in the notes.

"See the will of God as omnipresent and complete, the holy beat of the Sacred Heart throbbing within your own. Know and understand that surrender is not oblivion but a point of beginning and of greater joy. Now responsibility does not cease but begins anew, and man is yoked with eternal purpose—the shield of God's will."[2]

This is the message of El Morya, Lord of the First Ray of God's Will, "to the builders who seek Truth."

Most of our readers would agree that among the gifts of life's opportunity to man there is none greater than freedom. But do most of them know that the will of God is the sole source of man's freedom?

Indeed, the sanctity of the will is shared by all and treasured by the wise, while the ignorant among men seldom pause to consider what a precious gift they have in their hands.

What Is the Will of God?

Men may ask, "What is the will of God?"

"The will of God is everything," Morya says, "for it provides the spark that pushes back the darkness of sense consciousness, of ignorance and despair, while holding forth the torch of true illumination to the seeking soul, enabling each individual to find himself, lost in the passion of God's will."[3]

"The will of God is a security beyond belief, beyond faith, and even beyond manifestation, for it is the solemnly beautiful beaming of the tenderness of the Father's care for his creation. Left undisturbed and permitted to express the elements of their cosmic identity, individuals would see themselves leaping into the arms of perfect love, the perfect love of God. And the flashing of their divine identity would enable them to overcome all of those elements of the appearance world that have for so long distressed them."[4]

"The will of God, which seems so simple a thing, is the most complex organism in the universe. From it sprang full-blown the entire scheme of cosmos, worlds without end—circles, pinwheels, spiral nebulae in cosmos, and the whole sidereal sea, all glowing fire-gems responding to the ministrations of the divine will. Yet its cadences, like those of the melodic songs of a child, come forth with the simple beauty that adds meaning to each hour.

" 'How remote it all seems,' you say. Astronauts journeying out into space sense all of this immensity, but they cannot receive it within themselves; for they, too, have limited their consciousness. The dish of thought that they have made their portion is too finite and too small, albeit more vast by far than that of ordinary men in their narrow frame of reference....

"The will of God is the flawless diamond, it is the shining of the Divine Mind, it is the rushing of the wind of the Spirit, and it is the strength and laughter of Real Identity."[5]

"God sought to bestow, and the best gift he could give was the gift of his will; for by his will he framed the far-off worlds, and by his will he sustained the momentum of life within each cell. And so he heard the melody of the divine will. Some call it the music of the spheres; others perceive it in the faces of humanity; some cognize it in the revelations of science; others in the kingdoms of nature; while still others realize it in cloister. Retreating from the world, they hear it in the measured flow of the hours, in service and in prayer."[6]

The Great Divine Director says, "It should be understood that the will of God actually beats man's heart, stimulates his digestive system and provides the impetus for perfection throughout the physical domain. When interfering activities are allowed to intrude themselves upon the perfection of the divine pattern that is inherent in man—even within the cellular structure of his physical body—there is a jangle of inharmony, a friction between the perfect model and that which challenges the harmonious relationship of the parts with each other and with the whole—and disease follows. The quickening of man's entire consciousness and the harnessing of the four lower bodies for maximum efficiency is best accomplished, then, through his understanding of the nature of the divine will."[7]

Morya says, "Knowing the longing and the hunger of the souls of men for the Real, I am diligently evoking the symbols of His will to manifest in you as alertness of mind, willingness to change, and the courage to offer the self of mortality to the lovely designs of the Father's purpose."[8]

"Not My Will but Thine, Be Done!"

To surrender this will to another is to exhibit confidence of the first magnitude. There is something about holding the reins of life within one's own hands that gives men a special feeling of security, and this is as it should be. Yet we must acknowledge that there are times when an Intelligence higher than our own is needed to guide the will, and there are times when the surrender of the will to that Intelligence becomes desirable.

The declaration of Jesus "Nevertheless not my will, but thine, be done"[9] would be difficult for some to affirm. Those who have faith in God find it easier to surrender the will than those who yet entertain subtle doubts concerning His existence.

Hence, surrender of the personal will to the Divine is indicative not only of an abiding faith in the wisdom of God but also of a deep dedication to his purposes and a childlike trust in his unfailing love. The sweet surrender to the will of God gives man a serenity and a confidence that he can never know as long as he remains tethered to the human will with its stubbornness, its misconceptions and its fears.

El Morya continues his teaching on the will of God: "The

will of God, how clear and lovely—a beautiful dream filled with no thoughts of the human nightmare. The promise 'My grace is sufficient for thee'[10] becomes a tangible Reality as man is enclosed within the strength of God's will. When the hymn 'A Mighty Fortress Is Our God'[11] was released, it was to be a tribute to the divine will; and I think there is no greater goal for any man than to identify totally with this universal life-wave of cosmic creativity.

"Yet many do fear to surrender their own will to the Universal. They fear to lose their identity, when, in reality, they would but 'loose' their identity and find it again in the blessed sense of self-direction that exists in higher octaves of harmony.[12] For harmony is a divine sense, an afflatus of such vibrancy, buoyancy and oneness with all life, that heaven can never imagine how anyone who has tasted thereof can ever again return to the soil of carnal expression."[13]

"The fiat 'Not my will, but thine, be done' was not intended as a statement of sacrifice but one of heavenly-inspired wisdom. In the higher schools, this mantra of the Spirit is intoned invocatively so as to create the needed liaison between man and God. Whereas it is God's will that man intune with him, it is incumbent upon man to recognize that his responsibility demands search, willingness and an understanding of the self-created barriers that must be taken down so that the clarity of the will of God can come through."[14]

The God Meru gave this mantra to the students; it may be repeated by all who seek to do and to become God's will:

> Not my will!
> Not my will!
> Not my will, but thine, be done![15]

As you intone this mantra, know that many Ascended Masters are giving it with you.

Morya gives another mantra for those seeking the will of God: " 'The will of God is good.' The affirmation of this childlike statement, over and over again, is the means whereby the mind can be stilled and the mounting crescendo of human emotions diminished."[16]

The Opportunity of Free Will

Men are often faced with difficult choices in this valley of decision. And life will not always wait for them to make up their minds. Often a sudden demand will tax a man's entire resources. His total assets of mind, body and spirit are summoned into the decision-making process, and the decision he makes may well determine the course of his own life and the lives of millions.

Obedience to the will of God, even if it be blind obedience or a walking by faith alone, brings the reward of swift dominion through God-control that is consecrated to the highest precepts of the will of God. Obedience to the will of God puts one's entire being in alignment with both the will and consciousness of God. And therefore, illumination of a cosmic nature always follows an act of loving obedience, or obedience in love.

God gives to man the opportunity to exercise his free will, and at times he does not spell out to the evolving consciousness the exact way in which he should walk, for this would deprive man of the opportunity of finding the way through the process of intelligently, logically eliminating every alternative that is not the highest selection of the highest Good that is either known or available.

Step by step the mind of God allows child-man to prove for himself what is that wholly and acceptable and perfect will of God. Otherwise God would deprive man of his free will and assume the role of dictator or tyrant. Often man finds that because he has surrendered his free will to another, has allowed himself to come under the domination of others, that when he stands alone, his free will in his own hands, he trembles and is seized with fear, knowing not which way to go. He wishes, oh, how he wishes that God would simply say, "Do this," or "Do that." But this would absolve him of the responsibility of making the correct choice and of following in the footsteps of the Christ consciously, freely, determinedly.

When the avalanche of his fears has passed and man finds himself alone with God, he finds that he *is* God and that that free will that is in his hands is his power to create according to God-Good and His indomitable laws. Man is a god of his world, and the choices he makes will determine the fate of his world. By observing the effects, the consequences of his choices and his acts, he learns the responsibility of being God; and as he is willing to assume this responsibility, he becomes more and more of God and takes on more and more of the consciousness of God-Good. Thus his choices become the choices of God, and when all of his choices are God's choices, there no longer exists a differential between man and God; and so he is God-man, a good man fashioned after the divine likeness. No more frightened by the enormity of his responsibility, he wears the robes of his divine authority and his divine office.

Archangel Michael once said "I come to you to receive the faith that you have. Give me, then, your faith, and I will exchange it for my own."[17] On another occasion he said, "Give me your doubts. Give me your questionings. I will indeed give you my faith."[18] He made these statements because he knew that in times of testing, men of strong faith are not lacking in spiritual resources. These can and do rally to the occasion. But those who are without faith are often left stranded high and dry upon a desert island where they have isolated themselves.

We would agree with Saint Germain, who says, "The right use of free will is the essential difference between the spiritually exalted ones and those who are constantly whirled in a maelstrom of confusion."[19]

The Universal Presence of Holy Purpose

It is folly for anyone to deny the existence of God, of a Master Presence with a master plan who has conceived and brought into manifestation a universe of such vast precision and immutable harmony that it defies the explanation of cause and effect as accidental happenings. Morya teaches, "Each erg of cosmic energy that goes forth has the pattern of God's divine will impressed upon it; and as you receive it, you can perceive its divine plan, also, and your holy mission to use that energy for that which God gave it unto you.

"We are dedicated here in Darjeeling to the holy will of God, the purpose in all life. In each blade of grass, in each flower, in each dewdrop, there is holy purpose! Do you think God creates for naught, for idle time, for idle conversation? God creates for purpose. To find and know and keep that sacred covenant of his purpose is our holy charge, and we pass it unto you, even as ye are able to assist us in this mission.

"We know, precious ones, that nothing can interfere with the divine plan in heaven, and nothing can interfere with the divine plan upon earth—*if* mankind unascended so will it, *if* there are among mankind those who will stand and say, 'I AM come to do thy will, O God!'

"To find that holy will, to know the holy will—how it has been the love of our being for ages and ages—to serve the Presence of God, to serve his holy purpose! What higher calling is there? For God's will indeed illumines the plan of every ray of the divine spectrum. Every phase of divine appearing is governed by this holy principle, rooted in the mind of God, outpictured in the Christ mind in man, blossoming as the flower of the heart, the holy threefold flame."[20]

Morya asks: "What shall we say, then, to the careless ones who demand their own definitions and their definitions of definitions?

"We will say with God, 'I AM *Āgam,* the Unknowable. I AM the Infinite within who, in all of your winnings, can never be contained within the consciousness of sense or of perception.'

"Therefore the law of love would bestow upon man the means to contact and to know the will of God.

> It is an inward sense
> We must discover and impart,
> It is an inward sense
> That rends the veil before we start.
> We must convey our love to Him
> Who gives to us the grace to win,
> The power to see the flow of Truth,
> The sweetest comfort, eternal youth,
> And mighty power of Light to live—
> This is the radiance God does give.
> In kindred minds he will impart
> The holy will of God to start
> The process over once again.

"And thus we show that the will of God is a seed to be planted within the consciousness of the individual, that the will of God is substance, even as faith is, and that the will of God is the conglomerate stream of Reality—the issuance of purpose from the uncreated realm into the realm of the Created Essence."[21]

The Right Use of Free Will

Just as the divine will has determined the course of the universe, so the free will of man has determined the course of man's existence. It is indeed in the correct and incorrect use of the will that men and women, as well as nations and peoples, have determined the course of human events.

The channels carved by the collective will of the race determine the course of the flowing river of life. Whether you build a dam or a dike, divert the course of a stream or a river, or bottle the water and send it away, the waters of life will always follow the channels you select.

Chaos at any level is fed by the idiosyncrasies of men—their indecision, their inability or their unwillingness to cope with the mandates of their karma, their intolerance of one another's shortcomings and their habitual misapplication of life's basic principles. These have taken their toll upon the great mainstream of God's energy, which has flowed freely from the fount of life for the building of an abundant Golden Age civilization.

In ignorance men have diverted the stream of life, and they have wasted the natural resources that were their birthright. In so doing they have rejected the great privilege of making straight the way that leads to the fount of life—to the I AM Presence.

As Morya says: "For far too long man has yielded his birthright unto the false, the insecure and the transitory. But when he pauses to think of his Source, there should come to mind the best gifts of life—the ever-present thoughtfulness of God about his rate of progress, his advancement, his endowment, his protection and his ultimate fulfillment."[22]

Lord Himalaya expresses the same thought: "The best-laid plans of men must ultimately go astray unless they coincide with God's will. This is not a dictatorship; this is not even compulsion—it is the Law in action. If man had not been given the freedom to choose between his own course and the will of God, perfection would now be manifesting everywhere on earth. The fact that it does not is proof enough for those who require it that God has given free will to men. Only men of good will can return the gift to God by loving obedience and eternal determination!"[23]

The Master Jesus was one of these. Facing the crucifixion on the morrow, he knelt in prayer in the garden of Gethsemane. His was no ordinary consciousness revolving around a few individuals, a community or a nation. The Master's orbit was the universe, and his involvement as well as his commitment was with all of the people of this system of worlds. For upon his victory rested the fate of generations and worlds unborn.

In complete awareness of that which was to take place, the Master knew the sorrows that would come to those who sought to follow in his footsteps. Hence, he sweat "as it were great drops of blood."[24] His life energy poured out in the agony of his crucifixion for a suffering world, and the drama was played on the stage of the entire human consciousness.

At this moment of final testing, his impassioned fervor cried out in communion with the Father, with the Spirit of life everywhere: "Father, if thou be willing, remove this cup from me: nevertheless not my will, but thine, be done."[25]

The consecration of the Master's life was apparent in the singular devotion that he expressed in his hour of trial. And while it was no doubt the greatest of all tests, he met it according to the pattern of obedience to the will of God that had marked his entire mission.

It was, therefore, the capstone to a temple already builded without hands—not according to the human will but made after the Divine, eternal in the heavens. His passing of this test was the crowning achievement in his life's mission; for the triumph of the Spirit over the flesh was, is and always will be the triumph of man's obedience to the will of God.

Many admire the Master, even as many admire those who have achieved in various fields of human endeavor. But in the eyes of the Master, the greatest gift that the aspirant can offer to honor His name is the gift of emulation, the gift of following in his footsteps, of not only calling him "Lord," but also of giving obedience and heeding his words and direction. Did he not say, "If ye love me, keep my commandments"?[26]

In Imitation of Christ, Let Us Become the Christ

Pointing to the fact that man can become godlike (that he can actually experience the transfiguration of his consciousness as Jesus did) by patterning his thoughts after the Divine, El Morya asks, "If man thinks God's thoughts, are they ineffective because he is man?"[27] We know that the thoughts of God are a power in and of themselves, monads of his universal consciousness, seeds of his universal will.

When held in the heart of man, God's thoughts produce after their kind, and they transform man's will according to the patterns of the divine will. In answering Morya's question, then, we must admit that God's thoughts when held by man (the *man*ifestation of God) are just as effective as when they are held by God.

The imitation of Christ is an important aspect of discipleship, which, when faithfully practiced, will lead the pure in heart to the place where they will become the Christ and where they will be able to repeat his triumphant words "Nevertheless not my will, but thine, be done."

Serapis Bey, the great disciplinarian, teaches this principle to the candidates at Luxor in this wise: "Just as an actor may speak the lines of a play and enter into the identity of a living or an historical figure without ever becoming that individual, so mankind in the outer court of the temple may do homage in honest imitation of Christ-radiant men of past and present ages.*

"But imitation (unless the imitator becomes the one imitated) is no substitute for the actual vesting of the God-reality of the elect upon the radiant 'Light-form' that is man's blessed gift of opportunity. Descending from the heart of his own Divine Presence, this Light-form is intended to be the magnificent design for his entire world; and so it becomes when the outer consciousness sustains the perfection of God's energy by vesting it with the impressions of Reality."[28]

It is expected that candidates for the ascension will not only imitate the Christ but that they will also become the Christ by putting on the Light-form, the magnificent design of their identity, and by consciously qualifying it with God's pure thoughts about man—"the impressions of Reality."

Only One Mind, Only One Will

Scarcely able to recognize the presence of the LORD, men (out of habit) rebel at the thought of conforming to the will of God, much as they would rebel against conformity to human patterns. At all costs they must preserve their freedom to "do their own thing," they say, and above all they must not be conformists to any standard except their own. Men often feel that obedience is sacrifice, that religion is an imposition, that it binds them against their will, that it demands more than they are willing to give and that the service that is asked of them puts a damper on their personal happiness.

---

* Suggested supplementary reading: *The Imitation of Christ*, by Thomas à Kempis.

Knowing that Jesus exacted of his disciples the highest service to their fellowmen and obedience to the Laws of God as testimony of their love for the Christ, "why do men set up a counterfeit will and call it their own? Why do they engage in a continual struggle between the will of God and 'their own' will? In the answers to these questions is to be found the key to happiness for every part of life.

"When man understands that there is no need to struggle for a personal existence outside of God (because he is complete in God) and that, in actuality, there are not two wills—the will of man and the will of God[29]—but only the will of Truth and freedom, inherent within the very Spirit of Life that is the Spirit of God, then he will enter into the new sense of harmony and grace."[30]

If a man can reeducate his vision to behold the totality of his life's expression as the handiwork of God created as a thrust for a noble purpose, he will see that, in reality, the greatest sacrifice that he can make is to sacrifice the Higher Self to the lower self. This happens each time the human will is asserted in preference to the Divine.

"What folly it is that individuals feel separated from the will of God, as if they could not know it! For His will begins in the simplicity of a child and in the simplicities of nature. It is so natural and sweet that, in their sophistication, men often lose its tenets. The pathway to regaining it is the pathway the Master Jesus taught: 'Verily I say unto you, except ye become as a little child, ye cannot enter in.' "[31]

The Responsibility of Free Will

"There is suicide on earth, there are injustices, there are conditions that would make the angels weep!" Lanello says. "And people say, 'Why does God allow it?' It is part of the admixture of physical life, the astral plane and the levels where souls are suspended to work out their karma and their mission. The conditions that cause anything on earth are a part of the mathematical formula of the combined free will of all who live upon the planet.

"Free will *is* God. God *is* free will. Therefore, what free will has ordained, the God in you—as *you*—has ordained. Thus, you see, our religion that we share with the Ascended Masters comes down to the point of taking responsibility for being God on earth!"[32]

Hilarion, who was Saint Paul in a previous embodiment, explains a consequence of the gift of free will—that God cannot enter into our lives unless invited: "We are Ascended sons and daughters of God; you are unascended sons and daughters of God. All that separates us is the line of consciousness between the finite and the Infinite, between time and space and eternity. You can do many works that we cannot do; for by the law of Hierarchy, we cannot enter where the door is not open. We cannot enter unless the call has gone forth from someone in embodiment, someone who has a physical temple and thereby has the authority in the physical plane.

"When prayers are offered, they are always answered by the emissaries of Almighty God—legions of angels and a great company of saints and hosts of the LORD and Elohim and such an array of cosmic consciousness as you little dream of, as the veil has not been lifted from your eyes to see this great company of the hosts of the LORD. Whether the prayer of a child or of an aged one or the soft murmurings of the soul in the mother's womb longing for life, the Holy Spirit answers.

"Where there is no prayer, by cosmic law God cannot intervene for the safety of your lives and your property. There is no intercession unless you invite intercession. Understand this great truth of the Law: that God has given to unascended sons and daughters the authority for this plane of existence.

This ought to be obvious, considering what mankind have done with Terra.

"If God is a just God—and I assure you that he is—he would not have allowed such injustice except in keeping with his own Law by which he has committed himself to honor the free will of mankind, even if they employ that free will to their own destruction. There is only one way in which God can save the earth, and that way is by the individual surrender of free will to the will of God. The moment you declare, 'Not my will, but thine, be done, O LORD,'[33] you open the door, and God enters with that rushing mighty wind of the Spirit to take dominion in your life,[34] to set aright all that has gone astray from the path of righteousness.

"When you say in prayer, 'God, do this thing for me; nevertheless, not my will, but thine, be done,' then you give God the freedom to determine to answer your prayer in ways that perhaps are beyond your understanding; for the children of mankind often pray for things that they ought not to receive. And yet, because God is energy and God is Law, they often receive that which they ought not to receive."[35]

Saint Germain, our Knight Commander, says: "Remember, blessed ones, in past ages great advancement of a religious and social order has been externalized. It has not, however, always been sustained; neither has it endured so as to expand progressively with the unrolling of the scroll of time. The crumbling away of world cultures, either of the Spirit or of mundane science, like personal deterioration, results from inattention to one's Presence, lack of attunement with one's God Source, and a persistent enmeshment in vain pursuits exercised under the questionable and often spurious 'rights' of free will. Free will can exalt or debase according to how it is employed; and only if rightly used is it truly free.

"To sustain the personal chronology and habit patterns of

most lifestreams without periodic change of course would place all civilization in a rut of jeopardy. The world stage has been overturned countless times by karma and the law of divine justice in order to make it possible for civilizations to escape from the quicksand of vainly repetitious human ideas. The propensity to react to change will cease when the will of God is exalted and rightly understood to be an integral part of the inner birthright of each and every lifestream. The false will then be swallowed up and wholly transmuted in the dynamism of pure Truth....

"Today few among men possess the power to heal, to perform miracles of divine demonstration, levitation, precipitation and consecration that every Ascended Master naturally has. Yet these powers were once in the possession of many of us before our ascension; and they can be your gift to bless life today, if you will cease to limit yourselves in any way and recognize that the power to do these things is a natural one. Know also that men have been stripped of these powers by reason of their wrong concepts and gross selfishness.

"In restoring such powerful divine gifts to men, we are certain you will see that the cosmic law expects a great degree of Ascended Master integrity to manifest in you. One of the first requisites ... is the humble desire to emulate those standards of excellence and Cosmic Christ accomplishment that every Ascended Being has for so long highly esteemed and striven daily to express. This process is never a matter of strain or struggle—for it is ever a sense of struggle that makes the struggle—but it is a determinedly gentle, invocative feeling that inwardly beholds the Christ estate and then increases the desire to manifest it."[36]

"The will of God is your passport to heaven, and the will of God surrounds you at all times, waking and sleeping. It was to this will that the great Master Jesus called upon when he said, 'Our Father, who art in heaven…'[37] You, then, as children of the Most High God expressing the Christ purpose, must also pray and say, 'Not my will but thine be done.'[38] And then, when your will becomes the will of God in expression everywhere that you move, a change takes place within you, for you no longer suffer the pains of countering the will of God with your own human will. For your human will has become the will of God, and the resistance is broken down between the two. There is no struggle.

"Now it is absolutely true that the will of God does not struggle with the will of man. It is, to the contrary, the will of man that struggles with the will of God. For the will of God is a great sea of divine love and energy and illumination pouring forth at all times with the fullness and power of perfection. But the will of man is a sea of seething emotions and confusion and it is almost unpredictable."[39]

"No loss can occur when one serves the eternal will, for the revelation of the will of God shows the seeker the abundant face of Reality. One glimpse has been sufficient for many avatars, who were thereby exalted out of the socket of contemporary worldliness into positions of universal service and love.

"The greatest boon comes to those who surrender willingly with or without understanding, but always in the confidence of a faith that observes the universe and its myriad wonders and grasps with the simplicity of a child the Reality of universal science. Known by any name, God is still the Creator-Father of all life, and his will bears the fashion of acceptance by all of the emissaries of heaven."[40]

Forgiveness Is the Will of God

But what happens to those who refuse to surrender their will to God, to those who continue day in and day out to sacrifice the fruits of holiness and the essence of the soul to the Moloch of human pride and to the nets of social conformity in exchange for the fickle plaudits of men and the nod of mortal approbation?

These are excluded (because they have excluded themselves) from the hallowed circle of God's consciousness. Outside the walls of the Holy City they dance and play and make merry. Seemingly oblivious to the opportunities within, they do not even notice when the sons of God pass through their midst. But all the while they are using God's energy to bring forth images that are ungodly.

How long will the Creator endure their folly? When will the Form Maker break those forms and remake them after the image of the Divine? Does man's free will give him immunity from the law of recompense, or will his soul be eternally damned?

The scriptures declare, "The soul that sinneth, it shall die."[41] Is there no escape from the law of sin or from the judgments of heaven, no proviso for the return of the prodigal that his soul might not become a castaway? How does God see the pitiful plight of man, if indeed He sees it at all?

In order to answer the questions we have raised, El Morya tells us that "it is necessary that we establish in consciousness the concept of origins, for the majority of men's thought processes are patterned after the swing of the mind—to and fro. This pendulum motion, often stemming from the restlessness of men's emotions, is part of mankind's struggle for that identity that has already been bestowed upon them. But such movement can only swing men away from the peace of God and from his love.

"Let men who would discover the will of God realize that it is already a part of the universe; that the universe, in the macrocosmic sense, is already the perfection of God; and that each star, each cell and each atom was stamped with the Divine Image. The words 'Thou shalt have no other gods before me'[42] show the necessity for the Godhead to counteract the travesty of man's acceptance of fiats of imperfection. These have been issued by lesser minds and by the deceitful ones who are self-deceived."[43] Let us see how he will do this and yet preserve the soul of man for another day.

"In the Great Forever, in the beginningness of things, God saw Light, and he was Light. Out of his Light went forth the beauty of loving purpose, and in him was no darkness at all, nor could there be darkness there. This was the inviolate will of God—the same yesterday, today and forever.[44]

"The knowledge of Good and Evil, of duality, of the temporal and opposing factions that were within the range of the free will of the person—these came forth first as possibility and then as the looming shadows of karmic violation and disobedience to good will.

"The tenets of brotherhood were clearly stated in the Golden Rule: 'Do unto others as you would have them do unto you.'[45] But each violation produced its correspondent blot, its stain upon the page, and the Lords of Karma spoke: 'This departure from the Law of Good is but a repetition of the voices sent forth unto discord.' But there was an overthrust, a compulsion of the will of God, that sought to teach by the chastening of the Law, thus to avoid the repetition of error.

"The necessity of the will of God was clear. But while perfect love casts out all fear, for fear has torment,[46] what should be done for the impoverished ones, those who had lost their perfect love from the beginningness of God?

" 'Let them at least,' said the Great Ones, 'understand that God chastens those whom he loves,[47] and that he continues to love out of the bounty of his forgivingness.'

"Thus the will of God toward forgiveness was born in the

consciousness of man. It was a step toward the regaining of perfection; for as men understood that as they had sowed so should they reap,[48] a desire to have perfection arose within them. This desire to return to perfection through grace became the second corollary of the will of God.

"Now the children of men who had erred saw the need to correct the error of their ways and thus be restored to the old boundaries of perfection—the perfection of perfect love. The children of the Sun, who came forth bearing the white stones from the Temple of the Sun, evoked the mightiest response possible from the hearts of men; for in the hearts of men there was also a residual memory of the olden days when the Elder Race communed with the living God.

"Forgivingness, they saw, was eternal grace and the fire of purpose. Forgiveness, too, was the will of God. Thus the desire to return to perfect love flashed forth anew.

" 'Consider the lilies of the field; they toil not, neither spin....'[49] The cadences of the Master's words were dripping with the fires of that perfect love that is his perfect will."[50]

Thus the assayers of men's souls came into prominence. The Lords of Karma were elevated to their service, and the disposition of the will of God upon the planet took on a new note—the note of mercy, extended as opportunity, that man might return to the scene of his karma to reinvoke the will of God and to reestablish the patterns of perfection that he had lost. Mercy—the love of the will divine—how magnificent is the givingness of God!

Requirements of the Law of Mercy: Step by Step the Way Is Won

According to the plan of mercy, the soul of man need not become a castaway. The prodigal may return to a state of grace, and he may reclaim his divine inheritance.[51] But the requirements of the law of mercy must be met. When, dear reader, they shall say to you, "Tell us what are these requirements," tell them simply so that none will feel that going Home is an impossible dream.

(1) First, the errant son, determined to forsake the error of his ways, must go before his own God Presence and ask forgiveness for having departed from the path of righteousness (from the right use of God's energies and his Laws).

(2) Then he must surrender his human will unconditionally to the Divine and renew his vow to serve God with his total being.

(3) Next he must invoke the violet transmuting flame through his consciousness and through his imperfect creations. The flame will requalify the energies he has misused with their original purity, in order that he may reuse these same energies to fulfill his vows and for such noble purposes as are in keeping with the will of God.

(4) Then he must go forth in love and in wisdom to do the will of God in service to his fellowman, and he must daily keep the flame of the Holy Spirit blazing on behalf of the evolutions of this planet.

Then, dear reader, if they understand the simplicity of the Law, tell them the teachings of the Master Serapis on the subject of forgivingness—forgivingness as it is understood in the heart of God's flaming purity:

"When Jesus said, 'Father, forgive them; for they know not what they do,'[52] he spake of the multitudes who passed through the wide gate. The narrow gate must exclude the paltry errors of men, but they must be willing to recognize the fact that they have erred and to come to that contriteness of heart whereby we can impart to them safely and in divine measure the commands of the Infinite over the finite mind and being. The psalm of David 'The LORD is my shepherd; I shall not want. He maketh me to lie down in green pastures: he leadeth me beside the still waters. He restoreth my soul'[53] shows clearly in its comforting vocalization that the soul must be restored to her original Divine Image.

"Many men and women are not actually aware that the soul has been swept away from her eternal moorings. They feel that the soul has been temporarily lost and that of necessity some thaumaturgic process, spiritual formula or doctrine of salvation must be accepted and put to use by their lifestreams in order that they might obtain their eternal freedom.

"They seek, therefore, for a religion with a pattern they can accept that will provide for them, for all time to come, both forgiveness of sins and the gift of divine grace. Men do not realize that they themselves have lost their way and that it is they who must therefore find it again. They do not realize that their specific consciousness is involved in this losing of the way and that the consciousness that they have lost is the consciousness of the Divine One that they must personally regain.

"No litany or magical formula or even an imploration to the Deity of itself possesses the fullness of the power of realignment of the four lower bodies in conjunction with the balancing of the threefold flame. Realignment is attained through the simplicity of the Cosmic Christ mind that ever refuses to acknowledge that it has in any way been involved in a state of consciousness beneath the dignity of Truth and the majesty of the Godhead.

"The sickening beat of clenched fists upon human chests intended as a manifestation of abject humility to the Deity and the invocation of his mercy in time of trouble, where the true spirit of repentance is lacking, are of little effect in producing the state of God consciousness and divine awareness that the Law requires. The true internal sense of Cosmic Christ identification is one of beauty and rejoicing. It is the beautiful acknowledgment and perception of the laws of love and mercy; it is the acknowledgment of the tender intent of the Deity to raise the soul up the cosmic ladder of creation. Step by step the way is won until each one beholds for himself the pure longing of the Spirit that seeks to become one with the created being that the Spirit has made."[54]

Thus, in pursuing the requirements of the law of mercy, the supplicant must come to the place where he understands that "there is no room for speculative theological argumentation in the Godhead, for God is not aware in his pure consciousness of man's frightening descent into mortal involvement. Only the Holy Christ Self has this awareness and acts to mediate, in his advisory capacity to the Godhead, the total world situation"[55] and the total karmic patterns of the overcomer.

"Only by union with God's will can the world, one and all, come to peace and perfection in a relative sense, stretching toward the good things to come that spring forth in eternal life."[56]

Weaving the Seamless Garment through Gradual Surrender

When man begins to build upon the foundations of the divine will and its purposes, he opens the door to admit the Master Weaver into his world. Then, as the great shuttles of his life's energies flow to and fro, the seamless garment will be woven, and the fabric of his soul will expand to envelop the world.

The lure of the pleasures of the senses and the desire for

self-importance are traps into which the multitudes have fallen. When dealing with the human ego, there is a razor's edge that must be understood if men are to function within the framework of a practical perspective. If the ego lacks incentive, individuals are often unable to do good work. On the other hand, the undisciplined ego left to its own devices will parade its virtues before men and stifle the creative expressions of the soul in her outreach for spiritual progress.

There is a solution for those who are unable to surrender totally by a single act of the will. It is to replace, gradually, the undesirable qualities of the human ego with the desirable qualities of the Divine Ego. Let them take up the offer of the heavenly hosts to exchange their hatreds and their fears for God's love, their stubbornness and their perversions for his masterful control, their ignorance and greed for his illumination, their bigotry and pride for his divine direction, their disappointments and disillusionments for his vision of hope, their criticism and their misconceptions for the purity of his Truth, their defeats and backslidings for his victory, their sense of lack for his abundance and their disquietude for his peace.

Little by little, even cautiously, the individual turns over the reins of his consciousness to the Higher Self until, through the process of spiritual assimilation, his entire being is molded in the pattern of the Light-form. By using this method, the sense of struggle is avoided, and the violent reactions common to a dying ego do not manifest. For the transformation is so gradual that the ego, although it has given its consent, is not conscious of the fact that it is being displaced.

The Birth of the Divine Ego

Sometimes the fear of total surrender to the will of God comes from the mistaken idea that man's ego will be lost as a drop of water in the ocean, and it is feared that once the ego is lost, it will never be recovered. Let all learn that even more to be feared than the loss of the ego is the fattening thereof, for there is no greater tyrant than an unbridled ego.

The ego that has not submitted itself to the Christ will make demands upon one's total resources without ever returning one iota of benefit to the individual. The finite self, while laying claim to the treasures of the soul, will begrudge the time it spends in the pursuit of the things of the Spirit—which pursuit, while it will surely strip him of his human ego, will also bring him the greatest development of his Higher Self, his Real Ego.

Jesus diagrammed the dilemma of the human ego versus the Divine Ego when he said with utter simplicity, "Whosoever shall seek to save his life shall lose it; and whosoever shall lose his life shall preserve it."[57]

Those who still believe that the surrender of their free will means the giving up of their freedom should stop and think: Freedom is a quality of God! Did not the apostle say, "Where the Spirit of the Lord is, there is liberty"?[58] Freedom is our divine prerogative, even as freedom is our divine inheritance.

The Luciferian idea that in order to gain his freedom man must rebel against a tyrannical God is the lie that has confused the issues of man's entire existence and his reason for being. This is the lie that was spawned in order to make mankind lose the remembrance of the intimate and beautiful relationship that has always existed between Father and son.

Men fear the loss of their personal identity. But did not Paul say to the Colossians, "For ye [referring to the human ego] are dead, and your life is hid with Christ in God"?[59] If the individuality of the Real Man is "hid with Christ in God," then man will find himself only by plunging into the Being of God—and there in the flaming center of the Spirit of the LORD, he will find his true freedom.

The man who has surrendered himself unto God need never express a weak and palpitating human will. Nor should he express a weak and palpitating divine will, for the divine will is the strength of the Creator himself. Therefore, with certainty let men clasp the hand of the will of God as though they clasped one another's in the dark—and let them know that God's hand will lead them to the light of understanding, which surpasses all outer knowledge gained through the five senses.

The man who has surrendered himself to God knows that "the dream, the 'impossible' dream, becomes the Reality. And all that man has thought to be Real, insofar as his own relationship with the universe goes, is seen as a chimera—a shimmering illusion that comes from misqualified energy. In its place, in the place of the mirage of carnal identity with its shifting sands of manifestation, the Reality of the Christ-identity is seen as the will of God."

And he says to himself, "What difference does it make that there are opposing forces? The forces of Light are more dominant, the forces of Light are greater, the forces of Light are complete and eternal. They will stand when men are but dust and their present thoughts hollow echoes in the chambers of memory."[60]

After all is said and done, he comes to the realization that "Not my will, but thine, be done" is a fiat for all men. He sees that it does not mean the destruction of the human person; on the contrary, it can mean the construction of the divine person and the illumination of his actions in the Light of the will of God.

Amazing things happen when you discover the will of God as the flame in your heart, as something not opposing your identity or being but actually presenting the key and the formula to the fulfillment for your reason for being.

It is not that we have disobeyed some man-made law or something imposed from without when we stray from God's will. It is that we have ignored the impulse of the fire and the Light within. The power of God's will is the eternal blueprint of one's immortal destiny.

You find when you give the decree "I AM God's Will" (see page 407) in the understanding of surrender to God—as God is truly one's Real Self, one's real reason for being, one's identity—that all things come together in your life. You have peace you have never known before. You have faith that God will always lead you aright because you maintain the listening grace of Mother Mary, who followed God's will all the way to giving birth to the beloved Christ Child who is our Lord and Saviour.

The will of God is the most powerful step you can take in your life.

Your Divine Plan

People say, "What is my divine plan? What shall I do next? Shall I go here, shall I go there?"

Meta says: "Each man, each woman, each child upon the planetary body has a master plan, an opportunity, even as a seed holds the portent of the covering tree that becomes a haven for the birds of heaven to nest in. So the consciousness of each one is intertwined purposefully with the magnificent God intent that makes man to realize:

> "I AM the fullness of God's purpose!
> I AM the fullness of God's Light!
> I AM the vitality of the Central Sun!
> I AM the mastery of every electron,
>   of every atom of my being!
> I AM life indomitable!

I AM life overwhelming,
Grasping principles and flooding them forth
As the Being of God in finite form—
I AM Infinity coalescing its radiance
With the finite realm
And lifting it on wings of purpose
Into the fullness of the LORD
Who has said to his prophets,
'The earth is the LORD's and the fullness thereof.' "[61]

Serve the living God where you are. And when you serve him and you come into that rhythm of the heartbeat of God, you know the measured step, the measured cadence. You know where you must be. It becomes very evident that if you do not fulfill your niche in life, in your community or in your nation, some very important things may not get done. People may not be fed the nourishment they require.

You have talents. Unlock them. This is the purpose of the call to the will of God. It is the refinement of the diamond heart within you. It is the finding of that noble purpose you had in the Beginning.

"Who can know how to use his talents without first perceiving the flame of God's will? It is indispensable that you know the heart of the Father as it pertains to your life and to your going forth.

"You cannot choose a way upon earth and then say, 'O God, is this thy will?' after you enter into contracts and circumstances that cannot be altered because of karmic reasons. It is *before* the fact that you must invoke the will of God, not after the fact. For how do you expect that we shall help you once you have used your free will to do as you please? This is not divine order, and this is not good thinking, precious ones, to expect that we can alter your lives after you have taken the decisions.

"Therefore, when you arise, invoke that flame of holy will before you go forth to determine your actions for the day. Once you are embroiled and enmeshed in the outer world, we cannot interfere with the cyclic course that you have set up within yourself, for it must unwind according to the cause-and-effect pattern that you yourself have set up. E'en though God hath set the greater pattern, it cannot come into focus within you without your call, without your beckon, without your heart's attention to the flame of God's holy will, which we are so privileged and blessed to hold and nourish for you until such time as you are ready to call upon us.

"Let this sacred ritual, then, become part of your daily offering to the Most High God—that you reach to his heart to perceive and know all of the wonders of creation through the pathway of his holy will.

"And if you can remember but this sacred trust I give you this day, I shall not count my saying to have been in vain; for then I shall see and know that lives will be transformed, that many among you shall be sons of God brought unto captivity at the end of your embodiment through the ritual of your ascension. For if you truly walk the way of God's will, you cannot miss the Path, you cannot miss the calling of each of the seven rays, for each ray does follow that ordered cycle from the Father's heart."[62]

You came into embodiment with a purpose. You stood before Almighty God. You stood with your Christ Self. And God said, "Go to earth! Go be a comforter to life! Be a healer. Be a writer. Be a musician. Be a mother. Be a father. Be an example." And you have been seeking and searching to find the way, to realize your fiery destiny on earth, to be sure that this time, in this embodiment, you will accomplish the thing to which your soul was set before you took on the densities of these veils.

You *can* remember. You *can* go back. You *can* make contact with the will of God within. You *can* realize your reason for being. Find those whom you love and who love you. Find your area of service.

The teachings of the Great White Brotherhood bring to us the understanding why the great lights of history East and West—whether Jesus or Zoroaster, Buddha or Moses—were unique revolutionaries of God. They found the will of God. They adored that will. By embracing it they established, as it were, an electrode or a magnet within their beings. That magnet impelled the power of the Godhead. God anointed them. And millions of people following in their footsteps also found the key to the will of God.

The Universal Christ is in all of us. The same Christ that empowered Elijah and Elisha or the apostle Paul is also with you. It requires the awakening. It requires the devotion, the inner listening and the vow: "Lo, I AM come to do thy will, O God!"

Fit for the Kingdom

Illumination should always precede right action, for confidence that is begotten of spiritual understanding assists man in becoming one-pointed in his service. One-pointedness is a necessary virtue that should be invoked by those who would succeed on the path of service.

Those who develop singleness of mind and purpose will not be distracted by the world's thoughts, which beat at the door of self to test each man and see if he will go here and go there in search of the kingdom that is within. To those who desired to follow him, Jesus said, "No man, having put his hand to the plough, and looking back, is fit for the kingdom of God."[63]

Kuthumi echoes the sentiments of Jesus when he says: "Surrender must be beyond recall. Those who hold back part of the treasure and pleasure of life, those who still desire to live exclusively for themselves, fail to understand the law of sweet surrender. Does man surrender to God? Can God do more than surrender in return? Can he fail to recognize that the soul has offered himself in the service of the King? Shall not the King, then, empower him as his representative, as his ambassador? Shall the King not fight all of his battles and, by the Spirit of absolute justice, provide him with all of his rewards?"[64]

When temptations come—and come they will, if the initiate is to advance in the order of Hierarchy—he must cry out with a loud voice and with the full authority of his being say, "Get thee behind me, Satan."[65] Thus he will be following in the footsteps of the Christ who overcame the world. To challenge the stranger at the gate in the name of the I AM Presence is in keeping with the code of the Brotherhood, for a true emissary of God is never unwilling to show his credentials (his Light)—whereas the gray ones will take on an injured air and belittle the one who rightfully demands proof that they are all that they claim to be.

Invariably, the needs of the world will assert themselves before the aspirant for spiritual illumination. These will pull upon his time and energy through family, friends and the poor in spirit—who are always there, looking for someone to carry their karmic burden. Worldly opportunity will knock not once but many times—even as the opportunity to glorify the self in some new and glamorous religious experience.

The prophecy of the Christ must be remembered: "For there shall arise false Christs, and false prophets, and shall shew great signs and wonders; insomuch that, if it were possible, they shall deceive the very elect."[66]

Jesus admonished: "Wherefore if they shall say unto you, Behold, he is in the desert; go not forth: behold, he is in the secret chambers; believe it not. For as the lightning cometh out of the east, and shineth even unto the west; so shall also the coming of the Son of man be."[67] This shows clearly that the coming of the Christ to the consciousness of man will occur with the swift and sudden penetration of the diamond-shining mind of God. And he will come, not through another's attainment, but through the doorway of the receptive heart.

In the Book of Revelation we read: "He that is unjust, let him be unjust still: and he which is filthy, let him be filthy still: and he that is righteous, let him be righteous still: and he that is holy, let him be holy still."[68]

This passage indicates that the doorway to that which men call "death" is not necessarily a doorway to deification, to illumination or to progress, although we do not deny that the higher teachings can be communicated to those who are out of the body. The living Word clearly declares that those passing through the gate at the termination of their earthly life in a filthy state may well remain in that state; those who pass through in a holy state will remain holy.

Thus the will of God has ordained our best and surest means to progress in the here and now, rather than in the hereafter. The set of our sails today, the set of the rudder of life, determines the course of our ship for a long time to come. Whether men live once or through many embodiments, it is between the lines of birth and death that they must be concerned with the progress they can make as individuals in the fulfillment of their reason for being.

It is in this life, and not in the next, that they must bear in mind the words "Not my will, but thine, be done." We know that time will one day run out for all. Therefore, what we do, think, say and feel, and what we are is important—because it is declaratory to our own Christ Self, to our Divine Presence and to the Lords of Karma as to whether or not we are really concerned with obedience to the will of God, which is the doorway to immortal life.

The change men call death was instituted by God as an act of mercy that the chapters of men's existence might be terminated and they might subsequently be born again, free from the memories of the past. In the words of Kahlil Gibran, "A little while, a moment of rest upon the wind, and another woman shall bear me."[69]

The Abundant Life: Antidote for Human Stubbornness

El Morya explains: "Let men understand that it is not the Father's will that they should perish but that they should have abundant life.[70] When we begin to examine the great thoughts of God and the great will of God, when we begin to examine how great God is, we must see that cardinal to his greatness is the abundant life, the life that is eternal.

"It is fear—fear of death and fear of illusion—that has caused some men to fail to hold themselves in that state of consciousness wherein the will of God could manifest through them. They need to understand the very naturalness of cosmic purpose: God is life. They are manifesting temporal life, but they also possess, here and now, the seeds of eternal life in the very essence of the soul that God has given to them.

"The flaming Presence that directs them from above, their beloved God Presence, I AM, represents the fire of the will of God; and the will of God includes within itself the all-chemistry of cosmic purpose. Therefore, each department of life is brought under the direction of the central purpose of the will of God"[71] when man surrenders his will to God.

There is nothing more degrading to the soul than the perverted human will. Conversely, there is nothing more ennobling to the soul than the magnificent divine will. Time and again human beings have rebelled against the will of God and even against the will of their neighbors when they knew that the stand their neighbors took was representative of His will.

Human stubbornness is a perversion of the will of God. Human stubbornness is not a commodity you can exchange for Reality just when you are ready. Even as the snake sheds its skin, so man out of the fruit of divine wisdom would be very wise to shed stubbornness and substitute for it spiritual determination, constancy and steadfastness in service of the will of God.

"The human will presupposes it has the knowledge that it does not have. It bases most of its choices on human history and the observations of those whose own quality of observation is centered primarily around the physical and is seldom involved with the celestial.

"The human will identifies with the ego and seeks to support it in its passing aims. Men erect monuments to their vanities that endure in substance far beyond the tenure of their own times. But we are concerned with monuments of the Spirit.

"The will of God assures man that he will survive, for it is the will of God that those whom he has created should inherit his kingdom—but the rules of the game must be followed, for the Law of God is inexorable in its demands for perfection.

"Humans, cast in the role of imperfection, have been willing to discount the possibility of their attaining that measure of perfection that stems from God-realization. Let not your hearts be troubled, for with God all things are possible.[72]

"It is just as easy to serve the will of God—in fact it is far easier—than it is to serve the decaying will of man with its varying standards. The human will propels men to false aspirations at a dizzying rate of ascent and leaves them stranded without spiritual knowledge to plummet to their destruction.

"I would like to postulate, then, that the majority of men have no conception at all of what the will of God is; therefore they do not really know what they are opposing. The human will opposes the divine will because its aims are shortsighted. Men find it difficult to expand their thought beyond their days. They are prone to accept death as final and to identify with the physical form rather than with the Spirit that gives it life.[73]...

"Would it not be wise, then, for man, caught in the net of illusion, to examine the purposes of God, to know them, to understand and serve these mighty purposes in order to accelerate in his own personal evolution the divine plan and to foster the architecture of heaven for all mankind?"[74]

"In heaven's name, men of earth, do you think the Most High God created life to manifest as history shows it? And what of contemporary struggles twixt Church and State, race and race, class and class, and even man and man or man and woman?

"Does life seem so wonderful and the prospect of the future based on human trends so grand that you are fearful of submission to the will of the Eternal? I hope not, for in his will is comfort and strength for the ages as well as for today....

"Be ready mentally, spiritually and emotionally by an act of simple devotion or a feeling of awe to accept the will of God as a gladiator would a laurel wreath. Eras of achievement lie ahead—the planning of great cities, civilizations and humanitarian doings. But until the will of God becomes acceptable to men, until they can put aside their double-mindedness, they will remain unstable and fluctuating in their aims.[75]

"The terrors of their world exist first in their denial of God and secondly in their denial of his will. In order for the kingdom of God to manifest upon earth, it must first manifest in the heavenly consciousness.

"Let men think heaven and think God's will, let them deny the power of darkness, and the light of holy knowledge will show science and religion the way to happiness through finite days to infinite aeons of bliss for all. Thus God ordained it; thus man must seek to know!"[76]

Escape from Karma

"Each time a situation of imbalance occurs in your life," El Morya teaches, "as a chela on the Path you must see it as an opportunity in the present to right a wrong of the past. This is how you balance karma. This is how you relieve the soul of the burden of the synthetic image. Now life becomes a challenge! And you see that you are what you are—a living flame—regardless of what you think you are in those moments of encounter with the accumulations of past energy sowings. And so the law is fulfilled, 'Whatsoever a man soweth, that shall he also reap.'"[77]

"It is the will of God that mankind should escape wholly from their negative karma and receive only the benefit of their good karma. Individuals are not intended to walk upon this planet subject to limitation, to despair, to confusion, to any other vibratory action that is less than the Light of God. They are intended from the beginning of life to turn to their Source 'as the sunflower turns on her God.'[78] They are intended to turn and drink in and receive the rays outpoured from the Sun, and the rays are intended to raise them up toward the Light and restore them to their own Divinity. God sent forth the Light manifesting as the power of the ray of God. In the ancient Egyptian language the ray was called *ra* and they called God *Ra*.

"Beloved ones, you are all individualized rays from the heart of God. You are all intended to become one with God. You have heard this spoken of old, and yet the few who have believed it and have lived accordingly have become as we are—Ascended Beings."[79]

The Lord of the First Ray of the Will of God explains that "the tender shoots of aspiration budding within man's desire for spiritual attainment are more often blunted by the carnal mind than many would care to admit. Thus we perceive the constant struggle between the spirit and the flesh;[80] and we know somewhat the tools that are employed by the shadowed ones to thwart the would-be initiate in his search for God and in his longing to be of service in constructively molding the course of civilization as a co-creator with God. In this connection, let me point out that ordinary circumstances often contain gems of spiritual enlightenment that pass unnoticed because individuals become involved with the experiences passing before the screen of their minds instead of examining the stream of their consciousness and searching out the causes and effects of the events, from both a karmic and a generic standpoint.

"Karma, blessed ones, may be either good or bad. It is seldom neuter. Like rain falling on the continental divide, karma usually falls either to one side or the other. Therefore, while deeds may fall within the gray zone of a blending of good and evil, the Lords of Karma decide from the motive, the act and the cause-effect relationship with other parts of life into what category it shall be referred.

"We have known of many cases where individuals of good intent have unwittingly performed a disservice to their fellowmen. By the same token, there have been instances where those who have intended to act maliciously have instead brought a godsend or a great boon to those whom they desired to harm. Now we are certain that those who have sought with all their hearts to perform benignly and, through no fault of their own, have observed their benign intent go astray and manifest as ill effect will usually find no taint upon their record. Seldom, however, do such as these receive the great benefits that they would if the divine intent had been properly carried out.

"Let those who would understand the Law realize that even when men bow to good intent, it is their responsibility to follow its course of action and the plotting of its curve on the graph of life so that they may focus upon that good intent at all times and nurture it until it manifests fully in the world of another. This is a God-responsibility in consciousness, which, while it can be turned over to the Higher Mental Body (the Christ Self) for adjudication, does require the follow-up of some definite effort in order that it be consummated in the physical plane. However, those who plot and carry out ill-fated deeds calculated to harm or destroy their enemies or to bring disgrace to their neighbors and then find that circumstances have reversed their plans need expect no mercy from the Law simply because their malice did not mature. You see, the Law is so just and so complete that, when once understood, it becomes the true friend of every man.

"The aspects of personal genesis, of man's spiritual origin, differ from individual karma in that they embody the pure God-intent of the Creator who formed man in his image rather than the imperfections subsequently imposed upon that intent by the human consciousness. While these patterns of the Creator's intent, enmeshed within the very fabric of the soul, continually flash forth their impulses into the stream of man's consciousness, we find that the synthetic construction that has been placed upon human life—its values and its goals as seen through mortal eyes—is a conglomerate of adversity that must be reckoned with daily by every sincere seeker for God's flame of emancipation.

"If it were possible for man to close the valve of his karmic patterns and to open the valve of the pattern of his personal genesis, thus tuning in the pure Light waves of the Creator's design for his lifestream and tuning out the negative momentums of mortal involvements, a great deal of suffering could be avoided and an acceleration in soul evolution be achieved. There is no doubt that the daily exchange of the energy patterns of the human consciousness for those of the divine consciousness has played a major part in the ultimate victory of every saint and avatar and in their deliverance from mortal planes of manifestation into immortal realms of attainment and service.

"The time has come when greater understanding of the laws of the universe must be sought by the seeker for Truth. Men must not be content merely to scan the great hidden mysteries of life for selfish reasons and then misuse them in order to produce exotic experiences not in keeping with life's pure intent. For I am certain that the will of God possesses a power so far superior to that of the human will with its mundane patterns of sense consciousness that it would be folly to misuse it, even as it would be futile to attempt to describe its transcendent nature to those who have not experienced it themselves or at least glimpsed it in manifestation in their own lives. It is our wish, therefore, to stress the beautiful generic patterns of the Causal Body descending from the Godhead in cascades of power and beneficence and to show how these can be consciously appropriated by the devotee as well as by the seeker for oneness with his Divine Presence."[81]

Hercules gives us the answer to the question of how to escape karma: "What is a heap of karma? What is that mountain of karma? An anthill, I say! Take on the perspective of an Elohim. Look down upon that anthill you have created. Sweep it into the flame. Sweep it into the white-fire core of being. Take dominion over the mountain of karma. In the consciousness of an Elohim this is not the insurmountable, this is the glorious opportunity, grain by grain, to transmute, transcend, to define cycles of eternity, to release gratitude, to fill in, then, those nicks in the pyramid of life.

"I say, rush to the mountain of karma. Be swift, O my soul! Be swift, souls of God! Run to greet the morning. Run to greet the mountain. And rejoice with the strength of the Elohim, the wisdom, the love to put that mountain into the fire day by day. And thank the LORD God even for karma that keeps you in the planes of Mater on Terra: and thus you can be instruments of love to all life....

"Scale the mountain of karma! Transmute the mountain of karma into the pyramid of life, into the spiral of your ascension, then make that pyramid a mountain glistening white that all mankind might climb to make their own in the crystal summits of God-mastery."[82]

Moral Decisions Based on the Will of God

"The problem of absolutes is always at hand—absolute Evil and absolute Good. These conditions are so remote from the average person that their concern lies not in the absolute but in the relative. They are concerned not with the question 'Is it a condition that manifests Good or Evil?' but when making a moral decision they ask, 'Is it relatively good or evil by comparison to other conditions, and does it represent the best choice?'

"Understanding moral values, which are valid because they are based on Truth, will help men to understand that their progress must come from their present state and move forward. Too many are obsessed with the idea of a utopian ideal, which, because it is unobtainable, they use as an excuse for lowered standards....

"Cultivate, then, the spirit of Truth.[83] Invite an honest analysis of situations. This will not require hours of your time when it is evoked out of an honest heart. The will of God that has already engraven his wisdom and love upon your heart will enable you to draw reasonable standards toward which you may reach.

"God will not seem so remote, nor his will, when men are able to envision it as an extension of their own consciousness from present standards to those that are still higher. But when men consider their own standards to be above the stars, then like an animalistic cult, they grunt and groan, dance in circles and dissipate their energies in vanity.

"We are concerned that the will of God come into fuller manifestation in the world of men. But in a relative sense, one man's idea of the will of God may be a far lower standard than it is for another. Men must realize that some have higher standards than others and that some can attain higher goals. Life is not meant to be filled with criticism and condemnation, but it is an opportunity to thwart the human ego that must ultimately reflect God if it is to endure."[84]

The sweet surrender that can be felt in the declaration "Not my will, but thine, be done" does not spell an end to human choices. For God always returns control to those who surrender their all unto him, by giving them the precious opportunity to master their lives according to his precepts and his laws.

As the mother bird assists the fledgling to spread its wings and fly, so God is ever anxious for men to find that direction within themselves that he has implanted there as the treasure of his heart that they may develop and make their own.

His is a patient love; we call it mercy. He gives it to all. It is a quality that is never strained except by men who misappropriate God's patient love. The Father has no desire to usurp the free will of his children by intruding his assistance and counsel where these are not sought—and if he were to do so, he would be abrogating his own Law.

It is not his will that any should perish in the degradation of the misuse of their own human will, but neither is it his intent to control his children as puppets on a string. If this were his will, he would long ago have asserted it, for he who framed the universe certainly has the power to do so.

The Return to Reality through the Return to the Divine Will

God withholds from his children the full potential of his energies until they demonstrate their willingness to be obedient to his will. This is the altogether natural attitude of a father who does not allow his children to play with fire until they have learned to use it constructively.

God asks man to surrender his will unto him only until man can demonstrate, by his assimilation of and attunement with cosmic law, that he has put on the Father's own understanding of divine justice. Only then is God assured that man will use His will and His power to implement the universal intent, not only for the benefit of self and others but also for the benefit of all cosmos.

He who withholds his human will from surrender to the divine will only hinders his own entering into the kingdom and stays a little the progress of the whole world that waits daily for the sunrise. The greatest sunburst of all life is the will of God, which is indeed good for everyone.

His will trembles with the joy of the whole capsule of identity, full of grace and happiness. Without being centered in the will of God both within and without, man loses the meaning of his life and it vanishes—even as a waning moon falls beyond the horizon, leaving no shimmering trail upon the waters.

"The flashing forth of the renewal of the first covenant is the will of God; for it was this bond to which every soul who received the gift of individual life expression did once consent. The breaking of the bond of God's will has meant the parting of the way between Father and son. For the prodigal son has chosen to wander into the depths of maya to seek his fortune in the realm of illusion.

"Now we say, let us return to Reality, to the Father and to the heavenly will. Thus shall the fire purify each man's work[85] and the fiery trial cease in a pact of friendship with God."[86]

> "Long has the soul been dead
> In the night of personal delusion—
> The struggles, the accumulated karmic debts,
> And the great harms.
> Now the end has come
> In one solemn sweet surrender:
> I AM—Thou art—we are—
> All are One!"[87]

> "Rejoice, ye men of destiny!
> Rejoice, ye children of the free!
> Search on and on, be valiant still;
> For angel hands uphold his will."[88]

"And so this is my message to you this day. Even as we followed the star to the place where Jesus lay,* I come again, then, to point the way and to say to you that if you follow the

---

* In a previous embodiment Morya was Melchior, one of the three wise men of the East who followed the star that portended the birth of the Christ.

star of your mighty I AM Presence and pursue it well, if you heed not the whisperings of the Herods and the earthly kings and the earthly powers but move on to find the Christ Child where he lay, you shall find your divine calling and your mission. You shall perceive it and you shall know it.

"And in its knowing, the fiery essence of the will of God shall make it so beautiful and wondrous and magnificent in thy sight that thou shalt nevermore be able to refrain from outpicturing it in action. For this is the beauty of God's holy will—that it is so wondrous that man, once he has perceived it, cannot help but outpicture it! And if students of Light are not outpicturing the holy will of God, it is because they have not perceived it to begin with. For to know God is to know his will, and to know his will is to perform it upon earth."[89]

"The will is not a harsh overcoat for mankind to wear. It is not a rough garment. The will is a fine, refined garment of Light, more beautiful than any of you have ever worn, as pertaining and compared to human garments.

"And therefore, we await the hour of your enrobing, when the fullness of the will of God actually is draped around your four lower bodies and your form, hallowing those bodies and anointing them with all of the beauty of heaven until you will no longer be able to contain the joy that you feel. But it will propel you like an airplane propeller, raising you higher and higher and higher into the goals of your ascension until your physical form loses every vestige of age, every vestige of discord, every wrinkle, every gray hair, every appearance whatsoever that has been accepted by you in a lesser role, and the beauty of our eternal victory enfolds you in our hearts' love and Light as Ascended Beings.

"Then shall you know that I AM Morya El, Lord of the First Ray, Lord of Love as well as Lord of Will."[90]

A Sacred Adventure
by El Morya

Eternal Seekers,

In the beginning God created the heaven and the earth. And the earth was without form, and void; and darkness was upon the face of the deep. And the Spirit of God moved upon the face of the waters."[1] It is to this point that we would return in order to reveal the tenderness of the eternal will, for the light shone in the darkness and the darkness comprehended it not.[2] It is, then, to comprehension that we dedicate our closing release in this series on the will of God.

Thought is buoyant, but whose thought is more buoyant—man's or God's? If man thinks God's thoughts, are they ineffective because he is man? The affection of the will is its raison d'être. A will without affection is a nonentity. The natural affection of God for the creation is apparent within the creation, for the fire of creation is the affection of the will of God.

The ability to affect Matter and Spirit simultaneously is the prerogative of the divine will, which, in a lower harmonic range, is observed in part by evolving men. The laws of containment that govern time cycles and the enlargement of space involve the spreading apart of divine ideas from the center point unto the circumference of manifestation.

The tenderness of divine love refuses to yield itself to a moment of sympathy; for such indulgence would deny immortal opportunities, and it is even questionable that it would satisfy temporary thirst. Yet the mercy of the Law is functional and practical, and man is never deprived of grace by submission to the will of God. The grace that is sufficient for every day[3] is extracted from the universe by an act of will when that will concerns itself with glorifying God through outer manifestation and purpose.

The will of man is not capable of expanding self or substance, but dedication to the supreme purpose invokes the will that moves mountains. Man can do the will of God without knowing it, but by being conscious of himself as a part of the will of God he is able to fulfill his destiny in a more sublime way.

The talents and opportunities of life are given to man as stepping-stones toward spiritual achievement, and spiritual achievement is the only goal that is Real, hence worthwhile. Eternal life can best be enjoyed spiritually, for "flesh and blood cannot inherit the kingdom of God."[4]

The Form Maker, who is the Form Breaker, can also be the Form Remaker. No loss can occur when one serves the eternal will, for the revelation of the will of God shows the seeker the abundant face of Reality. One glimpse has been sufficient for many avatars who were thereby exalted out of the socket of contemporary worldliness into positions of universal service and love.

The greatest boon comes to those who surrender willingly with or without understanding, but always in the confidence of a faith that observes the universe and its myriad wonders and grasps with the simplicity of a child the reality of universal science. Known by any name, God is still the Creator-Father of all life, and his will bears the fashion of acceptance by all of the emissaries of heaven.

Every active power by which the universe is sustained and managed in the light of cosmic justice comes forth from him, and every spirit that he has created returns to him. Each spirit is intended to be made like unto him, hence in his image. Any lesser dominion is the having of "other gods before me."[5] Therefore, the holy will appears as the fullness of the swaddling garment of the Divine Man, the Son of Righteousness, with which the children of the Sun must be clothed.

Stand now to release thyself from the darkness that is in thee[6] and face the luminous orb of the Central Sun from whence all creation sprang. Mindful of his will for good and of his power to extend that will, realize that he is able to extend thy consciousness from its present state—to pick it up, to exalt it, and to draw it into himself by the magnetism of his grace—here and now, prior to thy release from sense consciousness.

Realize that he that keepeth all that *is Real*[7] about thee, having received thee momentarily unto himself, is also able to return thee to the present moment unaffected adversely but mightily affected inwardly by a fuller measure of the understanding of his will. Realize that the will of God can best be known by a spiritual experience. Desire, then, that experience. Desire to reach outwardly toward the Godhead in the Great Central Sun galaxy.

At the same time as thou art reaching inwardly to the implanting of the divine seed within thyself, it is the will to live within thyself that must unite with the will to live as God lives. This is the divine will within the heart of the Central Sun. This thou must understand and be united with.

If this be accomplished but once consciously, thy life shall ever thereafter be affected by an innate knowing, recorded within, of that which is the will of God. The phantoms and the ghosts that formerly made thee a stranger at the court of heaven will no longer hold power over thee as they once did. But man's reunion with the Sun can only be accomplished by an act of God. It is a cosmic event that can occur in the world of the individual only when he has proven himself ready for it.

I am a cosmic teacher, and I choose to appear to those who are able to see me with their spiritual eyes, to those who understand that my prime concern is the union of the heart of hearts within man with the Heart of Hearts within God. For me to provide descriptive passages of these wonders and to record them on paper would in no way compare to the glorious experience that can occur as you rise through the trackless air and far-flung reaches of space into a realization of the will of God that penetrates all substance and all nature.

You must be able to go deeply within, for not in outer accoutrements of name or fame or even in worldly intellect does man find the keys that will transport him to these higher reaches. We caution that great care must be exercised in this matter, for truly we are not concerned with the developing in men and women of untutored or unguided psychic experience.

We want this form of communion to be a rarity rather than a daily practice. It is something one should try no more often than once a year in just this manner, with the exception of those who have been mightily prepared by advanced training. For them there will unfold the necessary direction that will assist them in having vital experiences to guide them in their solar evolution.

You must understand that the will of God is a sacred adventure. I have said it thusly for a reason, for the average individual considers an encounter with the will of God a remote possibility.

He prays to have the will of God made known to him, but he does not understand that he can have an a priori glimpse of that will while yet in mortal form. He does not realize that the will that sees can also be seized, in part, as a treasure-house of consciousness and carried back into the domain of the life within. There the great lodestone of Truth acts as a divine revelator to reveal to each man from deep within his own heart what the will of God really is.

Above all, let him understand always that, complex and all-embracing though it may be, the will of God can always be reduced to the common denominator of love, life and light.

Forward we go together.

I AM simply, your

Morya

The Covenant of the Magi
by El Morya

Father, into thy hands I commend my being. Take me and use me—my efforts, my thoughts, my resources, all that I AM—in thy service to the world of men and to thy noble cosmic purposes, yet unknown to my mind.

Teach me to be kind in the way of the Law that awakens men and guides them to the shores of Reality, to the confluence of the River of Life, to the Edenic source, that I may understand that the leaves of the Tree of Life, given to me each day, are for the healing of the nations; that as I garner them into the treasury of being and offer the fruit of my loving adoration to Thee and to thy purposes supreme, I shall indeed hold covenant with Thee as my guide, my guardian, my friend.

For Thou art the directing connector who shall establish my lifestream with those heavenly contacts, limited only by the flow of the hours, who will assist me to perform in the world of men the most meaningful aspect of my individual life plan as conceived by Thee and executed in thy name by the Karmic Board of spiritual overseers who, under thy holy direction, do administer thy laws.

So be it, O eternal Father, and may the covenant of thy beloved Son, the living Christ, the Only Begotten of the Light, teach me to be aware that he liveth today within the tri-unity of my being as the Great Mediator between my individualized Divine Presence and my human self; that he raiseth me into Christ consciousness and thy divine realization in order that as the eternal Son becomes one with the Father, so I may ultimately become one with Thee in that dynamic moment when out of union is born my perfect freedom to move, to think, to create, to design, to fulfill, to inhabit, to inherit, to dwell and to be wholly within the fullness of thy Light.

Father, into thy hands I commend my being.

Sweet Surrender to Our Holy Vow
by El Morya

Meditation upon the God flame:
Our will to thee we sweetly surrender now,
  Our will to God flame we ever bow,
    Our will passing into thine
      We sweetly vow.

Affirmation of the God flame merging with the heart flame:
No pain in eternal surrender,
Thy will, O God, be done.
From our hearts the veil now sunder,
Make our wills now one.

Beauty in thy purpose,
Joy within thy name,
Life's surrendered purpose
Breathes thy holy flame.

Grace within thee flowing
Into mortal knowing,
On our souls bestowing
Is immortal sowing.

Thy will be done, O God,
Within us every one.
Thy will be done, O God—
It is a living sun.

Bestow thy mantle on us,
Thy garment living flame.
Reveal creative essence,
Come thou once again.

Thy will is ever holy,
Thy will is ever fair.
This is my very purpose,
This is my living prayer:

Come, come, come, O will of God,
With dominion souls endow.
Come, come, come, O will of God,
Restore abundant living now.

I AM God's Will

In the name of the beloved mighty victorious Presence of God, I AM in me, and my own beloved Holy Christ Self, I call to the heart of the will of God in the Great Central Sun, beloved Archangel Michael, beloved El Morya, beloved Mighty Hercules, all the legions of blue lightning and the Brothers of the Diamond Heart, beloved Lanello, the entire Spirit of the Great White Brotherhood and the World Mother, elemental life—fire, air, water and earth! To fan the flame of the will of God throughout my four lower bodies and answer this my call infinitely, presently and forever:

1. I AM God's will manifest everywhere,
   I AM God's will perfect beyond compare,
   I AM God's will so beautiful and fair,
   I AM God's willing bounty everywhere.

Refrain: Come, come, come, O blue-flame will so true,
Make and keep me ever radiant like you.
Blue-flame will of living truth,
Good will flame of eternal youth,
Manifest, manifest, manifest in me now!

2. I AM God's will now taking full command,
   I AM God's will making all to understand,
   I AM God's will whose power is supreme,
   I AM God's will fulfilling heaven's dream.

3. I AM God's will protecting, blessing here,
   I AM God's will now casting out all fear,
   I AM God's will in action here well done,
   I AM God's will with victory for each one.

4. I AM blue lightning flashing freedom's love,
   I AM blue-lightning power from above,
   I AM blue lightning setting all men free,
   I AM blue-flame power flowing good through me.

And in full faith I consciously accept this manifest, manifest, manifest! (3x) right here and now with full power, eternally sustained, all-powerfully active, ever expanding, and world enfolding until all are wholly ascended in the light and free!

Beloved I AM! Beloved I AM! Beloved I AM!

Notes

Books referenced here are published by Summit University Press unless otherwise noted.

Introduction

1. George Santayana, *Reason in Common Sense,* vol. 1 of *The Life of Reason* (1905; reprint, New York: Dover Publications, 1980), p. 284.
2. Will and Ariel Durant, *The Lessons of History* (New York: Simon and Schuster, 1968), p. 90.
3. John 8:58.
4. William Shakespeare, *As You Like It,* act 2, sc. 7, line 139; Thomas Heywood, *An Apology for Actors* (London: Nicholas Okes, 1612), p. 13.
5. Michael de Mantaigne, *The Works of Michael de Montaigne,* ed. William Hazlitt, 2nd ed. (London: C. Templeman, 1845), p. 348.
6. William Shakespeare, *Macbeth,* act 5, sc. 6, lines 24–25.
7. Ibid., lines 22–23.
8. Arnold J. Toynbee, *A Study of History,* abridgement by D. C. Somervell (New York: Oxford University Press, 1987), 1:243.
9. I John 4:4.

Chapter 1 · The Cult of Hedon

Opening quotation: II Tim. 3:1–2, 4.

SECTION 1 · THE PURSUIT OF HAPPINESS

1. Gen. 1:26.
2. Gen. 4:16, 17.
3. Practitioners of the Jewish mystical tradition known as Kabbalah reached the same conclusion. See Elizabeth Clare Prophet, *Kabbalah: Key to Your Inner Power* (1997), pp. 1–5.
4. John 1: 1, 3–4.
5. John 8:58.

Notes

6. Gen. 2:8.
7. Matt. 7:15.
8. "We hold these truths to be self-evident, that all men are created equal, that they are endowed by their Creator with certain unalienable Rights, that among these are Life, Liberty and the pursuit of Happiness." The Declaration of Independence, July 4, 1976.
9. Will Durant, *The Story of Philosophy* (New York: Pocket Books, 1961), p. 532.
10. Rev. 3:17.
11. Eccles. 1:9.
12. Saint Germain, "New Lamps for Old," in *Keepers of the Flame Lesson 4,* pp. 29–30.
13. The asteroid belt between Mars and Jupiter is what remains today of the planet Maldek, destroyed when its lifewaves waged a war ending in nuclear annihilation. A group of asteroids closer to the sun is the record and remains of the destroyed planet Hedron. The existence of a planet between Mars and Jupiter was predicted by Johann Titius and restated in 1772 by German astronomer Johann Bode based on the numerical progression of the distances of the then-known planets from the sun. Following the discovery in 1781 of Uranus, whose location conformed to Bode's law, astronomers began to search for the missing planet, finding instead the asteroid belt. About ninety-five of the thousands of asteroids, or minor planets as they are called, that have since been discovered in our solar system are part of this main asteroid belt between Mars and Jupiter. Astronomers have also discovered a group of asteroids whose highly elliptical orbits take them at times among the inner planets (Mercury, Venus, Earth, Mars) that are nearer to the sun. There is still much speculation among scientists over the origin of these minor planets; the two main hypotheses are that asteroids are either fragments of a planet that exploded or was destroyed, or they are particles that never condensed to form a planet.
14. For further information on the laggards and their activities on planet Earth, see Book 1 of the Climb the Highest Mountain series, *The Path of the Higher Self,* pp. 78–86.
15. Genesis chapter 5 records that those who lived before the flood of Noah (also known to us as the sinking of Atlantis) had life spans sometimes exceeding nine hundred years.
16. James 1:21.
17. Gautama Buddha, December 31, 1986, "The Golden Sphere of Light," in *Pearls of Wisdom,* vol. 30, no. 1, January 4, 1987.
18. Exod. 3:14.
19. John 16:33.
20. John 8:44.
21. Kuthumi, "The Mission of the Soul Must Be Understood," *Pearls of Wisdom,* vol. 10, no. 32, August 6, 1967.
22. Matt. 6:24.
23. Rom. 7:19, 21, 23.
24. Matt. 10:34.
25. Mark L. Prophet, *The Soulless One: Cloning a Counterfeit Creation*

(1981), p. 2.
26. James 1:21.
27. Gal. 6:7.

CHAPTER 1 · SECTION 2 · THE DRUG WAY OUT

1. Gen. 25:29–34.
2. Astrea, "Freedom from the Psychic World," in *Keepers of the Flame Lesson 24*, pp. 22–23.
3. Mark L. Prophet and Elizabeth Clare Prophet, *Understanding Yourself* (1999), p. 152.
4. Rev. 10:7.
5. See Book 1 of the Climb the Highest Mountain series, *The Path of the Higher Self*, pp. 441–43.
6. National Commission on Marihuana and Drug Abuse, *Marihuana: A Signal Misunderstanding* (1972), part one, section I.
7. J. M. Campbell, "On the Religion of Hemp," quoting the Makhvan, in *Indian Hemp Drugs Commission Report* (Simla, India: 1893–94), 3:252.
8. Gabriel Nahas, *Keep Off the Grass: A Scientist's Documented Account of Marijuana's Destructive Effects* (New York: Reader's Digest Press, 1976), pp. 14–15.
9. Ibid., p. 15.
10. Ibid.
11. Ibid., pp. 75–76.
12. Ibid., p. 76.
13. Ibid., p. 75.
14. Ernest L. Abel, *Marihuana: The First Twelve Thousand Years* (New York: Plenum Pub Corp., 1980), ch. 12.
15. Nahas, p. 20.
16. Ibid., p. 21.
17. Charles Baudelaire, "The Poem of Hashish," in *Artificial Paradises*, ch. 5, quoted in Nahas, pp. 17–18.
18. Scientists with data on risks of marijuana use often could not even get their results published. One researcher on marijuana reported in 1983 that "in the early part of the last decade, when medical authorities had *hard* data and relevant clinical studies to show that there were indeed dangers [associated with marijuana use], they kept their mouths shut. 'In the early '70s there was a powerful media blitz to convince the American public, particularly the young people, that marijuana was an innocuous drug,' remembers Carlton Turner, a research scientist who now serves as the director of the Drug Abuse Policy Office for the White House. 'It was a product you could enjoy without any downside effects. At the time it was extremely difficult to get any competent scientist to talk about it,' he added. 'Those scientists who took a strong position against marijuana in the early '70s were ostracized.'

"Reputations and careers were on the line. And even if that was not an issue, it was nigh impossible to get a hearing, let alone an impartial forum. Studies done and completed in the early '70s had to wait until the '80s to find an audience. 'Do you know when we finished this study?' Dr. Forest Tennant, by far one of the more prolific pot researchers, asked the reporter.... '1973!' He was referring to a report which demonstrated that American soldiers smoking large quantities of hash had gone as far down the road towards lung cancer in six months as cigarette smokers do in twenty years. 'We were going to publish it in the *Journal of the American Medical Association*. It was all set to be published and they said, "We're taking so much heat on this, we don't dare publish this." And so, we sandbagged the data.'" ("Pot Smoking in America: One Man's Journey," in *Heart* magazine, vol. 3, no. 2, p. 41.)

19. National Commission on Marihuana and Drug Abuse, *Drug Use In America: Problem in Perspective* (Washington, D.C.: GPO, 1972), ch. 1.

20. Jack Margolis and Richard Clorfene, *A Child's Garden of Grass (The Official Handbook for Marijuana Users),* (Los Angeles: Cliff House Books, 1974).

21. George Santayana, *Reason in Common Sense*, vol. 1 of *The Life of Reason* (1905; reprint, New York: Dover Publications, 1980), p. 284.

22. Jerry Rubin, "An Emergency Letter to My Brothers and Sisters in the Movement," *The New York Review*, February 13, 1969, p. 27, quoted in Erich Goode, *The Marijuana Smokers* (New York: Basic Books, 1970), ch. 4.

23. The National Institute on Drug Abuse lists the following effects of marijuana use: "The short-term effects of marijuana can include problems with memory and learning; distorted perception; difficulty in thinking and problem solving; loss of coordination; and increased heart rate. Research findings for long-term marijuana use indicate some changes in the brain similar to those seen after long-term use of other major drugs of abuse....

"A study of 450 individuals found that people who smoke marijuana frequently but do not smoke tobacco have more health problems and miss more days of work than nonsmokers. Many of the extra sick days among the marijuana smokers in the study were for respiratory illnesses.

"Even infrequent use can cause burning and stinging of the mouth and throat, often accompanied by a heavy cough. Someone who smokes marijuana regularly may have many of the same respiratory problems that tobacco smokers do, such as daily cough and phlegm production, more frequent acute chest illness, a heightened risk of lung infections, and a greater tendency to obstructed airways. Smoking marijuana increases the likelihood of developing cancer of the head or neck, and the more marijuana smoked the greater the increase. A study comparing 173 cancer patients and 176 healthy individuals produced strong evidence that marijuana smoking doubled or tripled the risk of these cancers.

"Marijuana use also has the potential to promote cancer of the lungs and other parts of the respiratory tract because it contains irritants and carcinogens. In fact, marijuana smoke contains 50 to 70 percent more carcinogenic hydrocarbons than does tobacco smoke. It also produces high levels of an enzyme that converts certain hydrocarbons into their carcinogenic form—levels that may accelerate the changes that ultimately produce malignant cells. Marijuana users usually inhale more deeply and hold their breath longer than tobacco smokers do, which increases the lungs' exposure to carcinogenic smoke. These facts suggest that, puff for puff, smoking marijuana may increase the risk of cancer more than smoking tobacco.

"Some of marijuana's adverse health effects may occur because THC impairs the immune system's ability to fight off infectious diseases and cancer. In laboratory experiments that exposed animal and human cells to THC or other marijuana ingredients, the normal disease-preventing reactions of many of the key types of immune cells were inhibited. In other studies, mice exposed to THC or related substances were more likely than unexposed mice to develop bacterial infections and tumors." (National Institute on Drug Abuse, *Infofacts* [2004])

The issue of chromosome damage and physical damage to the brain from marijuana usage is very controversial. Marijuana advocates claim that there is "no evidence" of either of these problems and tend to dismiss or ignore studies that do not support their position. Scientists seeking to do important research in the field have to deal with strong political forces on both sides of the issue. The pro-marijuana lobby is well financed and politically powerful—major contributors to organizations working to legalize marijuana have included the Playboy organization and billionaire George Soros. It is also supported by a multibillion-dollar industry of marijuana growers and paraphernalia manufacturers that wants to protect the image of its "product." (See note 18 above.)

It is worth remembering that the powerful tobacco lobby was able for decades to suppress scientific information about the damage caused by cigarette smoking and to promote the health "benefits" of its product.

24. THC, the psychoactive ingredient in marijuana, is a fat-soluble compound, and therefore has a long persistence in the body and preferentially collects in body tissues that have high levels of fats, such as the brain. (By comparison, alcohol, a water-soluble compound, is removed rapidly from the body, being no longer detectable in the urine after about six hours.)

THC is metabolized by the liver and removed from the bloodstream within hours, but the metabolites are stored in the body and excreted slowly over a period of days to months. In one Swedish study from 1989, the urinary excretion half-life of THC was found to range from one to ten days (Johansson E, Halldin MM. "Urinary excretion half-life of delta 1-tetrahydrocannabinol-7-oic acid in heavy marijuana users after smoking." *Journal of Analytical Toxicology.* 1989 Jul-Aug; 13[4]:218–23.). Studies using radioactively tagged THC have shown that metabolites are stored in the brain, gonads and fatty tissues (Nahas, p. 146). This means that someone who smokes marijuana only one or two times a month will always have levels of the drug in their system.

The long-term storage of THC in the body may be similar in some ways to the action of DDT, another fat-soluble chemical, which is concentrated and stored in the body's fat deposits, where it may persist for years. One way in which residues of drugs or other toxins stored in fat deposits may be removed from the body is by fasting, as the body switches its metabolism to breaking down fat reserves to provide energy. Some people have re-experienced while fasting some of the effects of drugs they had taken years before, as residues from fat deposits were released into the bloodstream. (This is one reason why it is advisable to be under the care of a healthcare professional when fasting for any extended period.)

25. For the story of this ancient mystery school established by Hercules and Amazonia, see the dictation by Amazonia from April 13, 1979.

26. The gifts of the Holy Spirit: (1) the gift of wisdom (2) the gift of knowledge (3) the gift of faith (4) the gift of healing (5) the gift of miracles (6) the gift of prophecy (7) the gift of discernment of spirits (8) the gift of tongues (9) the gift of interpretation of tongues. (I Cor. 12:8–10.)

27. Rev. 12: 15, 17.

28. The Second Book of Adam and Eve tells the story of the children of Jared, who were lured down the Holy Mountain of God by the children of Cain, who committed all manner of abominations and serenaded them with sensual music from the valley below. Jared was a descendant of Seth, the son born to Adam and Eve after Cain slew Abel. See "Prologue on the Sons of Jared" (taken from the Second Book of Adam and Eve), in Elizabeth Clare Prophet, *Fallen Angels and the Origins of Evil,* pp. 395–407. See also ch. 1, section 3, note 1.

29. Saint Germain, April 29, 1984, "The Ancient Story of the Drug Conspiracy," in *Saint Germain On Prophecy* (1986), book 4, pp. 95–97, 98–100.

30. See Rev. 13.

31. Saint Germain, "The Ancient Story of the Drug Conspiracy," pp. 108–19.

32. Centers for Disease Control, *Morbidity and Mortality Weekly Report,* 51:300 (2002); 1996 *Information Please Almanac,* p. 456.

33. Ibid.

34. Gen. 25:29–34.

35. Matt. 5:18, 26.

36. Archangel Jophiel, September 9, 1963, "The Power of the Angels of Illumination," in *Pearls of Wisdom,* vol. 25, no. 46, November 14, 1982.

37. El Morya, August 8, 1988, "The Light and the Beautiful," in *Pearls of Wisdom,* vol. 31, no. 77, November 13, 1988.

38. Saint Germain, "The Ancient Story of the Drug Conspiracy," pp. 101–2, 108, 129–30, 119–20, 102.

39. For information about the effects of refined sugar, see, for example, William Dufty, *Sugar Blues* (New York: Warner Books, 1986).

40. Some recommendations concerning fasting: Never fast if you are pregnant or a nursing mother. If you have a medical or mental health condition, consult your doctor before fasting. Fasting for more than

three days is not recommended unless you consult a health professional. If you feel lightheaded or disoriented or if you become ill while fasting, stop your fast and gradually return to solid foods.

The body eliminates toxins through the intestines, the skin, the lungs and the kidneys. You can increase the effectiveness of your fast by stimulating elimination through these avenues of cleansing. To aid elimination through the skin, brush your skin with a dry natural fiber brush. This will remove toxins and old layers of skin that clog the pores. Brushing also increases the action of the lymphatic system, which carries waste from the cells into the blood. The blood then delivers the waste to the kidneys, where it is converted to urine and deposited in the bladder.

To increase elimination through the lungs, breathe deeply and rhythmically, preferably outdoors, in the fresh air and sunshine. Give Djwal Kul's breathing exercise daily (see decree 40.09). To support the kidneys, drink calendula or dandelion leaf tea. Moderate exercise three times a day and a sauna or steam bath once a day for fifteen to twenty minutes will invigorate the mind and purify the body. When you come off a fast, a mild enema or colonic may be beneficial.

41. Matt. 17:21.
42. Heb. 12:29.
43. Lady Master Leto, January 2, 1972.

CHAPTER 1 · SECTION 3 · THE CULT OF PLEASURE

1. Some of the ancient history of the misuse of music is recorded in the Second Book of Adam and Eve, which tells the story of the sons of the fallen Cain playing sensual music to entice the children of Jared (a descendent of Seth) down from their Holy Mountain (their dwelling place in a level of higher consciousness):

"After Cain had gone down to the land of dark soil, and his children had multiplied therein, there was one of them, whose name was Genun, son of Lamech the blind who slew Cain. But as to this Genun, Satan came into him in his childhood; and he made sundry trumpets and horns, and string instruments, cymbals and psalteries, and lyres and harps, and flutes; and he played on them at all times and at every hour. And when he played on them, Satan came into them, so that from among them were heard beautiful and sweet sounds, that ravished the heart. Then he gathered companies upon companies to play on them; and when they played, it pleased well the children of Cain, who inflamed themselves with sin among themselves, and burnt as with fire; while Satan inflamed their hearts, one with another, and increased lust among them....

"Genun gathered together companies upon companies, that played on horns and on all the other instruments we have already mentioned, at the foot of the Holy Mountain; and they did so in order that the children of Seth who were on the Holy Mountain should hear it. But when the children of Seth heard the noise, they wondered, and came by companies, and stood on the top of the mountain to look at those below; and they did thus a whole year....

"Meanwhile the children of Seth, who were on the Holy Mountain, prayed and praised God, in the place of the hosts of angels who had fallen; wherefore God had called them 'angels,' because He rejoiced over them greatly. But after this, they no longer kept His commandment, nor held by the promise He had made to their fathers; but they relaxed from their fasting and praying, and from the counsel of Jared their father. And they kept on gathering together on the top of the mountain, to look upon the children of Cain, from morning until evening, and upon what they did, upon their beautiful dresses and ornaments....

"A hundred men of the children of Seth gathered together, and said among themselves, 'Come, let us go down to the children of Cain, and see what they do, and enjoy ourselves with them.' But when Jared heard this of the hundred men, his very soul was moved, and his heart was grieved. He then arose with great fervour, and stood in the midst of them, and adjured them by the blood of Abel the just, 'Let not one of you go down from this holy and pure mountain, in which our fathers have ordered us to dwell.' But when Jared saw that they did not receive his words, he said unto them, 'O my good and innocent and holy children, know that when once you go down from this holy mountain, God will not allow you to return again to it.'"

However, they would not heed the warning of Jared, nor that of his son Enoch, "but went down from the Holy Mountain.

"And when they looked at the daughters of Cain, at their beautiful figures, and at their hands and feet dyed with colour, and tattooed in ornaments on their faces, the fire of sin was kindled in them. Then Satan made them look most beautiful before the sons of Seth, as he also made the sons of Seth appear of the fairest in the eyes of the daughters of Cain, so that the daughters of Cain lusted after the sons of Seth like ravenous beasts, and the sons of Seth after the daughters of Cain, until they committed abomination with them. But after they had thus fallen into this defilement, they returned by the way they had come, and tried to ascend the Holy Mountain. But they could not, because the stones of that holy mountain were of fire flashing before them, by reason of which they could not go up again." (The Second Book of Adam and Eve, 20:1–4, 11–12, 15–16, 24–26, 30–33, reprinted in Elizabeth Clare Prophet, *Fallen Angels and the Origins of Evil* [2000])

2. Rev. 9.
3. Gen. 6:5, 13.
4. Gen. 1:28.
5. Ps. 110:4.
6. Matt. 25:1.
7. Gal. 6:7.
8. Quoted in Bernard Nathanson, *Aborting America* (New York: Doubleday, 1979), p. 235.
9. For a detailed analysis of the Ascended Masters' perspective on world population and the environment, see Book 1 of the Climb the Highest

Mountain series, *The Path of the Higher Self,* pp. 431–53.

10. I Cor. 6:19–20.

11. Loren Coleman, *Suicide Clusters* (Boston: Faber and Faber, 1987), p. 1.

12. See Goddess Meru, June 13, 1982, "The War against Marijuana," in *Pearls of Wisdom,* vol. 25, no. 35, August 29, 1982; God Meru, April 19, 1987, "To Plead the Cause of Youth," in *Pearls of Wisdom,* vol. 30, no. 19, May 10, 1987; God and Goddess Meru, June 30, 1991, "Run to the Heart of the Little Child," in *Pearls of Wisdom,* vol. 34, no. 34, July 7, 1991.

13. *Archangel Michael's Rosary for Armageddon,* released by Elizabeth Clare Prophet, is a one-hour service of prayers, decrees and hymns to invoke the assistance of Archangel Michael, the hosts of the LORD and the nine choirs of angels for the resolution of personal and planetary problems and for the binding of the forces of Evil attacking the children and youth of the world. As you give it, the armour and shield of Archangel Michael are immediately yours. Use this rosary for the exorcism of malevolent, nonphysical "forces of annihilation" affecting children, youth and adults alike, societies, economies, governments and nations. Available from Summit University Press in booklet and audio.

14. God and Goddess Meru, April 19, 1987, "To Plead the Cause of Youth," in *Pearls of Wisdom,* vol. 30, no. 19, May 10, 1987.

15. Lord Maitreya, July 2, 1978, "Find Your Way Back to Me," in *Pearls of Wisdom,* vol. 43, no. 34, August 20, 2000.

16. Eph. 6:11.

17. Mark L. Prophet, *The Soulless One,* pp. 30, 31–33.

18. El Morya, August 13, 1960, "I Would Ennoble You," in Mark L. Prophet and Elizabeth Clare Prophet, *Morya I* (Corwin Springs, Mont.: The Summit Lighthouse Library, 2001), pp. 38–39.

19. El Morya, "There Is Work to Be Done," in *Morya I,* pp. 47–48, 50.

CHAPTER 1 · SECTION 4 · THE RETURN TO EDEN

1. I Cor. 15:50.

2. I Cor. 15:55.

3. I Cor. 15:26.

4. Lord Lanto, "The Lamp of Knowledge," in *Keepers of the Flame Lesson 4,* p. 14.

Chapter 2 · Psychic Thralldom

Opening quotation: I John 4:1.

1. Sir Oliver Lodge, *Raymond, or Life and Death: With Examples of the Evidence for Survival of Memory and Affection after Death* (London: Methuen & Co, 1916).

2. Lewis Spence, *Encyclopedia of Occultism,* (New Hyde Park, N.Y.: University Books, 1960), s.v. "spiritualism."

3. For the story of the miraculous life of le Comte de Saint Germain (an

embodiment of the Ascended Master Saint Germain), see Mark L. Prophet and Elizabeth Clare Prophet, *Saint Germain On Alchemy* (1993); Isabel Cooper-Oakley, *The Count of Saint Germain* (Blauvelt, New York: Rudolph Steiner Publications, 1970).

4. Kuthumi, *Pearls of Wisdom,* vol. 6, no. 39, September 27, 1963.
5. Matt. 11:12.
6. One account of these events is recorded in an Austrian spiritualist publication *Licht des Jenseits oder Blumenlese aus dem Garden des Spiritismus,* vol. 2 (1867), pp. 175–89, 205–20, 240–53. A German documentary by Volker Anding titled *Das Spukhaus* (2003) dealt with attempts to find scientific explanations for the phenomena.
7. I Sam. 28:7–25.
8. II Cor. 11:14.
9. William F. Barrett, *On the Threshold of the Unseen: An Examination of the Phenomena of Spiritualism and of the Evidence for Survival after Death* (New York: E.P. Dutton & Co., 1917).
10. Frank Gaynor, ed., *Dictionary of Mysticism* (New York: Philosophical Library, 1953), s.v. "ectoplasm."
11. G. Henslow, *Proof of the Truth of Spiritualism* (New York: Dodd, 1928).
12. Job 22:28; Matt. 12:37.
13. Mark 10:17, 18; Matt. 19:16, 17; Luke 18:18, 19.
14. Matt. 27:51; Mark 15:38; Luke 23:45.
15. Luke 17:21.
16. Lord Maitreya, March 25, 1967, "AUM," in *Pearls of Wisdom,* vol. 27, no. 15, April 8, 1984.
17. I Peter 5:8.
18. II Cor. 11:13–14.
19. Matt. 6:23.
20. Gen. 3:6.
21. Gen. 1:26.
22. Gen. 2:6, 7.
23. Astrea, "Freedom from the Psychic World," in *Keepers of the Flame Lesson 24,* p. 23–27.
24. Luke 22:31.
25. II Cor. 11:13–14.
26. I Peter 5:8.
27. Rev. 22:11.
28. I Cor. 15:54.
29. I John 4:1.
30. Ps. 23:3.
31. This process is explained in *Keepers of the Flame Lesson 7.*
32. Kuthumi, *Pearls of Wisdom,* vol. 6, no. 39, September 27, 1963.
33. I Cor. 12:10.
34. John 14:10.
35. I Cor. 12:7–10.
36. Titus 1:10.
37. Isa. 8:19.
38. Exod. 7:8–12.
39. Ps. 103:15, 16.

40. Matt. 11:10.
41. Matt. 24:30.
42. El Morya, *The Chela and the Path* (1976), pp. 115–18.
43. Another, similar strategy of the dark forces is to claim that the Masters should be invoked by different names than the ones they have given. The Great Divine Director explains that the names of the Ascended Masters are keys to their Electronic pattern, to their consciousness and vibration. As each letter in the alphabet keys to a cosmic frequency and release, the combination of letters in an Ascended Master's name constitutes his personal keynote. In the case of well-known Masters such as Jesus Christ—whose name has been called upon by devotees for centuries—a great momentum of light has coalesced around the name, adding the devotion of unascended mankind to the momentum of light released by the name "Jesus." So powerful is this name of the Son of God that it may be used to the present hour to cast out demons and entities.

    Disregarding these facts, various channels in embodiment have allowed themselves to be duped by ambitious and calculating minds who, speaking from the lower astral planes, have proclaimed that Jesus Christ is no longer to be called Jesus, but another name. Likewise, these forces have announced that the names of the Great Divine Director, Saint Germain, Cyclopea and Lord Maitreya should be changed. The names given in each case were those of impostors who had long desired to usurp the office of these magnificent Cosmic Beings. Dangerous black magicians are they, who trick innocent victims into calling upon their own names while offering adoration to God in prayer, meditation and decrees. These beings then take the pure energies of the students and use them to perpetuate the black conspiracy upon the planet.
44. Lord Maitreya, July 2, 1978, "Find Your Way Back to Me," in *Pearls of Wisdom,* vol. 43, no. 34, August 20, 2000.
45. El Morya, April 16, 1995, "Clean House!" in *Pearls of Wisdom,* vol. 38, no. 26, June 18, 1995.
46. Astrea, "Freedom from the Psychic World," in *Keepers of the Flame Lesson 24,* p. 27.
47. Heb. 4:12.
48. Astrea, "Freedom from the Psychic World," in *Keepers of the Flame Lesson 23,* pp. 23–24.
49. I John 4:1.
50. John 16:23, 24.
51. Matt. 7:20.
52. Matt. 21:19.
53. Luke 11:52.
54. James 3:11.
55. El Morya, *The Chela and the Path* (1984), pp. 118–21.
56. Luke 15:12.
57. Josh. 24:15.
58. Akashic records: the recordings of all that has taken place in an individual's world are "written" by recording angels upon a substance and dimension known as akasha and can be read by those whose

spiritual faculties are developed.
59. Matt. 13:26.
60. Matt. 9:17; Mark 2:22; Luke 5:37, 38.
61. Rev. 21:2.
62. Eph. 1:7; Col. 1:14.
63. Job 19:26.
64. John 1:14.
65. Heb. 10:7.
66. Mark 1:11.
67. Heb. 7:17.
68. John 10:30.
69. Matt. 6:33.
70. Gal. 6:7.
71. Matt. 5:48.
72. I Pet. 5:8.
73. I Cor. 2:9. Astrea, "Freedom from the Psychic World," in *Keepers of the Flame Lesson 23,* pp. 25–32.
74. Exod. 20:5.
75. Astrea, December 30, 1968.
76. Matt. 6:34.
77. Mark L. Prophet, *The Soulless One,* p. 155.
78. Prov. 14:12. Ibid., p. 33.
79. Rom. 3:8.
80. Mark L. Prophet, *The Soulless One,* p. 156.
81. Matt. 12:50.
82. Phil. 2:5.
83. I Cor. 14:21, 22.
84. *Rocky Mountain News,* June 15, 1968.
85. *Rocky Mountain News,* June 17, 1968.
86. I John 4:18.
87. Cha Ara, February 19, 1967.
88. James 1:27.
89. Matt. 15:14.
90. II Tim. 3:7.
91. God Meru, July 26, 1964, "The Coat of Golden Chain Mail," in "The Radiant Word," *Pearls of Wisdom,* vol. 29, no. 15, April 13, 1986.
92. El Morya, December 28, 1969.
93. Serapis Bey, December 28, 1985, "The Descent of the Mighty Blue Sphere," in *Pearls of Wisdom,* vol. 29, no. 15, April 13, 1986.
94. Apollo and Lumina, June 25, 1995, "Turn This Civilization Around!" in *Pearls of Wisdom,* vol. 38, no. 31, July 16, 1995.
95. I Tim. 5:24.
96. John 3:19.
97. John 8:11.
98. Luke 15:11–32.
99. Jesus, "Unceasing Prayer," in Jesus and Kuthumi, *Prayer and Meditation* (1978), pp. 10–12.
100. Astrea, "Freedom from the Psychic World," in *Keepers of the Flame Lesson 23,* pp. 30–31.

Chapter 3 · Armageddon

Opening quotation: Rev. 12:7–9.

SECTION 1 · A PERSONAL AND PLANETARY BATTLE

Opening quotation: Eph. 6:12.

1. Gen. 1:26.
2. I John 2:18.
3. Rev. 13:8.
4. Eph. 6:12.
5. Eph. 6:13–17.
6. Luke 16:8.
7. El Morya, "To Watchmen upon the Wall: A Frontal Attack against the Christ Good in Man," *Pearls of Wisdom,* vol. 7, no. 16, April 17, 1964.
8. Isa. 13–14; 31:9. Rev. 14:8; 16:19; 17:5; 18.
9. El Morya, December 25, 1963, "There's No Place like Home," in *Morya I,* pp. 297–98.
10. Phil. 4:7.
11. Luke 17:20, 21.
12. Archangel Michael, January 1, 1996. "We Are Convinced of the Victory," in *Pearls of Wisdom,* vol. 46, no. 44, November 2, 2003.
13. Matt. 5:39; James 4:7.
14. Luke 18:1–8.
15. Matt. 6:34.
16. Deut. 33:25.
17. The decree is the most powerful of all applications to the Godhead. It is the command of the son or daughter of God made in the name of the I AM Presence and the Christ for the will of the Almighty to come into manifestation as Above, so below. It is the means whereby the kingdom of God becomes a Reality here and now through the power of the spoken Word. It may be short or long and usually is marked by a formal preamble and a closing, or acceptance. See Mark L. Prophet and Elizabeth Clare Prophet, *The Science of the Spoken Word* (1991).
18. Acts 7:58–60; 8:1–3; 9:1–31; 13–28.
19. Rom. 8:6, 7.
20. Matt. 4:1–11.
21. John 14:30.
22. John the Beloved, July 1, 1990, "Great Mystery of the Christos," in *Pearls of Wisdom,* vol. 33, no, 24, June 24, 1990.

CHAPTER 3 · SECTION 2 · EVOLUTIONS OF LIGHT AND DARKNESS

Opening quotation: John 8:23.

1. Matt. 3:11.
2. John 8:44.
3. This subject is explored more fully in the Great Divine Director's series of *Pearls of Wisdom* on the mechanization concept, which gives the

history of the activity that took place in the antediluvian period. These activities resulted in the destruction of much of the then civilized world and evoked from the Karmic Board the fiat that each seed should henceforth bear only after its kind. Prior to that time, the breeding of humans with animals produced monstrosities, which were destroyed by the flood. (See "The Mechanization Concept: A Manifesto by the Great Divine Director," *Pearls of Wisdom,* vol. 8, nos. 3–26); also published as Mark L. Prophet, *The Soulless One.*

4. Matt. 6:23.
5. This process is explained in more detail in book five of this series, *The Path of the Universal Christ,* pp. 91–94.
6. Ezek. 33:11.
7. Gen. 6:3.
8. Rev. 12:7–12.
9. Gen. 32:24–26; Hos. 12:4.
10. Gen. 19:1–11.
11. Judg. 13:3–21.
12. Franz Delitzsch, *A New Commentary on Genesis,* trans. Sophia Taylor, 2 vols. (Edinburgh: T. & T. Clark, 1888), 1:225.
13. Rev. 12:4.
14. The Book of Enoch was once cherished by Jews and Christians alike, but later fell into disfavor with powerful theologians because of its controversial statements on the nature and deeds of the fallen angels. The book was denounced, banned and cursed—and ultimately forgotten for a thousand years. In 1773, rumors of a surviving copy of the book drew Scottish explorer James Bruce to distant Ethiopia. True to hearsay, the Book of Enoch had been preserved by the Ethiopic church, which included this book in their canon alongside the other books of the Bible. Bruce secured three Ethiopic copies of the book and brought them back to Europe and Britain. Fifty years later, when the book's first English translation was produced, the modern world gained its first glimpse of the forbidden mysteries of Enoch.
15. Enoch 7:1–15. Unless noted otherwise, quotes from the Book of Enoch included here are from the translation of Richard Laurence, which may be found in its entirety (along with other Enoch texts) in Elizabeth Clare Prophet, *Fallen Angels and the Origins of Evil* (2000).
16. Enoch 8:1–9.
17. Enoch 9:1–14.
18. Enoch 10:15. Elizabeth Clare Prophet believes that the seventy generations have long passed and that this is the era of judgment. The offspring of the Watchers are unbound and have been loosed on the earth for the final testing of the souls of Light.
19. R. H. Charles, ed. and trans., *The Book of Enoch* (Oxford: Clarendon Press, 1893), pp. 148–50.
20. Enoch 15:8–10; 16:1.
21. For a detailed analysis of Biblical parallels to the book of Enoch and evidence that Jesus and the writers of the New Testament texts were familiar with this scripture, see Elizabeth Clare Prophet, *Fallen Angels and the Origins of Evil,* pp. 17–38.

22. Jude 4, 12–13.
23. Jude 14–15.
24. J. T. Milik, ed. and trans., *The Books of Enoch: Aramaic Fragments of Qumran Cave 4* (Oxford: Clarendon Press, 1976).
25. Some copies of the Greek Septuagint translated "sons of God" in this verse as "angels of God" (Charles, p. 62). The term "sons of God" is also used elsewhere in the Old Testament to indicate angels: see Job 1:6; 2:1. The "sons of God" in Deut. 32:8 *(Jerusalem Bible)* are in most cases understood by scholars to be angels—specifically, the guardian angels assigned to the nations. One theory has it that the Massoretic scribes of the sixth to tenth centuries thought that this idea might lead to the worship of these guardian angels, and therefore they changed the original Hebrew words "sons of God" (which they knew to mean "angels") to "children of Israel"—which then found its way into the King James Version of the Bible. Pre-Massoretic manuscripts recently discovered prove that "sons of God" was the original term in the Hebrew Scripture.

   It ought to be considered that the term "sons of God" might have originally referred to sons of God in heaven, Christed ones of whom Jesus was one. Some of these sons of God might have fallen, out of the misplaced ambition to create on earth by their Christic seed a super-race who could lead mere earthlings or the creation of the Nephilim on the paths of righteousness and to ultimate reunion with God. Though well-intended in their desire to upgrade the evolutions of the planet, these sons of God might not have had the divine approbation. Therefore the Watchers, once fallen and judged as unworthy of the ascent to God, having lost the sacred fire of their original anointing, would have determined in any case to dominate the scene of earth life with their superior intellect and overwhelming presence yet residual from their lost estate. If, in fact, the Watchers were the fallen sons of God and the Nephilim the fallen angels, we can understand both the difference of their modus operandi and reason for being and the dissimilarity of their natures that remains observable to the present.
26. Milik, p. 31
27. Julian Morgenstern, "The Mythological Background of Psalm 82," *Hebrew Union College Annual* 14 (1939), p. 106.
28. Ibid., pp. 106–7.
29. *Jerusalem Bible.*
30. Morgenstern, p. 107.
31. Book of Jubilees, 7:22; Milik, p. 178.
32. Morgenstern, pp. 84–85; 106, n. 135. See also J. H. Kurtz, *History of the Old Covenant* (Edinburgh: T. & T. Clark, 1859), p. 99.
33. Morgenstern, pp. 106–7, n. 135a.
34. Rev. 12:9.
35. II Pet. 2:4.
36. Dan. 12:1.
37. Montague Rhodes James, trans., "The Gospel of Bartholomew," in *The Apocryphal New Testament* (Oxford: Clarendon Press, 1924), p. 178.
38. James, trans., "The Book of John the Evangelist," in *The Apocryphal*

New Testament, p. 189.

39. Gen. 5:24.

40. Enoch 7:1, 2, 10; Gen. 6:1–3.

41. Enoch 15:8.

42. In their linkage of the ape with the seed of fallen angels they created the link between the animal and the human race that they later, as reincarnated Darwinians, used to prove their Darwinian theory of evolution, thus intimidating the children of the Light (the Christic seed) to believe that they are of the animal creation.

43. Gen. 6:5.

44. Enoch, December 29, 1980, "The Elect One Cometh—At the Convergence of Golden-Ratio Spirals Ascending and Descending," in *Pearls of Wisdom,* vol. 24, no. 5, February 1, 1981.

45. Deut. 2:11, 20; 3:11, 13; Num. 13:33; Josh. 12:4; 13:12; 15:8; 17:15; 18:16; I Sam. 17:4–51; II Sam. 21:16–22; I Chron. 20:4–8.

46. Mark L. Prophet, *The Soulless One,* pp. 107, 108, 110, 111.

47. Dan. 7.

48. Exod. 6:7.

49. Deut. 31:20.

50. Josh. 24:24.

51. Sanat Kumara, December 1979.

52. Satans (pronounced Seh-tánz): the race of the seed of Satan who long ago rose up against the I AM Race and "who have infiltrated every corner of this galaxy and beyond." Jesus Christ pronounced their judgment, concurrent with the final judgment of Satan, in this dictation given February 1, 1982. See Jesus, "The Final Judgment of Satan," in *Pearls of Wisdom,* vol. 25, no. 16, April 18, 1982.

53. Matt. 7:15.

54. Jude 1:14.

55. See ch. 1, section 2, note 28.

56. Lord Maitreya, February 4, 1979, "The Garden of Eden," Part 1, in *Pearls of Wisdom,* vol. 43, no. 37, September 10, 2000.

57. Gen. 3:1.

58. Lord Maitreya was the Guru in the mystery school that was known as the Garden of Eden. For additional explanation of this mystery school and the initiation of twin flames there, see Book 2 of the Climb the Highest Mountain series, *The Path of Self-Transformation.*

59. Gen. 3:4, 5. Sanat Kumara, *The Opening of the Seventh Seal* (Corwin Springs, Mont.: The Summit Lighthouse Library, 2001), pp. 286, 288.

60. John 3:3.

61. John 8:23.

62. Erich Fromm, "Necrophilia and Biophilia," in *War within Man,* Beyond Deterrence Series (Philadelphia: American Friends Service Committee, 1963), p. 9.

63. Matt. 23:27. The description "dead men's bones" may refer to the fact that the Watchers' temples, devoid of the Holy Spirit, were infested with discarnates, the cast-off sheaths of disembodied spirits.

CHAPTER 3 · SECTION 3 · THE CONSPIRACY OF GOG AND MAGOG

Opening quotation: Rev. 20:7–8.

1. Gen. 3:1–5, 14–15; Rev. 12.
2. Exod. 32:1–8.
3. Gen. 3:19.
4. In his dictation on October 10, 1971, the Great Divine Director gave the following teaching: "The mighty I AM Presence has the authority and the power to instantaneously arrest and reverse any cycle and to cause a complete erasing, a disintegration of it, right back to the twelve o'clock line.... I say to you, you must demand and command it in the name of the Christ—that every single cycle of every single cell and atom within your form that is not outpicturing the perfect cycles of the Christ consciousness is now dissolved, is now arrested and turned back by the authority of your God Presence! If you will but make that invocation each morning, you will find in a very short time that only the cycles of immortal life, and your divine plan fulfilled, and your ascension will prevail."
5. See Elizabeth Clare Prophet, *Predict Your Future: Understand the Cycles of the Cosmic Clock* (2004).
6. Matt. 15:24.
7. Rev. 21:16.
8. Find a quiet place where you will not be disturbed, light a candle, say a prayer, take out a clean sheet of paper and write your letter. When you complete the letter, burn it and ask the angels to take it to the realms of Light and deliver it to the Master.
9. The Great Divine Director, July 3, 1973, "The Future of a Planet Read from the Scroll of Cosmic History," in *Pearls of Wisdom*, vol. 17, nos. 5 & 6, February 3 and 10, 1974.
10. In the Hindu epics Mahabharata and Ramayana, Sanat Kumara, the Ancient of Days, is referred to as Karttikeya.
11. Rev. 19:11.
12. Sanat Kumara, July 28, 1968, "Architecture of the Spirit: Engrams of Light from on High," in *Pearls of Wisdom*, vol. 42, no. 34, August 22, 1999.
13. I Cor. 9:26.
14. Mark L. Prophet, *The Soulless One*, pp. 46–47, 48–52, 53, 54.
15. Archangel Gabriel, *Mysteries of the Holy Grail* (1984), pp. 57–61.
16. Matt. 19:16, 17.
17. Ezek. 38:2; Rev. 20:8.
18. Matt. 23:34–36; Luke 11:49–51; Rev, 16:6; 17:6; 18:24; 19:2.
19. Saint Clare of Assisi's special devotion to the Holy Eucharist saved her convent at San Damiano from a group of Saracens in the army of Frederick II who were on their way to plunder nearby Assisi c. 1240. As the soldiers scaled the convent walls, Clare rose from her sick bed and, according to one account, had the Blessed Sacrament set up in view of the enemy—prostrating herself before it and calmly praying aloud (other versions of the story state that Clare herself held up the

Sacrament while facing the infidels). At the sight of this, the advancing soldiers were suddenly seized with terror and took flight. Not long after, a larger group led by one of Frederick's generals returned to attack the town. Clare and the nuns prayed fervently through the day and night that Assisi might be spared. At dawn, a furious storm broke over the army's camp, scattering their tents and forcing them to flee in panic.

20. Rev. 14:1, 3.
21. See pp. 308–9.
22. Marxist insurgents known as the Khmer Rouge ("Red Cambodians") overturned the Western-backed Lon Nol government of Cambodia in April 1975 after nearly five years of fighting. Although there is no way of accurately counting, it is estimated that as many as three to four million Cambodians out of a population of some seven million were murdered or died from disease, malnutrition or forced labor during the four-year Khmer Rouge regime. Within hours of their take-over, the new leaders, calling themselves *Angka Loeu,* "Organization on High," began to implement a preplanned program of social change. Every man, woman and child in Phnom Penh, Cambodia's capital, was ordered at gunpoint to immediately leave the city (doctors were even stopped mid-operation) and head for the countryside. Survivors of the march later reported that those who could not keep pace were clubbed or shot.

As the days passed, the young children and elderly, the sick, wounded and pregnant were left on jungle trails to die. Soldiers of the former regime as well as professionals of any kind were slaughtered, often in barbaric ways, in an effort to "purify" the new society. All vestiges of modern society—from TV sets to radios, books and money in the banks—were destroyed, and the country was virtually cut off from the outside world except for contact with the Chinese, who provided some aid in the form of technical advisers and supplies.

Angka Loeu was intent on eradicating traditional concepts and patterns of family life as well. Parents were stripped of their right to discipline children, and children were encouraged to report on elders. Love was forbidden; even simple flirtation was punishable by execution. The Cambodian population, relocated in rural communes supervised by armed guards, was forced to work long hours planting rice and building irrigation systems.

In the wake of these brutal social and political upheavals, Democratic Kampuchea, as Cambodia was renamed in 1976, was ravaged by starvation and disease. One refugee called it "a country of walking dead." "Within a few days *Angka Loeu* had turned Cambodian society upside down," explain authors John Barron and Anthony Paul in *Murder of a Gentle Land* (New York: Reader's Digest Press, 1977). "The 'Organization on High' had advanced faster and further than any other revolutionaries of modern times toward the complete obliteration of an entire society." Among the handful of revolutionaries behind *Angka Loeu* were: Khieu Samphan, Hou Yuon, Hu Nim, Son Sen, Ieng Sary, Ieng Thirith, Koy Thuon and Saloth Sar (Pol Pot), who emerged as prime minister and leading figure in the government.

Frequent border conflicts in 1977 and 1978 between Cambodia

and Vietnam, enemies for centuries, escalated when the Vietnamese and a small group of Khmer Rouge rebels invaded Cambodia in December 1978. In early January 1979 it was reported that five columns of Vietnamese troops with thousands of guns and tanks were moving deeper into the country threatening to topple the regime of Cambodia's Prime Minister Pol Pot, who declared in a January 5 radio broadcast, "We pledge to fight them to the end to keep our national prestige." By January 7, the Vietnamese had taken Cambodia's capital, Phnom Penh, replacing Pol Pot with the Hanoi-backed People's Revolutionary Council.

23. Eph. 6:12.

24. Archangel Gabriel, *Mysteries of the Holy Grail,* pp. 155–57, 158–59, 160–61.

25. Dan. 11.

26. Jefferson Davis (1808–89), aided and abetted by the international bankers and power elite. See David Balsiger and Charles E. Sellier, Jr., *The Lincoln Conspiracy* (Los Angeles: Schick Sunn Classic Books, 1977); Burton J. Hendrick, *Statesmen of the Lost Cause: Jefferson Davis and His Cabinet* (New York: Literary Guild, 1939); Irving Katz, *August Belmont: A Political Biography* (New York: Columbia University Press, 1968).

27. See pp. 282–83.

28. On August 25, 1982, 800 Marines from 32nd Amphibious Unit arrived at Beirut port, joining French and Italian troops in a multi-national peace-keeping mission and specifically to oversee the evacuation of PLO forces. On September 10, after evacuation of 8,000 Palestinian guerrillas, the Marines left Beirut. On September 29: 1,200 Marines returned following the September 16–18 massacre of Palestinian civilians in Beirut refugee camps. The next year saw numerous attacks on American troops, culminating in an attack on October 23, 1983, where 239 Marines and sailors were killed by a suicide terrorist who drove an explosive-laden truck into a headquarters building full of sleeping Marines; minutes later in West Beirut, a second truck loaded with explosives crashed into a building housing French paratroopers, killing 58.

29. I Pet. 4:18; Mark 13:22–27.

30. Exod. 33:16; 34:14–16; Lev. 20:24, 26; Deut. 7:1–6; Ezra 9; 10; Neh. 13:23–30; II Cor. 6:17.

31. Gen. 11:27–31; 15:7; Neh. 9:7.

32. Matt. 13:24–30.

33. Sanat Kumara, July 3, 1983, "Of the Coming Race," in *Pearls of Wisdom,* vol. 42, no. 12, March 21, 1999.

34. Luke 11:50.

35. Biblical examples: Gen. 37:3–5, 17–28; Num. 22:1–6; Josh. 10:1–5; 11:1–5; II Sam. 10:6–19; II Chron. 20:1, 2; Ezra 4; Neh. 4:1–12; 6:1–14; Esther 3:8–15; Dan. 6; Matt. 27:1, 2, 12, 20; Luke 23:8–12; John 11:47–53; Acts 9:23, 24; 14:19; 16:16–24; 23:12–15; 25:1–7.

36. Archangel Uriel, October 7, 1983, "The Conspiracy of Gog and Magog," in *Pearls of Wisdom,* vol. 26, no. 52, December 18, 1983.

CHAPTER 3 · SECTION 4 · THE JUDGMENT

Opening quotation: Rev. 20:15.

1. Eccles. 1:4.
2. Rom. 8:6, 7.
3. Rev. 20:12, 13; II Cor. 5:10; 11:15.
4. Dan. 7:9, 13, 22; Rev. 4; 5; 6:16; 7:9–12; 14:3; 19:1–6; 20:11–15; 22:1, 3.
5. Rev. 21:7–8; 22:12–14
6. Mark 4:25.
7. Ps. 94:3.
8. John 9:39.
9. Luke 16:8; Matt. 10:16.
10. Matt. 13:24–30, 36–43.
11. John 5:22.
12. I Cor. 6:2–3; Luke 22:28–30; John 20:22, 23
13. Rom. 12:21.
14. Rev. 19:20; 20:10, 14, 15.
15. Ps. 103:15–17.
16. Sir Edwin Arnold, trans., *The Song Celestial or Bhagavad-Gita* (London: Routledge & Kegan Paul, 1948), p. 9.
17. Matt. 10:28.
18. The twin flame of the soul who passes through the second death must wait for another cosmic cycle when God will create out of his Electronic Presence another soul, who must then descend into form, master time and space, and ultimately reunite with the ascended twin flame after the ritual of the ascension.
19. Jesus and Kuthumi, "Reembodiment and the Law of Return," in *Keepers of the Flame Lesson 19,* pp. 14–16.
20. Matt.10:6; 15:24.
21. El Morya, July 2, 1979, "The Positioning of the Timbers Nation by Nation."
22. See Alpha, July 5, 1975, "The Judgment: The Sealing of the Lifewaves throughout the Galaxy," in *The Great White Brotherhood in the Culture, History and Religion of America* (1987), pp. 234–36, 239–49.
23. See Jesus Christ, February 1, 1982, "The Final Judgment of Satan," in *Pearls of Wisdom,* vol. 25, no. 16, April 18, 1982.

CHAPTER 3 · SECTION 5 · GALACTIC ARMAGEDDON

Opening quotation: Matt. 24:21.

1. See The Great Divine Director, "The Mechanization Concept," *Pearls of Wisdom,* vol. 8, nos. 3–26, January 15–June 27, 1965; also published in Mark L. Prophet, *The Soulless One.*
2. Sanat Kumara's dictation was delivered at the conclusion of a four-day seminar on "The Education of the Heart," which included exposés on the current state of education in America as well as lectures tracing the manipulation of education systems by the fallen ones going back as far as ancient Greece.

3. Heb. 11:6.
4. Sanat Kumara, February 26, 1980, "There Are Temples to Be Built: The Seven Holy Kumaras Release the Inner Electrode of Freedom."
5. I Cor. 15:53.
6. In *The Twelfth Planet* Zecharia Sitchin describes ancient Sumerian tablets that depict an extraterrestrial, superrace of gods called Nephilim who came to earth in spacecraft 450,000 years ago. After studying the earth to find an area suitable for spacecraft landings and colonization, the Nephilim, according to Sitchin, settled in Mesopotamia.

   About 300,000 B.C., according to Sitchin's thesis, the Nephilim decided to create a crossbreed—a mixture of their own seed with that of earth's primitive ape-man, *Homo erectus*. Ancient Sumerian texts tell the story of the creation by the god Ea (Enki) and the mother goddess, Ninhursag, of a race of primitive workers designed to perform the work of the gods on earth. Based on his study of these ancient texts, Sitchin believes that these Nephilim used genetic manipulation to accomplish this creation of a primitive race—extracting the eggs of female *Homo erectus* evolving on earth, fertilizing them with the "essence" or sperm of young Nephilim gods, and then reimplanting them in the wombs of birth goddesses. Sitchin theorizes that the product of this genetic engineering is what is known today as *Homo sapiens*.

   Sumerian texts speak of deformed beings produced by Enki and Ninhursag in revelry or mischief; Sitchin speculates that these were the result of the trial-and-error creation process that took place before the procedure was perfected and that this could be the explanation for the half-man/half-animal creations depicted on ancient temples in the Near East. See Zecharia Sitchin, *The Twelfth Planet* (New York: Avon Books, 1976), pp. 336–61; and *The Stairway to Heaven* (New York: St. Martin's Press, 1980), p. 102.
7. El Morya, April 18, 1965, "Nature, Take Thy Freedom," in *Morya*, p. 275.
8. Lady Master Venus, October 9, 1990, "The Hatred of the Divine Mother on Planet Earth," in *Pearls of Wisdom*, vol. 33, no. 40, October 14, 1990.
9. El Morya, October 11, 1964, "The Sword and the Stone," in *Morya: The Darjeeling Master Speaks to His Chelas on the Quest for the Holy Grail*, pp. 248, 251.

CHAPTER 3 · SECTION 6 · THE VICTORY

Opening quotation: Rev. 12:11.
1. Matt. 10:28.
2. Matt. 6:24; Luke 16:13.
3. Matt. 5:18.
4. Further explanation of the Second Coming may be found in book five of this series, *The Path of the Universal Christ*, pp. 121–33.
5. Jude 14.
6. For information about the retreats of the masters, see Mark. L. Prophet and Elizabeth Clare Prophet, *The Masters and Their Retreats*.

7. Archangel Michael, January 1, 1996, "We Are Convinced of the Victory," in *Pearls of Wisdom,* vol. 46, no. 44, November 2, 2003.

8. John 14:23.

9. Saint Germain, July 6, 1985, "The Gathering of the LORD's Chosen People," in *Pearls of Wisdom,* vol. 28, no. 34, August 25, 1985.

10. *Saint Germain On Alchemy* (1993), pp. 327–28.

11. Jesus, "Prayer as Communication with Purpose," in Jesus and Kuthumi, *Prayer and Meditation* (1978), pp. 29–30, 32.

12. Rev. 9:3, 7.

13. Dan. 10:13, 21; 12:1; Jude 9; Rev. 12.

14. The Blue Army of Our Lady of Fátima is a worldwide movement that claims over 22 million members in 100 countries dedicated to fulfilling the requests made by the Blessed Mother in 1917 at Fátima, Portugal, where she promised, "If my wishes are fulfilled, Russia will be converted,... and the world will enjoy a period of peace." During her six appearances to three shepherd children at Fátima, Mother Mary asked them to "say the rosary every day to bring peace to the world and an end to war.... Jesus wishes you to make me known and loved on earth. He wishes also for you to establish devotion in the world to my Immaculate Heart.... Make sacrifices for sinners and say often, especially while making a sacrifice: O Jesus, this is for the love of Thee, for the conversion of sinners and in reparation for sins committed against the Immaculate Heart of Mary." Following a frightening vision of hell revealed to the children, the Blessed Mother warned, "You have seen hell, where the souls of sinners go. It is to save them that God wants to establish in the world devotion to my Immaculate Heart. If you do what I tell you, many souls will be saved, and there will be peace.... When you see a night that is lit by a strange and an unknown light, you will know it is the sign that God gives you that He is about to punish the world with another war and with hunger, and by the persecution of the Church and the Holy Father. To prevent this, I shall come to the world to ask that Russia be consecrated to my Immaculate Heart, and I shall ask that on the First Saturday of every month communion of reparation be made in atonement for the sins of the world."

    Blue Army members pledge to offer reparation (sacrifices demanded by daily duty), to pray part of the rosary (five decades) daily while meditating on the mysteries, and to wear the Scapular of Mount Carmel as an act of consecration to Our Lady. On June 27, 1972, the Ascended Master El Morya called the Messenger Elizabeth Clare Prophet to begin giving the rosary and to walk the fourteen stations of the cross in fourteen-day cycles for the balancing of personal and planetary karma. Mother Mary has since dictated through the Messenger the Scriptural Rosary for the New Age (thirteen mysteries focusing the power of the eight rays and the five secret rays); the Fourteenth Rosary, the Mystery of Surrender; and the Child's Rosary.

15. See Mary's Scriptural Rosary for the New Age, in Mark L. Prophet and Elizabeth Clare Prophet, *Mary's Message for a New Day* (2003) and *Mary's Message of Divine Love* (2004); *The Fourteenth Rosary: The Mystery of Surrender,* booklet and 2-cassette album; and *A*

Child's Rosary to Mother Mary—15-minute scriptural rosaries for children and adults for meditation on the words and works of the apostles and for the adoration of God the Father, the Son and the Holy Spirit, and God the Mother, available from Summit University Press.

16. Archangel Gabriel, *Mysteries of the Holy Grail*, pp. 53–55, 63–64.

17. Omri-Tas, May 1, 1991, "A Violet Flame Sea of Light," in *Pearls of Wisdom,* vol. 34. no. 26, June 24, 1991.

18. Rom. 12:9.

19. Rose of Light, May 24, 1981, "The Visitation of the Heart," in *Pearls of Wisdom,* vol. 24, no. 65, May 1981.

20. For a more complete and scientific explanation of the spiritual implications of the Maltese cross in conjunction with the threefold flame, see "A Trilogy on the Threefold Flame of Life" in Mark L. Prophet and Elizabeth Clare Prophet, *Saint Germain On Alchemy: Formulas for Self-Transformation* (1993), pp. 265–345.

21. Zech. 4:6.

22. Rev. 12:15.

23. Rev. 12:16–17.

24. Rev. 2:17.

25. El Morya, "The Sword and the Stone," p. 254.

26. Dan. 12:1–3.

27. See p. 429, note 6.

28. There is a great deal of evidence that earth has been host to extraterrestrial visitors from many planetary systems. Some of this evidence is from archaeology and ancient legends; some from people of our own time who claim to have been contacted by these beings.

   For example, author Robert Temple in *The Sirius Mystery* notes the peculiar facts known to four of the Sudanese peoples who seem to have long held detailed knowledge of the star system of Sirius. From his investigations, Temple concludes that these primitive people drew their knowledge of an invisible star, called Sirius B, from extraterrestrials who landed on earth in ancient times. Sirius B is an astronomical pinprick compared to the vast star we know as Sirius. In Temple's view, contact with beings from Sirius' star system would also explain the seeming importance of Sirius in ancient Middle Eastern religions.

   One of the Sudanese peoples, the Dogon, believes that civilization on earth was founded by beings from the Sirius star and from its system called "Nommos," who were amphibious creatures. The Nommos are otherwise known as "the Monitors." Babylonian tradition seems also to preserve a record of these amphibious creatures, who are described as repulsive, disgusting and loathsome to look upon. See Robert Temple, *The Sirius Mystery* (New York: St. Martins Press, 1976).

   Among the many people who have claimed in recent times to have been contacted by extraterrestrials is a Swiss farmer who wrote of his experiences in *UFO: Contact From The Pleiades*. This book claims to record the statements of a "Pleiadian cosmonaut" called Semjase, who also allowed him to take photographs of his space ship. According to Semjase, the Pleiadians know they are not the only extraterrestrial lifewave involved with earth. During one of his contacts with the Swiss farmer, Semjase revealed that space travelers from 108 different civilizations (at last count) have visited earth.

In recent years, other UFO contactees have been given specific information about extraterrestrial races that claim to have visited the planet from Zeta Reticuli and other star systems.

Chapter 4 · Thy Will Be Done

Opening quotation: Heb. 10:7, 9.

1. Luke 12:32.
2. El Morya, "How Can I Know the Will of God?" in *The Sacred Adventure* (1981), pp. 37–38.
3. El Morya, "Not My Will, But Thine Be Done," in *The Sacred Adventure*, p. 79.
4. El Morya, "The Inviolate Will of God," in *The Sacred Adventure*, p. 27.
5. El Morya, "The Gift of His Will," in *The Sacred Adventure*, pp. 8–10.
6. Ibid., pp. 6–7.
7. The Great Divine Director, "Leadership, Take an Uncompromising Stand for Righteousness!" *Pearls of Wisdom*, vol. 11, no. 36, September 8, 1968.
8. El Morya, "How Can I Know the Will of God?" p. 50.
9. Luke 22:42; Mark 14:36.
10. II Cor. 12:9.
11. "A Mighty Fortress Is Our God." Words by Martin Luther, 1529; trans. Frederick Henry Hodge, 1852.

   A mighty fortress is our God, a bulwark never failing;
   Our helper he amid the flood of mortal ills prevailing.
   For still our ancient foe doth seek to work us woe;
   His craft and power are great, and armed with cruel hate,
   On earth is not his equal.

   Did we in our own strength confide, our striving would be losing,
   Were not the right man on our side, the man of God's own choosing.
   Dost ask who that may be? Christ Jesus, it is he;
   Lord Sabbaoth, his name, from age to age the same,
   And he must win the battle.

   And though this world, with devils filled, should threaten to undo us,
   We will not fear, for God hath willed his truth to triumph through us.
   The Prince of Darkness grim, we tremble not for him;
   His rage we can endure, for lo, his doom is sure;
   One little word shall fell him.

   That word above all earthly powers, no thanks to them, abideth;
   The Spirit and the gifts are ours, thru him who with us sideth.
   Let goods and kindred go, this mortal life also;
   The body they may kill; God's truth abideth still;
   His kingdom is forever.

12. John 11:44.

13. El Morya, "Not My Will, But Thine Be Done," p. 73–74.
14. Ibid., p. 82.
15. God Meru, November 27, 1966.
16. El Morya, "The Inviolate Will of God," p. 20.
17. Archangel Michael, "America, Awake!" February 14, 1963.
18. Archangel Michael, July 4, 1971.
19. Saint Germain, *Pearls of Wisdom*, vol. 4, no. 21, May 26, 1961.
20. El Morya, October 17, 1965, "Holy Purpose," in *Morya*, p. 326.
21. El Morya, "The Gift of His Will," pp. 11–12.
22. El Morya, "The Ownership of God's Will," in *The Sacred Adventure*, pp. 57–58.
23. Lord Himalaya, *Pearls of Wisdom*, vol. 3, no. 38, September 16, 1960.
24. Luke 22:44.
25. Luke 22:42; Mark 14:36.
26. John 14:15.
27. El Morya, "A Sacred Adventure," in *The Sacred Adventure*, p. 105.
28. Serapis Bey, "The Eternal Brotherhood," in *Keepers of the Flame Lesson 13*, p. 5.
29. Saint Paul called the will of man "the law of sin" that was in his members (in his consciousness). He recognized the presence within himself of a power apart from God, and he knew that as long as he permitted this force to remain in the inn of his being, it would war against the "law of his mind" or the will of God. He also said, "Where the Spirit of the Lord is, there is liberty," showing that when one disarms himself of all opposition to God and seeks the very presence of his Spirit as the only Reality, then he is free from all lesser manifestations. (Rom. 7:23; II Cor. 3:17.)
30. El Morya, "The Ownership of God's Will," p. 59.
31. Luke 18:17. El Morya, "The Inviolate Will of God," p.30.
32. Lanello, December 27, 1981, "Taking Responsibility for Being God on Earth," in *Pearls of Wisdom*, vol. 25, no. 6, February 7, 1982.
33. Luke 22:42; Mark 14:36.
34. Acts 2:2.
35. Hilarion, January 25, 1976, "The Known God Whom I Declare to Be the I AM THAT I AM," in *Pearls of Wisdom*, vol. 19, no. 42, October 17, 1976.
36. Saint Germain, "Cease to Limit Yourselves in Any Way," in *Keepers of the Flame Lesson 7*, pp. 9–11.
37. Matt. 6:9; Luke 11:2.
38. Luke 22:42; Mark 14:36.
39. El Morya, December 30, 1961, "Not My Will, But Thine Be Done!" in *Morya I*, pp. 112–13.
40. El Morya, "A Sacred Adventure," pp. 108–9.
41. Ezek. 18:4.
42. Exod. 20:3.
43. El Morya, "The Inviolate Will of God," pp. 25–26.
44. Heb. 13:8.
45. Luke 6:31.
46. I John 4:18.

47. Prov. 3:11, 12; Heb. 12:5, 6.
48. Gal. 6:7.
49. Matt. 6:28.
50. El Morya, "The Inviolate Will of God," pp. 21–25.
51. Luke 15:11–24.
52. Luke 23:34.
53. Ps. 23:1–3.
54. Serapis Bey, "Step by Step the Way Is Won," in *Dossier on the Ascension,* pp. 71–73.
55. Ibid. p. 73.
56. El Morya, "How Can I Know the Will of God?" p. 46.
57. Luke 17:33.
58. II Cor. 3:17.
59. Col. 3:3.
60. El Morya, "The Inviolate Will of God," pp. 27–28.
61. Ps. 24:1. Meta, May 16, 1971, "Confess God's Purpose by Your Life in Action," in "The Radiant Word," *Pearls of Wisdom,* vol. 15, no. 24, June 11, 1972.
62. El Morya, October 17, 1965, "Holy Purpose," in *Morya,* pp. 326–27.
63. Luke 9:62.
64. Kuthumi, "Universal Light Carries Man to the Altar of Transmutation," in Jesus and Kuthumi, *Prayer and Meditation,* p. 102.
65. Matt. 16:23; Mark 8:33; Luke 4:8.
66. Matt. 24:24.
67. Matt. 24:26, 27.
68. Rev. 22:11.
69. Kahlil Gibran, *The Prophet* (1923; reprint, New York: Alfred A. Knopf, 1964), p. 96.
70. Matt. 18:14; John 10:10.
71. El Morya, "The Inviolate Will of God," pp. 28–30.
72. John 14:1; Matt. 19:26.
73. II Cor. 3:6.
74. El Morya, "The Human Will," in *The Sacred Adventure,* pp. 89–91, 94.
75. James 1:8.
76. El Morya, "Not My Will, But Thine Be Done!" pp. 81–84.
77. Gal. 6:7. El Morya, "Chelas of the White-Fire Core," in *The Chela and the Path,* p. 34.
78. Thomas Moore, "Believe Me, If All Those Endearing Young Charms," stanza 2. El Morya was embodied as the Irish poet Thomas Moore (1779–1852).
79. El Morya, October 14, 1960, "As the Sunflower Turns on Her God," in *Morya I,* pp. 55–56.
80. Rom. 7–8.
81. El Morya, "A Message from the Lord of the First Ray," in *Keepers of the Flame Lesson 17,* pp. 7–9.
82. Hercules, March 16, 1975, Scaling the Mountain of Hierarchy," in *Pearls of Wisdom,* vol. 21, no. 10, March 5, 1978.
83. John 14:16, 17; 15:26; 16:13; I John 4:6.
84. El Morya, "The Human Will," pp. 94–97.

85. I Cor. 3:13.
86. El Morya, "The Ownership of God's Will," p. 67–68.
87. El Morya, "How Can I Know the Will of God?" p.42.
88. El Morya, "A Message from the Lord of the First Ray," in *Keepers of the Flame Lesson 17*, p. 10.
89. El Morya, October 17, 1965, "Holy Purpose," in *Morya*, p. 327.
90. El Morya, October 2, 1960, "There Is Work to Be Done," in *Morya I*, p. 50.

"A SACRED ADVENTURE," BY EL MORYA

Previously published in *The Sacred Adventure*, pp. 105–14.
1. Gen. 1:1, 2.
2. John 1:5.
3. II Cor. 12:9.
4. I Cor. 15:50.
5. Gen. 1:26, 27; Exod. 20:3.
6. Matt. 6:22, 23.
7. Ps. 121:4.

FOR MORE INFORMATION

Summit University Press books are available at fine bookstores worldwide and at your favorite on-line bookseller. For a free catalog of our books and products or to learn more about the spiritual techniques featured in this book, please contact:

Summit University Press
PO Box 5000
Corwin Springs, MT 59030-5000 USA
Telephone: 1-800-245-5445 or 406-848-9500
Fax: 1-800-221-8307 or 406-848-9555
www.summituniversitypress.com
info@summituniversitypress.com

Glossary

Terms set in italics are defined elsewhere in the glossary.

Adept. An initiate of the *Great White Brotherhood* of a high degree of attainment, especially in the control of *Matter*, physical forces, nature spirits and bodily functions; fully the alchemist undergoing advanced initiations of the *sacred fire* on the path of the *ascension*.

Akashic records. The impressions of all that has ever transpired in the physical universe, recorded in the etheric substance and dimension known by the Sanskrit term *akasha*. These records can be read by those with developed *soul* faculties.

Alchemical marriage. The soul's permanent bonding to the *Holy Christ Self*, in preparation for the permanent fusing to the *I AM Presence* in the ritual of the *ascension*. See also *Soul; Secret chamber of the heart.*

All-Seeing Eye of God. See *Cyclopea.*

Alpha and Omega. The divine wholeness of the Father-Mother God affirmed as "the beginning and the ending" by the Lord *Christ* in Revelation (Rev. 1:8, 11; 21:6; 22:13). Ascended *twin flames* of the *Cosmic Christ* consciousness who hold the balance of the masculine-feminine polarity of the Godhead in the *Great Central Sun* of cosmos. Thus through the *Universal Christ* (the *Word* incarnate), the Father is the origin and the Mother is the fulfillment of the cycles of God's consciousness expressed throughout the *Spirit-Matter* creation. See also *Mother.*

Ancient of Days. See *Sanat Kumara.*

Angel. A divine spirit, a herald or messenger sent by God to deliver his *Word* to his children. A ministering spirit sent forth to tend the heirs of *Christ*—to comfort, protect, guide, strengthen, teach, counsel and warn. The fallen angels, also called the dark ones, are those angels who followed Lucifer in the Great Rebellion, whose consciousness therefore "fell" to lower levels of vibration. They were "cast out into the earth" by Archangel Michael (Rev. 12:7–12)—constrained by the karma of their disobedience to God and his Christ to take on and evolve through dense physical bodies. Here they walk about, sowing seeds of unrest and rebellion among men and nations.

Antahkarana. The web of life. The net of *Light* spanning *Spirit* and *Matter,* connecting and sensitizing the whole of creation within itself and to the heart of God.

Archangel. The highest rank in the orders of *angels.* Each of the *seven rays* has a presiding Archangel who, with his divine complement or Archeia, embodies the God consciousness of the ray and directs the bands of angels serving in their command on that ray. The Archangels and Archeiai of the rays and the locations of their *retreats* are as follows:

First ray, blue, Archangel Michael and Faith, Banff, near Lake Louise, Alberta, Canada.

Second ray, yellow, Archangel Jophiel and Christine, south of the Great Wall near Lanchow, north central China.

Third ray, petal pink, deep rose and ruby, Archangel Chamuel and Charity, St. Louis, Missouri, U.S.A.

Fourth ray, white and mother-of-pearl, Archangel Gabriel and Hope, between Sacramento and Mount Shasta, California, U.S.A.

Fifth ray, green, Archangel Raphael and Mary, Fátima, Portugal.

Sixth ray, purple and gold with ruby flecks, Archangel Uriel and Aurora, Tatra Mountains, south of Cracow, Poland.

Seventh ray, violet and purple, Archangel Zadkiel and Holy Amethyst, Cuba.

Archeia (pl. **Archeiai**). Divine complement and *twin flame* of an *Archangel*.

Ascended Master. One who, through *Christ* and the putting on of that mind which was in Christ Jesus (Phil. 2:5), has mastered time and space and in the process gained the mastery of the self in the *four lower bodies* and the four quadrants of *Matter*, in the *chakras* and the balanced *threefold flame*. An Ascended Master has also transmuted at least 51 percent of his karma, fulfilled his divine plan, and taken the initiations of the ruby ray unto the ritual of the *ascension*—acceleration by the *sacred fire* into the Presence of the I AM THAT I AM (the *I AM Presence*). Ascended Masters inhabit the planes of *Spirit*—the kingdom of God (God's consciousness)—and they may teach unascended souls in an *etheric temple* or in the cities on the *etheric plane* (the kingdom of heaven).

Ascension. The ritual whereby the *soul* reunites with the *Spirit* of the living God, the *I AM Presence*. The ascension is the culmination of the soul's God-victorious sojourn in time and space. It is the process whereby the soul, having balanced her karma and fulfilled her divine plan, merges first with the Christ consciousness and then with the living Presence of the I AM THAT I AM. Once the ascension has taken place, the soul—the corruptible aspect of being—becomes the incorruptible one, a permanent atom in the Body of God. See also *Alchemical marriage*.

Aspirant. One who aspires; specifically, one who aspires to reunion with God through the ritual of the *ascension*. One who aspires to overcome the conditions and limitations of time and space to fulfill the cycles of karma and one's reason for being through the sacred labor.

Astral plane. A frequency of time and space beyond the physical, yet below the mental, corresponding to the *emotional body* of man and the collective unconscious of the race; the repository of mankind's thoughts and feelings, conscious and unconscious. Because the astral plane has been muddied by impure human thought and feeling, the term "astral" is often used in a negative context to refer to that which is impure or psychic.

Astrea. Feminine Elohim of the fourth ray, the ray of purity, who works to cut *souls* free from the *astral plane* and the projections of the dark forces. See also *Elohim; Seven rays.*

Atman. The spark of the divine within, identical with *Brahman;* the ultimate essence of the universe as well as the essence of the individual.

AUM. See *OM.*

Avatar. The incarnation of the *Word.* The avatar of an age is the *Christ,* the incarnation of the Son of God. The *Manus* may designate numerous Christed ones—those endued with an extraordinary *Light*—to go forth as world teachers and wayshowers. The Christed ones demonstrate in a given epoch the law of the *Logos,* stepped down through the Manu(s) and the avatar(s) until it is made flesh through their own word and work—to be ultimately victorious in its fulfillment in all souls of light sent forth to conquer time and space in that era.

Bodhisattva. (Sanskrit, "a being of *bodhi* or enlightenment.") A being destined for enlightenment, or one whose energy and power is directed toward enlightenment. A Bodhisattva is destined to become a *Buddha* but has forgone the bliss of *nirvana* with a vow to save all children of God on earth. An Ascended Master or an unascended master may be a Bodhisattva.

Brahman. Ultimate Reality; the Absolute.

Buddha. (From Sanskrit *budh* "awake, know, perceive.") "The enlightened one." Buddha denotes an office in the spiritual *hierarchy* of worlds that is attained by passing certain initiations of the *sacred fire,* including those of the *seven rays* of the Holy Spirit and of the five secret *rays,* the raising of the feminine ray (sacred fire of the *Kundalini*) and the "mastery of the seven in the seven multiplied by the power of the ten."

Gautama attained the enlightenment of the Buddha twenty-five centuries ago, a path he had pursued through many previous embodiments culminating in his forty-nine-day meditation under the Bo tree. Hence he is called Gautama, the Buddha. He holds the office of *Lord of the World,* sustaining, by his *Causal Body* and *threefold flame,* the divine spark and consciousness in the evolutions of earth approaching the path of personal Christ-hood. His aura of love/wisdom ensouling the planet issues from his incomparable devotion to the Divine *Mother.* He is the hier-arch of Shamballa, the original *retreat* of *Sanat Kumara* now on the *etheric plane* over the Gobi Desert.

Lord Maitreya, the *Cosmic Christ,* has also passed the initia-tions of the Buddha. He is the long-awaited Coming Buddha who has come to the fore to teach all who have departed from the way of the Great *Guru,* Sanat Kumara, from whose lineage both he and Gautama descended. In the history of the planet, there have been numerous Buddhas who have served the evolu-tions of mankind through the steps and stages of the path of the *Bodhisattva.* In the East Jesus is referred to as the Buddha Issa. He is the World Saviour by the love/wisdom of the Godhead.

Caduceus. The Kundalini. See *Sacred fire.*

Causal Body. Seven concentric spheres of *light* surrounding the *I AM Presence.* The spheres of the Causal Body contain the records of the virtuous acts we have performed to the glory of God and the blessing of man through our many incarnations on earth. See also *Chart of Your Divine Self;* color illustration facing page 76.

Central Sun. A vortex of energy, physical or spiritual, central to systems of worlds that it thrusts from, or gathers unto, itself by the Central Sun Magnet. Whether in the *microcosm* or the *Macrocosm,* the Central Sun is the principal energy source, vortex, or nexus of energy interchange in atoms, cells, man (the heart center), amidst plant life and the core of the earth. The Great Central Sun is the center of cosmos; the point of integration of the *Spirit-Matter* cosmos; the point of origin of all physical-spiritual creation; the nucleus, or white fire core, of the *Cosmic Egg.* (The God Star, Sirius, is the focus of the Great Central Sun in our sector of the galaxy.) The Sun behind the sun is the spiritual Cause behind the physical effect we see as our own physical sun and all other stars and star systems, seen or unseen, including the Great Central Sun.

Chakra. (Sanskrit, "wheel, disc, circle.") Center of *light* anchored in the *etheric body* and governing the flow of energy to the *four* *lower bodies* of man. There are seven major chakras corresponding to the *seven rays,* five minor chakras corresponding to the five secret rays, and a total of 144 light centers in the body of man.

Chart of Your Divine Self. (See color illustration facing page 76.) There are three figures represented in the Chart. The upper figure is the *I AM Presence,* the I AM THAT I AM, the individualization of God's presence for every son and daughter of the Most High. The Divine Monad consists of the I AM Presence surrounded by the spheres (color rings) of *light* that make up the body of First Cause, or *Causal Body.*

The middle figure in the Chart is the Mediator between God and man, called the *Holy Christ Self,* the *Real Self* or the *Christ* consciousness. It has also been referred to as the Higher Mental Body or one's Higher Consciousness. This Inner Teacher overshadows the lower self, which consists of the *soul* evolving through the four planes of *Matter* using the vehicles of the *four lower bodies*—the *etheric* (memory) *body,* the *mental body,* the *emotional* (desire) *body,* and the *physical body*—to balance karma and fulfill the divine plan.

The three figures of the Chart correspond to the Trinity of Father, who always includes the *Mother* (the upper figure), Son (the middle figure) and Holy Spirit (the lower figure). The latter is the intended temple of the Holy Spirit, whose *sacred fire* is indicated in the enfolding *violet flame.* The lower figure corresponds to you as a disciple on the *Path.*

The lower figure is surrounded by a *tube of light,* which is projected from the heart of the I AM Presence in answer to your call. It is a cylinder of white light that sustains a forcefield of protection twenty-four hours a day, so long as you guard it in harmony. The *threefold flame* of life is the divine spark sent from the I AM Presence as the gift of life, consciousness and free will. It is sealed in the *secret chamber of the heart* that through the love, wisdom and power of the Godhead anchored therein the *soul* may fulfill her reason for being in the physical plane. Also called the Christ Flame and the Liberty Flame, or fleur-de-lis, it is the spark of a man's divinity, his potential for

Christhood.

The silver cord (or *crystal cord*) is the stream of life, or *lifestream*, that descends from the heart of the I AM Presence to the Holy Christ Self to nourish and sustain (through the *chakras*) the soul and its vehicles of expression in time and space. It is over this 'umbilical cord' that the energy of the Presence flows, entering the being of man at the crown and giving impetus for the pulsation of the threefold flame as well as the physical heartbeat.

When a round of the soul's incarnation in Matter-form is finished, the I AM Presence withdraws the silver cord (Eccles. 12:6), whereupon the threefold flame returns to the level of the Christ, and the soul clothed in the etheric garment gravitates to the highest level of her attainment, where she is schooled between embodiments until her final incarnation when the Great Law decrees she shall go out no more.

The dove of the Holy Spirit descending from the heart of the Father is shown just above the head of the Christ. When the son of man puts on and becomes the Christ consciousness as Jesus did, he merges with the Holy Christ Self. The Holy Spirit is upon him, and the words of the Father, the beloved I AM Presence, are spoken: "This is my beloved Son, in whom I AM well pleased" (Matt. 3:17).

Chela. (Hindi *celā* from Sanskrit *ceta* "slave," i.e., "servant.") In India, a disciple of a religious teacher or *guru*. A term used generally to refer to a student of the *Ascended Masters* and their teachings. Specifically, a student of more than ordinary self-discipline and devotion initiated by an Ascended Master and serving the cause of the *Great White Brotherhood*.

Chohan. (Tibetan, "lord" or "master"; a chief.) Each of the seven *rays* has a Chohan who focuses the *Christ* consciousness of the ray. Having ensouled and demonstrated the law of the ray throughout numerous incarnations, and having taken initiations both before and after the *ascension*, the candidate is appointed to the office of Chohan by the Maha Chohan (the "Great Lord"), who is himself the representative of the Holy Spirit on all the rays. The names of the Chohans of the Rays (each one an

Ascended Master representing one of the seven rays to earth's evolutions) and the locations of their physical/etheric focuses are as follows:

First ray, El Morya, Retreat of God's Will, Darjeeling, India

Second ray, Lanto, Royal Teton Retreat, Grand Teton, Jackson Hole, Wyoming, U.S.A.

Third ray, Paul the Venetian, Château de Liberté, southern France, with a focus of the *threefold flame* at the Washington Monument, Washington, D.C., U.S.A.

Fourth ray, Serapis Bey, the Ascension Temple and Retreat at Luxor, Egypt

Fifth ray, Hilarion (the apostle Paul), Temple of Truth, Crete

Sixth ray, Nada, Arabian Retreat, Saudi Arabia

Seventh ray, Saint Germain, Royal Teton Retreat, Grand Teton, Wyoming, U.S.A.; Cave of Symbols, Table Mountain, Wyoming, U.S.A. Saint Germain also works out of the Great Divine Director's focuses—the Cave of Light in India and the Rakoczy Mansion in Transylvania, where Saint Germain presides as hierarch.

Christ. (From the Greek *Christos* "anointed.") Messiah (Hebrew, Aramaic "anointed"); "Christed one," one fully endued and infilled—anointed—by the *Light* (the Son) of God. The *Word*, the *Logos*, the Second Person of the Trinity. In the Hindu Trinity of Brahma, Vishnu and Shiva, the term "Christ" corresponds to or is the incarnation of Vishnu, the Preserver; Avatāra, Godman, Dispeller of Darkness, *Guru*.

The term "Christ" or "Christed one" also denotes an office in *hierarchy* held by those who have attained self-mastery on the *seven rays* and the seven *chakras* of the Holy Spirit. Christmastery includes the balancing of the *threefold flame*—the divine attributes of power, wisdom and love—for the harmonization of consciousness and the implementation of the mastery of the seven rays in the chakras and in the *four lower bodies* through the Mother flame (the raised *Kundalini*).

At the hour designated for the *ascension,* the *soul* thus anointed raises the spiral of the threefold flame from beneath the feet through the entire form for the transmutation of every atom and cell of her being, consciousness and world. The saturation and acceleration of the *four lower bodies* and the soul by this transfiguring light of the Christ flame take place in part during the initiation of the *transfiguration,* increasing through the resurrection and gaining full intensity in the ritual of the ascension.

Christ Self. The individualized focus of "the only begotten of the Father, full of grace and Truth." The *Universal Christ* individualized as the true identity of the *soul;* the *Real Self* of every man, woman and child, to which the soul must rise. The Christ Self is the Mediator between a man and his God. He is a man's own personal teacher, master and prophet.

Color rays. See *Seven rays.*

Cosmic Being. (1) An *Ascended Master* who has attained cosmic consciousness and ensouls the *light*/energy/consciousness of many worlds and systems of worlds across the galaxies to the Sun behind the *Great Central Sun;* or, (2) A being of God who has never descended below the level of the *Christ,* has never taken physical embodiment, and has never made human karma.

Cosmic Christ. An office in *hierarchy* currently held by Lord Maitreya under Gautama *Buddha,* the *Lord of the World.* Also used as a synonym for *Universal Christ.*

Cosmic Clock. The science of charting the cycles of the *soul's* karma and initiations on the twelve lines of the Clock under the *Twelve Hierarchies of the Sun.* Taught by Mother Mary to Mark and Elizabeth Prophet for sons and daughters of God returning to the Law of the One and to their point of origin beyond the worlds of form and lesser causation.

Cosmic Egg. The spiritual-material universe, including a seemingly endless chain of galaxies, star systems, worlds known and unknown, whose center, or white-fire core, is called the *Great Central Sun.* The Cosmic Egg has both a spiritual and a material center. Although we may discover and observe the Cosmic Egg from the standpoint of our physical senses and perspective, all of the dimensions of *Spirit* can also be known and experienced within the Cosmic Egg. For the God who created the Cosmic Egg and holds it in the hollow of his hand is also the God flame expanding hour by hour within his very own sons and daughters. The Cosmic Egg represents the bounds of man's habitation in this cosmic cycle. Yet, as God is everywhere throughout and beyond the Cosmic Egg, so by his Spirit within us we daily awaken to new dimensions of being, soul-satisfied in conformity with his likeness.

Cosmic Law. The Law that governs mathematically, yet with the spontaneity of Mercy's flame, all manifestation throughout the cosmos in the planes of *Spirit* and *Matter*.

Crystal cord. The stream of God's *Light,* life and consciousness that nourishes and sustains the *soul* and her *four lower bodies.* Also called the silver cord (Eccles. 12:6). See also *Chart of Your Divine Self*.

Cyclopea. Masculine Elohim of the fifth ray, also known as the All-Seeing Eye of God or as the Great Silent Watcher. See also *Elohim; Seven rays.*

Deathless solar body. See *Seamless garment.*

Decree. A dynamic form of spoken prayer used by students of the *Ascended Masters* to direct God's *light* into individual and world conditions. The decree may be short or long and is usually marked by a formal preamble and a closing or acceptance. It is the authoritative *Word* of God spoken in man in the name of the *I AM Presence* and the living *Christ* to bring about constructive change on earth through the will of God. The decree is the birthright of the sons and daughters of God, the "Command ye me" of Isaiah 45:11, the original fiat of the Creator: "Let there be light: and there was light" (Gen. 1:3). It is written in the Book of Job, "Thou shalt decree a thing, and it shall be established unto thee: and the light shall shine upon thy ways" (Job 22:28).

Dictation. A message from an *Ascended Master,* an *Archangel* or another advanced spiritual being delivered through the agency of the Holy Spirit by a *Messenger* of the *Great White Brotherhood.*

Divine Monad. See Chart of Your Divine Self; I AM Presence.

Electronic Presence. A duplicate of the *I AM Presence* of an Ascended Master.

Elohim. (Hebrew; plural of *Eloah,* "God.") The name of God used in the first verse of the Bible: "In the beginning God created the heaven and the earth." The Seven Mighty Elohim and their feminine counterparts are the builders of form. They are the "seven spirits of God" named in Revelation 4:5 and the "morning stars" that sang together in the beginning, as the Lord revealed them to Job (Job 38:7). In the order of *hierarchy,* the Elohim and *Cosmic Beings* carry the greatest concentration, the highest vibration of *Light* that we can comprehend in our present state of evolution. Serving directly under the Elohim are the four hierarchs of the elements, who have dominion over the elementals—the gnomes, salamanders, sylphs and undines.

Following are the names of the Seven Elohim and their divine complements, the ray they serve on and the location of their etheric *retreat:*

First ray, Hercules and Amazonia, Half Dome, Sierra Nevada, Yosemite National Park, California, U.S.A.

Second ray, Apollo and Lumina, western Lower Saxony, Germany

Third ray, Heros and Amora, Lake Winnipeg, Manitoba, Canada

Fourth ray, Purity and *Astrea,* near Gulf of Archangel, southeast arm of White Sea, Russia

Fifth ray, *Cyclopea* and Virginia, Altai Range where China, Siberia and Mongolia meet, near Tabun Bogdo

Sixth ray, Peace and Aloha, Hawaiian Islands

Seventh ray, Arcturus and Victoria, near Luanda, Angola, Africa

Emotional body. One of the *four lower bodies* of man, corresponding to the water element and the third quadrant of *Matter;* the vehicle of the desires and feelings of God made manifest in the being of man. Also called the astral body, the desire body or the feeling body.

Entity. A conglomerate of misqualified energy or disembodied individuals who have chosen to embody evil. Entities that are focuses of sinister forces may attack disembodied as well as embodied individuals.

Etheric body. One of the *four lower bodies* of man, corresponding to the fire element and the first quadrant of *Matter;* called the envelope of the *soul,* holding the blueprint of the divine plan and the image of *Christ*-perfection to be outpictured in the world of form. Also called the memory body.

Etheric octave or etheric plane. The highest plane in the dimension of *Matter;* a plane that is as concrete and real as the physical plane (and even more so) but is experienced through the senses of the *soul* in a dimension and a consciousness beyond physical awareness. This is the plane on which the *akashic records* of mankind's entire evolution register individually and collectively. It is the world of *Ascended Masters* and their *retreats,* etheric cities of *light* where *souls* of a higher order of evolution abide between embodiments. It is the plane of Reality.

The lower *etheric plane,* which overlaps the astral/mental/physical belts, is contaminated by these lower worlds occupied by the false hierarchy and the mass consciousness it controls.

Etheric temple. See *Retreat.*

Fallen angels. See *Angels.*

Father-Mother God. See *Alpha and Omega.*

Four Cosmic Forces. The four beasts seen by Saint John and other seers as the lion, the calf (or ox), the man and the flying eagle (Rev. 4:6–8). They serve directly under the Elohim and govern all of the Matter cosmos. They are transformers of the Infinite Light unto souls evolving in the finite. See also *Elohim.*

Four lower bodies. Four sheaths of four distinct frequencies that surround the *soul* (the physical, emotional, mental and etheric bodies), providing vehicles for the soul in her journey through time and space. The etheric sheath, highest in vibration, is the gateway to the three higher bodies: the *Christ Self,* the *I AM Presence* and the *Causal Body.* See also *Physical body; Emotional body; Mental body; Etheric body.*

Great Central Sun. See *Central Sun.*

Great Hub. See *Central Sun.*

Great White Brotherhood. A spiritual order of Western saints and Eastern adepts who have reunited with the *Spirit* of the living God; the heavenly hosts. They have transcended the cycles of karma and rebirth and ascended (accelerated) into that higher reality that is the eternal abode of the soul. The *Ascended Masters* of the Great White Brotherhood, united for the highest purposes of the brotherhood of man under the Fatherhood of God, have risen in every age from every culture and religion to inspire creative achievement in education, the arts and sciences, God-government and the abundant life through the economies of the nations. The word "white" refers not to race but to the aura (halo) of white *light* surrounding their forms. The Brotherhood also includes in its ranks certain unascended *chelas* of the Ascended Masters.

Guru. (Sanskrit.) A personal religious teacher and spiritual guide; one of high attainment. A guru may be unascended or ascended.

Hierarchy. The universal chain of individualized God-free beings fulfilling the attributes and aspects of God's infinite Selfhood. Included in the cosmic hierarchical scheme are *Solar Logoi, Elohim,* Sons and Daughters of God, ascended and unascended masters with their circles of *chelas, Cosmic Beings,* the *Twelve Hierarchies of the Sun, Archangels* and *angels* of the *sacred fire,* children of the *light,* nature spirits (called elementals) and *twin flames* of the *Alpha/Omega* polarity sponsoring planetary and galactic systems.

This universal order of the Father's own Self-expression is the means whereby God in the *Great Central Sun* steps down the Presence and power of his universal being/consciousness in order that succeeding evolutions in time and space, from the least unto the greatest, might come to know the wonder of his love. The level of one's spiritual/physical attainment—measured by one's balanced self-awareness "hid with *Christ* in God" and demonstrating his Law, by his love, in the *Spirit/Matter* cosmos —is the criterion establishing one's placement on this ladder of life called hierarchy.

Higher Mental Body. See Chart of Your Divine Self.

Higher Self. The *I AM Presence;* the *Christ Self;* the exalted aspect of selfhood. Used in contrast to the term "lower self," or "little self," which indicates the *soul* that went forth from and may elect by free will to return to the Divine Whole through the realization of the oneness of the self in God. Higher consciousness.

Holy Christ Self. See *Christ Self.*

Human monad. The entire forcefield of self; the interconnecting spheres of influences—hereditary, environmental, karmic— which make up that self-awareness that identifies itself as human. The reference point of lesser- or non-awareness out of which all mankind must evolve to the realization of the *Real Self* as the *Christ Self.*

I AM Presence. The I AM THAT I AM (Exod. 3:13–15); the individualized Presence of God focused for each individual *soul.* The God-identity of the individual; the Divine Monad; the individual Source. The origin of the soul focused in the planes of *Spirit* just above the physical form; the personification of the God Flame for the individual. See also *Chart of Your Divine Self;* color illustration facing page 76.

I AM THAT I AM. See *I AM Presence.*

Kali Yuga. (Sanskrit.) Term in Hindu mystic philosophy for the last and worst of the four yugas (world ages), characterized by strife, discord and moral deterioration.

Karmic Board. See *Lords of Karma.*

Keepers of the Flame Fraternity. Founded in 1961 by Saint Germain, an organization of *Ascended Masters* and their *chelas* who vow to keep the flame of life on earth and to support the activities of the *Great White Brotherhood* in the establishment of their community and mystery school and in the dissemination of their teachings. Keepers of the Flame receive graded lessons in *cosmic law* dictated by the *Ascended Masters* to their *Messengers* Mark and Elizabeth Prophet.

Kundalini. See *Sacred fire.*

Lifestream. The stream of life that comes forth from the one Source, from the *I AM Presence* in the planes of *Spirit,* and descends to the planes of *Matter* where it manifests as the *threefold flame* anchored in the heart *chakra* for the sustainment of the *soul* in Matter and the nourishment of the *four lower bodies.* Used to denote souls evolving as individual "lifestreams" and hence synonymous with the term "individual." Denotes the ongoing nature of the individual through cycles of individualization.

Light. The energy of God; the potential of the *Christ.* As the personification of *Spirit,* the term "Light" can be used synonymously with the terms "God" and "Christ." As the essence of Spirit, it is synonymous with *"sacred fire."* It is the emanation of the *Great Central Sun* and the individualized *I AM Presence*—and the Source of all life.

Logos. (Greek, "word, speech, reason.") The divine wisdom manifest in the creation. According to ancient Greek philosophy, the Logos is the controlling principle in the universe. The Book of John identifies the *Word,* or Logos, with Jesus Christ: "And the Word was made flesh, and dwelt among us" (John 1:14). Hence, Jesus Christ is seen as the embodiment of divine reason, the Word Incarnate.

Lord of the World. *Sanat Kumara* held the office of Lord of the World (referred to as "God of the earth" in Rev. 11:4) for tens of thousands of years. Gautama Buddha recently succeeded Sanat Kumara and now holds this office. His is the highest governing office of the spiritual *hierarchy* for the planet—and yet Lord Gautama is truly the most humble among the *Ascended Masters.* At inner levels, he sustains the *threefold flame,* the divine spark, for those *lifestreams* who have lost the direct contact with their *I AM Presence* and who have made so much negative karma as to be unable to magnetize sufficient *Light* from the Godhead to sustain their *soul's* physical incarnation on earth. Through a filigree thread of light connecting his heart with the hearts of all God's children, Lord Gautama nourishes the flickering flame of life that ought to burn upon the altar of each heart with a greater magnitude of love, wisdom and power, fed by each one's own *Christ* consciousness.

Lords of Karma. The Ascended Beings who comprise the Karmic Board. Their names and the *rays* that they represent on the board are as follows: first ray, the Great Divine Director; second ray, the Goddess of Liberty; third ray, the Ascended Lady Master Nada; fourth ray, the *Elohim Cyclopea;* fifth ray, Pallas Athena, Goddess of Truth; sixth ray, Portia, Goddess of Justice; seventh ray, Kuan Yin, Goddess of Mercy. The Buddha Vairochana also sits on the Karmic Board.

The Lords of Karma dispense justice to this system of worlds, adjudicating karma, mercy and judgment on behalf of every *lifestream*. All *souls* must pass before the Karmic Board before and after each incarnation on earth, receiving their assignment and karmic allotment for each lifetime beforehand and the review of their performance at its conclusion. Through the Keeper of the Scrolls and the recording *angels*, the Lords of Karma have access to the complete records of every lifestream's incarnations on earth. They determine who shall embody, as well as when and where. They assign souls to families and communities, measuring out the weights of karma that must be balanced as the "jot and tittle" of the Law. The Karmic Board, acting in consonance with the individual *I AM Presence* and *Christ Self,* determines when the soul has earned the right to be free from the wheel of karma and the round of rebirth.

The Lords of Karma meet at the Royal Teton Retreat twice yearly, at winter and summer solstice, to review petitions from unascended mankind and to grant dispensations for their assistance.

Macrocosm. (Greek, "great world.") The larger cosmos; the entire warp and woof of creation, which we call the *Cosmic Egg*. Also used to contrast man as the microcosm ('little world') against the backdrop of the larger world in which he lives. See also *Microcosm.*

Mantra. A mystical formula or invocation; a word or formula, often in Sanskrit, to be recited or sung for the purpose of intensifying the action of the *Spirit* of God in man. A form of prayer consisting of a word or a group of words that is chanted over and over again to magnetize a particular aspect of the Deity or of a being who has actualized that aspect of the Deity. See also *Decree.*

Manu. (Sanskrit.) The progenitor and lawgiver of the evolutions of

God on earth. The Manu and his divine complement are *twin flames* assigned by the *Father-Mother God* to sponsor and ensoul the Christic image for a certain evolution or lifewave known as a root race—*souls* who embody as a group and have a unique archetypal pattern, divine plan and mission to fulfill on earth.

According to esoteric tradition, there are seven primary aggregations of souls—that is, the first to the seventh root races. The first three root races lived in purity and innocence upon earth in three Golden Ages before the fall of Adam and Eve. Through obedience to *cosmic law* and total identification with the *Real Self,* these three root races won their immortal freedom and ascended from earth.

It was during the time of the fourth root race, on the continent of Lemuria, that the allegorical Fall took place under the influence of the fallen angels known as Serpents (because they used the serpentine spinal energies to beguile the soul, or female principle in mankind, as a means to their end of lowering the masculine potential, thereby emasculating the Sons of God).

The fourth, fifth and sixth root races (the latter soul group not having entirely descended into physical incarnation) remain in embodiment on earth today. Lord Himalaya and his beloved are the Manus for the fourth root race, Vaivasvata Manu and his consort are the Manus for the fifth root race, and the God and Goddess Meru are the Manus for the sixth root race. The seventh root race is destined to incarnate on the continent of South America in the Aquarian age under their Manus, the Great Divine Director and his divine complement.

Manvantara. (Sanskrit, from *manv,* used in compounds for *manu,* + *antara,* "interval, period of time.") In Hinduism, the period or age of a *Manu,* consisting of 4,320,000 solar years; one of the fourteen intervals that constitute a *kalpa* (Sanskrit), a period of time covering a cosmic cycle from the origination to the destruction of a world system. In Hindu cosmology, the universe is continually evolving through periodic cycles of creation and dissolution. Creation is said to occur during the outbreath of the God of Creation, Brahma; dissolution occurs during his inbreath.

Mater. (Latin, "mother.") See *Matter; Mother.*

Matter. The feminine (negative) polarity of the Godhead, of which the masculine (positive) polarity is Spirit. Matter acts as a chalice for the kingdom of God and is the abiding place of evolving *souls* who identify with their Lord, their *Holy Christ Self.* Matter is distinguished from matter (lowercase *m*)—the substance of the earth earthy, of the realms of maya, which blocks rather than radiates divine *light* and the Spirit of the *I AM THAT I AM.* See also *Mother; Spirit.*

Mental body. One of the *four lower bodies* of man, corresponding to the air element and the second quadrant of *Matter;* the body that is intended to be the vehicle, or vessel, for the mind of God or the *Christ* mind. "Let this [Universal] Mind be in you, which was also in Christ Jesus" (Phil. 2:5). Until quickened, this body remains the vehicle for the carnal mind, often called the lower mental body in contrast to the Higher Mental Body, a synonym for the *Christ Self* or *Christ* consciousness.

Messenger. Evangelist. One who goes before the *angels* bearing to the people of earth the good news of the gospel of Jesus Christ and, at the appointed time, the Everlasting Gospel. The Messengers of the *Great White Brotherhood* are anointed by the *hierarchy* as their apostles ("one sent on a mission"). They deliver through the *dictations* (prophecies) of the *Ascended Masters* the testimony and lost teachings of Jesus Christ in the power of the Holy Spirit to the seed of *Christ,* the lost sheep of the house of Israel, and to every nation. A Messenger is one who is trained by an Ascended Master to receive by various methods the words, concepts, teachings and messages of the Great White Brotherhood; one who delivers the law, the prophecies and the dispensations of God for a people and an age.

Microcosm. (Greek, "small world.") (1) The world of the individual, his *four lower bodies,* his aura and the forcefield of his karma; or (2) The planet. See also *Macrocosm.*

Mother. "Divine Mother," "Universal Mother" and "Cosmic Virgin" are alternate terms for the feminine polarity of the

Godhead, the manifestation of God as Mother. *Matter* is the feminine polarity of *Spirit,* and the term is used interchangeably with Mater (Latin, "mother"). In this context, the entire material cosmos becomes the womb of creation into which Spirit projects the energies of life. Matter, then, is the womb of the Cosmic Virgin, who, as the other half of the Divine Whole, also exists in Spirit as the spiritual polarity of God.

Nirvana. The goal of life according to Hindu and Buddhist philosophy: the state of liberation from the wheel of rebirth through the extinction of desire.

OM (AUM). The Word; the sound symbol for ultimate Reality.

Omega. See Alpha and Omega.

Path. The strait gate and narrow way that leadeth unto life (Matt. 7:14). The path of initiation whereby the disciple who pursues the *Christ* consciousness overcomes step by step the limitations of selfhood in time and space and attains reunion with Reality through the ritual of the *ascension.*

Pearls of Wisdom. Weekly letters of instruction dictated by the *Ascended Masters* to their *Messengers* Mark L. Prophet and Elizabeth Clare Prophet for students of the sacred mysteries throughout the world. *Pearls of Wisdom* have been published by *The Summit Lighthouse* continuously since 1958. They contain both fundamental and advanced teachings on *cosmic law* with a practical application of spiritual truths to personal and planetary problems.

Physical body. The most dense of the *four lower bodies* of man, corresponding to the earth element and the fourth quadrant of *Matter.* The physical body is the vehicle for the *soul's* sojourn on earth and the focus for the crystallization in form of the energies of the *etheric, mental* and *emotional bodies.*

Rays. Beams of *Light* or other radiant energy. The Light emanations of the Godhead that, when invoked in the name of God or in the name of the *Christ,* burst forth as a flame in the world of the individual. Rays may be projected by the God consciousness of ascended or unascended beings through the *chakras* and the third eye as a concentration of energy taking on numerous God-qualities, such as love, truth, wisdom, healing, and so on. Through the misuse of God's energy, practitioners of black magic project rays having negative qualities, such as death rays, sleep rays, hypnotic rays, disease rays, psychotronic rays, the evil eye, and so on. See also *Seven rays.*

Real Self. The *Christ Self;* the *I AM Presence;* immortal *Spirit* that is the animating principle of all manifestation. See also *Chart of Your Divine Self.*

Reembodiment. The rebirth of a *soul* in a new human body. The soul continues to return to the physical plane in a new body temple until she balances her karma, attains self-mastery, overcomes the cycles of time and space, and finally reunites with the *I AM Presence* through the ritual of the *ascension.*

Retreat. A focus of the *Great White Brotherhood,* usually on the *etheric plane* where the *Ascended Masters* preside. Retreats anchor one or more flames of the Godhead as well as the momentum of the Masters' service and attainment for the balance of *light* in the *four lower bodies* of a planet and its evolutions. Retreats serve many functions for the councils of the *hierarchy* ministering to the lifewaves of earth. Some retreats are open to unascended mankind, whose *souls* may journey to these focuses in their *etheric body* between their incarnations on earth and in their finer bodies during sleep or *samadhi.*

Root race. See *Manu.*

Sacred fire. The Kundalini fire that lies as the coiled serpent in the base-of-the-spine *chakra* and rises through spiritual purity and self-mastery to the crown chakra, quickening the spiritual centers on the way. God, *Light,* life, energy, the *I AM THAT I AM.* "Our God is a consuming fire" (Heb. 12:29). The sacred fire is the precipitation of the Holy Ghost for the baptism of souls, for purification, for alchemy and transmutation, and for the realization of the *ascension,* the sacred ritual whereby the *soul* returns to the One.

Samadhi. (Sanskrit, literally "putting together": "uniting") In Hinduism, a state of profound concentration or absorption resulting in perfect union with God; the highest state of yoga. In Buddhism, samadhis are numerous modes of concentration believed to ultimately result in higher spiritual powers and the attainment of enlightenment, or nirvana.

Sanat Kumara. (From the Sanskrit, "always a youth.") Great *Guru* of the seed of *Christ* throughout cosmos; hierarch of Venus; the Ancient of Days spoken of in Daniel 7. Long ago he came to earth in her darkest hour when all light had gone out in her evolutions, for there was not a single individual on the planet who gave adoration to the God Presence. Sanat Kumara and the band of 144,000 souls of light who accompanied him volunteered to keep the flame of life on behalf of earth's people. This they vowed to do until the children of God would respond to the love of God and turn once again to serve their Mighty *I AM Presence*. Sanat Kumara's retreat, Shamballa, was established on an island in the Gobi Sea, now the Gobi Desert. The first to respond to his flame was Gautama *Buddha*, followed by Lord Maitreya and Jesus. See also *Lord of the World*.

Seamless garment. Body of *Light* beginning in the heart of the *I AM Presence* and descending around the *crystal cord* to envelop the individual in the vital currents of the *ascension* as he invokes the holy energies of the Father for the return home to God. Also known as the deathless solar body.

Secret chamber of the heart. The sanctuary of meditation behind the heart *chakra*, the place to which the *souls* of Lightbearers withdraw. It is the nucleus of life where the individual stands face to face with the inner *Guru*, the beloved *Holy Christ Self*, and receives the soul testings that precede the alchemical union with that Holy Christ Self—the marriage of the soul to the Lamb.

Seed Atom. The focus of the Divine *Mother* (the feminine ray of the Godhead) that anchors the energies of *Spirit* in *Matter* at the base-of-the-spine *chakra*. See also *Sacred fire*.

Seven rays. The *Light* emanations of the Godhead; the seven *rays* of the white Light that emerge through the prism of the *Christ* consciousness.

Siddhis. Spiritual powers such as levitation, stopping the heartbeat, clairvoyance, clairaudience, materialization and bilocation. The cultivation of siddhis for their own sake is often cautioned against by spiritual teachers.

Solar Logoi. *Cosmic Beings* who transmit the *Light* emanations of the Godhead flowing from *Alpha and Omega* in the *Great Central Sun* to the planetary systems. Also called Solar Lords.

Soul. God is a *Spirit,* and the soul is the living potential of God. The soul's demand for free will and her separation from God resulted in the descent of this potential into the lowly estate of the flesh. Sown in dishonor, the soul is destined to be raised in honor to the fullness of that God-estate which is the one Spirit of all life. The soul can be lost; Spirit can never die.

The soul remains a fallen potential that must be imbued with the reality of Spirit, purified through prayer and supplication, and returned to the glory from which it descended and to the unity of the Whole. This rejoining of soul to Spirit is the *alchemical marriage* that determines the destiny of the self and makes it one with immortal Truth. When this ritual is fulfilled, the highest Self is enthroned as the Lord of Life, and the potential of God, realized in man, is found to be the All-in-all.

Spirit. The masculine polarity of the Godhead; the coordinate of *Matter;* God as Father, who of necessity includes within the polarity of himself God as *Mother,* and hence is known as the *Father-Mother God.* The plane of the *I AM Presence,* of perfection; the dwelling place of the *Ascended Masters* in the kingdom of God. (When lowercased, as in "spirits," the term is synonymous with discarnates, or astral *entities;* "spirit," singular and lowercased, is used interchangeably with soul.)

Spoken Word. The *Word* of the Lord God released in the original fiats of Creation. The release of the energies of the Word, or the *Logos,* through the throat *chakra* by the Sons of God in confirmation of that lost Word. It is written, "By thy words thou shalt be justified, and by thy words thou shalt be condemned" (Matt. 12:37). Today disciples use the power of the Word in *decrees,* affirmations, prayers and *mantras* to draw the essence of the *sacred fire* from the *I AM Presence,* the *Christ Self* and *Cosmic Beings* to channel God's *light* into matrices of transmutation and transformation for constructive change in the planes of *Matter.*

The Summit Lighthouse. An outer organization of the *Great White Brotherhood* founded by Mark L. Prophet in 1958 in Washington, D.C., under the direction of the *Ascended Master* El Morya, Chief of the Darjeeling Council, for the purpose of publishing and disseminating the teachings of the Ascended Masters.

Threefold flame. The flame of the *Christ,* the spark of life that burns within the *secret chamber of the heart* (a secondary *chakra* behind the heart). The sacred trinity of power, wisdom and love that is the manifestation of the *sacred fire.* See also *Chart of Your Divine Self;* color illustration facing page 76.

Transfiguration. An initiation on the path of the *ascension* that takes place when the initiate has attained a certain balance and expansion of the *threefold flame.* Jesus' transfiguration is described in Matthew 17:1–8.

Tube of light. The white *Light* that descends from the heart of the *I AM Presence* in answer to the call of man as a shield of protection for his *four lower bodies* and his *soul* evolution. See also *Chart of Your Divine Self;* color illustration facing page 76.

Twelve Hierarchies of the Sun. Twelve mandalas of *Cosmic Beings* ensouling twelve facets of God's consciousness, who hold the pattern of that frequency for the entire cosmos. They are identified by the names of the signs of the zodiac, as they focus their energies through these constellations. Also called the Twelve Solar Hierarchies. See also *Cosmic Clock.*

Twin flame. The *soul's* masculine or feminine counterpart conceived out of the same white fire body, the fiery ovoid of the *I AM Presence.*

Unascended master. One who has overcome all limitations of *Matter* yet chooses to remain in time and space to focus the consciousness of God for lesser evolutions. See also *Bodhisattva.*

Universal Christ. The Mediator between the planes of *Spirit* and the planes of *Matter.* Personified as the *Christ Self,* he is the Mediator between the Spirit of God and the *soul* of man. The Universal Christ sustains the nexus of (the figure-eight flow of) consciousness through which the energies of the Father (Spirit) pass to his children for the crystallization (*Christ*-realization) of the God Flame by their soul's strivings in the cosmic womb (matrix) of the *Mother* (Matter).

Violet flame. Seventh-ray aspect of the Holy Spirit. The *sacred fire* that transmutes the cause, effect, record and memory of sin, or negative karma. Also called the flame of transmutation, of freedom and of forgiveness. See also *Decree; Chart of Your Divine Self;* color illustration facing page 76.

Word. The Word is the *Logos*: it is the power of God and the realization of that power incarnate in and as the Christ. The energies of the Word are released by devotees of the Logos in the ritual of the science of the *spoken Word.* It is through the Word that the *Father-Mother God* communicates with mankind. The Christ is the personification of the Word. See also *Christ; Decree.*

World Teacher. Office in *hierarchy* held by those Ascended Beings whose attainment qualifies them to represent the universal and personal *Christ* to unascended mankind. The office of World Teacher, formerly held by Maitreya, was passed to Jesus and his disciple Saint Francis (Kuthumi) on January 1, 1956, when the mantle of *Lord of the World* was transferred from *Sanat Kumara* to Gautama *Buddha* and the office of *Cosmic Christ* and Planetary Buddha (formerly held by Gautama) was simultaneously filled by Lord Maitreya. Serving under Lord Maitreya, Jesus and Kuthumi are responsible in this cycle for setting forth the teachings leading to individual self-mastery and the *Christ* consciousness. They sponsor all *souls* seeking union with God, tutoring them in the fundamental laws governing the cause-effect sequences of their own karma and teaching them how to come to grips with the day-to-day challenges of their individual dharma, the duty to fulfill the Christ potential through the sacred labor.

Mark L. Prophet and Elizabeth Clare Prophet are pioneers of modern spirituality and internationally renowned authors. Among their best-selling titles are *The Lost Years of Jesus, The Lost Teachings of Jesus, The Human Aura, Saint Germain On Alchemy, Fallen Angels and the Origins of Evil* and the Pocket Guides to Practical Spirituality series, which includes *How to Work with Angels, Your Seven Energy Centers* and *Soul Mates and Twin Flames*. Their books are now translated into more than twenty languages and are available in more than thirty countries.